THE CITIES OF ST. PAUL
THEIR INFLUENCE ON HIS LIFE AND THOUGHT

PLATE XIII.

Seat of the Mevlevi Dervishes: the Religious Centre of Iconium

THE
CITIES OF ST. PAUL

THEIR INFLUENCE ON HIS
LIFE AND THOUGHT

THE CITIES OF EASTERN ASIA MINOR

BY

W. M. RAMSAY

BAKER BOOK HOUSE
Grand Rapids, Michigan

Reprinted 1979 by
Baker Book House Company
from the 1907 edition published by
Hodder and Stoughton, London

ISBN: 0-8010-7601-3

This volume is part of the ten-volume
William M. Ramsay Library
ISBN: 0-8010-7685-4

PHOTOLITHOPRINTED BY CUSHING - MALLOY, INC.
ANN ARBOR, MICHIGAN, UNITED STATES OF AMERICA
1979

PREFACE

THE subject of these lectures has proved much larger than was anticipated in my original plan, and I have been obliged to omit the Pauline Cities of the Aegean coasts, important as they were in St. Paul's career, and to refrain from discussing his words and metaphors, as I had hoped to do in Part VII.

Parts III.—VI. treat the same subject as was handled in Chapters XII.—XV. of the Introduction to the *Historical Commentary on the Epistle to the Galatians;* but, whereas there the aim was to collect all the information that could be gathered about the Galatian cities, here the object is to understand the character of each as an experiment in the amalgamation of Asiatic and European in a social organism, and to appreciate the unity which runs through its history from century to century.

I add a confirmation of the view stated in p. 204 f. as to the veil being the authority of the woman in

Oriental society. In the Hebrew marriage ceremony, as it is celebrated in modern Palestine, I am informed that the husband snatches off the bride's veil and throws it on his own shoulder, as a sign that he has assumed authority over her.

Considerable parts of this book have appeared as articles, especially in the *Contemporary Review* and the *Expositor*. With the large tax levied on my time and strength by college duties in winter and exploration in summer, the task of composing a book would be beyond my powers, were I not able in this way to take it in parts, working up each as opportunity offers, but having always the general plan in mind. Several of the articles were written in trains or remote places, but they were composed long before they were written. Most of them have been greatly modified and, I hope, improved in their present form.

W. M. RAMSAY.

CONTENTS

PART I

PART II

PART III

PART IV

PART V

PART VI

PART VII

ILLUSTRATIONS

PLATES

CUTS IN THE TEXT

MAPS

Fig. 11A.—Head of the Goddess of Tarsus. Obverse of Fig. 11, p. 144.

Fig. 19A.—The God of Antioch-on-the-Cydnus (Tarsus). Reverse of
Fig. 19, p. 160.

ERRATA.

Insert references to the above on pp. 144 l. 12, 160 l. 10, 161 l. 15, 187
l. 12.   Insert on p. 140 l. 12 reference to p. 435.

P. 357, l. 5 : delete 33.

P. 358, l. 4 : *for* 34 *read* 33.

P. 360, l. 7 : delete 34.

PART I.

PAULINISM IN THE GRÆCO-ROMAN WORLD.

PAULINISM IN THE GRÆCO-ROMAN WORLD.

§ I. INTRODUCTION.

MY first words must be an apology for the character of my opening paragraph: but the circumstances make an auto-biographical introduction the most suitable in this place and in this University, as furnishing an explanation and a justi-fication of the choice of subject in these lectures.

It has always appeared to me the most fortunate factor in the whole course of my education that in the last part of my undergraduate life immediately after spending a year in read-ing with unusual care the most developed stage of Aristotle's philosophy, I was compelled by the Law of the University —much against my own will—to study the letter of Paul to the Galatians, and to learn in practical experience that the Law is a schoolmaster to prepare one for freedom, "rough, but a good nurse of youths," to use the words of Homer, whereas on the contrary a premature entrance into the life of apparent freedom can only be the beginning of a life-long slavery. Freedom, as Paul taught, must be the culmination of a long preparation under servitude to the Law; otherwise it can only be injurious, and cannot even be freedom, but only a worse form of servitude. Degeneration is the inevit-able result of servitude, whether it be servitude to an external master or to one's own insufficiently educated nature. My subject in the first part of these lectures is mainly to pass

(3)

under review the form which Paul gave to the ancient theory of the universal degeneration in history, and the cure which alone he judged sufficient to turn degeneration into progressive development.

Reading the most remarkable and the most intensely individual of the Pauline Epistles as the completion of a study of Greek philosophy, I felt that in Paul, for the first time since Aristotle, Greek philosophy made a real step forward. Such was the impression made during my reading for the schools. Now after thirty-one years I have to state to you the issue of that idea, which seized hold of my mind in undergraduate days and has gripped me ever since. I shall not attempt to treat it with philosophic delicacy and subtlety, for that is beyond my power. I state only the broad rough views of one who looks at what men did and how States rose and fell.

While it is impossible to discuss Paul's views on philosophy or on history without touching on his religious opinions, our subject is primarily historical, and our aim is for the moment to set aside, as far as may be, the religious aspect of Paul's ideas, and to regard him as a force and a leader in history.

The main point and issue is this: Ancient civilisation perished almost utterly; comparatively few specimens of its literature survived; far the larger part of its institutions and methods in the organisation of society disappeared entirely from practical life, and can barely be guessed at now, as some saner ideas of the ancient world are being recovered. When one looks at the terrible suffering that accompanied the inroads of the worst tribes of destroying barbarians, from the Huns to the Mongols, when one remembers the wanton and reckless destruction of almost everything that the ancient civilisation had constructed, the utter loss of so much that was useful and beautiful, so much in social life that had to be slowly recovered, and has as yet been by no means all recovered, in order to make life good and healthy and sound, it seems as if history were the game of a wanton child playing with its toys and wasting or throwing them away as it tired of them. What can explain, and what can repair the week-long sack of the greatest city of the Middle Ages by the Mongols, the annihilation by ignorant savages of the biggest collection of the remains of the ancient world, and all that this total wreck means to the civilised world? Is there reason in this, or mere blind chance and foolish caprice?

To Paul it seemed that there was reason in it. He, like the great Hebrew prophets, foresaw it, denounced its causes, recognised its purpose, and announced the remedy. The sack of Bagdad was but part of the last act in a long course of degeneration. The degeneration had been in process before the time of Paul. It was not the attacks of savages from without that destroyed the ancient civilisation and almost all the many great benefits it had wrought out for mankind; it was the inherent and innate faults of that civilisation. A new foundation was needed on which to build up civilised life. Paul showed what the foundation must be. He taught how the transformation of the old system and the improvement of the foundation could be gradually effected. For some centuries it seemed possible that the transformation and regeneration might be effected peacefully. But, as he declared, and as the result showed, there was no alternative except either regeneration or death. He appreciated well, and declared emphatically that the old system had an element of good (§ 2); but without fundamental reform it could not be preserved. It was rotten to

the heart   So said Paul; and so must every one feel who
studies the innermost character of ancient society; so most
emphatically said the ancients themselves.   The Hellenistic
kingdoms of the East struck out many admirable devices
in society and in administration, or else borrowed them from
the older Oriental States and improved them as they took
them; the Roman Empire appropriated many of these
devices and wrought them into its own vast system of
government; but neither in Hellenistic nor in Roman times
did these admirable devices rest on a broad enough and safe
enough basis.

In the philosophy of Paul, the Eastern mind and the
Hellenic have been intermingled in the closest union, like
two elements which have undergone a chemical mixture.
In every sentence, in every thought, you can feel the Oriental
element, if you are sensitive to it, and you are also aware of
the Western, if you are perceptive of Hellenism; but you
become aware only of that which you are qualified by nature,
by training, and above all by inclination, to perceive.   Hence
the extraordinarily opposite opinions held by modern
scholars about the writings of Paul.   The great majority of
scholars are sentient only of the Judaic element.   They feel
the Jew in him.   They feel that every paragraph and every
idea in his writings is such as only a Jew could have conceived and composed.   And so far they are perfectly right.
From first to last throughout the whole fabric of his being
Paul was Hebrew.   But they err in thinking that this is the
whole matter, and that they have understood Paul completely when they have been aware of the Hebrew.

They have not approached the problem with a wide
enough nature.   They have come to Paul with their mind
dipped in Hebraism and Orientalism, thinking only of this,

sensitive only to this side of his character. They seem never to have sufficiently familiarised themselves with the Græco-Roman world as it was in the first century of our era. They have been educated in the old Hellenism of free Greece, and in the civilisation of Rome. But I rarely find in them any sympathy with, or understanding of, hardly any thought about, the Hellenism that overran the world of Western Asia, adapted itself to Asia, widened itself to the wider sphere, and changed its character profoundly in the adaptation. Nor do they convey the impression that they have thought much about the subtle tinge or flavour that Rome had imparted to the Græco-Oriental civilisation. Rome had not Romanised or sought to Romanise the Eastern Provinces. Rome was content to organise and to govern them, to preserve peace in an orderly population and make it contribute to the strength of the Empire as a whole. But in doing this it had perceptibly influenced the tone of the Eastern Provinces. Romans were the aristocracy of the Eastern world.

For example, glance at two pictures, which Luke passes before us in the Acts, of events which occurred within his own knowledge and in part before his own eyes. Here you have photographs, as it were, taken from real life as it was lived in the Roman Provinces of the first century after Christ. Nothing more vivid and more informing has been preserved to us in the records of the period. Not to recognise this life-like character is to write oneself down as unfit to appreciate and to understand the living world of that age. When two wanderers, unknown and assumed to be of the poorest class, were imprisoned in a Roman colonial city, the chains fell off them at the words " we are Romans ". A Roman Tribune heard that an Egyptian brigand was being torn in pieces by an infuriated mob in Jerusalem; he rescued the vagabond in order to exercise Roman justice on him, and as a first step was proceeding to have him flogged, when the prisoner mentioned that he was a Roman by birth; the officer at once became his apologetic protector and friend. No further questions were put in either case; no proofs were required; the mere claim was enough, and constraint and ill-treatment were ended. Incidentally the question suggests itself : Was there not something in the very manner and tone of the claim which carried conviction in spite of unfavourable external appearances? Was there not something Roman about the Roman? At any rate, this privilege and authority made the rank not merely honourable, but also practically advantageous, and hence rose the keen desire to obtain it which is shown in the Acts xxii. 28. Now in any society the aristocratic class exercises a certain vague, yet very real, influence on the tone of every other class; and especially must this be the case in a society like that of the Roman provinces, where every person of good position might look forward to the attainment of the coveted rank as a possibility in his career. The Romans at this period gave the tone of society; it was different two centuries later, when the national and the Oriental spirit had revived and grown powerful.

All these varied influences were at work in the Græco-Asiatic cities of the Empire; and they produced a type of man and of thought which hardly seems to be dreamed of by those interpreters of Paul, who appreciate the Hebrew element in him and discern nothing else. But, if we first familiarise ourselves with the society in which Paul grew up, in which he spent most of his life, and for which he in his mature years felt that he was specially suited, and if we approach him from that side, we shall feel everywhere in his work the spirit of the Tarsian Hellene. So Canon Hicks, who knows the Hellenic cities of Asia as few scholars do, feels the Hellenic training and experience apparent throughout the Pauline letters. So the late Ernst Curtius, the historian of Greece, felt in the letters the Hellenic tone.[1]

The testimony which struck me most of all was the opinion expressed by two of the most learned Jews of modern time, with whom I happened to be talking more than ten years ago in the house of one of them. The conversation chanced to turn on Paul and on the letters attributed to him. They were both perfectly certain that none of the Pauline letters could be genuine, because there is much in them which no Jew could write. These were scholars whose opinion on any matter connected with Judaism in the early Christian centuries stands very high in the estimation of the whole world. They know old Jewish feeling from the inside with an intimacy which no Western scholar can ever attain to. They appreciated the non-Jewish element intermingled in the writings of Paul. They rightly recognised that no mere Jew could write like that; but instead of inferring that Paul was more than a mere Jew in education and mind, they argued that he, being (as is commonly assumed and maintained by modern scholars) a pure and narrow Jew, could not have written those letters.

The plan of the first part of these lectures is, first to state the fundamental principles of Paul's historical survey; next to contrast his view with the modern method; thirdly, to point out that his view in some degree may be regarded as a development of Hellenic thought; fourthly, to show the relation in which his thought and the cure which he proposed for the degeneration of society stood to the Roman world of his own and of succeeding time.

§ II. The Pauline Philosophy of History.

I should, in the first place, ask you to glance at the Philosophy of History, as Paul declares it. To him the Philosophy of History was the History of religion, for in his view there is nothing real except God, things are permanent and firm only as they partake of the Divine. All else is evanescent, mere illusion and error and uncertainty.

It is in his letter to the Romans that Paul gives clearest expression to the view which he took of human history; but the same view underlies all his thought, and springs inevitably from his attitude towards God and human nature, expressing itself in his perception, gained through Greek philosophy, of the never-ceasing flux and change in all things and of the one law that gives reality and permanence amidst this mutability. His view, as set forth in Romans i. 19 ff., is that there existed in the world from the beginning a certain amount of real perception of and true knowledge about God and His nature and His relation to mankind. By observing, studying, and gradually understanding the facts and processes of the external world, men became aware of the power and divinity of God, which were manifested therein.

But the deliberate action of man vitiated this fair beginning. The reason lay in idolatry. This cause obscures the first true and good ideas of men as to the nature of God; and thus the Divine Being is assimilated to and represented by images in the shape of man who is mortal, and birds and quadrupeds and reptiles. In idolatrous worship a necessary and invariable accompaniment was immorality; you can never have one without the other. This grows from bad to worse in physical passions, and corrupts the whole nature and character of man.

In the following parts I shall try to give a picture of the character of the Eastern Hellenic cities by which Paul was most affected.

We must clearly understand at the outset, both the intensity of Paul's hatred for idolatry, and the reason and nature of that hatred. His view, as we have stated it on his own authority and approximately in his own sentences modernised, is not a mere expression of religiosity, as it is apt to appear to the superficial reader. Nor is it a mere abstract philosophic dictum respecting the great ontological problem of the nature of God. It is, indeed, a necessary consequence of his fundamental view. Since the only reality in the world is God, any serious error about the nature of God, *i.e.*, any idolatry, must distort our conception of the world and of external nature. That is, however, in itself a mere abstract philosophic opinion, and might remain so. Paul abhorred idolatry as the enemy of mankind, because he perceived the law of growth in human nature. This error of idolatry must work itself to its issue in the character and life of the man. As Paul looked over the heathen world, which he knew since his birth practically, both from the inside as a Roman and a Tarsian Hellene, and from the outside as a Hebrew, he saw how it acted in the society where he was born. He saw that it must necessarily, and that it did actually, work itself out in a distortion of the whole life of society and of the individual, falsifying the political situation, frustrating all preparation for the future, making the whole fabric of the State unhealthy, rendering the life and thought of the individual diseased and decadent. If you examine the history of any nation, you can see how the State becomes unhealthy, how its right development is stopped, how it is prevented from getting

rid of evils and dangers in its constitution, by error as to the
nature of God and the true relation of man to God.   Such
is Paul's view.

Accordingly, to the first Pauline principle:

The Divine alone is real : all else is error :

we can now add Paul's second principle:

A Society, or a Nation, is progressive in so far as it hears
the Divine voice : all else is degeneration.

This second principle throws us into the midst of history, the
growth and change of politics, the struggle of man with man
and nation against nation.   It is the province of the historian
to trace the steps and facts of life through which the degeneration or the progress works itself out and makes itself manifest.

Progress, *i.e.*, the perception of truth, is, according to the
Pauline view, open to all men.   Men are never so utterly
corrupt that a return to truth is impossible.   If they only
wish it, they can choose the good and refuse the evil.   The
Gentiles are ignorant of the Law as it was revealed to the
Jews, but some of them, through their better nature, act of
themselves according to the Law, and are a law unto themselves : the practical effect of the Law is seen in their life,
because it has been written by nature in their hearts, and they
have a natural sense of the distinction between right and
wrong, between good and evil; and their conscience works
in harmony with this natural Law in their hearts, prompting them to choose the right action, and making them
conscious of wrong-doing if they choose the wrong course
(Rom. ii. 14 f.).   This beginning of right never fails utterly in
human nature, but it is made faint and obscure by wrong-
doing, when men deliberately choose the evil and will not
listen to the voice of God in their hearts.

Yet even at the worst there remains in the most corrupted man a sense that out of this evil good will come. The remarkable and difficult passage, Romans viii. 19-22, states this emphatically. We all are in some degree aware that evil is wrong, because it is painful, and the pain is the preparation for the birth of better things. The eager watching expectancy of the universe (as of a runner with his eye fixed on the goal, or of a wrestler about to come to grips with his adversary) waiteth for the revealing of the sons of God. For the creation was subjected to vanity, not of its own will, but by reason of man who subjected it, and in this subjection there arises a hope that the creation itself also shall be delivered from the bondage of corruption so as to attain unto the liberty of the glory of the children of God. For we know that the whole creation in all its parts is groaning in the birth-pangs from which shall emerge a better condition, and we also who are Christians and have already within ourselves the first practical effects of the Spirit's action, are still in the pain and hope of the nascent redemption.

This Pauline doctrine bursts the bonds of the narrower Judaism, and rises to a higher and broader outlook. Such a philosophic view could not have been thought out in the form which Paul gave it without a training in Greek philosophy. It is not inconsistent with the best side of Hebrew thought and prophecy; but it was utterly and absolutely inconsistent with the practical facts of the narrower retrograde Judaism in his time. The man who thought thus could not remain permanently in harmony with the bigoted Pharisaic party in Jerusalem,[2] which was inexorably opposed to the early followers of Christ, not because they were Christian, but because they were progressive and growing out of the narrow old Judaism.

It was only in maturer years that Paul became fully conscious of this truth; but as he became able to formulate it clearly to himself and teach it to others, he also became aware that it had been implicit from the beginning in his thought. He had it in his nature from birth. It was fostered by the circumstances of his childhood. He had come in contact with pagans, and knew that they were not monsters (as they seemed to the Palestinian zealots), but human beings. He was so indebted to them, that he felt bound, in return for what he had learned from them, to go and tell them of the truth which had been revealed (Rom. i. 14). He had learned by experience of the promptings to good, of the preference for the right, of self-blame for wrong-doing, which were clearly manifest in their nature. He had also been aware of that eager longing for the coming of something better, of a new era, of a Saviour, of God incarnate in human form on the earth, which was so remarkable a feature in Roman life before and after his birth.

The third principle of the Pauline philosophy of history, therefore, may be thus expressed:

> *All men and every human society can hear the Divine voice; but they must co-operate ere the communication can take place.*

There was, in Paul's opinion, a certain amount of progressive force, a certain perception of Divine truth, in the pagan world; and this was entirely caught up and incorporated in his teaching, which was the complete revelation of God. As I believe, he deliberately and consciously aimed at bringing together on the higher plane of Christian thought and life all that was true and real in the pagan world; and the passages which I have quoted above from his own writings show that he believed that much in the pagan thoughts and hopes was good and true.

It is true that he nowhere defines his intentions with respect to the contemporary world except in the strictly religious point of view. He nowhere clearly states his attitude to the pagan world apart from its religious and moral aspects (which were to him abhorrent and detestable), but he acknowledges that he had learned from it, that he was indebted to it, that he was bound to pay his debt, and that his young Churches should regulate with wisdom their conduct to the pagan world around and buy to the full all that was profitable for them from the opportunity that the world afforded ; "whatsoever is true, or holy, or just, or pure, or courteous, or reputable, all excellence, all merit, include these in the account books of your life," from whatever origin they come, they are for you.

But it was not his object in any of his writings to set forth such general ideas. They are all occasional writings, devoted to the immediately pressing problems of his correspondents. Yet from the counsel about details the general principles of his policy are recoverable. Also we may fairly use in evidence the subsequent influence of Paul's teaching as seen in the following centuries.

§ III. THE PAULINE CONTRASTED WITH THE MODERN METHOD.

Regarding the Pauline view as a scientific or philosophic theory of the progress of history, one observes at once how diametrically opposed it is to the fashionable modern scientific conception about the right method in the investigation of ancient religion. The modern method is based on the assumption that there takes place normally a continuous development in religion, in thought, and in civilisation, since primitive times; that such a development has been practically universal among the more civilised races; that, as to certain less civilised races, either they have remained stationary, or progress among them has been abnormally slow; that the primitive in religion is barbarous, savage, bloodthirsty and low in the scale of civilisation, and that the line of growth normally and usually is towards the milder, the more gracious, and the nobler forms of religion; that the primitive type of religion can be recovered by studying the savage of the present day, and that the lowest savage is the most primitive.

Nowadays we are all devotees of the theory of development: it is no longer a theory, it has become the basis and guiding principle of our thought and mind: we must see development everywhere. But it is necessary to be very sure first of all that we have got hold of the right law of development in history; and we are sometimes too hasty. We can easily arrange religions in a series from the lowest to the highest, and we are wont to assume that this series represents the historical development of religion from the most primitive to the most advanced. The fetish, the totem and the sacred animals, and so up step by step to Jehovah and the Ark of the Covenant. Is that the true line?

You observe that the assumptions here are very serious. Is the modern savage really primitive? Paul would have said that he represents the last stage of degeneration, that he is the end and not the beginning, that he has lost almost everything that is really primitive, that he has fallen so completely from the ancient harmony with the order of nature and sympathy with the Divine as to be on the verge of death, and an outrage on the world and on human nature.

Who is right, Paul or the moderns? For my own part, I confess that my experience and reading show nothing to confirm the modern assumptions in religious history, and a great deal to confirm Paul. Wherever evidence exists, with the rarest exceptions, the history of religion among men is a history of degeneration; and the development of a few Western nations in invention and in civilisation during recent centuries should not blind us to the fact that among the vast majority of the nations the history of manners and civilisation is a story of degeneration. Wherever you find a religion that grows purer and loftier, you find the prophet, the thinker, the teacher, who is in sympathy with the Divine, and he tells you that he is speaking the message of God, not his own message. Are these prophets all impostors and deceivers? or are they speaking the truth? Is it not the fact of human history that man, standing alone, degenerates; and that he progresses only where there is in him so much sympathy with and devotion to the Divine life as to keep the social body pure and sweet and healthy?

The appeal must be to facts. Let us cast a glance back over Mediterranean history and the evolution and vicissitudes of its civilisation. On the Mediterranean lands and waters you have for thousands of years the centre of human civilisation and knowledge, and there best of all you can detect the principle of growth in human history.

The outstanding achievement of the East Mediterranean world, the great service which the peoples of the Levant rendered to mankind, was that they conquered nature and made it obedient and useful to man. The Mediterranean lands are not like the great plains of the Canadian North-West, productive almost spontaneously, gifted by nature

with a great depth of rich soil.   They are to a large extent
hilly or even mountainous; a considerable portion of them
is bare and rocky ; where there is soil it is in great part so
dry as to be absolutely useless without artificial irrigation ;
the rich valleys are rarely extensive,,and large part of those
valleys was originally marsh.   Almost everywhere a vast
amount of labour and a high degree of skill, forethought and
knowledge had to be applied before the soil became useful
to man and able to support a large population.

If the old Mediterranean lands are dotted all over with
great monuments, mostly of a religious character, graves of
large size or elaborately ornate temples, pyramids, etc.,
which astonish the modern mind as it estimates the amount
of work and time and skill that must have been expended
on them, it is no less the case that the expanse of ancient
history is dotted over with the records of great engineering
works serving the uses of man, works which astonish us not
only by the vast amount of hand labour performed with
simple tools in their construction, but far more by the re-
sources, the wide outlook, the power of adapting means to
gain a far-distant end, the habit of living for the future and
expending labour, not to win one's daily bread, not even to
provide the year's supply of corn or to acquire immediate
wealth, but to achieve works which could be only remotely
profitable or serviceable.   How was the knowledge acquired
which made mankind able to devise and plan out such great
schemes as the draining of the Bœotian plain or the Lernæan
marsh, the forming of a discharge for the waters of many
upland land-locked valleys in Asia Minor and Greece, and
later in Italy, the regulation of the course of considerable
rivers, the cutting of a carriage road across great mountains
like that which goes through the Cilician Gates?

The ancients tell us that the later works of this kind were done by historical persons like the Emperor Claudius and Curius Dentatus, or by half-historical figures like Servius Tullius. When you go back a few centuries earlier, you find purely mythological names, as, for example, that of Mopsus, Apollo's prophet and the divine guide of Apollo's colonising people, clinging to such great works of improvement or defence. When you go back to works still more remote in time, you learn that they were performed by the god himself, as for example, Herakles: the ancient mind here felt that it had got beyond human power, and it took refuge with God.

On a first glance one might be inclined to say that in the nearer past, to which historical record extended, the man who had achieved the work was remembered and named, and only for the enterprises of a remoter time, of which the record had perished, did the popular fancy create a Divine originator. Up to a certain point this is true. It is a way of stating the facts which is superficially accurate, but which misses the real deep-lying truth. How superficial, how fundamentally untrue it is to say that the Emperor Claudius drained the Fucine Lake. He inherited the knowledge which others had accumulated; he had learned from the experience of generations and ages past that such enterprises were possible; he set in motion the mass of skilled labour which had been organised before his time. He deserves all credit for what he did; he had mastered this lesson of the past. But only in a very modified sense can the draining of the lake be attributed to him. The same is the case with every man who has the credit for any of those great and beneficent works, and who in part deserves the credit. It was the slowly gathered wisdom of the past that both made those works possible, and taught intelligent administrators what there was to gain in the distant future by the effort and expenditure needed to accomplish them. The treasured and gathered wisdom of the past inspired the design and achieved the execution of all those works. In administration the knowledge of what can be done and what will be worth doing is all-important.

And so the ancient accounts, which invoked the aid of the God, expressed, after all, in a certain sense and properly understood, the truth. The God to whom the people looked for guidance and counsel, was, so to say, the imaginative embodiment or personification of the accumulated experience and the growing wisdom of the race. Anything that originated from a knowledge wider than the range of man himself was, in a real sense, the work of the God, performed through the Divine impulse and under the Divine guidance.

Less striking, but really almost more wonderful, than the great feats of early engineering, is the high development of ancient agriculture, arboriculture, and domestication and improvement of the useful animals. I happenèd to be talking two days ago to Dr. W. G. Rutherford,[3] my contemporary as an undergraduate. He had been reading the old Roman work on agriculture, and was full of admiration of the wisdom and knowledge that lay behind Cato; what centuries of experience and observation were implied in the rules of agriculture that the old Censor prescribed.

Most impressive of all to me personally is the cultivation of the olive, beyond all others the tree of civilisation. From the day you plant the tree, about sixteen to eighteen years must pass before it begins to produce any return, seventeen years of care, work, and unremunerative preparation. What a high standard of real civilisation, what stability and order, what true wisdom must there be in the society where men can wait so long in full confidence that he who sows will reap. And what wealth is imparted to an otherwise unproductive region by the olive. Professor Theobald Fischer, who has studied the geographical and economic botany of the Mediterranean lands with special care, mentions some typical examples of what can be done for a country by the cultivation of the olive. In Southern France, in the Arrondissement Grasse, one-third of the country is planted with olives and supported a population of 60,000 in the year 1880, the other two-thirds which grew no olives contained a population of 10,000; in the olive-growing district of Tunisia, 150,000 people live in an area of 600 square kilometres, but close by are districts inhabited by five or six people to the square kilometre.[4]

In agriculture we find the same historical principle of evolution as in the great engineering works, which widened the area of agriculture. Elsewhere I have attempted to trace the religious character of the rules of domestication of animals, agriculture, horticulture, as well as of the rules regulating the conduct of men in their social relation, to ensure the sanitation and cleanliness of town life.[5] Everywhere you come back to the same first cause. The Divine power and wisdom was popularly believed to have taught, nourished and preserved both man and society. God, or rather the Goddess, for early man regarded the mother, their teacher and their guide, as the type of the Divine power in its beneficent character, is wise, bountiful and tutelary; man is merely obedient and receptive. In the operations of agriculture, unskilled work, such as man could apply, was of small avail. The really important factor was divinely given, *viz.*, knowledge and skill, prudence and forethought. The mere labour of man was useless and unproductive without this guiding wisdom; and the wisdom was embodied in the rules and ritual prescribed by religion.   Thus directed, the labour of many generations raised great tracts of barren land to the highest standard of productiveness.   When the guidance ceased, what was the result?[6]   Look for a moment at the present state of the Eastern Mediterranean lands in comparison with their wealth and inexhaustible productiveness in ancient times.   Much—indeed the greater part—of the land which was once so highly cultivated produces little or nothing; it has gone back to its primitive condition.   You can traverse coast-lands for hundreds and hundreds of miles continuously, where practically nothing is grown, or could in the present state of the soil grow, except the minimum of wheat and barley to feed a very scanty population and their few poor horses and cattle, and where not a single tree is now cultivated.   Yet those very districts were in ancient times proverbial for richness and wealth.   Nothing can now be hoped for there—not merely is there no certainty that he who sows will reap, but also capital will in modern times never be used in enterprises where so many years must elapse before any return can be looked for.   We must have quick returns; but civilisation was not made by people who were bent on quick returns.

Our survey of the Mediterranean lands reveals no sign of development.   It shows us only a process of degeneration and decay, and offers little hope of revival in the present economic system.   Now in which state of society is the greater wisdom seen, in the old state which by long toil, directed to a distant future end, made that country rich and populous, or in the present system which necessarily renounces such tasks because the return on outlay is so distant? One of the sure signs of a well-ordered and stable society is that in it the remoter future can be preferred to the immediate profit; and Browning states the true principle:

> Oh, if we draw a circle premature,
>   Heedless of far gain,
> Greedy for quick returns of profit, sure
>   Bad is our bargain!

But it is in this period which we have just been contemplating that the modern scientific study of religion expatiates. Here it finds its favourite field for exercise and its most gratifying examples. Here it finds the evolution of religion from the savage to the civilised state by a natural process of growth from the primitive to the higher. When the Mediterranean religion according to the modern fashionable theory was little, if at all, above the religious idea of the modern savage, history[7] shows that it was producing the Mediterranean agriculture and prosperity. When it had had plenty of time to develop, the prosperity ceased, and agriculture through neglect became impossible, and civilisation was destroyed over great part of the Mediterranean world. One who looks at the facts must ask whether religion naturally develops from the lower to the higher stage, or whether Paul was not right in declaring that religion tends to degenerate among men. So far as the history of the Mediterranean lands reaches I find only degeneration, corrected from time to time by the influence of the great prophets and teachers like Paul.

Whether there lies behind this historical period a primitive savage period, I am not bold enough or skilful enough to judge. I can only look for facts in the light of history. I dare not rush into the darkness that lies behind. The

primitive savage, who develops naturally out of the stage
of Totemism into the wisdom of Sophocles and Socrates, or
he who transforms his fetish in the course of many generations through the Elohistic stage into the Jehovah of the
Hebrews, is unknown to me.   I find nothing even remotely
resembling him in the savages of modern times.   I cannot
invent for myself a primitive savage of such marvellous
potentialities, when I find that the modern savage is devoid
of any potentiality, in many cases unable to stand side by
side with a more civilised race, a mere worthless degenerate
who has lost even his vital stamina, in other cases, when he
can survive, showing at least no capacity to improve except
through imitation of external models.   If you seek in the
modern savage an analogous case to the early Mediterranean
beginners of civilisation, you must take your savage as you
find him.   It is an unscientific process to invent a primitive
savage, who resembles the modern in the lowness of his religious ideas, but differs from him by a wealth of potential
development in religion and civilisation.

But, it may be said, in ancient Greece and in early Hebrew
history, you find numerous examples of Totemism and other
savage religious customs and ideas.   That is perfectly true.
But, in the first place, these are the dead twigs, the weak
offshoots which were unfit to live, on the tree of Hellenism.
You may as well seek the explanation of the splendid tree in
those failures, which abound everywhere when you examine
it closely, as seek the reason for the splendid development of
Hellenism and Hebrew religion in those faults and abortions
and errors.   Hellenism flourished and grew, not in virtue of,
but in spite of, those facts which show the mind of the savage
and the degenerate.   Those facts are all mere instances of
degeneration.   Degeneration is not confined to the later ages

or to any one age of religious history. It lies deep in human nature. It is as old as man. It has been going on in all religions and in all ages from the beginning; and you find examples of it in all ages down to the present time.

Moreover, it is not the case that all superficial appearances, say, of Totemism, are really examples of it. A dear and honoured friend of mine, long since dead too young, under whose tuition I was nearly thirty years ago an enthusiastic student of M'Lennan and devotee of Totemism and all that appertains thereto, used to regard the serpent as the totem of the family of David. I have heard him often converse on this topic with the eloquence, the conviction, and the easy mastery of vast learning that made him almost unique among scholars, while he demonstrated with singular persuasiveness that the Brazen Serpent of the Wilderness was the family totem elevated for the veneration of the nation. But I find nowhere that the modern totem of a family is raised aloft for the veneration of other families : these have their own totems. It is characteristic of all degeneration in religion that the devotees of each cult guard it jealously as a private possession, which they must keep to themselves lest others should share in its possession and diminish the advantages of its present possessors. Had the serpent been a family totem, it would not have been made national. While I quite admit that the Brazen Serpent was an instance of savage ritual at an early period in Hebrew history, I cannot admit that it was the totem of one family or one tribe. Not all serpent worship is Totemism.

Accordingly, consideration of the actual facts leads back to the same beginning as that which Paul assumes. In the remotest period of Mediterranean history to which human research can at present penetrate, if it restricts itself to the

observation of facts and the drawing of cautious warrantable
inferences from the facts—in that earliest period we have
come, not to savages and Totemism and all the paraphernalia
of primitive religion, as many of the moderns picture it to
themselves and to their pupils, but to a theocracy, to an
agency of prophets who make known the will of the goddess
to her people, to a well-justified belief in the motherly wisdom
of the Divine being and the truth-speaking of the prophets.
We have come also to many sporadic examples of Totemism
and other customs and ideas of the modern savage.   The
savage has been and is always with us in history.   But these
are merely the signs and fruits of degeneration.   It was not
through them that the old religion obtained and kept its
hold on the minds of men.   As they, in the process of increasing degeneration, became stronger and more frequent,
the religion lost in great degree its influence, or retained its hold only on the least educated in the form of
popular superstitions.   Its power to guide, to teach, and to
do good was what gave it originally its power over the
minds of men.   What was true in it made it live : the
symptoms of savagery in it made it die.   There were bull-
roarers and other paraphernalia or savage ritual in the
Eleusinian worship, but it was not these that made it a power
in Greek life and caused it to be respected and lauded by
Sophocles and Socrates.   The method of studying ancient
religion which concentrates attention on these signs of
savagery and degeneracy loses sight of everything which
makes ancient religion worthy of the historian's study.
These barbarous and degenerate elements existed, and there
was not sufficient vitality in the people and in the religion to
eliminate them.   The race of prophets died out.   The needed
sympathy with the Divine nature ceased.   The degeneracy

spread unchecked, until the coming of Christianity and the reaction against Christianity imparted a new life and vigour to the old paganism.

The modern theory is expressed in its sharpest and most extreme terms by my friend M. Salomon Reinach, in the *Revue des Etudes Grecques*, 1906, p. 344, where he criticises M. Paul Foucart on the ground that he " a trop perdu de vue, ou n'a peut être pas reconnu le caractère primitif et magique du rituel éleusinien. *Tout rituel primitif est à l'origine magique.*" The words which I have italicised go further than some modern scholars who adopt a similar method of study and reasoning would be willing to follow him; but they are a logical statement of the principle involved in the modern method : Religion begins in magic and gradually elevates itself to a higher stage of thought.

On the contrary, the view to which I have found myself gradually driven is that magic is incident to the degradation of primitive religion ; religion must either develop to a higher stage or degenerate, but cannot remain stationary ; in a society where the standard of thought and moral judgment is rising amid part of the community, any old religious idea or rite which persists among the unprogressive and uneducated masses tends to lose the higher possibilities which once were latent in it, to be hardened into a lifeless superstition, and to become a magic ritual or formula. Take for example the idea characteristic of early Hellenism that the gods are jealous of too great and outstanding success or power or happiness falling to the lot of any man, and interfere to prevent this even by slaying the man, and that it is wise and prudent for man to propitiate them by voluntarily sacrificing part of his possessions. This primitive idea is capable of being either developed in a good way or degraded into a debased and debasing superstition. On the one hand, it became in the hands of the tragedians the deepest principle of the Greek drama, that great success produces pride, pride crime, crime punishment, and punishment wisdom, which is expressed in various forms in the action of many tragedies. On the other hand, it was degraded into the fear of the evil eye and of baleful influence in other forms, which ever lie in wait for men and must be guarded against by charms and protective symbols or gestures. Such degradation is extremely early, and the degraded forms are thought to be primitive by those who assume the principle of development from the lower to the higher; but they are really secondary, not primitive.

This may serve as an example of the general law, which the present writer has attempted to work out in more detail for Greece and Asia Minor, showing how the really primitive religion was a consecration of the rules and practices that were useful for the individual and for society, these rules being determined by the experience and growing wisdom of the race and enforced by the religious sanction, so that "the life of a simple community was ordered and prescribed from birth to death in a series of religious formulæ for conduct, personal purity, relation to others in the family and in the community, management of the household and of agriculture and farm economy, etc." [8]   Many causes tended to prevent development to the higher stage, and where not developed such religious formulæ become debased and misunderstood, as the most superficial glance into the rules of purity, for example, or the distinction of clean and unclean foods, would show. Yet even so late as the age of Paul a considerable residuum of wisdom and usefulness remained in those ritualistic rules, and convinced him that in the beginning men were sensitive to the Divine truth, until their perception was confused and clouded by idolatry.

That Paul was right in regarding this part of the religious law of the Pagans as true and Divine we can hardly doubt or deny, when we observe how much harm has been caused to society by the loss of it. Much of that healthy teaching, which was enforced on all as obligatory religious ceremonial, has ceased in modern time to be known to or practised by the poor and ill-educated classes. This widespread ignorance and neglect of the fundamental principles on which comfort, health and happiness in life depend, is now a serious danger, even among the most civilised nations. It must be acknowledged that the tendency of the Christian Church to concentrate its teaching on theoretical dogma and Church ritual, and to lose hold on the practical household life of the people, has contributed to spread this ignorance by allowing the ancient stock of household wisdom to fall into oblivion and even actively discouraging it as involved with superstition. It would be easy to quote cases in which modern Christian missionaries have done grave injury to their converts by forbidding them to continue old and wise sanitary practices, because they had been enforced by pagan religious law and took the form of service to a pagan deity.

Beginning the study of Greek Religion as a follower of Robertson Smith and M'Lennan, and accepting the Totemist theory as the key of truth, I was forced by the evidence to the view that degeneration is the outstanding fact in religious history, and that the modern theory often takes the last products of degeneracy as the facts of primitive religion. Having attained this view I recognised that it was the basis of the Pauline philosophy. In this Paul adopted the opinion current in pagan society and in pagan philosophy. The

view practically universal in the ancient world was that decay
and degeneration was the law of all things; that the Golden
Age lay in the beginning and every subsequent period was
a step further down from the primitive period of goodness,
happiness and sympathy with the Divine nature. We are
too apt to pooh-pooh this ancient doctrine as merely an old
fashion, springing from the natural tendency of mankind to
praise the former times and ways. But it was much more
than this. It was the reasoned view of the philosophers.
It coloured almost all Greek and Roman literature. It lay
deep in the heart of the pagan world. It produced the tone
of sadness which is hardly ever absent from the poetry of
Greece and Rome, heard as an occasional note even in its
poems of pleasure. A feeling like this cannot safely be set
aside as false. It must be explained; and the only explanation is that it arose from the universal perception of the fact
that the history of the Mediterranean world was a story of
degeneration and decay.

§ IV. St. Paul and Hellenism.

In contrast to the artificial system which modern theory
tries to impose on the study of religion, Paul saw the natural
and true principle through which alone religion and life can
develop and in the want of which they must degenerate. In
the process of history you observe that, in the few nations
and periods where there has been progress in any department
of life, some impulse and inner power has been at work,
some strong desire which incites the mind, forms the character
and directs the activity of the nation or of a sufficient number
of leading men in the nation. Paul generalised this principle.
He saw that the intense desire for truth and reality is the
fundamental fact in life, and that reality is God; and he

found in Christ the power that can rouse this desire and make it live among men permanently, instead of appearing sporadically on rare occasions and for a brief period.

The view of life taken by a practical nature like Paul's is determined by and suited to the age and the surrounding facts ; and, in order to understand him rightly, we must recognise how his thought had grown out of Hellenism, how it was related to Judaism, and how it sought to direct the Roman Imperial system. But we must remember that the idea of growth and development conditions his view and gives form to all his thought; and unless we appreciate this, we shall never comprehend the effect which his teaching had on the world.

The Hellenism with which Paul came in contact had greatly changed from the Hellenism of the classical period. It had lost that delicate grace which makes it unique in the world's history, but which was fragile, evanescent and irrecoverable, belonging to a certain peculiar collocation of racial and historic conditions, and unable to survive when those conditions changed. But it had become hardier, more practical, more common-place, and more capable of influencing the world. The grace of the older Hellenism as it arose under rare conditions, has always been a power that affected only the few. The later Hellenism had adapted itself to the world in general.

Since the time of Aristotle, Hellenism had been essaying a new and stupendous task, which was forced on it in the development of Mediterranean history. Greece had gone forth to conquer the East: Greek education and ideals were attempting to establish themselves in Western Asia. The attempt was successful in a remarkable degree, because Hellenism adapted itself to the new problems which it had to solve: it did not seek to impose itself in rigid purity on its Asiatic subjects, but profoundly modified itself in the school of practical life.   With the armies of Alexander, Seleucus, and Ptolemy marched also the philosophy and the literature and the art of Hellenism.   It was merely one symptom of a wider impulse that Alexander carried everywhere with him the poems of Homer.   Perhaps it was only a pseudo-historic fancy of later time which invented the story that a bronze statuette of Hercules by Lysippus accompanied all his marches, adorned his dinner-table, and was affected with emotion at his death; but the tale embodies the historic truth that those marches made Greek art a factor in the development of human life as far East as the Indus and the city of Bactra.

Greek philosophy, hitherto circumscribed in its ideals, tried to embrace within its scope the wider problems of a larger world-life; but the attempt could not be successful at the first essay.   Neither Epicureanism nor Stoicism—the one too Greek the other too Asiatic in its tone, but neither of them touching the finest chords of the Hellenic or the Oriental mind—attained a level higher than mere abstract philosophising.   Human thought cannot lead human life; it must ever lag behind practice, and gather power and truth from the world of real work and the practical solution of real problems.   None of those earlier attempts at a fusion of Greek and Oriental thought had any grasp of the principle of development, of which Aristotle in his most advanced stage had caught more than a glimpse.   Except through this principle it was impossible to unite Greek and Oriental thought.   It was equally impossible in practical life simply to amalgamate European and Asiatic society as they were: the two had to grow together into a new organisation.

Paul is penetrated from first to last with this idea. He looks at everything as in a process of growth, not as a hard stationary given fact. The true life is a making towards perfection through growth, culminating in fruit. How frequently there appears in his letters this thought of producing fruit, a development leading towards an issue in riches and usefulness. The good seems never to occur to his mind as a mere quality, but as a law of progress. Even where this thought is not explicitly brought out in the words, the analogy of other places may usually be taken as sufficient proof that, when he is speaking of riches, he thinks of it as the issue of a process of growth : so, for example, Phil. i. 11, "filled with the fruit of righteousness," Phil. i. 22, "to live is Christ and to die is gain," must both be understood as expressions of the gradual consummation of a process of living, *i.e.*, of striving towards an end. Phil. iv. 17, " I seek for the fruit that increaseth to your account," gives the picture of the accounts carefully kept in a day-book of the results coming in day by day and steadily increasing as time passes and the growth of character and power proceeds. His whole philosophy rests on this idea of growth and development. The world is always to him fluid and changing, never stationary. But the change is towards an end, not mere flux without law : it is either degeneration towards death or increase towards perfection and true life; it is the purpose of God working itself out in the affairs of men, a truly Greek idea which can be traced in the highest expression of its literature, beginning from Homer, who sums up the whole drama of the *Iliad* as the consummation of the purpose of Zeus ($\Delta\iota\grave{o}\varsigma$ $\dot{\epsilon}\tau\epsilon\lambda\epsilon\acute{\iota}\epsilon\tau o$ $\beta o\upsilon\lambda\acute{\eta}$, I. 4). After Aristotle Greek philosophy ceased to have any firm grasp of this idea, till it reappears as the determining form of Paul's whole thought.   Moral excellence is to him not a mere quality; it is a purpose to be attained, an end to be reached, a prize to be won by a course.

This character in the Pauline thought was what first struck me, as was mentioned already, during my last studies as an undergraduate in this University.   It seems to me wholly inconceivable in a mere narrow Hebrew, and wholly inexplicable without an education in Greek philosophy.   We find some indication of it in the few scraps of Athenodorus the Tarsian, which have been preserved by Seneca, such as " know that you are free from passions only when you have reached the point that you ask God for nothing except what you can ask openly".   Here true freedom of mind is conceived as an end to be attained, not as a quality naturally belonging to the mind in the beginning ; and another passage of considerable length quoted by Seneca shows distinctly that conception of life as a warfare and a struggle, which both Paul and Seneca express in remarkably similar terms.

Now, as was stated at the outset, it is not my purpose to discuss the relation between the philosophy of the Greeks and the philosophy which may be traced as the basis of Paulinism, a task for which the power and the inclination are lacking.   The aim of these lectures is to examine how the practical service in the development of mankind which Hellenism performed for the world, was taken up as an element in the Pauline reorganisation of society.

Hellenism has led the way of civilisation in many things ; but for the well-being of society there are two pre-eminent services which it has rendered to the world, and in which it stands almost alone : it showed how the freedom of the individual should be consistent with an ordered and articulated government, and it organised a system of State education. The relation in which Paul stands to both of these Hellenic ideals demands consideration.

That the unfettered development of the individual was the aim of Hellenism, and that the cities in which the Hellenic ideal was best realised were those in which freest play was given to the individual to live his own life according to his own judgment, needs merely to be stated ; it is a matter of universal agreement. There you have at once the strength and the weakness of Hellenism in the practical world of government. No other ancient people aimed so steadfastly as the Greeks at freedom as the greatest good in life, and while it must be confessed that the order and even the safety of the State were sometimes jeopardised in the pursuit of individual freedom, and the freedom tended to degenerate into licence and caprice, yet there was a certain atmosphere of liberty in a Greek city which is invigorating to breathe even in the pages of history, and which seems to have lasted even in remote lands and alien surroundings so long as any shadow of Hellenic society remained. We may state a single example, instructive yet too little noticed.

The contrast between the easy freedom of a Græco-Italian city and the rule of the strict and paternal government of a Roman city was still apparent in 95 A.D. This we learn from Statius, a poet not of the highest class, yet possessed of a real affinity for and an intense love of the beautiful, alike in external nature, in art, and in human character : he therefore saw what was best in contemporary Italian life, and we get from him a far more favourable as well as a far truer idea of that life, than from Juvenal, a disappointed man, or from Martial with his fondness for all that is ugly. The picture which Statius paints of Neapolis throws a light on the character of real Italian society, which we could never get from those two contemporary poets. We gather from it that a Greek-Italian town like Neapolis stood in much the same contrast with Roman system, as the free life, the almost capricious liberty and licence, in an English city shows to life in a German town, admirably ordered but bound by painfully strict rules. He praises in Neapolis the freedom of thought and word such as one finds in the dramatic poetry of Menander, a freedom in which Grecian licence mingles with and is toned by the strict principle of Rome: in Neapolis order reigned without virulence or wrangling in the law-courts, and the people found their law in their own character and practised equity without the compulsion of magistrates like those of Rome.

It is especially in writing to a group of Galatian cities that Paul insists on the idea of freedom. He urges them to stand fast in the freedom with which Christ set them free, and not be entangled again in a yoke of bondage. He reminds them that they were called for freedom. He uses the words "free," "freedom," "set free," eleven times in this short Epistle of six chapters. He has those three words only

7	times in Romans,	with	16	chapters
8	„ „ Corinthians,	„	29	„
2	„ „ the other letters,	„	43	„

While this indicates that there was some special need for insisting on this idea in writing to the Galatians and that freedom of spirit was an element which much required to be fostered in their character, it also shows that the idea was an essential and fundamental part of the social order as Paul understood it. The four South Galatian cities were more Asiatic, less moved by long familiarity with freedom of life and thought. In the case of the Romans Paul insists less on this idea ; Roman liberty was old in Rome ; and in writing to Greek cities of the Aegean lands, where liberty had been only too apt to degenerate into licence, it was more needful to insist on the importance of order, self-restraint, contentment, abnegation, than of freedom. So, even where Paul treats what is fundamentally the same topic, it is noteworthy that he does it with a different suggestion according to the character and past experience of his correspondents.

But, it may be said, the freedom on which Paul insists as a fundamental part of the Christian life, is only freedom from Jewish ritual; not freedom generally in political and social and philosophical relations. The reply is that freedom in one direction tends to produce freedom of mind in general, as human nature will have it; and moreover I would go so far as to maintain that Paul was conscious of the wider idea, even while in the first instance he is talking of its special application to the immediately pressing side of the case. The illustrations, the reiteration of the contrast between freedom and slavery, in the Galatian letter, show that the wider application could not be absent from the mind of either the writer or the readers. It is difficult and dangerous to narrow an idea in the interpretation of a great thinker and statesman, just as it is difficult and dangerous to narrow it in practical life, for a people which is educated to freedom in one direction will widen it all round. No man can set bounds to the growth and generalisation of a fruitful idea in the practical life of the world ; every autocrat has found it so, except if he succeed in a universal massacre, and if he leaves only one survivor, it may be fatal to his intentions. And so likewise in the thought and words of Paul, there is no fallacy of interpretation more dangerous than to maintain

that he was thinking only of some narrow religious question
or controversy, and had no conception of the wider application in the range of life which his words and thought admitted.   Yet there is no fallacy more common than this
among modern scholars, owing to their caution (in many
respects a healthy caution) against reading into Paul's words
more than was clearly and certainly meant by them.   But
it must be remembered that Christianity was not a philosophic theory, where one must be so strict in interpretation,
but a power in the life of the world ; that it must grow and
widen by the law of its being ; and that a firm grasp of this
law of growth is the determining and characteristic fact in
the thought of Paul.   Here we can appeal to subsequent
history.   Where Pauline ideas have been strongly operative,
there freedom in thought and life has been most conspicuous.
Where you have a people enslaved by ecclesiasticism or
obedient and devoted to autocracy, there Paul is a mere
empty name, a mere Saint who is revered without any
attempt to understand him.

Moreover we can trace this Pauline idea back to its origin
in the teaching of Christ.   No Saying of Christ's has been
more frequently quoted than that which is preserved by
Matthew alone, xi. 28-30, where the easy yoke and light
burden, which Christ imposes on men, are contrasted with
the heavy burden which others lay on them.   This is the
contrast between freedom and slavery.   Man cannot escape
the burden ; he must be restricted and tied down in a certain
degree; but the bonds and the weight which Christianity
imposes leave the bearer really free.

That this Saying of Christ's was familiar to Paul is
proved by the frequency with which he brings together two
words which are specially characteristic of it.   The words

are " meek " and " lowly " : and they are brought together in
Ephesians iv. 1, 2, Colossians iii. 12, 2 Corinthians x. 1 :
sometimes the adjectives, sometimes the nouns are used, for
Paul does not quote the exact words, but the thought lies in
his mind, and moulds his expression. Take for example the
last case : " I entreat you by the meekness and gentleness of
Christ, I who in your presence am lowly among you ". One
cannot escape the inference that the force of this appeal
depends on the readers' knowledge that meekness and lowli-
ness were of the character of Christ, in other words on their
knowledge of the Saying. Paul had been blamed by them
as poor-spirited : he reminds them that, as Christ was meek,
so he himself is lowly. The passage is forcible only to those
who knew that Christ had called himself meek and lowly.

This Saying guided the expression of those who championed the cause of freedom against the Judaising party in
the early Church. Peter protested against putting a *yoke*
upon the neck of the disciples, which they themselves could
not bear ; and the Council in Jerusalem resolved to lay upon
them no greater *burden* than these necessary things. The
emphatic words are always caught from the Saying, which
thus leads up through the Council and its Decree to the
Galatian Epistle. Paul, as he encouraged and urged the
Galatians on to freedom, was consciously working out the
appeal and the encouragement which Christ made in that
Saying, Matthew xi. 28-30.

A different fate has befallen those words of Christ from
the words of Paul. The former have been generally taken
in the universal sense, as referring to all the burdens and
troubles of life, whereas Paul's freedom has been construed
too narrowly as meaning only freedom from the hard and
fast rules of the Jewish Law. But the truth is that both

sayings have the double application, in the first instance to the burden and yoke of the Law and the freedom therefrom, in the second instance to the general idea of all burdens and trials and of wider freedom of life and thought. Christ stated as explicitly as Peter or James or Paul, that the Pharisees' rules bound upon men burdens heavier than they could bear. Christ and Paul alike generalised the thought into a universal principle of freedom and ease. It is because the Saying of Jesus is so patently and undeniably universal, and because it was evidently so much in Paul's mind, that we have the assurance and proof that he too took this contrast of bondage and freedom (which is the leading thought in the letter to the Galatians) in the wider as well as in the narrower sense.

We are therefore justified in maintaining that Paul felt a strong sympathy with the freedom of life and thought which marked the Greek society, and amid which he had grown up in Tarsus—which no one that has ever experienced it can willingly abandon ; and we are justified in asserting that the freedom which he champions in the letter to the Galatians was the freedom which the world owes to the Greek civilisation, a freedom, however, " in which Grecian license mingles with and is toned by Christian principle," if I may quote with one modification the description given by Statius.

In the second place Hellenic civilisation had formed a system of public education in an unsurpassed and almost unequalled way. The weakness of the Roman State was that it neglected education. The Jews developed a system of home education, in which certain religious and family and national influences were impressed on the child in a marvellous fashion, so that they permanently moulded his character : and the supreme influence was exercised by the festival, at once a national and a family celebration, of the Passover, and the teaching about its meaning and origin which the head of each house on that annual occasion imparted to all members of the household. But Hellenism evolved a national and public education, intellectual and physical, of remarkable character; and it was in later times and in the Græco-Asiatic cities that this system can be observed in greatest perfection. There can be no doubt that the vitality of those cities depended on their careful attention to public education. The character and details of the system belong still to the domain of the archæologist, for they are only being slowly recovered from the ruins of the Græco-Asiatic cities. The general principle is clear and certain.

The question is, what position Paul took up on this point. Did he regard education as a necessary element in a properly arranged society? Did he aim at making an educated, or was he satisfied with an uneducated, Church?

The answer follows at once from his ideal of freedom. Freedom is the growth of education : it does not really exist for the uneducated man, who cannot emerge from a state of servitude. Now true Christianity demands an educated people. It is the religion of educated minds, and it can never appeal to a rude barbarian race with that marvellous effect of instantaneously elevating and ennobling them to a certain degree, which Mohammedanism has often been able to attain. The pure, simple, stern, definite law conveyed in the Mohammedan faith can seize the mind of an ignorant and barbarous race. Christianity seems to miss it, except in so far as it begins by educating it.

Above all, that is true of the Pauline teaching. Its very essence lies in education. To say that is simply to repeat in another way what has been already said about Paul's insistence on the fundamental truth that the higher life is a growth, a development, a process of attaining to an end desired and struggled for. This growth is the education of the intellect and the character. The sarcasm that Paul pours forth on the Sophia, the philosophy, of the wise Corinthians, and the contrast that he points between their philosophic subtlety and the simplicity of true religion, have often led to the mistaken view that he disparaged education and preferred an uneducated religion. But this view misses the sarcasm of Paul's Letters to the Corinthians. It is not education that he hates, but false and abstract education ; for no person speaks so harshly about bad education as the educational enthusiast and reformer. What he really says to the Corinthians is that they must strip themselves of their false knowledge, cease to pride themselves on their spurious wisdom, recognise their own ignorance, before they can begin to acquire true education. They had never learned that the beginning of true knowledge lies in the recognition of one's ignorance.[9] The work of a true educator was " to fit spiritual words to spiritual ideas, to speak Sophia among the mature, the Sophia of God, the Divine system of true philosophy, the deep-lying scheme in which the intentions of God in the world find expression " (1 Cor. ii. 6 f., 12 f.). In writing to the Corinthians Paul was not depreciating the value of education, but warning them against the fault to which they were prone, *viz.*, philosophic verbalism and juggling with words.

It may be argued that Paul refers little to teachers and the organisation of teaching, that the word "teaching" is not a characteristic word in his writings, and that therefore, whatever he may have thought, he showed no care for the practical realisation of his ideas about education. But the formal organisation of teaching was a matter of practical detail, which lay outside the scope of his letters. In the *Pastoral Epistles*, where he approaches nearest to the subject of the practical organisation in a Christian society, the word "teaching" becomes a characteristic term, occurring fifteen times in those three short letters, whereas it occurs only four times in all the rest of his writings. Moreover, Paul may well have been alive to the dangers to which all schools and systems of teaching, lower and higher alike, are exposed: on the one hand they are too apt to become formal, stereotyped, conservative, lifeless; on the other hand Greek education, in an even greater degree than English, was too literary and abstract, too remote from the world of real life.

§ V. Hellenism and Hebraism.

In the mind of Paul a universalised Hellenism coalesced with a universalised Hebraism. If the Hebrew and the Hellenic ideals are both widened to embrace the whole human race, they must either be able to coalesce or the one must destroy the other: there is no third alternative.

That the thought of Paul was intensely and thoroughly Hebrew is, of course, a fixed beginning to start from; this needs no argument, for it rests on the practically universal agreement of scholars. Yet there exists a widespread opinion that the Hebrew side of Paul's mind is the whole, and that you can comprehend his aims and thoughts fully by approaching him solely from the Hebrew side; and on account of that strong opinion, expressed emphatically for example by Professor Harnack often in quite recent writings, many regard it as mere presumption to state a different view. But I cannot understand Paul as purely a Hebrew: his words and his life present on that supposition an insoluble enigma, and the course of history remains equally unintelligible.

I am assuming the possibility of combining in one mind
the aims and ideals of the East and the West. Here again
I find myself in opposition to a fashionable opinion. There
is a tendency in modern times, especially in this country, to
consider that the Oriental and the European mind are
absolutely contrary to each other, and to regard it as an
impossibility that Asiatic and European should mix in a
stable and contented common society. "Oil and Water" is
the proverb that every superficial observer will quote. This
opinion is mainly of modern manufacture. The truth that
underlies it, and which some more accurate speakers state
plainly, is that you cannot by pure compulsion and domination make Orientals into Europeans, any more than you can
make Europeans into Orientals. The West cannot simply
rule over the East, or the East over the West. The governing power must be above both; and each must approximate
to and adapt itself to the other by learning from the other.

The most marked and dangerous symptom of degeneration
in modern civilisation is the strengthening of racial antipathy,
which now exists to an extent that was formerly unknown.
In ancient history that deep-seated racial hatred plays little
part; the enmity of Greek and Jew is the worst example of
it, and this was never carried to anything like the extreme
that the *Judenhetze* has attained in mediæval and in modern
Europe. But race-hatred and colour-hatred are under present
conditions forming barriers far more impassable than ever
existed in ancient times; and the so-called irreconcilability
of Asiatic and European is one of those artificial modern
products.

The war between civilisation and barbarism, the battle
between the Gods and the Giants (to use the Greek mythological expression of the thought), is always going on: it can

never reach an end. The opposition reappears in new
forms, as soon as the old forms are decided; and this exaggeration of racial pride and intensification of racial hatred
is one of the modern forms which barbarism has assumed in
its war against civilisation and progress. You see it in the
railway station at Buda-Pesth, where in a great international
halting-place there is no inscription permitted in any
language except Magyar. You see it in the entrance hall
of an American hotel, where the clerk refuses admission to
a well-educated and well-dressed man because a tinge of
blue in the finger-nails betrays a slight intermixture several
generations back of negro blood. You see it on a great
scale in India, where the lesson has not been learned, or
has been learned to the wrong issue, that permanent rule
of one race over another must fail unless they can to some
degree approximate and unite.

The Roman Provinces in the Asiatic continent furnish one
example on a great scale to prove that the modern view is a
fallacy. In the great Hellenistic cities of Asia the union of
Asiatic and European in an orderly and well-balanced society
was accomplished, first by the wise policy of the Greek
kings and afterwards by the Roman rule. A high level of
adaptive and inventive capacity characterised those great
Græco-Asiatic cities, and among their mixed population
many excellent devices for the better ordering of society
originated in the Hellenistic age. The narrow limits within
which the old and purely Greek ideal of a City-State was
confined had made it hard, and it would have remained
isolated and barren, unless it had been worked out on a
broader stage in the Græco-Asiatic cities. Under the compelling power of necessity amid the intercourse of East
and West, development began in the realm of fact and life.

It has never been sufficiently noticed how much of improved
Roman method (and even of modern method) in administration was taken directly by the Imperial government from
Hellenistic models.   A rational chronology, based on a
national not merely a municipal principle, is, so far as I know,
first traceable in Asia Minor and Syria ; and it is one of those
simple matters of everyday usage, whose familiarity blinds
us to its immense importance.   Even alone such a creation
of good method is an inestimable service to mankind ; but
such a creation never stands alone.   The practical sense
which does this does many other things.   The Imperial
system of tax-collection, the substitution of which for the
old Republican system of farming by the great financial
magnates and corporations was one of the greatest benefits
that the Empire conferred on the Roman world, was simply
taken over from the Hellenistic states in the Eastern Provinces.   Numerous devices of the Roman commercial law
as developed by the praetors were borrowed from Hellenistic
practice with very slight modifications (which were not
always improvements), *e.g.*, in respect of wills, contracts, etc.
—a fact of which some recent writers on the Epistle to the
Galatians and its legal aspect continue to remain ignorant.

But far the most important fact of all was that in the
mixed Hellenistic Empires, and especially in the Seleucid
Empire, the wider idea of a nation and of national patriotism
was beginning under the compulsion of necessity to replace
the narrower Greek idea of the City-State and of a purely
municipal patriotism.   The wider idea was still faint and
weak, but its germ was growing, destined to be taken up and
fostered by the stronger and better amalgamated Empire
of Rome.   Philosophy followed hard on the heels of fact.
Greek thought, and especially the Stoic philosophy, was not

insensible to this wider and nobler idea of a unity and brother-hood that transcended the limits of a city or a tribe ; but the conception of universal brotherhood remained as yet an abstract and ineffective thought, devoid of driving power to move the world.

The Judaic conception was equally narrow with the pure Hellenic ideal, equally hard and barren when it persisted too long in its isolation, but also equally capable of rich growth. It saw one people of God, while all others were outcasts. The Judaism of the Diaspora was already working its way practically towards demonstrating the irrationality and im-possibility of that narrow principle. Every Jewish family, which possessed the right of citizenship in a Greek city or the higher right of Roman citizenship, was in practice deny-ing the principle to which its members still clung in theory. The teaching of Jesus rose high above such a narrow idea. The Apostles by slow steps were moving out of it : whether the impulse which forced them on would have been sufficient to raise them entirely above it of themselves cannot be known, for events took another course. The greater idea seized on Paul, penetrated and ruled his whole nature, and made him on a sudden able to see the whole truth and compelled him to live in it. He perceived in a flash of illumination that the universal Hellenism and the universalised Jewish right of inheritance to God's promise and grace, must be co-exten-sive ; that each was the complement of the other. He made the other Apostles see this, at least sooner than they would themselves have understood it. The barrier was broken once for all. The universalism of Christianity completed the transformation of Hellenism.

§ VI. THE EMPIRE AS THE WORLD'S HOPE.

As has been pointed out in § III., the opinion which was almost universally held in ancient time, alike by philosophers, by poets, and by society in general, was that all history was a progress towards decay, a degeneration from good to bad. In the view of both Greeks and Romans the Golden Age of the world lay in the beginning of history, far back in the remote past; and since then the world had been passing through a series of ages, each new one worse than the preceding.

There was one remarkable exception to the unanimity of ancient feeling. There existed during the last fifty years before Christ a disposition to regard the rise of the Roman Imperial system as the inauguration of a new and better era in the history of the world. In this respect, as in so many others, the Empire presented itself as the rival of Christianity, attempting to solve the same social problems by means which were superficially similar, however unlike they were fundamentally.

It was part of the ancient view that there could be no remedy for the evils of the world except through the help of Divine power. This view was taken both in the Christian and the Imperial hope and in the popular despair. As Paul said, so also those heralds of the Empire maintained, when things are at their worst then comes the divinely sent aid. The hope of a cure through the new Empire was born out of the most desperate straits to which the Mediterranean world had yet been reduced, *viz.*, the Civil Wars and the apparently imminent ruin of the one great remaining power of order in the civilised world. The terrible and widespread suffering entailed by the Civil Wars proved, just as the

Pauline view declared (§ II.), the birth-pangs of a new hope, which appeared in the form of a deity incarnate in human form upon the earth: on this god, whether he was named Mercury, or Apollo, or Jupiter, rested the salvation of the Roman world.

This Imperial hope was undoubtedly fostered and engineered as a political device. Poets were used and rewarded for singing it, and orators were encouraged to employ it in their public speeches. But it was more than a device of clever party manipulation. It had a natural origin and a basis in human nature and human needs. The best way to understand its character is to examine carefully the poem in which it first appears, the famous Fourth Eclogue of Virgil, which was the first clear and articulate expression of the hope. This poem indubitably exercised considerable influence in giving form and definition to the vague emotion which was stirring in the popular mind at the time when the Empire was in preparation, felt by many, and expressed by one great writer.

The Fourth Eclogue had its origin in an interesting episode of literary history; and, if it were regarded solely from the literary point of view, it might almost be called an occasional poem. But what might have been a mere occasional poem in the hands of a lesser poet, became in passing through the mind of Virgil a work of far wider and higher character. The thought must have been simmering in his mind for a considerable time before it was expressed; though the form was suggested by an occasion in literary intercourse. It is, therefore, essential to a right comprehension of this Eclogue that it should be studied in its origin. Only in this way can its relation to the popular conceptions of the time be understood.

4

It was through the relations between Virgil and Horace, so friendly and for the latter so important, that this poem of Virgil's took its actual form.[10]   Horace was an officer, who served in the army of Brutus and Cassius, and took part in the disastrous battle of Philippi, which wrecked the aristocratic and republican party, late in the year 42 B.C. He fled from the rout of Philippi and returned to Italy, where he found that the estate at Venusia which he had inherited from his father had been confiscated and assigned (like many other Italian estates) to the soldiers of the victorious armies. He came to Rome, where, as he says,

> Bereft of property, impaired in purse,
> Sheer penury drove me into scribbling verse.

The metropolis was the only place which at that time offered a career to a young man conscious of literary power, and compelled to seek a living thereby.   Horace had now neither property nor patron nor influential friend.   As an adherent of the defeated and unpopular party, the young poet's career was doubly difficult ; and we could not suppose that his republican and aristocratic sentiments were blazoned by him in Rome when he settled there.   That he now concealed his political feelings is proved by the fact that he found employment as a clerk in one of the government offices : a pronounced aristocrat would not have received, and would hardly have asked, such a position.

Horace's mind was not that of a zealot or an extremist. He had fought for the side which he believed in, and he accepted the result of the fight.   The question for him was settled, and he now accommodated himself unreservedly to the new situation.   Moreover, he had unquestionably lost his faith in his former party, from causes at which the historian can guess without any difficulty.   He recog-

nised that it was incapable and dead, and that Rome
had nothing to hope from it, even if it had been successful
in the fight. Every reader of his works knows that such
was his feeling, and such was the widespread feeling of the
Roman world. Men recognised that the degeneration of
the Mediterranean world had proceeded one stage further,
and that the Republic had failed decisively to govern the
vast Empire which it had conquered. Horace represents
the general opinion of the pagan world. He stands in the
world of men, not above it (as Virgil did); he expresses its
sentiments from a sane, common-sense point of view; and,
as he emerged from penury, he attained a high level of
wisdom, propriety and self-respect in his outlook on the
world, and a singularly easy and graceful yet dignified
expression of popular philosophy and worldly experience.
From him we gather the best side of popular sentiment
and popular philosophy, as they were trained in the stern
school of life.

In one of Horace's poems the popular estimate of the
situation in which the Roman world was placed found full
expression. This poem is the Sixteenth Epode, which
stands at the end of the first period of his literary activity,
and prepares the entrance on his second period. In the
first period he was the hungry wolf, the impoverished and
disappointed writer, who had felt the injustice of the world
and was embittered by his experience. In the Sixteenth
Epode he pours forth unreservedly the disappointment,
which he and the people generally felt about the existing
situation of the Roman world. The long civil wars had
sickened and disgusted the popular mind, except in so far
as they had brutalised it into positive enjoyment of the
apparently endless series of intestine wars and massacres,

each more bloody than its predecessor.   The Roman Empire
and Roman society were drifting steadily towards ruin, and
their motion onwards towards the abyss was becoming ever
more rapid.

This consciousness of degeneration and approaching ruin
generally turned to utter despair.   No hope was apparent.
The Roman people had outgrown its old religion, and had
found no new religion to take its place.   Hence there was
no religious consolation for it, no God to whom it could look
for help and salvation.   To which of the deities should the
Roman people turn: what prayer would avail to importune
Vesta and the old Divine patrons of the State and compel
them to help the city and the Empire in their need?   So
asks Horace in the second Ode of the first book, a poem
written at a considerably later date, when he thought he had
found a new God and a present help.   He replies that a new
God was required to save the world.   But in the first period
of his literary work he had no hope.   He had not even a
political party to which he could join himself and for which
he could fight.   He had lost his old faith in the Republican
party, and found nothing to replace it; the mind of man
craved for the help of God, and there was no God known to
it.   So Horace consoled himself by an excursion into the
land of fancy and of dreams.   The Romans, as he says, had
now only one chance left.   They could abandon their country,
and go far away from Italy into the Western Ocean, to find
that happy land of which legend tells and poets sing, where
the Golden Age of quiet and peace and plenty is always
present, because here the degeneration which had affected
the whole Mediterranean world had never begun.   And so
the poet calls upon all true men and good patriots to abandon
their country, to desert Rome, and sail forth into the Atlantic

Ocean, seeking a "new world to redress the balance of the old world"—to dwell in

> The rich and happy isles
> Where Ceres year by year crowns all the untill'd land with sheaves,
> And the vine with purple clusters droops, unpruned of all her leaves;
> Where the olive buds and burgeons, to its promise ne'er untrue,
> And the russet fig adorns the tree, that graffshoot never knew;
> Where honey from the hollow oak doth ooze, and crystal rills
> Come dancing down with tinkling feet from the sky-dividing hills;
> There to the pail the she-goats come, without a master's word,
> And home with udders brimming broad returns the friendly herd.
>
> . . . .
>
> For Jupiter, when he with brass the Golden Age alloy'd,
> That blissful region set apart by the good to be enjoy'd;
> With brass and then with iron he the ages sear'd, but ye,
> Good men and true, to that bright home arise and follow me! [11]

Evidently, this fanciful description of the Golden Age in the Western Isles, with the advice to the Romans to take refuge there, does not express any serious belief. Horace and the popular mind generally had no cure to suggest for the malady of the State. To them the world of reality had sunk beyond salvation, and human life had degenerated into a riot of bloodshed and strife. Only in dreamland was there any refuge from the evils of actual life. Horace is here only "the idle singer of an empty day," singing in the brief interval between the last massacre and the next one. There is no faith, no belief, no reality, in the poem, because the poet had no religion, while the popular mind felt in a vague fashion that God alone could help now, but knew no God to turn to. In this poem despair was seeking a moment's oblivion, and cheating itself with the false words of hope.

But, while there is no reality in the proposed remedy, no one can doubt or has ever doubted that the poem is political, and touches on the real facts of the Roman situation. This was what the people thought and felt and vaguely said. The old Rome could not stand: the Republican and aristocratic party, which had fought to maintain the old Rome, was mistaken and practically dead, and its policy had utterly failed. The poem is really the expression of a despairing acquiescence in the tyranny of the Triumvirate and the autocracy of the coming Empire.   This was the reluctant and despairing view with which Tacitus a century later (and many for whom Tacitus speaks) regarded the government of the Flavian Emperors: a Republican constitution, though theoretically the best, was too good for the Roman people, and the autocracy was the only government that was practically possible. And, after a similar fashion, in the Sixteenth Epode Horace abandoned definitely his Republican views, to dream about freedom and to acquiesce in the slavery of a military despotism.

For our purpose the most important feature of the Epode is its expression of the general opinion that no salvation could be hoped for except through some superhuman aid. Man, left to himself, had degenerated and must degenerate. As we have already seen, this was the almost universal pagan view.   St. Paul makes this view the starting-point of his philosophy and history: God alone can give help and preserve true civilisation.   In this the Apostle of the Gentiles agrees with the almost universal Gentile thought.   What he adds to it is the evangel of the way, revealed first to the Hebrews imperfectly, now perfectly to all men.

We see, then, that the opinion of Virgil stands by itself, practically unprecedented in pagan literature.   How did this idea of hope of an immediate and present salvation through a new-born child take form in his mind?

It may be assumed, for the moment, that chronology and general conditions permit the supposition that Virgil's poem

started from and gave the answer to Horace's.[12]   The late
Professor Kiessling, of Berlin, pointed out that Virgil in this
poem caught up and echoed two of Horace's phrases.   It
seems beyond doubt that

nec magnos metuent armenta leones

is not independent of Horace's

nec ravos timeant armenta leones ;

and similarly that Virgil's

ipsae lacte domum referent distenta capellae ubera

has some connection with Horace's

illic iniussae venient ad mulctra capellae
refertque tenta grex amicus ubera.

Two contemporary poets, known to one another, each (as
we may be certain) familiar with the other's work, do not
write in this way by accident.   The resemblance is intentional, and was regarded, both by themselves and by the
world, as a compliment paid by the imitator to the imitated.
The question might be raised, however, which was the
imitator ; and there is a certain probability *a priori* that
Horace, as the younger and less distinguished, was the
imitator ; for we know of other places in which beyond
doubt that was the case.   But in this instance Kiessling
concludes 'that Virgil was the one who echoed Horace ; and
his reasoning from internal evidence seems conclusive.
Moreover Virgil's poem was written in the year 40 B.C., and
(as is universally accepted) in the latter part of the year ;
whereas Horace's poem, which arose out of the horrors
and suffering of the bloody Perusian war and expressed the
feeling of repulsion excited thereby in the poet's mind, can
hardly be placed later than the early months of 40 or the end
of 41 B.C.   The imitation is a graceful compliment paid by

the older and more famous poet to his young and as yet little known contemporary.

We can appreciate how much the compliment meant to Horace, and understand that the language of the Ode which he addressed many years later to Virgil is not hyperbolic, but perfectly sincere and well-deserved. It was the kindness and courtesy which Virgil showed to Horace when still struggling with poverty that endeared the older poet to the younger ; and this spirit of kindness and courtesy prompted Virgil to pay this graceful compliment, which may be regarded as the beginning of the friendship between the two poets. That friendship opened the door of society to Horace. After a time Virgil introduced him to Maecenas, who became his patron and intimate friend.   In the sunshine of moderate prosperity his character expanded and blossomed into the genial temper of his maturer work. A deep gulf, caused by a profound difference of tone and spirit, separates Horace's later from his earliest work. While he was struggling amid hard fortune, he was bitter and narrow. What he quickly became after he met Virgil, the world knows and appreciates.

Now, looking at the Fourth Eclogue from this point of view, let us place it beside the Sixteenth Epode, and see what meaning it gathers from the collocation. Horace had said that no hope for the Romans existed, except that they should abandon Italy and Rome, to seek a happy life in the islands of the Western Ocean. Virgil replies that the better age of which Horace dreams is here in Italy present with them, now just beginning. The very words in which Horace had described a fabulous island and a legendary Golden Age are applied by Virgil to describe Italy as it will soon be, as the child already born in Italy will see it. What are mere fanciful marvels when told about an unknown isle of the Ocean becomes real in the imaginative vision of Virgil, for they are being now realised in Italy under the new rule, through the power of the peace and good order and wise administration, settled government and security of property, which have been established in the country.

Reading the two poems together, and remembering that they were written within a year of one another by two friends, one cannot doubt that they were companion and contrasted pieces, responding one to the other. They say to Rome respectively: "Seek your happiness by fleeing far into the Western Ocean"; and "Your happiness is now being wrought out before your eyes in Italy". A glance suffices to show the intention to any one who has eyes to see. But in literary criticism inability to perceive more than one has been taught and habituated to see is a feature of some of the most learned scholars.

Virgil is the prophet of the new age of Italy. He was always thinking about Italy and imagining what it might be made by the application of prudence, forethought, and true knowledge. The object of the Georgics is to describe what Italy might become, if agriculture were wisely and thoroughly carried out. "You have all you need in Italy, the most beautiful and the best country of the whole world, if you will only use it right." The intention of the poem is to force this lesson home to the Roman mind.

The practical and skilful administration of Augustus appealed to Virgil. He saw that Augustus had wise plans, and skill to carry them into effect. He was a convinced adherent and apostle of the Emperor; and in this poem he sets forth the Gospel of the new Empire. The union of science and government had made the Mediterranean world

fertile. The science had originally been supplied by the theocratic order, when the accumulated experience and growing
wisdom of a people was concentrated at the hieron of each
district, where the Goddess educated and guided, nourished
and tended her people. The union of science and government was now beginning to make Italy perfect under the
new Empire ; that union would soon destroy every noxious
plant and animal, produce all useful things in abundance
from the soil, tame all that was wild, improve nature to an
infinite degree, make the thorn-tree laugh and bloom with
flowers : it would naturalise at home all that was best in
foreign lands, and thus render Italy independent of imports
and so perfectly self-sufficient that navigation would be
unnecessary.

In this last detail we have one of those startlingly modern
touches which so often surprise us in Roman literature.
Virgil would have no free trade.   The ideal he aimed at
was that Italy should depend on itself alone, and not on
sea-borne products.   His ideal is here different from and
narrower than the Imperial.   He does not think of binding
the lands of the whole Empire into a unity, as the Emperors
desired ; he wishes only that Italy should learn to produce
everything for itself and that thereafter the " estranging sea "
should separate once more the lands, and navigation should
cease.   He probably had not thought of all that was implied
in this ideal.

That the Fourth Eclogue stands in close relation with the
new Empire is obvious.   It is the wise new system of rule
that is to produce these blessed results for Italy.   But
there is as yet no trace of the autocratic idea in the poem.
The future Emperor is neither named nor directly alluded
to : he was still only one of a small coalition, the Triumvir-

ate, and his name was Octavianus. The title Augustus was bestowed upon him many years afterwards, in 27 B.C.

Virgil thinks of the continuance, in an improved form, of the old Roman system of constitutional government by magistrates (*honores*), of the political career open to all Romans in the old way, and of the military training which was the foundation and an essential part of the Roman education. War must continue for a time, in order that the young Roman may be educated in the true Roman fashion. But it will be foreign war, carried on in the East; new Argonauts must explore and conquer and bring under the Roman peace the distant Orient; a new Achilles was now sailing for another Troy in the person of Antony, who was charged with the government of the whole East and the conduct of the Parthian war. The triumvirate, Antony, Octavian and Lepidus, was not in appearance an autocracy : it was, in name at least, a board of three commissioners for establishing the Republic, professedly a temporary expedient to cure the troubles of the State. To speak or think of a single Emperor, or to connect the salvation of Rome with any single human being, was treason to the triumvirate, and was specially out of place at the moment when Virgil was writing, shortly after the peace of Brundisium had established concord and equality between Antony and Octavian. In the Eclogue a more obvious allusion is, in fact, made to Antony than to Octavian, for every one at the time recognised Antony in the new Achilles who was starting for an eastern war : the provinces east of the Adriatic Sea were under Antony's charge, and a Parthian war was in progress.

But, while Antony is more directly alluded to, the thought that incites the poem and warms the poet's enthusiasm is the wise and prudent administration of Italy by Octavian.

That is the real subject.   The enlightened forethought of
Octavian and Agrippa made their rule the beginning of a
new era in Italy ; and Virgil looked forward to a continuous
growth in the country.

Still less is there any dynastic thought in the Fourth
Eclogue.   The idea that an expected son of Octavian, or the
son of any other distinguished Roman, is alluded to, is ana-
chronistic and simply ridiculous.   Every attempt to identify
the young child mentioned in the poem with any actual child
born or to be born has been an utter failure, and takes this
Eclogue from a false point of view.   The idea of some
literary critics is that the poem celebrates the expected birth
of a son, who unfortunately for the poet turned out to be a
daughter.   This idea is really too ludicrous for any one but
a confirmed literary and " Higher " Critic.   A poet does not
work so ; even a " poet laureate " could not work under such
conditions.

Least of all is there any idea in the Fourth Eclogue of
deifying either Octavian personally or a son of his who might
hereafter be born.   That view is not merely untrue to the
existing facts of the conjoint government and the union of
Octavian and Antony.   It misunderstands and misrepresents
the development of the Imperial idea and the growth (or
growing perversion) of thought in Rome ; it places Virgil on
a plane of feeling far too low ; it is a hopeless anachronism
in every point of view.   Schaper, in a very interesting paper,
pointed out many years ago that the deification of Augustus
and his son and his dynasty was wholly inconsistent with
the composition of the Eclogue so early as B.C. 40.   The
paper was convincing and, in a certain way, conclusive.   But
instead of drawing the inference that the deification of the
dynasty is a false idea, read into the poem under the preju-

dice caused by the development of history in the years
following after A.D. 40, he propounded the impossible theory
that the poem was composed at a later time, *i.e.*, in the
period ending June B.C. 23, when Augustus was governing
no longer as triumvir, but as consul, and was practically sole
master of the Empire, though maintaining the Republican
forms and the nominal election of another consul along with
himself.   To support this theory, Schaper eliminated the
allusion to Pollio's consulship, which fixes the composition
to the year 40 B.C., reading *Solis* instead of *Polio* (for that,
as he maintained, was the correct spelling).   To make this
theory possible chronologically, and reconcile it with the
date of the publication of the Eclogues not very long after
40 B.C., Schaper supposed that the Fourth Eclogue was composed at a later date and inserted in a revised second edition
of the Eclogues.[13]

These impossible buttresses of Schaper's theory were
universally rejected; the faults of his paper distracted attention from its real merits; and the perfectly unanswerable
argument from which he started was tacitly set aside, as if it
shared in the error of the theory which he had deduced
from it.

The truth is that the poem belongs to an earlier stage of
thought than the worship of Augustus; and the Divine idea
in it was still so vague that it was readily capable of being
interpreted in accordance with subsequent history.   But it
was equally capable of being developed in a different direction and in a nobler and truer style.   Had the Pauline idea
of Christianity as the religion of the Empire been successfully
wrought out during the first century, the Fourth Eclogue
would have seemed equally suitable to that line of development.   The later popular instinct, which regarded the poem

as a prophecy of the birth of Christ, was not wholly incorrect. The poem contained an inchoate idea, unformed and vague, enshrining and embodying that universal need which indicated "the fulness of time" and the world's craving for a Saviour. The Roman world needed a Saviour; it was conscious of its need; it was convinced that only Divine intervention could furnish a Saviour for it. Paul was fully aware that this universal craving and unrest and pain existed in the Roman world; and he saw therein the presage of the birth of Divine truth. "The whole creation groaneth and travaileth in pain until now."

The political side of the Fourth Eclogue is emphatically marked, and was indubitably recognised at the time. The poem suited the situation, and it glorified the wise policy of Augustus. We are not blind to this side of the facts, which (as I believe) suggested to Maecenas and Augustus how much strength might be gained for the Imperial movement by associating it with the new ideas which Virgil expressed. But the significance of this aspect should not blind us to the fact that this alone is insufficient to explain the genesis and the full meaning of the poem. It was not simply a political pamphlet in verse, though it had political significance.

What then was the origin of the poem? Apart from the political idea, the Fourth Eclogue is a vision of the true Italy, of Italy as it ought to be and might be. With the eye of a poet and the certainty of a prophet Virgil sees this new Italy in actual process of coming into being, and describes what he sees.

There are two things which determine the evolution of this ideal picture in Virgil's poem. He is perfectly sure that the glorified and idealised Italy of his vision is being realised at this very time and before the eyes of living men, and he connects that realisation with a new-born child. These are two ideas to which no real parallel can be found in preceding Greek or Roman literature. The Better Age had been conceived by the Greeks as lying in the past, and the world's history as a progress towards decay. Even where a cycle of ages was spoken of by the Greek philosophers, it was taken rather as a proof that no good thing could last, than as an encouragement to look forward to a better future. Now Virgil's new age, though spoken of in his opening lines as part of a recurring cycle, is not pictured before his view as evanescent; it is coming, but its end is not seen and not thought of by him.

How does Virgil arrive at his firm conviction that the best is last, and that the best is surely coming, nay, that it now is? We cannot regard it as arising entirely from his own inspiration, springing mature and full-grown, like Athena from the head of Zeus. Rather we must attempt to trace the stages in its development to the perfect form which it has in this poem.

Again, the association of a young child with this coming age is something entirely alien to Greek and Roman thought. It springs from a sense of a Divine purpose, developing in the growth of the race and working itself out in the life of other new generations, a thought not in itself foreign to the philosophical speculation of Greece, but developed here in a form so unusual that it imperatively demands recognition and explanation.

The idea that the nation may and must look forward to a happier future, pledged by Divine promise, was too delicate for the Greek philosophers, though one finds it to a certain degree in the poets. Nowhere can we find any previous

philosophy or religion that had grasped the thought firmly
and unhesitatingly, except among the Hebrew race.   To the
Hebrew prophets, and to them alone, the Better Age lay
always in the future :

> The best is yet to be,
> The last of life, for which the first was made.

The Hebrews always recognised that the Divine purpose
reserved for them a future better than the past, and they
alone associated the coming of the Better Age with the birth
of a child.   We must, I think, look to the East and to
Hebrew poetry for the germ from which Virgil's poem
developed, though in the process of development ideas
derived from other sides determined its growth and
affected its character.

Looking at the poem from another point of view, we recognise that it is a metrical experiment, which Virgil tried
in this one case and never repeated.   Its metrical character
seemed to him appropriate to his treatment of this one
subject; but he found no other subject which it suited, and
he considered that the true development of the heroic verse
lay in another direction.

Landor, in his criticisms on Catullus's twelfth ode, has the
following remarks on the metrical character of this Eclogue :
" The worst, but most admired, of Virgil's Eclogues, was
composed to celebrate the birth of Pollio's son in his con-
sulate.   In this Eclogue, and in this alone, his versification
fails him utterly.   The lines afford one another no support.
For instance this sequence (lines 4-6) : —

> Ultima Cumæi venit jam carminis ætas.
> Magnus ab integro sæclorum nascitur ordo.
> Jam redit et Virgo, redeunt Saturnia regna.

Toss them in a bag and throw them out, and they will fall

as rightly in one place as another. Any one of them may come first; any one of them come last; any one of them may come immediately; better that any should never come at all." But in his criticism (apart from the fact that the force of lines 4-6 would suffer seriously if they were transposed, though grammar and metre might be uninjured) Landor has not observed that Virgil in this poem is deliberately trying an experiment in order to obtain a special effect. We do not maintain that the ruling metrical form would be suitable for ordinary Latin use, but its employment in this case is obviously intentional, and dictated by the subject; it is no case of accidental failure in versification. But Virgil recognised that it did not suit the Latin genius, and he never repeated it. He used it here, because the subject was not purely Latin: prophecy of this kind was not akin to the Latin temperament or the Latin language.

The two most distinguishing and salient metrical characteristics of this Eclogue are, first, that the stops coincide more regularly with the ends of lines than in any other passage of Virgil, so that to a large extent each single verse gives a distinct sense; and, secondly, that in a number of cases the second half of the line repeats with slight variation the meaning of the first half, or, when the sense is enclosed in two hexameters, the second repeats the meaning of the first. These characteristics are unlike any previous treatment of the hexameter. As to the first, it is true that in the earliest stages of Virgil's metre the stops are placed at the ends of lines to a much greater extent than in its later stages. But there is a general agreement among Latin scholars that the Fourth Eclogue is not the earliest; and even compared with the earliest, its metre is seen to be something peculiar and apart.

These characteristics are distinctly those of Hebrew poetry ; and it appears to me that the metrical treatment of this Eclogue can hardly be explained except as an experiment made in imitation of the same original, from which sprang the central conception of the Better Age surely approaching, and inaugurated by the birth of a child. Virgil found the idea and the metrical form together; that is to say, he did not gather the idea from a secondary source, but had read it (in translation) as expressed by a great writer, whose poetic form dominated his mind for the moment. Only a writer of the loftiest poetic power could have so affected the mind of Virgil. We notice, too, that the peculiar metrical form is most marked where the expression approaches the prophetic type, while in the descriptive parts the metre is closer to the form common in the Eclogues.

That such an origin for Virgil's idea is possible, will be doubted by no one who takes properly into account both the width of his reading, and the influence which the strange and unique character of the Jewish nation and religion (and here the religion made and was the nation) already had exerted and was exerting on the Græco-Roman world. That is a subject over which there hangs, and must always hang, a thick veil ; but enough is known to give us increasing certainty, as time goes on, that the fascination which Judaism exerted on a certain class of minds was very strong, and its influence on Roman society far greater than is apparent in the superficial view which is permitted us in the dearth of authorities.

Finally, the often quoted analogies with several passages of the prophet Isaiah afford some indication as to the identity of the great poet whose words, either in a Greek translation or in extracts, had come before Virgil, and influenced the development of his thought. It is true that there are numerous points in this Eclogue which go back to Greek models. The ideas taken up by Virgil from a Semitic source are developed in a mind rich with Hellenic knowledge and strong with a vigorous Italian life. Virgil is never a mere imitator except in his most juvenile work ; he reforms and transforms everything that he has learned from his great instructors. It is an Italian idyll that he has given us, not a mere transplantation of a foreign idea, or of any number of foreign ideas.[14]

The Hebrew idea of a growth towards a happier future through the birth of a Divine child was simmering in his mind, when Horace's despairing poem declaring that no happiness for Rome could be found except in voluntary exile to the Islands of the West caught his attention, and drew from him a reply. As a convinced and enthusiastic supporter of Augustus, he declared that peace and happiness were being realised in Italy by the wise rule of the Triumvir. With this he interwove the almost universal thought of his contemporaries that Divine aid alone could afford real and permanent improvement in the condition of the State ; and this Divine aid expressed itself to him in the form that he had caught from the Hebrew poetry.

Whom then did Virgil think of as the child ? He must have had some idea in his mind. There can be no doubt as to this, if we simply look at the genesis of the Imperial cult. The power of that cult lay in a certain real fact, the majesty and dignity and character of the Roman people, which was assumed to be represented by the Emperor as the head of the State. Augustus permitted worship of himself only in the form of a cult of " Rome and Augustus ". To a Roman like Virgil in B.C. 40, the Divine child, who embodies the future of Rome, who has to go through the education of war and magistracies (as the poem declares), could only be

" Rome," *i.e.*, the Roman people collectively, the new generation of Rome, born under happier auspices and destined to
glory and advancement in power and in happiness.   As
Virgil apostrophises the one Roman as typical of the race
and its destiny in the famous line, often quoted, *tu regere
imperio populos, Romane, memento,* and as Macaulay imitating
him uses the same figurative speech, " Thine, Roman, is the
pilum," to paint the Roman racial character, so here the
Latin poet, with the Hebrew thought of a child in his mind,
can describe the birth and infancy of the future Roman as
taking place under the usual natural conditions.

A correct appreciation of this poem makes us better understand the origin and character of the Roman Empire, and
the problem which had to be solved in its construction.
The poem is the apotheosis of the Empire, but not of autocracy.   The Divine idea in it is wider than the narrow limits
of Roman or of pagan thought.   But it is vague as well as
wide : it is nobler than paganism in proportion as it is vague
and wide.   Owing to its vagueness it was susceptible of more
than one interpretation ; and in the lifetime of Virgil it was
interpreted as the Gospel of the Empire ; and it was made
the starting-point of a half-artificial, half-genuine literary
movement, which set up the New Empire as the Divine
power on earth, a movement fostered by Maecenas and
brilliantly expressed with more than half-belief by Horace.

But the Divine idea of the poem was true enough to be
also capable of being developed in a different direction and
in a nobler style.   The Eclogue stands at the parting of the
ways, and has not yet set foot on the worse path which was
soon afterwards chosen.   In it there lay much more than
Virgil was himself conscious of.   He did not see, as we now
can recognise, that the necessity for a common religion lay

before the Empire. In fact, as we saw, he did not grasp
fully the Imperial idea. His ideal was Italian, not Imperial.

In this, as in so many other ways, the Imperial system
offered a strange and striking parallel to the Pauline system.
They were two attempts to achieve a similar end by means
which in some respects strongly resembled each other. The
need of an incarnate God to save the world, the gathering up
in the new system of all that was excellent in older history,
were Imperial as well as Pauline ideas. The unity and
brotherhood of the whole Roman world was the goal towards
which Imperial policy was consciously tending. To attain
the goal a common religion was needed, and Augustus found
himself, against his own will and wish, forced to make an
Imperial religion. His attempt to restore to life the dead
ceremonial of the old Roman worship proved, as he could
not but recognise, utterly inadequate. The Provinces could
never have been brought to adopt the childish ritual of the
Arval Brothers, the Salian priests, the Lares, and so on.
The majesty of Rome incarnate in the reigning Emperor
was presented to Augustus by the popular choice as the
common religion of the Empire.

There were in this way two religions proposed for the
Empire; the Imperial cult was demanded by the populace,
the new universal religion of Christ was offered by the in-
sistent voice of Paul. The Emperors, if they refused the
latter, must accept the former; but it was not until the reign
of Domitian that the Imperial worship was frankly and
ostentatiously adopted, when the Christian alternative had
been refused and proscribed absolutely. Augustus, who was
forced to organise the Imperial cult in the Provinces as a
support of the State, was always a little ashamed and afraid
of it; and he prohibited it in Italy. His successors, with

the exception of Caligula, a half-insane person, but insane with the idea of autocracy, were affected in some degree by the same feeling. Some regarded it as a mere political fiction. Domitian began to take a real pride and pleasure in it.

§ VII. PAULINISM IN THE ROMAN EMPIRE.

If Paul was attempting to gather together into his ideal of a Christianised society all that was true and Divine in the older world of thought and life, the Roman Empire was working at the same problem on the practical side. We have just seen how it caught up from the Hellenistic states many excellent devices in administration and wrought them into its own system. That is typical of the Imperial policy. The Empire was universal in its intentions : the Emperor, father of his country the Empire, sought to turn to the advantage of his children all that had been discovered or invented in the past, and to improve upon it. Thus there existed the same antithesis as we have just seen in § V. A universal Paulinism and a universal Empire must either coalesce, or the one must destroy the other. The question which history had to determine was whether the two powers should be hostile or should coalesce.

The Empire was trying to weld the separate nations into a great Imperial unity, and to substitute the Roman idea of " Province" for the older idea of " Nation," or rather to make the term " Nation," Ethnos in Greek, the translation of the Latin Provincia. It is needless and impertinent here to describe or praise the skill with which the Empire attempted this task, gradually widening the area of Roman citizenship by taking into it those who stood out conspicuous in the Provinces for ability, public service, education and wealth.

What is pertinent to our purpose is to observe that Paulinistic Christianity offered itself as the power which alone could make the unity vital and effective. It was the soul which might give life to the body of the Empire, a body which the Emperors were trying to galvanise into life by the religion of Roman patriotism, the worship of the Roman majesty as incarnated in the Emperors. It had now to be determined whether the Empire would accept the chance of permanent vitality that was offered to it.

The history of the Empire needs to be rewritten from this point of view: the relation of the government to the new universal religion determined the vicissitudes of its fate. The historians who write the story of the Empire devote an occasional footnote, or a paragraph, or a special chapter to what are called the "Persecutions". They miss entirely the deeper facts of the situation. The one overwhelming factor in the situation of the Empire was its relation to the Church: in their reconciliation lay the only hope of permanent strength for the Roman State: all other considerations were secondary. A large portion of the most hardworking, eager, and resolute people in the most progressive Provinces—in some the overwhelming majority—were estranged from the government and exposed to an intermittent and incalculable risk of suffering, torture and death. This portion was, on the whole, the educated middle class, the real strength of the State. The government, by estranging this class, was throwing itself unreservedly on the support of the soldiers.

It is patent to all that the deep-lying weakness and ever-present danger of the Empire was two-fold. In the first place the Imperial authority was originally based on military power; and the soldiers gradually learned that they could make or unmake the sovereign as they pleased. The

Churches of Paul offered the corrective to this evil, and made it possible to reform the foundations of the Empire by basing it on the support of the educated middle class throughout the Roman world, a solid and permanent platform for the State to rest on.

The second danger to which the Empire was exposed, and which right policy would have aimed at diminishing and eliminating, arose from the enormous preponderance of an uneducated populace. This danger was all the more serious because the sovereign power nominally lay in the hands of the people, and the uneducated populace formed an overwhelming majority of the whole people. The theory of the Imperial constitution was that the people entrusted the supreme power to the Emperor, as Champion of the Commons in virtue of his tribunician authority, and received back the power from his hands at death or resignation or dethronement, until they chose to entrust it to another. It should have been the prime duty of the Empire to educate the populace so that it might become a rational, not an irrational and incalculable force. A government which rested firmly on the agreement of an educated people would have been saved from the ever-present menace of the soldiery, whom the Emperors dreaded while they leaned upon them.

The Pauline Church in the Empire would have put an end to the danger, and strengthened the State as it spread. The educated middle class who constituted the Church would have grown, and reached more deeply and widely into the uneducated masses, raising them to its level. The ignorant proletariate would have been automatically diminished, as the Church increased and absorbed into itself the ignorant by educating them. The Roman State possessed remarkable

elasticity and was quite equal to the task of adapting itself
to this progressive development.

Such was the Pauline policy. The Imperial policy—apart
from some exceptional cases—was to neglect education, but
to feed and amuse the populace, a process which steadily
degraded and brutalised it more and more. The vital question for the State was which of these policies was to gain the
upper hand. The Pauline policy would have saved the
ancient civilisation by reforming the State. The policy which
was actually carried into effect by the Emperors ruined the
State by destroying education.

Some of the Emperors were impelled to carry out this
ruinous policy by mere opportunism and blindness to the
future. They saw that the populace must be kept quiet
from day to day by catering for its body and its soul.
The first necessity for the government was to keep in stock
a large enough supply of food in Rome to prevent famine ;
this was arranged by a State department, for with the insufficient means of transport that then existed, private enterprise
could not be relied on (as is possible in modern times) to
pour into the city food enough to serve a million of inhabitants. The people was encouraged to think of nothing but
games and amusements, lest it should think of more serious
things, and waken to a sense of responsibility. A riot in
Rome must at all costs be prevented, for a riot was the one
greatest and most immediate and incalculable danger to
which the State was exposed. The Emperors were therefore
strongly tempted to take this easiest way of staving off the
danger by humouring the populace ; but the issue was in the
long run fatal.

More able and prudent Emperors dreaded the Pauline
Church, because they recognised that ultimately it must be a

foe to autocracy. The Christians were, in the last resort, the reforming party: the Emperors felt that reform must affect their own power. Whereas an uneducated populace could never use the power that it nominally possessed, and must entrust it to an autocrat, a people trained to think and to feel responsibility might seek to use it themselves and perhaps destroy the autocratic system. The Church, therefore, presented itself to the imagination of the greatest and most far-seeing Emperors as their most dangerous rival; and, as a whole the Imperial policy was inexorably opposed to the reforming party; the ablest, wisest and most patriotic in spirit of the Emperors approved (though sometimes very reluctantly) the policy of repression and persecution, and the salvation which Paul offered to the Roman State was rejected. As they rejected the salutary policy, the only alternative was to continue the other policy of cajoling and brutalising the people by charity, cheap food and lavish amusements.

A certain number of the Emperors were disposed to leave free scope to their great rival, the Pauline Church. Their motives can hardly be determined, and were doubtless various; modern historians of the Empire, prevented by the fashionable blindness from seeing the real character of the situation, do not even attempt to estimate the motives which prompted these Emperors. Some apparently who had no regard for the Roman glory, were actuated by mere idleness and carelessness, and were disposed simply to let things go. Others perhaps were prompted by a sort of enlightened selfishness: they saw that the danger to the autocracy from the Church would come too slowly to affect themselves, and acquiesced in the aggrandisement of a power which could not do them personally any harm. But there were some cases in which, as I cannot but think, a more

generous and a wider policy was consciously chosen. Some
of the Emperors felt that a course of action which was alienating and trampling upon the educated middle classes of the
Empire could not be right or salutary, and attempted on
statesmanlike grounds to abandon the persecuting policy and
to initiate a conciliation between the autocracy and the reform movement; but their attempts were in all cases quickly
put down. The spirit of Roman determination to brook no
rival and accept no reform that came from without was too
strong.

How far did Paul understand and foresee the issues that
were nascent in the Empire during the first century? Who
can say exactly how far a great statesman can foresee in
detail the distant consequences of rejecting the salutary
measure that he advocates? It is enough to say that he sees
the cure for existing evils, and advocates with all his might
the only possible remedy, and warns the State that ruin is
the only alternative. So much we can say that Paul saw
and did. And the vague mythopoetic perception of the
people recognised the statesmanlike intention of Paul, and
formed a legend connecting him with the other great contemporary stateman, Seneca, a minister to whom the blindness
of modern and the strong prejudice of ancient historians
have rendered scant justice. The period of Seneca's tenure of
power is marked by a wise and generous tolerance, which
would, if continued, have prevented the persecutions and saved
the Empire, and which was fully appreciated by Paul and
his historian Luke. Such was the spirit of Seneca's brother
Gallio, whose decision in the case at Corinth constituted a
precedent so important as to be almost a charter for the
Christians, until it was overturned by the decision of a
higher tribunal. It is a remarkable fact that a Roman Jew

of Tarsus and a Roman Phoenician of Spain should between
them have come so near to saving the Roman State by the
wise policy which the one preached and to which the other
allowed free scope and growth.   The wise and right policy
was begun: it ruled for a time: it underlies the whole of
Paul's letters : Luke and 1 Peter protest against a change of
policy.   Never was a case where the wise statesmanship
came so near being adopted permanently over the whole
civilised world.

But it was not to be.   That the recklessness of Nero
reversed the policy of Seneca was not in itself a serious
matter, for all Nero's acts became invalid at his death.   But
the clear insight of Vespasian confirmed, or rather legally
instituted, the proscription of Christianity ; and the ablest
and greatest Emperors accepted and enforced the policy of
Vespasian, though like him for a long time they did so only
in a half-hearted and inconsequent fashion.   The Emperors
staked their fate against the Church, and they lost.

In the third century the character of the question is most
clearly seen.   Alexander Severus had attempted a reconciliation by enthroning Christ in the Imperial pantheon ; Philip
the Arabian, Zenobia the Palmyran, aimed at the same end
in various ways ; but no conciliation was possible.   It was a
question between the military power and the thinking middle
class, and it became also a question between two rival religions.   The State worship of the Emperors proved too
feeble, as a mere sham religion ; and Mithraism was made
the religious banner of the later pagan Empire and the faith
of the soldiers.   Mithras or the Galilean : such was the later
form of the question ; and on the whole the West was mainly
for Mithras, the East mainly for Christ.

The centre of gravity of the whole Empire shifted towards

the East. The city of Rome was no longer the heart and brain and seat of life for the Empire. The Provinces were growing every year in importance, and the East especially so. The pre-eminence of the city of Rome was becoming in some degree a mere popular superstition and an antiquarian survival. Now the Christian Church was the fullest expression of this new spirit in the Roman world, the refusal of the Provinces to accept the tone of Rome. Through Christianity the Provinces conquered Rome and to a certain degree re-invigorated the Empire. The shifting eastward of the capital of the Empire was in reality an acknowledgment of the strength of the new religion, for the East was mainly Christian, while the power of the government, and of the army, and of Mithraism, the triune enemy, lay mainly in the West.

Diocletian was able to see the fact, though not the reason. Constantine saw both the fact and the reason: he had a truer, because a wider, view. Born and nurtured in childhood in the pagan West, he lived and was educated for many years as a hostage of State in the Christian East. He acquired through this double experience a knowledge of both systems. Like Paul he had assimilated in some degree the spirit both of the East and of the West. Because he understood both, he could judge better between them. He gauged the power of both forces. Whether from far-seeing ability to estimate the future, or from genuine conviction—who shall be able to judge?—he made his choice. Diocletian had moved the capital from Rome into Asia. Constantine founded the New Rome on the Bosphorus, and the Christian Empire began.

But it was too late. The policy of massacre on a vast scale, inaugurated by {Decius, had been carried out too thoroughly by Diocletian and his co-emperors; and it produced its usual ruinous consequences. A State which is supported on massacre is doomed. An official Christianity was victorious, but Pauline Christianity had perished, and Paul was now a mere saint, no longer Paul but St. Paul, forgotten as a man or a teacher, but remembered as a sort of revivification of the old pagan gods. Paulinistic Christianity disappeared almost entirely from the world for a time; but it was not dead; it was only waiting its opportunity; it revived when freedom of thought and freedom of life began to stir in Europe; and it guided and stimulated the Protestants of the Reformation.

§ VIII.   Conclusion.

It seems needless to point out that this Pauline idea is incomparably wider than Jewish, and that the simple narrow Hebrew, who is set before us as Paul by many modern scholars, could never have conceived it. The Jewish mind was content to recognise the infinite power of God and the utter powerlessness of men before Him: He is the potter; we are the clay. What is the manner in which God deals with man, how He works out His purpose in the world, whether there are steps and stages in the process of His action, and if so, what are these stages, of all such questions the Semitic mind seemed naturally careless. It was enough to know the fact; investigation of the manner was needless and even impertinent: as Abt Vogler says in Browning, so the Jews thought,

> The rest may reason and welcome: 'tis we musicians know.

Curiosity and investigation of that kind was Greek, not Semitic; and there can be no doubt that Paul learned it in the Greek cities, and above all in Tarsus. This was the great debt that he owed to the Greeks (Rom. i. 14).   Partly, doubtless, through the formal education needed to fit him for the sphere in which he was born, the Græco-Roman world, partly through unconscious assimilation of the atmosphere and spirit that breathed through Hellenised Tarsian society, his mind had been widened far beyond the narrow limits of the stereotyped Judaism.   In fully conscious thought during his maturer years he broadened both Judaism and Hellenism till they were co-extensive with the world and co-incident with one another.

To specify all the influences that worked on Paul in his youth would be to discuss completely the situation of the Jewish citizens in the Græco-Asiatic cities of the Roman Empire, a task far beyond the present writer's powers, and one that transcends the bounds of known evidence.   In brief it may be said that those influences were some theoretical, some practical.   The education and method of Greece had deeply affected Paul's mind, as has just been stated.   The practical surroundings of municipal life in a self-governing free city like Tarsus had also profoundly influenced him. These forces had been acting on him for generations, for he was heir to all that his ancestors had learned in their position as Tarsian citizens (see Part II.).   The habit of electing their own rulers, of free sovereign discussion of their own interests in public meeting, of making or voting on their own laws, of living the unfettered life of Greek citizens, moulds the character of men.   This we may assume, but we cannot weigh it or measure its effect by any mathematical formula.

Our plan will be to describe the Hellenic cities in which Paul lived and worked, to attempt to determine the varying tone and spirit of each, so far as our insufficient knowledge of its history reaches, and thus to show at least the variety of experience through which Paul passed.

Jerusalem, of course, does not figure in our list. Its force was reactionary; and the years which Paul spent there in his youth were years during which the Hellenic tendencies in his nature lay dormant and probably were weakened.

Syrian Antioch, undoubtedly, exercised considerable influence in moulding Paul's mind. There he first came in contact with a young Church of the new kind wider than the Palestinian congregations. But it is not our intention to devote any consideration at present to Antioch. Luke gives us no detail whatsoever about the city. He speaks only of the congregation, and even in regard to it he mentions little except names and generalities. In his narrative at Antioch there is nothing that even remotely suggests personal knowledge and eyewitness. No incident lives before us, until we come to the scene when Barnabas and Saul were sent forth to the first missionary journey; and here there is nothing that specially belongs to Antioch. It is a universal scene, that belongs to the Church as a whole, not to the city in which it chanced to take place. Moreover, the present writer has never been able to visit the city, and has no personal knowledge of the localities; and a study at second-hand would be out of keeping with the rest of this book.

There remain Tarsus and the four Galatian cities. Luke gives no details about Paul's life in Tarsus. One must conclude that he had no personal knowledge of the city; and Paul's relation to it would be a blank to us, were it not for what he himself tells about it.

The interest of Luke lies in the Aegean lands and on the sea. He is stamped as a Greek by the range and the limits of his personal predilections. Even about the Galatian cities he has not very much to relate that is detailed or picturesque. But the inauguration of the Galatian work at Pisidian Antioch and the scenes at Lystra are in the best style of his narrative, where every word is addressed to the eye as well as to the mind. A study of the Aegean cities would be the fitting completion of the book ; but that task would need another volume.

Incidentally, one must ask whether the contrast between the slightness and vagueness of the Syrian and Cilician history, and the fulness and copiousness of detail in the Aegean lands and waters, which were familiar to Luke, does not prove that he had no personal knowledge of Syria and of Cilicia. In regard to an ordinary author, the inference would be unhesitatingly drawn. Why not in regard to Luke ?

Finally, some inferences will be drawn in the concluding part as to the influence of the Hellenic city life on Paul's personal character.

PART II.

TARSUS.

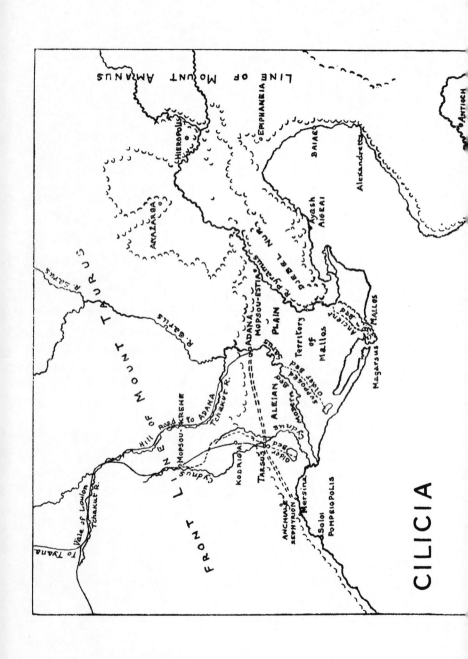

CILICIA

TARSUS.

§ I. INTRODUCTION.

IN the introductory verses of his Letter to the Galatians—
that wonderful preface to the most remarkable letter that
ever was written—St. Paul gives an historical sketch of his
own life, as he looked back on it with the experience of a
lifetime and the insight of a thoroughly reasoned religion
to direct and intensify his vision. He describes the chief
stages in his life from its beginning. What had been mis-
guided and ignorant almost sinks out of view: he remembers only the steps by which his knowledge of truth
and his insight into the real nature of the world had grown.
The many years in which he had been a leader and chief
among the Jews, with his mind shut up within the circle
of Jewish ideas and aspirations, are summed up in a brief
sentence; and he passes on to the epoch-making event in
his career, the real beginning of his life, "when it was the
good pleasure of God, who separated me, even from my
mother's womb, and called me through His grace to reveal
His Son in me, that I might preach Him among the
Gentiles".

It is a widely spread view that in these words the Apostle
is merely expressing the infinite power with which God
chooses His instruments where He will, selecting persons
even the most unlikely and apparently unprepared and
unsuited to be His ministers, and putting into them the

(85)

power to execute His will.   But such an interpretation is
inadequate and far from complete.   It is true that here, as
everywhere, Paul lays the strongest emphasis on the limitless power with which God selects His agents and instruments ; but neither here nor anywhere else does he
represent this power as being used in an arbitrary fashion,
of which man cannot understand the reasons or the method.
The choice of himself was the final execution of a design
which had been long maturing in the purpose of God, and
which was worked out step by step in the process of events.
Already before his birth Paul had been chosen and set
apart as the Apostle of the Gentiles ; and, when the proper
moment had arrived, the revelation took place, and the
design of God was made consciously present in the mind
and heart of the man.   It was not a sudden and incalculable
choice of a human instrument.   It was the consummation
of a process of selection and preparation which had begun
before the man was born, but of which he had at first been
wholly unconscious—so unconscious that he had spent his
energy in fighting vainly against its compelling power.
Only in later time, as he reviewed his life, he could see the
preparatory stages in the process, beginning before his
birth; the purpose of God had matured its design by the
selection through a long period of means useful to the
ultimate end.

The conception is more Greek than Hebrew.   A purely
Jewish mind would have been content to emphasise the infinite power of God, who chooses an instrument for His purposes wherever He will.   It is characteristic of the Greek
education not to be content with this almost fatalistic conception, but to scrutinise the manner and the steps by which
the Divine purpose works itself out.   The Greek mind re-

gards the evolution of the will of God as a process which takes place under the conditions of space and time, *i.e.*, as a process of history. We see this idea running through Greek literature; and in the same way as the action of the *Iliad* presents itself to Homer as the series of events by which "the counsel of Zeus wrought out its accomplishment" (see Part I., § IV.), so Paul conceives the counsel of God working out its accomplishment in the circumstances of his birth.

If we attempt to interpret his mystic religious statement in the language of history, it means that the family, the surroundings, and the education of Paul had been selected with the perfection of a Divine purpose to make him fit to be what he was designed to be, the Apostle of the Gentiles. There was one nation, one family and one city, out of which the Apostle must arise. The nation was the Jewish; but the family was not Palestinian, it was Tarsian. Only "a Hebrew sprung from Hebrews" could be the Apostle of the perfected Judaic faith; but he must be born and brought up in childhood among the Gentiles, a citizen of a Gentile city, and a member of that conquering aristocracy of Romans which ruled all the cities of the Mediterranean world. The Apostle to the Gentiles must be a Jew, a Tarsian citizen, and at the same time a Roman. If that be not the meaning of Paul's words, the historian may abandon altogether the task of interpreting them, for they cease to have any historical application. But his words, here and everywhere, are instinct and alive with historical force. Every sentence is a summary of historical development. But Paul sees and speaks on the plane of eternal truth; and the historian has to render his words, only half seeing, half understanding them, "with stammering lips and insufficient sound," into those which may describe the steps of that development as they are conditioned by time in the process of history.

Tarsus was the city which should produce the Apostle to the Gentiles. Why was that city chosen? Again we must recognise that the choice was no arbitrary selection of an unlikely and unsuitable place. Tarsus was, through its nature and circumstances, the proper city. That it was the one suitable place has been borne in on the present writer during long study of the conditions of society and the geographical environment of the Cilician land and cities. It was only after the observation of this remarkable adaptation had gradually fixed itself in his mind, taken root there, and made for itself definite expression in language, that he found the same thought fully expressed in the words of Paul himself. In the *Historical Commentary on the Epistle to the Galatians*, those words were left by the writer un-noticed and unexplained, because they were to him still uncomprehended and obscure. Now they appear full of light and historical meaning.

Wherein lay the peculiar suitability of Tarsus to educate and mould the mind of him who should in due time make the religion of the Jewish race intelligible to the Græco-Roman world, and should be able to raise that world up to the moral level of the Hebrew people and the spiritual level of ability to sympathise with the Hebrew religion in its perfected stage? It lay in the fact that Tarsus was the city whose institutions best and most completely united the oriental and the western character. When Greece went forth under Alexander the Great to conquer the East, the union of oriental and occidental was attempted in every city of western Asia. That is the most remarkable and inter-esting feature of Hellenistic history in the Græco-Asiatic

kingdoms and cities.[1]   But none of those cities, though all
were deeply affected in varying degrees by their Asiatic
surroundings and the Asiatic element in their populations,
seems to have been so successful as Tarsus in establishing a
fairly harmonious balance between the two elements.   Not
that even in Tarsus the union was perfect: that was impossible so long as the religions of the two elements were
inharmonious and mutually hostile.   But the Tarsian state
was more successful than any other of the great cities of
that time in producing an amalgamated society, in which the
oriental and the occidental spirit in unison attained in some
degree to a higher plane of thought and action.   In others
the Greek spirit, which was always "anti-semitic," was too
strong and too resolutely bent on attaining supremacy and
crushing out all opposition.   In Tarsus the Greek qualities
and powers were used and guided by a society which was,
on the whole, more Asiatic in character.

With this idea in our mind, we proceed to study the
character and the social conditions of the city of Tarsus.
It would be vain and profitless to study the city simply as
it was in the childhood of Paul.   We can understand its
character and influence at that period only by studying its
development and the law of its growth.   How had it been
formed into its condition at the Christian era?   What
elements were there in its population?   What fortunes had
befallen the people and moulded them already before their
birth?   What influences of sea and air, of plain and
mountain, of intercourse and warfare with others, had
through many generations affected their nature and determined their character?[2]

The attempt to put together a picture of Tarsus and its
people in the first century after Christ would be entirely

vain, owing to the paucity of information, were it not for
the intensity of municipal patriotism among the citizens of
an ancient city.   In modern times that character is not
sufficiently remembered by many scholars, who are misled
by the modern facts.   In most Scottish cities of the present
day knowledge of, and interest in, their early history belong
only to a few antiquaries : the mass of the citizens know
and care nought about such matters.   In Aberdeen, for
example, the speaker in the Town Council, who wishes to
persuade his audience, does not quote early history ; if he
were to begin a speech by appealing to his hearers' pride
in "the Red Harlaw," some would hardly know what he
meant, others would regard him as an amiable enthusiast
whose opinion about present business could be of no possible
value.   Patriotism is far from weak in the heart of such
citizens, though they are a little ashamed of manifesting it
outwardly, and suspicious of, or amused by, those who show
it more openly ; but their patriotism is mainly for their
country and their race, not for their own town.

But to the ancient Greek citizen his city absorbed all his
patriotism.   His city, not his country as a whole, was his
"fatherland" (yet see p. 46).   He was keenly interested in
its past, and he actively participated in managing its present
government.   A citizen who was not active and interested
in his own State was disliked and contemned in general
opinion ; and the unwillingness of the early Christians to
perform the religious acts required in all political duties,
and their consequent abstention from politics, intensified the
disapproval which the pagan mob felt for them.   The patriotism of the ordinary citizen gained intensity through the
narrowness of its scope.   All that his patriotism embraced
was constantly present to his senses, and forced every day

and every hour on his attention. He could not get away from its claims. It surrounded him from infancy, educated him in boyhood, and opened to him all his opportunities of activity in manhood. It was to a large extent co-extensive with, and inseparable from, his religion ; in fact, the true Greek theory was that religion should be entirely co-extensive with patriotism ; but human nature was too strong for theory, and it was impossible to restrict a man's religion within the circle of his duties towards the State, though the Greek view tended to regard as superstition all that lay outside of, and too deep for, that circle.

Only by an effort can the modern mind begin to appreciate how strong and real was the influence that the more striking facts of past history, and its half-religious, half-political legends, exerted on the ancient citizen. These were to him present and real influences, guiding his action and moulding his mind : they formed the standard to which the orators and philosophers, who wished to move the mind of the citizens, must accommodate their words ; and each orator selected from past history with such skill as he possessed the points suitable for his own purposes. One single example will serve to show the enormous influence of historical legend on the ancient cities. It was probably a Greek poet of Sicily who invented in the sixth century a connection between ancient Greek history and the young city of Rome, already powerful under its kings ; for Greek views demanded that any strong external State should be brought into relations with old Greece. Thus arose the fancy that Rome was founded by Trojan refugees, fleeing from their city when Agamemnon captured and burned it. Yet this utterly groundless, and non-Roman idea became gradually accepted by Rome herself ; it was used as an incident in the great national historical epics of Naevius and Ennius, and finally was made the plot of Virgil's *Aeneid*, the most perfect literary expression of Roman sentiment and Roman pride. It won its way to the Roman mind, though attributing a foreign origin and a fugitive ancestry to their people, mainly because it was a convenient political instrument. The ancient mind required, and always found or invented, a justification in past history and religion for all political action ; and, when the Romans began to exercise influence in the Greek world, they justified their interference by their right, guaranteed by old Greek authors, to carry on to completion the historical drama which had begun with the war of Troy and their own expulsion by the Greeks. On this ground they justified their interposition to protect their kindred in New Ilium against the Græco-Syrian king early in the third century (282 B.C.). Legend, half-religious, half-political, is here exhibited as a powerful and vital force in the ancient mind.

Popular belief and legends with regard to the foundation and past history of a Hellenic city are, therefore, important as a means of understanding the mind of the people, who believed and circulated them. The example just given shows that the value of the evidence is entirely unconnected with historical truth. What the citizens were saying at any time about their own past reveals what was their mind about present matters at that time, what they prided themselves on, what they claimed to be, what were the topics which might be appealed to by orators and teachers desirous of influencing their action. As at Rome, so in Tarsus and Iconium and other Hellenic cities, totally different and inconsistent legends circulated with regard to their origin : these tales came into existence at different times, in different states of feeling, and among different constituent elements in the complicated fabric of municipal society and politics.

§ II. THE SITUATION OF TARSUS.

Tarsus (which still bears its ancient name slightly modified, Tersous) is situated in the Cilician plain, 70 to 80 feet above sea level, and about ten miles from the southern coast. Behind it towards the north, fully two miles distant, the hills begin to rise gently from the level plain; and they extend back in undulating and gently swelling ridges, intersected by deep water channels, until they lean against the vast and lofty range of Taurus, about thirty miles distant to the north.

Cilicia lies between Taurus and the sea, and comprises the level sea plain, the undulating alluvial hills, and the front of the ridge of Taurus. The bounds on the north varied in different periods of history. In the Roman time (with which we are here chiefly concerned) they were fixed high up on the face of Taurus, about 500 feet below the summit of the front ridge.[2a] At this point, and not at the actual summit, is the natural geographical boundary between the Cilician land, steamy with the moist heat of its well-watered soil, and the broad, lofty and inclement mountain region of Taurus, backed by the high central plateau of Anatolia; and therefore it may rightly be regarded as the true frontier of the country. The exact point is indicated by inscriptions on the rock walls of the narrow pass which is famous in history under the name of the " Cilician Gates". The situation will be more fully described in § IV.

The combination of these three kinds of country was highly advantageous to the Cilician cities and people. The cities, Tarsus and the rest, were situated in the low plains, only a few feet above sea level. The moist heat of the fertile soil and oppressive atmosphere would have been unfavourable to vigorous municipal or commercial life. But the considerable extent of undulating ground, often very fertile and generally well wooded at the present time, which intervened as foot-hills between the sea plain and the Taurus mountains, offered a far more pleasant and healthy abode during the summer heat; while the high glens and plateaus of Taurus were admirable sanatoria.

Those foot-hills, therefore, were a valuable part of Tarsian territory, and really essential to its prosperity; and the remains of ancient life show that the opportunity was thoroughly used by the people. There is, in truth, a second Tarsus on the hills, about nine to twelve miles north of the city proper, probably a town which was partly used for summer residence, but still a large and strong town with regular fortifications on a great scale, permanently occupied by a considerable population—indeed a much stronger city than Tarsus on the level plain, which was devoid of any proper acropolis (as Dion Chrysostom mentions).

These ruins, which extend westwards from the north road for several miles up to the deep gorge of the river Cydnus, are evidently mainly Roman; and the very name which was given to them in the third century can be determined. On the west edge of the ruins the Roman road leading north from Tarsus to the Cilician Gates is spanned by a triumphal arch, styled with boastfulness characteristic of the Tarsians (see § XXII.) by the Latin term *quadrigæ*, though probably no four-horse car was ever placed upon it. This monument gave its name to the whole district

PLATE I.

Tarsus, the Hill Country behind, and the snow-covered Taurus in the background.

To face p. 94.

around; and the name appears in Greek as Kodrigai on coins of Tarsus, struck about A.D. 200. From these coins we learn that games of the Olympian fashion were celebrated in honour of the Emperor Severus at Kodrigai, which is called the " Boundary of the Cilicians," and was therefore on the north side of Tarsus towards the Cilician Gates. Severus had marched south into Cilicia along the road from the Gates, and we may presume that the triumphal arch was erected at the place where the road approached the town. On the plateau near the arch games might well have been held, especially during the heat of summer.

This upper town formed a really important factor in Tarsian history. It was mainly instrumental in maintaining unimpaired through many centuries the vigour and energy of the citizens. Tarsus, lying low in the plain, sheltered by Taurus from the invigorating northerly breezes, which are so important in maintaining the salubrity of Anatolia, would inevitably be a relaxing and enervating place ; but the close neighbourhood of the hills brought an invigorating residence within easy reach of the mass of the population.

The healthy condition of ancient Greek cities generally was due partly to the water supply, partly to the cleanliness which was a matter of religious duty, enforced by the gods of the streets whose images stood there, and partly to the love of the people for country residence and for outdoor life. That, in choosing the sites of the great Greek cities of Asia, much attention was paid to the character of the atmosphere and the neighbourhood of invigorating high ground, is evident to all who have seen and noted their situation. The population of Asia Minor is, and has probably always been, appreciative of this character. The natives even now, unobservant and resigned and careless as they are, will often distinguish between the invigorating atmosphere of one town and the oppressive, heavy air of another at no great distance in a worse situation.

In respect of the danger of malaria the case of Tarsus was similar to that of Perga, and even worse. Perga stood on a slightly elevated plateau by the river: Tarsus lay on the dead level plain, only a few feet above the lowest level of the river Cydnus, and exposed to inundation as soon as the water rose in flood. Both are sheltered in the same way by the northern mountains ; both face the sea and the sun. In my *Church in the Roman Empire*, p. 62 f., this character of Perga is described. A distinguished French scholar has denied that Perga could have been exposed to malaria, on the ground that the thorough cultivation of the soil in ancient times must have made it healthy. It is all a question of degree. Cultivation will do much to diminish the malarious character of a district; but the Pamphylian soil was so fertile because it is by nature abundantly moist. Irrigation, where needed, is easy. Wherever this abundant moisture and fertility characterise the sea-plain in this extremely hot country, fever is prevalent and the climate is depressing, while insect pests make human life wretched for a considerable part of the year. The bad effect is exaggerated by neglect and the increase of marshes ; but it is unavoidable and only partially curable.

Now, since the country south of Tarsus has been allowed to relapse into its primitive state of marsh, the climate of the city is doubtless more oppressive and enervating than it was in the Roman time, when the marshes had all been drained and the country was entirely under cultivation. But, at the best, the situation of Tarsus must always have

PLATE II.

Two views of a Triumphal Arch on the Roman Road, twelve miles north of Tarsus: from the south. (A view from the north is given in *Pauline and Other Studies*, Plate XIII.)

To face p. 96.

made the climate relaxing; and the city could not have retained the vigour that made its citizens widely famous in the ancient world, without the hill town or hill residence so close at hand, which prevented the degeneration of the Tarsian spirit through many centuries.

But this hill town was not a place of summer residence only. It seems to have grown from a mere wayside[3] station and an open summer resort into a real fortified city, a second Tarsus. The fortifications were probably constructed during the decay of the Roman Empire, when invasions were a constant danger, and a stronger defence than the city of the plain was required. It seems possible that this hill town is the Tarsus which the Bordeaux Pilgrim mentions, twenty-four Roman miles south of the Cilician Gates. This is far too short for the distance between the Gates and the city of the plain. Perhaps the Pilgrim stopped at the hill town, while Tarsus on the plain decayed in the wars, and was rebuilt by Haroun-al-Rashid.[4]

Tarsus was certainly a very large city in the Roman times. The information of intelligent and observant residents is that, wherever you dig, from the hills two miles north of the present town to the lake and marsh five or six miles south, you come upon remains of the ancient city. With the residents on the hills, the population of the Tarsian State is likely to have been not less than half a million. Thus it was, as Basil describes it, a metropolis for three provinces, a centre of communication for Cilicia, Cappadocia, and Assyria.

The fortunes and history of Tarsus were determined by three geographical conditions: (1) its relation to the rest of the Cilician plain, (2) its connection through the river Cydnus with the sea, and (3) its position commanding the end of the principal pass across the Taurus mountains to the central plateau and the western and northern parts of Anatolia, one of the great routes which have determined the history of the Mediterranean world, the pass of the Cilician Gates.

§ III. Tarsus and the Plain of Cilicia.

The country of Cilicia is, roughly speaking, triangular in shape, the apex on the north-east being formed by its mighty boundary mountains, Amanus, running due south and separating Cilicia from Syria and Commagene, and Taurus diverging to the south-west and dividing the country from Cappadocia and Lycaonia. Those two great mountain walls approach close to the sea, which forms the third side of the Cilician triangle.

If we neglect as less important two narrow strips of coast land at the eastern and western ends of Cilicia, and if we leave also out of count the foot-hills that lie against the mountains and make a full half of the whole land, Cilicia consists of two very rich plains, the upper or eastern, which is divided from the sea by a ridge of hills (Djebel-Nur), and the lower or western, which is in the strictest sense a maritime plain. The eastern plain is the valley of the river Pyramus. The western is the valley of three rivers, the lowest course of the Pyramus, the Sarus, and the Cydnus;[5] and on the three rivers were situated the three great cities, Mallos on the Pyramus, Adana on the Sarus, and Tarsus on the Cydnus. The mutual relations and rivalries of these three cities have determined the history of the maritime plain of Cilicia.

Another side of Cilician life, the opposition between the western plain with its capital Tarsus and the eastern plain with its capital Anazarba, will not concern us much in the

PLATE III.

Jonas Pillar and the Cilician Sea, near Issus.   The slope of Djebel Nur rises on the right.
To face p. 98.

present study. It was an important feature of the later
Roman period, the second and following centuries after
Christ; but it exercised no appreciable influence in determining the character of the Pauline Tarsus, with which we
are now engaged.

The west Cilician plain has been gradually won from the
sea in the course of ages. It was formed mainly by the
great river Sarus, which bears through the centre of the plain
to the sea the united waters of two great rivers of the
plateau, the Karmalas and the Sarus proper. The formation of the plain has probably been assisted by several
successive slight elevations of the level of the land (shown
by a succession of old sea beaches, which mark out the
shape of the former gulf, now become the western plain);
but, mainly, the plain has been deposited by the Sarus.
This plain, like the country as a whole, is triangular in
shape, with the sea as its base, and its apex in a recess of
the hills. It contains about 800 square miles of arable land,
with a strip of sand-hills and lagoons about two to three
miles wide along the coast.

At the apex of the plain, on the north, the river Sarus
enters this lower plain, and winds its circuitous way in a
great sweep towards the sea, which it now reaches very near
the mouth of the Cydnus at the western edge of the plain.
At an early period it probably joined the Pyramus, which,
entering the western plain by a narrow pass between the
Taurus foot-hills and the Djebel-Nur, keeps close at the
present day to the base of the latter, and winds back towards the sea, on the extreme eastern limit of the plain.[6]
But the Sarus deserted that old junction centuries before
the time of Christ, and formed its own way to the sea
through the centre of the plain. It probably found entrance

to the sea at different points as the centuries passed by, and
its mouth is now, certainly, much further west than it was
in the Pauline period. At that time it apparently flowed
not directly into the sea, but into a large lagoon, still well
marked, about nine miles east of the mouth of the Cydnus
and fifteen miles west of the old Pyramus mouth. This
lagoon was half divided from the sea by a bar of sand.
Thus the Sarus had no navigable entrance from the sea;
and a city situated on the river Sarus could have no direct
maritime connection. Adana, therefore, the city on the
Sarus, was situated far up the river, near the apex of the
plain. The river was and still is navigable there, but
navigation must have been only for purposes of local communication, not of sea-going traffic.

Taking into consideration the foot-hills as well as the sea
plain, we see that Adana lies near the centre of Cilicia, in a
very favourable situation for ruling the country when sea
navigation is unimportant. Hence it is the natural capital
of the country under Turkish rule. A lofty rocky hill
forms an excellent and strong acropolis, crowned now by
the buildings of the American Mission. From those buildings there is offered a wonderful view ; on the south, across
the apparently limitless level plain, the sea cannot be distinguished ; on the north and west one looks over the lower
foot-hills to the long snow-clad wall of Taurus. Eastwards
the view is almost more varied and impressive.

From Tarsus no such view can be got. The city lies
so low that the mountains are for the most part concealed
behind the hills; and there is no rock marked enough to
serve as an acropolis. Pl. II. shows the best outlook.[7]
But from the hills a few miles northward, and especially
from the acropolis of the hill city, a marvellous view is pre-

sented, extending along the mountain walls of Taurus and of Amanus, and across the Gulf of Issus to the Syrian mountains and the promontory behind which lie Seleucia and Antioch.

Adana and Tarsus are cities of inevitable importance ; and both retain their ancient name to the present day. Mallos, on the Pyramus, has lost its people and its name. Its very site is still unsettled and a subject of controversy. It owed its greatness in early history to circumstances that have long ceased to exist. At the beginning of history it stands forth as the principal harbour of the Cilician land, and the chief seat of Greek influence and trade. The Pyramus then offered the only well-defined river entrance on the Cilician coast with a natural harbour, whereas Tarsus had to make its harbour, and Adana never could have enjoyed easy maritime communication.

As was necessary in primitive times, when piracy was a never-ceasing danger, Mallos was built, not on the sea, but some way up the river. Strabo mentions that it stood on a hill, and thus points out its position, for there is only one hill near the mouth of the Pyramus. West of the ancient mouth and east of the modern mouth a little ridge of hills (now called Kara-Tash) [8] rises on the seashore. This ridge was probably once an island in the Cilician gulf, and afterwards it formed the eastern promontory at the entrance to the gulf. As the land rose and the sea receded, the Pyramus passed out along its northern and western base into the sea. The city of Mallos was situated on the northern slope of the hill, away from the sea and looking towards the river. In this situation, one understands why Scylax regards it as an inland city, up the river, while both Strabo and the Stadiasmus describe it as belonging to the coast, and Strabo pointedly contrasts it with the inner country.

The river Pyramus, like the Sarus, has silted up its former mouth, and now flows in a different channel. About twelve or fifteen miles above the ancient mouth, where the old course turned off towards south-west, keeping close along the northern edge of the Mallos hills, the river now bends sharply back to the east and flows into the bay of Ayash (the ancient Aigeai), which it is rapidly filling up with the soil deposited from its waters. Accordingly the site of Mallos must now be looked for on the western side of the modern river, and at some considerable distance from the bank.

Between the rivers Cydnus and Pyramus lies the famous Aleian plain, deposited in large degree by the river Sarus which flows through it and has gradually formed it. A plain formed in this way must in an earlier stage of history have been a succession of swamps and waste land, only half won from the sea, with the Sarus struggling to find a painful and devious way through it. Long after the Pyramus had found a well-defined channel down past the site of Mallos to the coast, the Sarus was wending its difficult course through those marshy lowlands towards the sea. Homer has preserved for us in the fifth book of the *Iliad* the memory of that early time, when he relates the tale of Bellerophon :

> When at last, distracted in his mind,
> Forsook of Heaven, forsaking humankind,
> Wide o'er the Alêian plain he chose to stray,
> A long forlorn uncomfortable way.

This writer evidently understood the Aleian plain to be a melancholy waste, untraversed by any path, uninhabited by man, a scar upon the smiling face of the land, where a melancholic madman might " wander alone, eating his own soul, avoiding the paths of man ".[9] But in the classical period of history it was a great stretch of especially fertile and rich land. Strabo distinguishes the Aleian plain from the coast-land, because the former was cultivated and rich, while the latter was mere sand and lagoon and cane-brake. The troops of Alexander the Great were able to march right across the plain, which was well suited for the movement of cavalry in the fourth century before Christ and doubtless during many centuries earlier.

In contrast to these accounts the Homeric lines preserve a true memory of more ancient days, brought to the harbours of the west by the early Greek sailors who traded to the port of Mallos ; and the tale probably carries us back to a time far older than the ninth century B.C., and opens before us a page in the history of the gradual formation of the central Cilician river and the Cilician plain. How far human agency co-operated with nature by defining and embanking the river channel is a question on which proper exploration would doubtless throw some light. Those great engineering operations by which rivers were regulated and marshes were drained, as *e.g.*, the Yang-tse-kiang, the Po, the Nile, the Boeotian marsh Copais, and many mountain glens in Greece and Anatolia, lie far back at the beginning of civilisation in the southern countries.

The Aleian plain was divided between the three great cities ; but undoubtedly the largest part belonged to Mallos. Hence Mallos is probably the harbour which is meant by Herodotus, vi. 95, when he tells that the great army sent by Darius against Greece in 490 B.C. marched to the Aleian plain in Cilicia and encamped there, until the fleet arrived and took them on board.

The early history of Tarsus was determined by competi-

tion with its two rivals. It outstripped them in the race
at last; but Mallos was at first the great harbour and the
principal Greek colony of Cilicia. An alliance between
Mallos and Adana was natural, because the path from
Mallos to the north and the inner plateau lay through
Adana, and its trade was dependent on the friendship of
the inland city. Each had much to gain from alliance
with the other. On the other hand the interests of Tarsus
were opposed to both Adana and Mallos. Tarsus, as a
harbour, competed with the latter, and as commanding its
own path to the inner plateau it competed with the former. This struggle for superiority continued through the
Greek period, and traces of it remain in the orations which
Dion Chrysostom delivered at Tarsus in the beginning of
the second century after Christ. But Tarsus grew steadily
greater and more powerful, while its two rivals seem to
have finally been forced to accept a lower rank, leaving the
supremacy of the western plain to their more vigorous
competitor.

If I may judge from the holes which I saw in the ground
here and there, the plain near Tarsus consists of a stratum
of rich fertile soil resting on a bottom of gravel and pebbles.
The stratum of soil is thin at the edge of the hills on the
north and gets deeper as one goes south towards the sea.
The rivers flow on the gravel and pebbles. Perhaps the
same kind of formation may extend over the whole Aleian
plain.

It is sometimes stated that the ruins of the ancient
Tarsus are covered by the silt of the river to the depth of
15 or 20 feet. I could find no proof that any recent river
deposit overlies the old level of the city, nor that the
remains of ancient life are covered so deep, except on a

sort of hill or mound on the south-west of the modern
buildings, which seems to be entirely modern, caused by
the earth accumulating over ancient remains. Such a
mound always tends to gather over an uninhabited site.
But in the inhabited part of Tarsus the modern level seems
not to be more than a few feet above the ancient. This
may be inferred from the depth at which the pebble and
gravelly bottom is struck in digging, for the level of
this bottom has probably not varied since the overlying
stratum of loam was deposited in the geological process of
formation.

As regards the command of a large extent of fertile
territory, Tarsus though well equipped, was not equal to
either of her rivals. The superiority which she ultimately
achieved over them was due to other causes.

§ IV. Tarsus, the River and the Sea.

The glory and the ornament of Tarsus was the river Cydnus, which flowed through the middle of the city. Dion
Chrysostom, in the first of his two orations delivered at
Tarsus somewhere about A.D. 110, makes fun of the pride
and affection with which the Tarsians regarded their river;
they loved to hear from strangers the praises of its beauty
and of the clearness of its water, and when it flowed dark
and muddy, they anxiously explained to visitors the reason.
He speaks rather depreciatingly of the situation and natural
surroundings of Tarsus, and declares that it is inferior to
many cities in respect of river and climate and conformation
of land and sea and harbour and walls.[9a] The river, which
runs clear and bright among the hills, soon grows muddy
after it enters the rich deep soil of the plain. Dion implies
that its water as it passed through the city was ordinarily

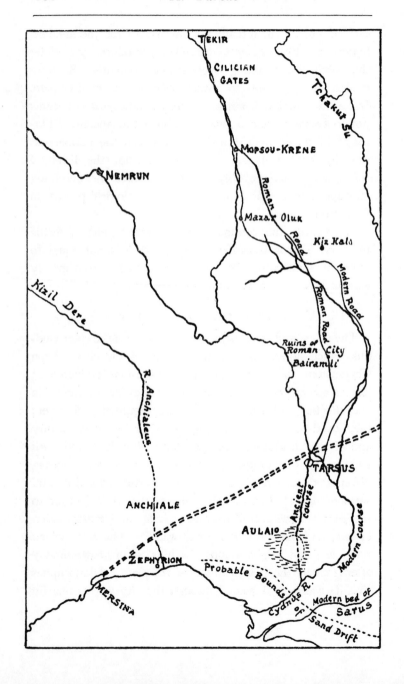

clear. This was certainly the case. In its short course
through the thin soil north of the city it did not come much
in contact with the mud, but flowed in a wide gravelly bed.
Only when in flood did it carry down with it mud and soil,
and rush through the city in a dark and turbid current.
But below the city, where the soil is deeper, it soon became
laden with mud, and acquired permanently the yellowish
opaque colour of the Tiber at Rome.

The question as to the character of the bed of the Cydnus
is complicated by the change that has occurred in the course
of the river. It was liable to inundation, as it drained a
large extent of hill and mountain country, down which its
numerous feeders rushed rapidly after heavy rain and poured
a sudden flood into the city. Probably the danger was
guarded against during the most prosperous period of Tarsian
history by operations facilitating the outflow. At least Dion,
while he refers to the turbid colour of the river in flood,
does not mention the danger of inundation in his very
candid and searching enumeration of the natural defects
of the city. Afterwards less care was shown in keeping
the channel clear and open, and in the time of Justinian,
between 527 and 563 A.D., a flood did so much harm to the
city, that the Emperor formed a new channel in which the
river now runs. Probably this channel was intended merely
to divert the superabundant water, for the purpose of keeping
the level within the city uniform and safe. But the result
was that, in the neglectful times which followed, the channel
within the city gradually became choked, and the whole
body of water was diverted into the new course. It was
not till about the fourteenth or fifteenth century that the
process was completed. Earlier travellers saw the river
flowing in part through the city, in which its channel can

still be traced (especially in the southern parts) by the depression in the level, and by remains of the embankments and bridges seen by living witnesses during excavations for building purposes. The modern watercourse on the west side of the town, often mistaken by travellers for the original bed of the river, is wholly artificial and quite distinct from the old channel (as can be seen by following it up to the point where it is taken off from the Cydnus).

It was not necessary for Justinian to make a new channel all the way to the sea. A watercourse flowed down parallel to the Cydnus past the eastern side of the city. All that was necessary was to make a cutting from the Cydnus, beginning from a point about a mile north of the modern town, and diverging gradually from it towards the other bed, which it joins on the east side of the modern city. This watercourse was too small for the large body of water that afterwards came to run through it; and hence in modern times there are annual floods and great part of the country south of the city is sometimes inundated. In May, 1902, we could hardly make our way down by the west side of the Cydnus towards the sea, and the horses had to wade a long distance through fairly deep water that covered the fields.

The artificial character of the channel in which the Cydnus now flows on the north and north-east sides of the city is plainly shown in the so-called "Falls of the Cydnus," a little below the point where the modern course diverges from the ancient bed. The rocks over which the stream falls contain numerous ancient graves, and many of these are underneath the ordinary level of the water and visible only when the river is at its lowest.

While the river in its modern course never touches the

PLATE IV.

Falls of the Cydnus (the new River of Justinian) on the north side of Tarsus.

See p. 107.

PLATE V.

The Cilician Gates.

To face p. 108.

See p. 113.

town, and artificial canals carry the water to irrigate the gardens and turn the cotton mills and other machinery in Tarsus, the ancient Cydnus flowed right through the city. Strabo, Dion, Xenophon, and other authorities agree in this statement. About two miles or less below the city there is formed in the wet season a small lake, which generally disappears in summer. This lake forms in a slight depression on the former bed of the river, as the flow of the water is impeded by modern conditions; but no such lake was permitted to form when Tarsus was a great city.

About five or six miles below the town the ancient Cydnus flowed into a lake. This lake is fed by natural springs in its bed (as I was informed by good authorities), and must always have existed. Its ancient name was Rhegmoi or Rhegma; and the name must be taken as a proof that it was at one time a lagoon, into which the sea broke over a bar of sand. Thus at some remote period, the memory of which was preserved by the name, the river had no proper mouth to discharge itself into the sea (resembling in this respect the Sarus, as described above, § III.). But in the time of Strabo, and doubtless for centuries previously, the lake was separate from the sea, and communicated with it only through the lower course of the river. Strabo describes the lake as a widening of the river. There was doubtless then, as now, a belt of sand and dunes between the lake and the sea, though it remains uncertain whether the belt was as broad then as it now is.

The lake was the harbour of Tarsus. Here were the docks and arsenal. Here most ships discharged, though light galleys, like that which carried Cleopatra, could be navigated up into the heart of the city. Round three sides of the lake, probably, extended the harbour town, which

___

was called Aulai.[10]   The city did not extend to the southern
side of the lake ; not a trace of it has been found on that
side ; but the buildings extended in an almost unbroken
succession from the lake to the city.

The conformation of the country shows that the Cydnus
must have flowed in a comparatively straight course south-
wards through the plain into the lake.   The exact line of
its old channel cannot always be traced, but its general
course is evident.   In the centre of the city, however, it
made a sharp bend eastwards for a short distance, and then
turned south again.   Its old channel in this bend is quite
clearly visible within the modern town ; and a more careful
survey might suffice to place its whole course on a map with
exact certainty.

The Cydnus flows with a much swifter current down a far
less level course than the Sarus.   The railway, which passes
a short mile north of Tarsus, is a few feet higher above the
sea at Tarsus than at Adana (63 feet), and therefore, while
the Sarus has a meandering course of fifty or sixty miles
from Adana to the sea, the Cydnus falls a little more in its
course of about eleven miles.   But the fall is greatest above
the city, less within it and far less below it.   Even the upper
lake or marsh cannot be much above sea level, and the lower
permanent lake is probably little, if at all, higher than the
sea, except when it is swollen by rains and by overflow
from the modern river on the east.

At an early period of history a great deal of labour and
skill must have been expended on the channel of the Cydnus
and on the lake in order to regulate and limit them, and to
improve the navigation.   The once useless lagoon was converted into a convenient harbour, open to ships through
the mouth of the river, yet completely shut in and safe

against sudden attack from the sea. Nature had aided the
work by forming a broader belt of sandy sea-shore and
transforming the lagoon into a lake. But engineering skill
was required to improve the lower course of the river, to
facilitate its flow and prevent inundation, to deepen and em-
bank the channel and to drain the marshes, as well as to
border the lake with the quays and dockyards which Strabo
describes. The lake was certainly smaller in ancient times
than it now is, and proportionately deeper. The river probably issued from it at the south-eastern end and found its
way into the sea through the same mouth as at the present
day, though the present communication from the lake to the
modern river is by a cutting about a hundred yards north of
the probable former channel of the river.

This brief survey shows what was the foundation on which
rested the love and pride with which the Tarsians regarded
their river. The Cydnus is very far from being a beautiful
or a grand stream. Nature was not originally kind to
Tarsus. Nothing can be drearier or more repellent than the
stretch of land and river between the city and the sea, as
the modern traveller beholds it. No amount of skill could
ever make it beautiful. Dion certainly was thoroughly
justified when he said to the Tarsians that as regards
natural surroundings and advantages, they were inferior to
numberless cities. But their river was their own in the sense
that their own skill and energy had made it. They had
transformed that dreary stretch of half-inundated lands,
fringed by sand-heaps along the sea, into a rich, well-
drained and well-watered plain, holding in its bosom a vast
city through which ran for miles a river capacious of the
merchandise of many lands—a city with its feet resting on
a great inland harbour and its head reaching up to the hills.

This is only one of the numberless cases in the ancient world in which a great engineering operation lies far away back at the beginning of the history of a city or a district. The effort and the struggle for victory over nature in such cases seem to have started the population on a career of success, teaching them to combine and to organise the work of many for a common benefit, and showing in the result how union and toil could make their city great and its inhabitants respected.

When once the Cydnus had been regulated and navigation made possible, Tarsus was placed in a very favourable situation. It was (as Thucydides says) a necessity for the early trading cities that they should lie at some distance from the sea in order to be safe from pirates. Tarsus was situated at the head of the navigation of a river, which it had by its own work and skill made navigable; and it took full advantage of its position. Though not most favourably situated by nature to be the distributing centre for Cilicia, and the road centre for communication with other lands, it entered into competition with rivals that were more favoured by nature, and by another great piece of engineering placed itself in command of the best route from Cilicia to the north and north-west across the Taurus mountains. Tarsus cut the great pass, called the Cilician Gates, one of the most famous and the most important passes in history.

§ V. Tarsus and the Cilician Gates.

The broad and lofty ridge of the Taurus mountains divides Cilicia on the south from Cappadocia and Lycaonia on the north. The Taurus is cut obliquely from north-west to south-east by a glen, down which flows a river called Tchakut Su, rising in Cappadocia and joining the

Sarus in Cilicia near Adana.   The glen of the Tchakut
water offers a natural road, easy and gently sloping through
the heart of Taurus.   It is generally a very narrow gorge,
deep down amid the lofty mountains; but it opens out
into two small valleys, one near the northern end, the Vale
of Loulon or Halala, 3,600 feet above the sea, the other
about the middle of its course, the Vale of Podandus, 2,800
feet.   At the east end of the Vale of Loulon the glen is
narrowed to a mere slit barely wide enough to receive the
Tchakut water, and the road has to cross a hill ridge for
about four or five miles.   Apart from this there is no difficulty, until, a few miles south-east from the Vale of Podandus, the glen ends before the southern ridge of Taurus,
which rises high above it, like a broad, lofty, unbroken wall.
The river Tchakut finds an underground passage through
this wall; and the railway will in some future age traverse
it by a tunnel, and emerge on the foot-hills in front of
Taurus, and so come down on Adana.   But the road has
to climb over this great wall, and nature has provided no
easy way to do this.   The earliest road, which is still not
altogether disused, went on south-eastwards direct to Adana,
ascending the steep ridge and descending again on the
southern side: it has never been anything but a hill path,
fit for horses but not for vehicles.   This was the path by
which Mallos and Adana originally maintained their
communication and trade with the Central Plateau of
Anatolia.

The enterprise of the Tarsians opened up a waggon road
direct to their own city.   A path, which was in use doubtless from the earliest time, leaves the Tchakut glen at
Podandus (2,800 feet) and ascends by the course of a small
stream, keeping a little west of south till it reaches and

8

crosses the bare broad summit (4,300 feet), where Ibrahim
Pasha's lines were constructed in the war of 1836; then it
descends sharply 500 feet beside another small stream, till
it reaches a sheer wall of rock through which the stream
finds its way in a narrow gorge, the "Cilician Gates".
Nature had made this gorge just wide enough to carry the
water, and the rocks rise steep on both sides to the height
of 500 or 600 feet. Except in flood, men and animals
could easily traverse the rough bed of this small stream.
But the pass began to be important only when the Tarsians
built a waggon road over the difficult hills from their city
to the southern end of the Gates, and then cut with the
chisel in the solid rock on the west bank of the stream a
level path through the gorge. Thus the pass of the
"Cilician Gates" became the one waggon road from Cilicia
across the Taurus, and remained the only waggon road
for many centuries.

We naturally ask at what period these great engineering
works were achieved; but no direct evidence is attainable,
except that a waggon road leading south across Taurus
from Tyana was in existence before the march of the Ten
Thousand (401 B.C.), and this waggon road must necessarily be the road through the Cilician Gates. For my own
part, though strict evidence has not been discovered and
certainty is unattainable, I feel confident that the waggon
way through the Cilician Gates had been cut and a permanent frontier guard stationed there centuries before that
time. The probability that this was so will appear in the
following sections.

This survey of the natural conditions by which Tarsian
development was controlled has brought out clearly that
the great history of the city was not due to the excellent

qualities of river, climate, sea or harbour placed at its disposal with lavish kindness by nature. In those respects it was inferior, as Dion says, to very many cities. It had subdued nature to its purposes, it had made for itself river and harbour and access to the sea, and a great engineered road across the mountains; and through the kindness of nature it could compensate the stifling moist heat of the plain by the lighter and cooler atmosphere of the hills or the sharper air of the upper Taurus regions. It had learned to conquer nature by observing the laws and methods of nature. It was the men that had made the city.

Such was the great inheritance which they bequeathed to their descendants. An inheritance of the fruit of courage and energy like this is a great thing for a people, and a just cause of pride: the Tarsians of the later Greek and Roman times were stimulated and strengthened by the consciousness of their descent from the men of earlier times. That is clearly implied by the language of Strabo and Dion; and it is expressed in the words of St. Paul, as may be gathered from Luke's account of the stormiest scene in his chequered and adventurous career, when he replied to the Roman Tribune, " I am a Jew, Tarsian of Cilicia, citizen of no mean city ". One would have expected him to claim the Roman rights, as indeed he did a few moments later; but the first words that rose to his lips came direct from his heart and expressed the patriotism and pride in his fatherland, his *patria*, that lay deep in his nature.[11]

The city that was his fatherland and his home mattered much to Paul. It had a place in his heart. He was proud of its greatness. He thought of the men who had made it and bequeathed it to his time as men connected by certain ties with himself (Rom. i. 14).

Who were those men? Of what stock was the people who thus made their own river and harbour?

§ VI. THE IONIANS IN EARLY TARSUS.

According to the view stated above, the formation of that important pass over Taurus, one of the great triumphs of early civilisation over the conditions of nature, was simply a stage in the long struggle between Tarsus and its pair of allied rivals, Mallos with Adana, for control of the markets of the country. From this point of view it becomes clear also that Tarsus first became a harbour and a sea power, and afterwards proceeded to open up the land road as a means of developing its commerce.

The conformity of the facts, as thus stated, with the character of Greek trading enterprise at numberless points round the Mediterranean and Black Seas, is striking. Surely the development of Tarsus must imply a mixture of Greek blood and race in the city. This idea is confirmed and definitely proved by the fact that the first station north of Tarsus, on the way to the Gates, bore the name of Mopsou-krene, the Fountain of Mopsus. Mopsus was the religious impersonation and expression of the expansive energy of the Greek colonies on the Cilician and the neighbouring Pamphylian and Syrian coasts. Such colonies always went forth under divine guidance, and this guidance regularly proceeded from a single centre, *viz.*, one of the abodes of prophetic inspiration which the Greeks called Oracles. In the best known period of Greek history the Delphic Oracle was the chief agent in directing the streams of Greek over-flow and colonisation in the various lines along which it spread. But the Cilician colonies were founded at an earlier time, when the Delphic Oracle had not yet established such a widespread influence. The divine guidance that marked out the way to the Cilician land proceeded from an Ionian centre, *viz.*, the Oracle of Clarian Apollo near Colophon. Mopsus is the expression (according to the anthropomorphic method of Greek popular thought) of the orders of Apollo of Claros, in obedience to which trade and settlement on the Levant coasts set forth from the shores of Lydia and Caria.

Mopsus was the leader and guide of the expansive energy of Mallos, as well as of Tarsus; and the town which was founded on the road from Mallos to inner and Eastern Cilicia was called Mopsou-estia, the Hearth of Mopsus. Mopsus was a far more important figure in the religion of Mallos than in that of Tarsus. He slipped out of the latter to such an extent that no other trace of his former existence there is known to us besides the village of Mopsoukrene. The reason can only be that the Greek element and the Greek religion were weaker in Tarsus than in Mallos; and this is shown by other facts. But the presence of Mopsus in Tarsian local nomenclature is a complete proof that the Greek element was influential at a very early time in that city.

This Greek expansion was designated in old Oriental and Semitic tradition as "the sons of Javan," *i.e.*, the "Ionian" traders. "The sons of Javan" are the Greek race in its progress along the Levant coasts eastwards, which brought the Ionian Greeks within the sphere of knowledge and intercourse of the Semites.

The very ancient Ionian connection of Tarsus is set forth in that important old geographical document, preserved to us in Genesis x. 4 f. : "The sons of Javan : Elishah, and Tarshish, Kittim and Dodanim (or better, Rodanim).

Of these were the coasts of the nations divided in their lands, every one after his tongue; after their families, in their nations." The most probable interpretation of this list is still that of Josephus: Kittim is Cyprus (Kition, the leading city of early time), and Tarshish is Tarsus. That Rodanim means the settlers of Rhodes seems to follow naturally (Dodanim being rejected as a false text).[12] Elishah has been very plausibly explained as the land of Alasia or Alsa (mentioned in the Tel-el-Amarna tablets), which, as is generally agreed, lay somewhere in the Syrian-Cilician-Cyprian coast region; and this explanation must, in the present state of our knowledge, supersede all others (though, of course, certainty is not yet attainable on such matters).

Bearing in mind the close connection between the Aleian plain and Mallos, and the way in which Herodotus seems to assume as self-evident that Mallos was the harbour of the Aleian plain (see § III.), we must admit the probability of Professor Sayce's suggestion that Alasia is the Aleian plain, with its harbour and capital Mallos.[13] This identification would discover in the list of Gen. x. 4 the two great harbours of ancient Cilicia and the two great islands off the south coast of Asia Minor. These four were "the sons of Javan," the four Greek foundations which first brought the Ionian within the ken of the nations of Syria and Palestine.

The objections made by modern scholars to the identification of Tarsus and Tarshish, and the rival theories which they propose, seem utterly devoid of strength or probability. To suppose that Tartessos, or any other place in Spain, formed part of the list in Genesis x. 4, is geographically meaningless and historically impossible; and the theory that the Etruscan people (Tyrsenoi) was meant is nearly as bad. To say that Tarsus was not founded when this document was written is to pretend to a knowledge about the beginnings of Tarsus which we do not possess, and to set undeserved value on the foundation legends stated by Strabo and others (see § VIII.). It is also objected that the Aramaic spelling of the name (as shown on the coins) was with -r z- and not -r s h-; but great changes and varieties in the spelling of foreign geographical names are frequently found in other cases. This Cilician or Anatolian name was spelt Tarsos by the Greeks, Tarzi- in Aramaic, and Tarshish in the document of Genesis x.

It may also be urged in objection that the Greek colonies of Cilicia seem to have been Dorian, whereas Genesis x. 4 speaks of "Ionian". But who would venture, in the face of the recent discoveries which have upset all our old ideas about early Greece, to dogmatise about the meaning of "Ionian" in the second millennium B.C., or to say that "Ionians" could not have founded colonies in Cilicia so early as that? We cannot say anything more definite than that "the sons of Javan" were the Greek settlers and traders as known to the people of Phœnicia or Syria, before the distinction between Ionian and Dorian had any existence among the Greeks. On the Dorian character in Cilicia, and its late origin, see § XII.

It would be out of place here to discuss the questions that rise out of the various uses of the name Tarshish in the Old Testament; nor am I competent to do so. But it is important for our present purpose to note that the exports from Tarshish to Tyre included silver, iron, tin, and lead (Ezek. xxvii. 12; Jer. x. 9). Silver and lead are found in abundance in the Taurus mountains, close to the route of the Cilician Gates, and the mines have been worked there from time immemorial. Iron has been found and worked from an extremely early time in the northern or Pontic region of Cappadocia, and it is commonly held by scholars that the use of iron for the benefit of man originated there. The Pontic production was carried south by the Cilician Gates to Tarsus. Tin is, however, not known to be found in Asia Minor.

Assuming the identification of Tarshish and Tarsus, we find the same name in various slight modifications, lasting from the second millennium before Christ, through the Assyrian, Persian, Greek, Roman, Arab, Egyptian, and Turkish domination, down to the Tersous of the present day. Tarsus, always half Oriental, adapted itself readily to every Oriental ruler, and preserved its continuous individuality under all. While it would not be justifiable, in the conflict of opinion, to draw weighty historical inferences at present from the identification, we can at least infer that "the sons of Javan" are allowed by general opinion to have had a footing somewhere on the east Levant coasts in the second millennium at Alasia and Kittim. If so, they must have had landing places or ports in Cilicia, and these can hardly have been elsewhere than on the rivers at Mallos and Tarsus.

With this early origin of Tarsus we shall find that all the evidence is in perfect agreement. The reasons for thinking that the early Tarsus was one of "the sons of the Ionian" are as strong as can be expected in that period of history. But this expression must be properly understood. It is not intended to mean that Ionian Greeks were the first people that formed a settlement at Tarsus. Tarsus was doubtless one of those primeval towns, like Damascus and Iconium, which have been such since settled habitation and towns began to exist in the countries. It is, indeed, highly probable that the earliest Tarsus was situated on the outer hills, about two miles north of the present town, because defensive strength was one of the prime necessities for early towns, and only on the hills could this be attained.

Nor do we mean that the early Ionian Tarsus was inhabited solely by Ionian Greeks.   There was rarely, if ever, a case in which Greeks formed the sole population of a city which they founded in a foreign land.   The strength and permanence of the Greek colonies were due to their power of assimilating the native population, and imparting to it something of their own genius and aspirations; but a mere settlement of unmixed aliens on a foreign shore would have been unable to maintain itself against the untempered hostility of a native population nearly as high in capacity and vigour as the aliens themselves.   All analogy points to the conclusion that this Ionian colony was a mixed town, not a pure Ionian settlement.

With regard to that early time, we must content ourselves for the present with analogy and indirect argument.   Until Cilicia is better known and more carefully studied, its earliest history must remain almost a þlank, just as its mediæval history also is enveloped in obscurity.

§ VII.   Tarsus as an Oriental Town.

As has been stated in § VI., it seems to be certain and admitted that the ancient document in Genesis x. bears witness to an extension of Ionian, *i.e.*, very early Greek influence along the Asiatic coasts in the second millennium B.C. ; for modern authorities are agreed that some at least of "the sons of Javan" are to be found on the south coast of Asia Minor, or in the Levant islands.   The following millennium shows a retrograde movement in the extent of

Greek influence, and a distinct strengthening of the Asiatic power and spirit, in this region; and this strongly affected the fortunes of Tarsus.

Such ebb and flow in the tides of influence of East on West, and West on East, has always characterised the movement of history in the borderlands, and especially along the land roads across Asia Minor, that bridge of nations stretching across from Asia to Europe, and along the sea-way of the southern coast. At one time Europe sweeps over great part of Asia, and seems on the point of overrunning the whole continent; but always Asia recruits its forces, rolls back the tide of conquest, and retaliates by engulfing parts of Europe. If Alexander marched to the Indus and his successors ruled over Bactria and Afghanistan, the Arabs marched to the banks of the Loire and the Turks to the walls of Vienna, and all of them made only evanescent conquests. Europe cannot permanently subdue Asia, nor Asia Europe.

Thus from an Ionian colony Tarsus became an Oriental city, and in this character it is revealed to us in the oldest historical records in which it is mentioned. The earliest reference to Tarsus occurs on the Black Obelisk of Shalmaneser, king of Assyria: he captured this with other towns about the middle of the ninth century B.C., and at this time may be dated (so far as evidence or probability reaches) the first entrance of a thoroughly Asiatic race into the country west of Mount Amanus.

Neither the domination of the Assyrians, nor that of the Medians afterwards,[14] nor the rule of the Persians from the sixth century onwards, was likely to cause much change in the organisation of the country or the character of the cities. Those Oriental states, only loosely knit together even near the centre, exercised their power over such outlying provinces chiefly by means of governors, who represented the king in his suzerainty over the native chiefs and townships, while the latter retained much of their old authority within their own territories. The change that occurred in the state of Tarsus was due not to the governing foreign empire, but to internal causes and especially to the decay of the Greek element, which was absorbed into the native population.

The reinvigoration of Orientalism, or rather the weakening of the Western spirit of freedom and self-assertion in

Fig. 1.—Reverse of coin struck at Tarsus by the king of Cilicia shortly before 400 B.C.; inscribed Tarz in Aramaic letters.

Cilicia, is marked by the growth of a native Cilician dynasty of petty kings, who ruled Cilicia under the Persian kings as overlords; thus the Cilicians were the servants of the servant of the Great King. Kingship, which was alien and repellent to the ancient spirit of the European races, was congenial to an Oriental people. So, for example, when the last king of a Cappadocian dynasty died, the Romans offered the people their freedom. The Cappadocians, who did not know what freedom was, begged for a king. The Romans marvelled that any people could prefer slavery to freedom, but treated them after their own character and appointed a king to rule over them.

Accordingly in 401, when Xenophon crossed Cilicia with the Ten Thousand Greeks of the younger Cyrus's army, he found a king Syennesis, whose capital was apparently Tarsus. A Cilician king of the same name had co-operated with the king of Babylon in making peace between Cyaxares the Mede and Alyattes the Lydian in 585 B.C., a second is mentioned about 500 B.C., and the same or a third Syennesis fought in Greece under Xerxes in 480 B.C. On the other hand, when Alexander the Great entered Cilicia in 334 B.C., there seems to have been no king of Cilicia, but only a Persian officer directly governing the country. The kings, therefore, must have been put down ; and this in all probability was due to the growth of stricter organisation in the Persian empire, and stricter exercise of the power of the Great King in the outlying provinces through his representatives or satraps. The action which Syennesis and his queen Epyaxa took in 401 in favour of Cyrus against king Artaxerxes may perhaps have shown the danger involved in suffering Cilicia to be governed by subordinate tributary kings, and led to the suppression of the kings and the introduction of a new system with more direct control. At any rate, it may be stated with confidence that the Persian kings inherited the system from the Assyrian (and perhaps the Median) domination, and, after permitting it to continue for fully a century and a half, put an end to it soon after 400 B.C. As to the character of the Cilician kingdom, and the constitution of Tarsus as its capital, nothing is recorded.

The repetition of the name Syennesis has suggested to some modern inquirers that this name was, like Pharaoh, a

title mistaken by the Greeks for a personal name.   It seems
however quite probable that the Cilician kings may have
been really priest-dynasts, such as are known to have long
ruled at Olba among the Cilician or Isaurian mountains, and
at other places in the eastern regions of Asia Minor.[15]   The
priestly power naturally tended to grow greater in times of
disorganisation ; and the Assyrian kings may probably
have found it convenient to rule through the leading priest,
who was quite ready to suit himself to their requirements
and buy temporal power at the price of service to a foreign
sovereign.   Now the priest's authority was based originally
on his position as representative on earth of the supreme
god of the district : the priest wore the dress and bore the
name of the god.[16]   If the origin of the Cilician kingship
were of this kind, it may be thought probable that Syennesis
was a Divine name, rather than a title, and that the kings at
their accession lost their own name and assumed the priestly
name taken from the god, as *e.g.*, the priests at Pessinus
assumed the name of Atis.

The coinage of this Oriental Tarsus, while showing the
strong influence of the Hellenic element in the population,
also reveals the weakening of that influence.   The coins
belong to the fifth and fourth centuries, and were evidently
struck, not by a self-governing city of the Greek kind, but
by kings and by Persian satraps.[17]   Yet even here a certain
Greek character is apparent.   Some of the earliest coins are
more Hellenic in feeling than the later.   Occasionally there
occurs a revival of Hellenic character, accompanied by the use
of Greek letters on the coins ; but the latest coins of Tarsus
under the Persian domination, though imitated from Greek
models, were strongly Oriental in character, wholly devoid
of the true Hellenic spirit, and bore purely Aramaic legends.

The earliest coins attributed to Tarsus are as old as the sixth century, and prove that the city had "commercial relations with Lydia or the Ionian coast-towns," which is in harmony with the views stated in § VI., as to the character of the old Ionian Tarsus. But as the attribution to Tarsus of these coins (which are usually left unclassified) is not universally accepted,[17a] it is best to leave them out of reckoning here. These coins are more thoroughly Greek than the Tarsian coinage of the following centuries; but this is precisely what a study of the city's history leads us to expect.

The warrior armed in the Greek fashion, shown in Fig. 1, is a common type on the coins struck under the Cilician kings; the figure still retains much of the Greek spirit, though the name of Tarsus is written in Aramaic letters. On the obverse of the coins the king himself is shown, quite in the Oriental style, as a horseman galloping, wearing the Persian head-dress. A coin like this reveals much. There is the regal government symbolised by the king, who wears on his head the authority granted by his overlord the Persian Great King. That some share of the old Greek spirit remained in the population appears from the warrior on the reverse. The city had still some shadow of individuality and in a sense independence, *i.e.*, it was not a mere unit in the dominion of the king, but retained something in the way of self-administering authority: this seems to be shown by the legend, which names "Tarsus," not "Cilicia". But the government was Oriental, like the letters of the legend, not Greek. All this suits well, and even necessitates, the supposition, that a free constitution had once existed in Tarsus and was gradually dying out under Oriental rule. A free constitution could not have originated at that period, except through the influence of Greek colonisation. Civic freedom was unknown and inconceivable in Oriental towns; it was a gift of the Greeks to the world.

The double character of the city, as at once Cilician and Persian, is shown by a coin (Fig. 17 in § IX.) with the Tarsian god and the Persian god occupying each one side: it was struck under the satrap Tiribazus, 386-380 B.C. This coin is described in connection with the religion of Tarsus, § IX.

Pharnabazus, satrap of the regions near the Hellespont from about 412 B.C. onwards, struck many coins in Cilicia,

Fig. 2.—Coin struck at Tarsus by Pharnabazus, 379-374 B.C. The inscription, Pharnabazus Cilicia, on the reverse is in Aramaic; but the heads of the goddess and the warrior are of the Greek type.

doubtless at Tarsus, when he was on duty occasionally in that province, arranging the expedition against Egypt between 379 and 374 B.C. There is a marked recurrence to Greek types on these coins. The head of the goddess or nymph on the obverse, with necklace and earrings, her streaming hair bound by a sphendone (a band resembling a sling), was imitated from the famous and lovely representation of Arethusa by the artist Kimon on coins of Syracuse. The head of a warrior, wearing a highly ornate crested Attic helmet, with a chlamys fastened by a brooch round the neck,

is also of the Greek type. The long intercourse of Pharnabazus with the Greeks of the west coast of Asia Minor made
him employ Greek artists and types ; but the legends are in
Aramaic letters, with some few exceptions which bear the
name of Tarsus in Greek. It would be out of place to seek
for any specially Tarsian character on coins struck by a non-
Cilician satrap on such occasional sojourn in the land.

On the coin of Datames, satrap of Cilicia, 378-2 B.C. (Fig.
3), the reverse type is wholly Oriental. A Persian archer,

FIG. 3.—Coin struck by the satrap Datames, 378-372 B.C. Obverse : the
Lord of Tarsus with his name Baal-Tarz in Aramaic letters. Reverse:
the satrap in Persian costume with his name, Datames, in Aramaic.
The letters are read as Tarkamos by some writers, a name very suitable
for a native of East Anatolia, but hardly for a Persian satrap.

doubtless the satrap himself, wearing the Oriental trousers
and long sleeved tunic under a cloak, sits on a chair, examin-
ing an arrow which he holds in both hands, while his quiver
lies on his lap and his bow is before his knee. In front of
him is the winged solar disk in Persian form. Behind him
is his name in Aramaic letters. The Oriental character of
this type is evident by comparison with the Parthian coins
of many centuries later, on which the Parthian king is represented by a figure in many respects similar; an example is

shown in the *Letters to the Seven Churches*, p. 59. But on
the Tarsian coin the art has not wholly lost its Greek skill :
on the Parthian coin it is thoroughly barbaric.

The reverse of this coin shows the Baal of Tarsus. The
figure is of Greek attitude and Greek origin ; but it had long
been naturalised in Tarsus, and the accompaniments are Oriental, like the name and the letters in which it is inscribed.
The memory that this was the representation of the Hellenic

Fɪɢ. 4.—Coin struck by Mazaeus, 366-333 B.C. Obverse : the Lord of Tarsus
with the usual Aramaic inscription. Reverse: the Syrian Gates and
lion attacking bull ; Aramaic inscription, " Mazaeus (satrap) of Trans-
Euphratesia and Cilicia ".

Zeus had become very faint in Tarsus, if it survived at all.
See § IX., where this figure is more fully described.

In this coin the one side is Anatolian, while the other is
Persian. The city was Perso-Cilician, and the coin reflects
the double character.

Several coins of the satrap Mazaeus, 361-33 B.C., are shown
in Figs. 4, 5, 6, and 9, 10, § IX. Fig. 4 shows a lion devouring
a bull, a favourite Tarsian type (seen also in Fig. 15), with
the satrap's name and title in Aramaic letters, and a curious
device of two parallel battlemented walls, which is probably
to be interpreted as a representation of the " Gates " between

Cilicia and Syria.   In this congeries of unconnected symbols
there is not a trace left of the Hellenic spirit, which made
every coin-type express some single idea.[17b]   The Aramaic
legend "Mazaeus (governor) over Eber-nahara and Cilicia"
may explain the double type, as symbolising the double region
over which the satrap ruled.   Eber-nahara was "the country
beyond (*i.e.*, west of) the river (Euphrates)"; and the Syrian
Gates commanded and guarded the pass leading across Mt.
Amanus from Eber-nahara to Cilicia.

FIG. 5.—Coin struck by the satrap Mazaeus, 361-333 B.C.   This coin
may belong to Magarsus, not Tarsus.

On the obverse of this coin the Lord of Tarsus is represented in very slight variation from the preceding (see § IX.).

In Fig. 9, § IX., the type is a variation of Fig. 4.   The
lion pulls down a stag.

Another coin of the same satrap (Fig. 5) shows the head
of a goddess, similar in character to the Greek Athena : she
wears an Attic helmet with a strange triple crest, also earrings and necklace.   The obverse has another slight variation
of the most characteristic Tarsian type, the Baal of Tarsus.
The goddess, to the old Anatolian mind the chief envisagement of the Divine power, does not remain a prominent

figure on Tarsian coins; but she was, doubtless important in the ritual. That she should be an armed goddess, assimilated to Pallas Athena, is characterisic of the East Anatolian religion, as distinguished from the Central Anatolian or Phrygian form [see Hastings' *Dictionary of the Bible*, v., p. 134 (2)].

A third coin of Mazaeus (Fig. 6) shows a lion walking; above his back is a star; beneath his feet is a large crescent. The collocation of types is Oriental and not Hellenic. The obverse is the usual Lord of Tarsus, with Aramaic legend.

FIG. 6.—Coin struck by Mazaeus, 369-333 B.C. The name of the satrap is inscribed in Aramaic letters.

The coinage of an ancient city is a miniature of its history; and in these specimens the transition of Tarsus into a thoroughly Anatolian and Oriental city can be clearly read.

§ VIII. LEGENDS OF EARLY TARSUS.

During fully five centuries therefore Tarsus was merely a town under Oriental domination. The Assyrian rule left a strong impression on the historical memory, which created various legends veiling, but not wholly concealing, the real facts of that time.

Such legends about the early history of a city commonly take the form of foundation narratives: they describe the circumstances in which the city was founded. It is a mistake, however, to understand that they were intended to describe the beginning of the city. The ancients used the term " foundation " in a loose way to indicate any important change, or anything that could be regarded as the beginning of a new period in the history of the city. In honorary inscriptions of the later time the title " Founder " meant little more than benefactor: any person that gave a building or an institution or a donation was styled a founder of the city. As was pointed out in § VI. it is an error to argue that Tarsus did not exist at the time when the document quoted in Genesis x. was composed, because the foundation of the city is assigned to a later period. The city was, in a sense, founded over and over again ; but its beginning goes back to the beginning of human history in Cilicia.

When the Assyrians entered Cilicia about 850 B.C., Tarsus was one of the cities that they conquered. It therefore existed in the pre-Assyrian period. Solinus, a writer who often preserves good traditions,[18] says that, before it was conquered by the Assyrians, the empire of Cilicia extended to the borders of Egypt and included Lydia, Pamphylia, Cappadocia, Armenia, and Media. This statement, which once would have been thought absurd, is now seen to be a vague memory of the historical fact that the Hittite Empire, with its capital in Asia Minor, once extended from Lydia to the borders of Egypt, and that Cilicia was part of that Empire. And possibly the statement of Solinus may be hereafter still further justified, if it be found that the capital of the Hittite Empire was at one time within the bounds of Cilicia.[19]   Tarsus was certainly a flourishing city in this pre-Assyrian time, which may be called the Anatolian period; and its religion seems to have retained strong traces of that early civilisation. To that time belongs the early Ionian settlement in Cilicia; but it is vain to speculate about the history of that period, and we must await the progress of discovery, which seems now imminent.

About the Assyrian Tarsus we have no information except in the form of foundation legends. Alexander Polyhistor [20] says that Sennacherib, king of Nineveh (705-681 B.C.), was the founder. A more Hellenised form of the legend, related by Strabo and many others, makes Sardanapalus the founder of Tarsus, and tells how he recorded on his tomb at Anchiale, fourteen miles south-west from Tarsus, that he had built those two cities in one day. The story ran that on this tomb was a statue representing Sardanapalus snapping his fingers, with an inscription in Assyrian letters: "Sardanapalus, son of Anakyndaraxes, built Anchiale and Tarsus in one day. Eat, drink, and play, for everything else is not worth this (action of the fingers)." The poet Choirilos versified the sentiment, and Aristotle quoted it, remarking that it was more worthy to be written on the grave of an ox than on the tomb of a king. There is some difference among the ancient authorities as to whether this monument was in Anchiale or in Nineveh; but the authority of Aristoboulos may be accepted that it was really at Anchiale. It was an easy error to transfer the monument of an Assyrian king from Anchiale to Nineveh. The opposite process could not have occurred to any one.

The form of this legend shows that it is founded partly on a historical fact, *viz.*, the Assyrian domination, and partly on the misunderstanding of a work of art, probably a relief, in which a male figure was represented with right hand raised in front of the face. This gesture which appears in the relief at Fassiler (Fig. 7), was readily misinterpreted by the Greeks in later time as denoting the snapping of the fingers; and the words attributed to Sardanapalus in the legend express the sentiment which, as

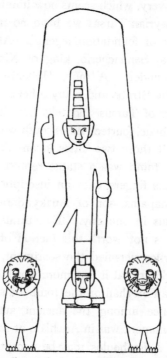

FIG. 7.—Stele at Fassiler on the border of Lycaonia and Pisidia. The goddess with her lions; the god plants one foot on her head.

later people fancied, corresponded to the gesture in the relief. The "Assyrian" letters were either cuneiform, or, more probably, Hittite hieroglyphics; and were certainly quite unintelligible to the Greeks at the time when this legend took form.

Thus on a real monument at Anchiale was founded this mere legend, in itself devoid of any truth or historic value, and yet veiling real historical facts.

Other legends current locally show that some memory of the old Ionian city was preserved in Tarsus. Athenodorus, the great Tarsian philosopher in the time of Augustus, says that the original name of the city was Parthenia, a purely Greek name, and that it took this name from Parthenius, grandson of Anchiale, the daughter of Iapetos, *i.e.*, Japhet. The Oriental idea that Javan, the "Ionian," was son of

Fig. 8.—Perseus in Greek type, as shown on Tarsian coins.

Japhet (Gen. x. 2) has been transformed by Greek fancy into this legend, which thus connects the two cities, Anchiale and Tarsus, with Japhet and the Ionians.

Strabo, again, says that the people whom the Greeks called Cilicians had borne at first the name of Hypachaeans, but afterwards got the name Cilicians from Cilix, son of Agenor, king of Phœnicia. It is very common to find the successive changes in the history and population of a town expressed in legend as a series of changes of name. In this case the thoroughly Greek-sounding name, Hypachaeans, is an echo of the old Ionian settlement in Cilicia, and Cilix represents an Asiatic immigration or revival.

Other legends current in later time at Tarsus made Perseus or Heracles the founder of Tarsus. Perseus and Heracles seem to be two names applied by the Greeks to a hero or god of the locality, whose influence in very similar forms can be traced very widely through the eastern parts of Asia Minor. This local hero was treated as a religious expression of historical relations and racial facts; and probably it might be found, if evidence had been preserved as to the course of Tarsian history, that the same Anatolian Divine figure was expressed by the Greek element in Tarsus at one time as Perseus (Fig. 8) and at another time as Heracles.

The Tarsian legends and beliefs regarding Heracles are unknown. He occurs on coins only in stereotyped Greek forms, and he is mentioned by Dion Chrysostom, speaking to the Tarsians, as "your leader," or "ancestor" (Archegos, which is used in the sense both of "leader in a migration" and "ancestor and founder of a race"). (Compare Fig. 44.)

The legends of Perseus at Tarsus are better attested; they are often represented on coins of the city, though in an obscure and as yet unexplained form, quite different from the ordinary Hellenic representations of that hero. Perseus (Figs. 8, 14-16) appears sometimes in company with a fisherman, sometimes greeting Apollo or adoring the image of that god, which is placed on a lofty column, or carrying the image on his right hand. These types show a strange mixture of Greek and Oriental ideas; and there is apparent in the forms a vague suggestion of strangers, *viz.*, an immigrant and a native people, meeting one another. This East Anatolian Perseus has a half Greek look, and he is found in localities such as Iconium, where no very early Greek immigrants can possibly have penetrated. The choice of name may perhaps be due, in some vàgue, unreasoning, and now unintelligible way, to the Persian domination. But it is necessary to regard, not only the historical, but also the religious side of these legends and their expression on the coins ; and therefore we must at this point glance at the religion of Tarsus, which was as composite as the population. The religion of such a city was, in a sense, an epitome of its experience and a summary of its entire history ; and therefore a study of its religion is indispensable in attempting to understand its character and its population.

§ IX. THE RELIGION OF TARSUS.

The religion of Tarsus is an extremely complicated subject, and the information which has been preserved is far too scanty to permit anything like a satisfactory account of it. Several steps in its development can be distinguished with certainty: others are probable: but many are quite obscure.

We have observed in Part I., § II., that Paul recognised in the pagan religion a certain element of truth and Divine insight. This he had learnt in Tarsus. It was in the religion of the city that he had first become aware of certain fundamental ideals of good amid the vast accretion of abomination and evil built up round and over those initial ideas ; and this fact lends a special interest to the religion of Tarsus. It is not our object to describe the evil, the vice and the deception involved in it as a practical working factor in the life of the later city. Much of that evil was due to degeneration, part of it was inherent from the beginning, because the initial ideas were after all very imperfect. In happier circumstances, it might have been possible that a succession of prophets and thinkers should succeed in strengthening the truth and eliminating the evil of the original ideas; but true development had been denied to the Tarsian cult. As the embodiment and expression of the experience of the people, it had taken into itself the evils of a mixed population, of a rude conquering soldiery and an enslaved populace; and it had long ago ceased to satisfy the minds of the more educated pagans. Yet even in the latest most degraded stage it had not lost entirely the ideas of Divine truth, which had originally given fcrm to it, as the popular perception recognised "the witness of himself" which the beneficent God had granted, "in that he did good and gave from heaven rains and fruitful seasons and filled the hearts of men with food and gladness". These are the words in which Paul expressed to the rude Lystran people in a simple way, such as they could understand, the thought which he expounded in more philosophic terms in his letter to the Romans.

In the growth of an ancient city no religious fact was ever wholly lost. When immigrants or colonists settled there, they brought their own religion with them, but they did not destroy the previously existing religion any more than they exterminated the older population. An amalgamation took place between the religions of the old and the new people; as *e.g.*, at Athens, when a race of Poseidon-worshippers settled beside and among the older worshippers of Athena, a certain male figure, named Erechtheus, who formed part of the Divine group in the Athena-religion, was in the State cultus identified with Poseidon, and thus Athena and Poseidon-Erechtheus were associated in a joint worship and a common temple.

In Tarsus we can say with certainty that the early Ionian immigrants found an older population and an older religion already in possession. Certain elements in the later Tarsian religion can be distinguished as being in all probability pre-Ionian, others as Ionian. The Assyrian domination doubtless affected the religion of the country. The Persian period left unmistakable traces, which appear on the coins. The new foundation of the Hellenic Tarsus about 170 B.C. must inevitably have given a distinctly more Hellenised aspect to the State cultus, though it had little, if any, effect on its real nature. The Greek element in the new population readily adopted the national cult, identifying their Greek gods with the Tarsian deities, and merging their own rather formal religion in the more real worship of the Tarsian gods. Only the Jewish element remained separate, and did not affect the State religion, though it certainly must have affected strongly the character and views of many individuals, and produced that circle of believing or devout persons of pagan origin, who in every city surrounded the Synagogue. It was precisely because the Jewish religion was so incapable of amalgamation with the others that the Hellenes of those cities complained : the Jews really stood outside of the city union. In Tarsus, so far as the scanty evidence justifies an opinion, the Jews seem to have been regarded in a less degree than elsewhere as an alien element.

The principal deity in Tarsus was the one who is styled on coins with Aramaic legends of the Persian and early Seleucid period, Baal-Tarz, the Lord of Tarsus. He also appears frequently on coins of the Hellenic Tarsus, and sometimes in the Roman Imperial time. He is represented in the character and position appropriated to Zeus in Greek art, sitting on a chair, resting his raised left hand on a long upright sceptre, and holding out in his right hand objects varying on different coins and at different periods, but most frequently either an ear of corn and a bunch of grapes, or a figure of Victory. The latter, which is more Hellenic, is more frequent in the Roman time, the corn and grapes are commonest in the earlier period, and mark this god as the old Anatolian deity, the giver of corn and wine. The censer for fumigation, which sometimes stands beside him (Fig. 3), marks him as the god of purification. On the top of the sceptre, or on his hand, sits often the sacred bird, the

Fig. 9.—Coin struck by the satrap Mazaeus, 361-333 b.c. " Baal-Tarz," the Lord of Tarsus. Reverse : lion killing a stag.

eagle. The strange, and quite non-Hellenic border, in which the statue of the god is framed in Fig. 3, is thought to be a rude way of indicating the temple which was his abode on earth. (Figs. 9, 10, see also Figs. 3, 4, 6 in § VII.)

Like Zeus in Greek art, this Tarsian god is sometimes represented as standing ; but the regular type is that of the sitting deity.

This god represents, beyond all doubt, the old Tarsian conception of the Divine power as male. Under Semitic influence he became Baal-Tarz, under Greek influence he was identified with Zeus. But he was older than the Aramaic and the Greek name; and we must look at the original Anatolian envisagement of this god.

These symbols, corn-ears and grapes, are carried in the hands of the god, who is sculptured of colossal size on the rocks above the great springs at Ibriz, on the north side of Taurus. He is there represented as the Peasant-God, dressed simply in short tunic, high boots, and tall pointed head-dress with horns in front, bearing in his hands the gifts which he has bestowed on mankind by his toil, the corn and

FIG. 10.—Coin of Mazaeus " Baal-Tarz ". Reverse: lion killing a bull.

the grapes. Sculptured there long before the Hellenic period of Central Anatolian history, he shows only the native character, without a trace of Greek influence, but with a strong Assyrian element. This god of Ibriz is the embodiment of the toiling agriculturist, who by the work of his hands has redeemed the soil for tillage, gathered out the stones from it, conducted the water to it, ploughed it and sowed in it the corn, or planted it with trees and tended them and cleaned them till they bear their fruit.[20a]

But that is not the Lord of Tarsus. The deity who sits

on a chair, wearing simply the loose himation, which could only impede active exertion, and holding the sceptre, is not the Peasant-God, who by the labour of his hands has produced the corn and the wine, but the supreme god who gives rain and fruitful seasons and their products, who without exertion by the simple word of his power bestows his benefits on mankind.

This distinction between the supreme deity and the working god was one that lay deep in the Anatolian religion. It was expressed by thé rude people of Lystra when they saluted Barnabas and Paul as gods. Paul was to them Hermes, and Barnabas was the supreme god and father Zeus : such at least are the names in the Greek translation, for we unfortunately are denied the names that were employed in the Lycaonian language. I cannot illustrate the distinction better than by quoting a few lines written in 1895.[21] " The same qualities which mark out Paul to us as the leader, marked him out to the populace of Lycaonia as the agent and subordinate. The western mind regards the leader as the active and energetic partner ; but the Oriental mind considers the leader to be the person who sits still and does nothing, while his subordinates speak and work for him. Hence in the truly Oriental religions the chief god sits apart from the world, communicating with it through his messenger and subordinate. The more statuesque figure of Barnabas was therefore taken by the Orientals as the chief god, and the active orator, Paul, as his messenger, communicating his wishes to men. Incidentally, we may notice both the diametrical antithesis of this conception of the Divine nature to the Christian conception, and also the absolute negation of the Oriental view in Christ's words to His disciples, ' whosoever would become great among you shall be your minister; and whosoever would be first among you shall be your servant'" (Matt. xx. 26).

This distinction was appreciated by the Greeks in their expression of the Anatolian religion. The supreme god is usually called by the name of their supreme deity, Zeus. The working god is in the south-eastern cities of Asia Minor most frequently identified with Heracles, the hero labouring under a cruel taskmaster, who slays monsters, drains marshes, and gives fertile land to agriculture; but he is also envisaged under other aspects, especially as Apollo the seer of the Divine will, or Hermes the messenger who intimates the Divine purpose to men.

But it is never the case that those envisagements of the Divine nature are fixed and stereotyped. On the contrary they are fluid, shifting, often in a way interchangeable, even though they are so strongly distinguished. Thus the supreme god in Anatolia is the giver of signs and revealer of his will, as Zeus Semanticus, and the giver of corn and wine and the fruits of the earth and all things good and beautiful, as Zeus Karpodotes and Zeus Kalokagathios. So the Lord of Tarsus holds in his hands the corn and the grapes, which at Ibriz the Peasant-God bestows upon his votaries. The working god, the subordinate, was as a rule conceived as the son, the supreme god as the father. But in the cycle of the life of the gods, the father is the son, and the son the father. "The bull is the father of the serpent, and the serpent of the bull": such was the expression in the Phrygian mysteries; and it well illustrates the element abominated by St. Paul as the cause of the degradation and hatefulness of the popular religion. But, in spite of the fluid character of these Divine ideas, it is possible in a certain degree to separate them and to contemplate each by itself in the

Tarsian religion and the religion of south-western Anatolia generally.

We distinguish the young and active deity in a figure of thoroughly Oriental type, common on Tarsian coins throughout Greek and Roman times: he stands on a winged and horned lion, wearing a tall pointed head-dress, with bow-case on his shoulder and sword girt at his side: he holds forward his right hand, often with a branch or a flower in it, while with his left he grasps a double-headed battleaxe.

Fig. 11.—Reverse of coin of second or first century B.C. The god "of the Tarsians" on winged and horned lion. Obverse: head of the City goddess.

The branch marks him out as the god of purification, who teaches the ceremonies and rules for the expiation of guilt and the cleansing of impurity. The flower is perhaps the symbol of curative power, as Mr. J. G. Frazer points out. There is in this representation much that suggests an analogy with the Greek Apollo, the god of purification and of curative power. (See Figs. 11, 12.)

This representation is an old Anatolian type, untouched by Greek influence. In the holy chamber at Boghaz-Keui a similar young god is represented on the rock wall (Fig. 12).

He stands immediately behind the Goddess-mother, as she faces the supreme god in the ceremony of the Holy Marriage. It caused no difficulty to the ancient mind that the young god was, in one sense, to be the fruit of that marriage; the

Fig. 12.—Rock-sculpture at Boghaz-Keui.

gods are always living; they are always with us; yet they are born and they die. The fluidity and impalpability of the ancient conceptions of the Divine nature cannot be bound down by logic or by the conditions of time. The Holy Marriage takes place every year: it is in a sense the cause and the guarantee of the life of Nature. But the gods are outside of time, symbolic, ever changing, and yet ever the same. No more did it trouble the ancient sense of morality that the young god is also, in a sense, the favourite and paramour of the Mother-goddess. It was all symbolic of the life of the changing year: there was no question of morality involved originally, though such questions came to be involved as the old religious ideas and rites degenerated.

The resemblance between this ancient Anatolian type and the representation of the Tarsian youthful god are very marked. There are indeed certain differences in detail. The young Tarsian god often holds in his right hand the same flower, which at Boghaz-Keui is carried by the supreme god who stands facing the Mother-goddess in the Holy Marriage. The tall head-dress (like that of the modern Turkish dervish orders), which the god at Boghaz-Keui wears, is very much shortened in the Tarsian type. But these are unessential changes. The curative power is attributed in the one case to the Divine father (as very frequently in other parts of Anatolia the god identified with the Hellenic Zeus was regarded as the healing power), and in the other case to the son. It might equally be, and often was, assigned to the Mother-goddess. The power of healing was a universal Divine attribute. The addition of the bow to the equipment of the young god at Tarsus may be due to change in the methods of war, and was perhaps made in the Persian time. It will be observed that the chin of the god at Boghaz-Keui is very short, whereas in Greek art the chin was portrayed much more strongly: this is a characteristic of the pre-Hellenic art on the plateau of Asia Minor.

It is highly probable that one of those two old Anatolian gods of Tarsus was called Sandon, and the other Tarku;

but it is necessary to guard against assigning too positively one name to one figure. The term Disandan, which is a variant of Sandon, would suggest that Zeus and Sandon corresponded best to one another, and that Sandon was the envisagement of the Divine nature as fully grown, Tarku as youthful. But it must always be remembered that these Divine conceptions pass into one another and are not permanently separate. When Ammianus, xiv. 8, says that Tarsus was founded by Perseus son of Danae or by Sandan a rich noble from Aechium, we may infer that the story in its original form had identified Perseus and Sandon as the immigrant hero who founded Tarsus; and this implies that Sandon was the youthful active god. Numerous authorities mention that Heracles was identical with Sandon; and we shall find ourselves obliged to regard the Tarsian Perseus and Heracles as two heroised forms of the same Anatolian deity. But the name was, in the ancient conception, an unimportant detail: the Divine names shifted and changed in a most perplexing way, just as did the attitude in which the god was represented: the god who sits above all as supreme may at any moment become energetic as the Divine power in action, and be represented as standing and putting his power into activity personally. The essential matter was the Divine nature and power: the particulars and details were non-essential and changeable.[21a]

Both Tarku and Sandon (or Sandes) are often found as elements in Cilician personal names.

Archæological discovery has not yet began to throw any light on old Tarsian religion or history. The large unsightly mass of concrete called popularly the Tomb of Sardanapalus is, according to the architect Koldewey,[21b] the core of the platform that supported a Roman temple.

This Tarsian god is often shown on coins of the Roman Imperial time within a curious structure, which most probably represents a portable shrine. It is a pyramidal structure resting on a broad platform, and the god on his lion stands upon the pedestal inside the pyramidal covering. On the top of the pyramid often perches the divine eagle. Sometimes the pyramid is shaded by a semicircular canopy supported by two young beardless men wearing tunics: the

Fig. 13.—Coins of Tarsus Metropolis, struck under Marcus Aurelius, 161-180 A.D., and under Decius, 249-251 A.D. The god as he was borne through the streets to the funeral ceremony.

men stand on the platform on which the structure rests. (See Figs. 13 and 21.)

This quaint representation must probably be regarded as an attempt to show in the small space of a coin a large erection, which was a feature in an annual procession in honour of the god. Some of the coins attempt, and some do not attempt, to show the human beings, doubtless young men chosen from the city, who bore a canopy over the holy structure. The whole was carried through the streets on a great platform; and we must presume that it was drawn by animals or by a train of devotees.

Now there was a festival at Tarsus, in which the burning of a pyre was the chief ceremony; and this took place in honour of a god, whom Dion Chrysostom calls Heracles. The pyre was constructed for the occasion, and the god was burned in it as the crowning scene of the ceremonial. The periodic burning of the god represented his translation to heaven.[22] The eagle, which bore the Trojan Ganymede to heaven, perched on the apex of the pyramid in the Tarsian rite. We are therefore forced to the conclusion that the image of the god, as it was borne through the streets to this pyre, the centre of one of the greatest Tarsian religious festivals, was the object so often represented on the coins of the city.

The character of this deity, the weapons which he carries, and his death on a funeral pyre, all combined to force on the Greeks the identification with their own Heracles. This they could not possibly avoid. The Tarsian deity is on the coins generally draped in a long tunic reaching to the feet, but sometimes nude. The former appearance may be taken as true to the actual religious presentation; the latter is a Greek touch, helping to make out the analogy with Heracles. At the same time the analogies with Apollo, which have been already pointed out, made it quite possible also to identify this Tarsian deity with Apollo. The fluid, wavering religious fancy of the Greeks saw no difficulty in the double identification.

These two figures, the Lord of Tarsus and the Sandon of Tarsus, we take as primitive Anatolian, part of the oldest religion of the city, which lasted through all stages of history with little alteration until the Christian period, different gods, yet in reality only two envisagements of the one ultimate deity, regarded as male.

The great number and variety of representations of Heracles on coins of Tarsus and other cities of south-eastern Anatolia may all be interpreted through the play of Greek artistic fancy with the type of the young Anatolian deity. They appear in all periods from the beginning of the fourth

FIG. 14.—Coin of Tarsus Metropolis, struck under Gordian III., 238-242 A.D. Archaic image of Apollo on a tall column: in front, an altar with bull lying before it. Perseus and the City goddess adoring. (See p. 154.)

century B.C. downwards. This was the favourite Hellenisation of the native god, but not by any means the only one.

Although no early representation of him is known, we must recognise a god of the early Ionian settlers in an Apollo of archaic character, who often appears on coins of the Imperial time, a nude figure grasping in his hands, one by the forelegs and one by the ears, two dogs (or wolves, perhaps), which hang down to the ground on each side of him. Representations of Artemis and Apollo of this type were common in archaic Greek times. They are rather pre-Hellenic and Oriental than Hellenic in character, and are peculiarly suitable to a really pre-Hellenic people such as the old Ionians were.

The animals which Apollo holds are usually regarded as wolves, and the god is styled Lykeios, the Wolf-god, by the numismatists. But it is evident that in the Hellenistic period the animals were considered to be dogs, for Lycophron calls the two prophets Mopsus and Amphilochus, "the dogs of Apollo". The poet adopted a popular identification of the two Apolline prophets with the two animals whom the god grasps in his hands.

We shall probably not err, if we regard this Apollo of the old Ionians as the Apollo with the trident, whom Dion Chrysostom mentions in his first Tarsian Oration. The Tarsian Apollo, as the god of a sea-faring people, bore the trident of Poseidon the sea-god. The life and ways of a people were thus envisaged in their conception and representation of their god. In their god they saw themselves, their own life and their own experience. They regarded this Apollo as the Divine founder of the city, its hereditary god (Patrôos) and its helper (Boêthos) : see below, p. 156.

It may be assumed as highly probable that this old Ionian Apollo, the god of the Clarian Oracle, who had guided the migration by his advice and led it to the Cilician coast-lands across the sea which he ruled with his trident, was brought into connection with the old Anatolian ritual of Tarsus by identification with the native god of purification and healing power (which is always regarded as a form of prophetic interpretation). We have no direct proof of this, as we have no ancient representation of this Tarsian Apollo ; but the facts speak for themselves. Just as, in the example at Athens, quoted on p. 138, Poseidon the god of an immigrant race was introduced into the old native worship of the goddess Athena by identification with a Divine being of the entourage of Athena, so at Tarsus the god of the immi-

Fig. 15.—Coin of Hadriana Tarsus, struck about 120-180 A.D. Perseus holding on his extended right hand the archaic image of Apollo Boêthos (as in Fig. 14). The hero wears the chlamys and holds the bent knife called harpe. The Tarsian emblem, lion attacking bull, as in Fig. 4.

grant Ionians was identified with the native god of similar character.

Moreover, the Tarsian Apollo is on the coins brought into close relation with another impersonation of the native god, *viz.*, Perseus. It is a common thing in religious myth to connect with the god a hero, who is really a sort of repetition of the god on a lower plane nearer the level of human nature : so *e.g.*, Heracles varies in the Greek conception between a god and a hero. All the numerous representations of the hero Perseus on coins of the south-eastern region of Asia Minor are probably to be taken in connection with this young native god. Perseus is the immigrant hero, who is connected artificially with the older religion of the country. He represents a new people and a new power. In him probably are united features both of Persian and of Greek character; but the Greek element seems to predominate strongly. He comes from the side of the sea; he is specially connected with Argive legend; but he comes also as the horseman, who crosses the sea by flying over it. It may be

Fig. 16.—Coin of Tarsus Metropolis, First, Greatest, Loveliest, struck under Gordian III., 238-242 A.D. Fisherman showing a large fish to Perseus; the hero in usual attitude with harpe and chlamys.

supposed that a religious envisagement which gave mythical justification to the Persian rule by connecting a Persian hero with the native religion, was caught up by the later Greek colonists in the Seleucid period and Hellenised so far that little was left of the Persian idea. We conclude therefore that the native Tarsian god in his heroised form was identified with Perseus by the Greeks of the later Hellenistic Tarsus. The Anatolian Perseus is the mythical envisagement of the intruding population, which gave religious legalisation to its settlement by this religious fiction.

This explanation of the nature of the East Anatolian Perseus will be found to suit his character in Iconium, where also he is an important figure, and (as I believe) in other places

Now the coins of Tarsus often show Perseus in close connection with the old Ionian Apollo. In Fig. 15 he stands holding on his extended right hand the statue òf Apollo. Similar examples are common, in which a god envisaged in a later form bears his own image in a more archaic embodi-

FIG. 17.—Coin struck by the satrap Tiribazus, 386-380 B.C. Ahura-mazda rising from the winged solar disk. The god carries in his hands a garland and a lotos-flower.

ment, or stands beside it (see *e.g.* the *Cities and Bishoprics of Phrygia*, ii., p. 692 f.). The obverse of this coin bears the head of Heracles, so that the coin brings together the three connected Divine figures, Pèrseus, Apollo, and Heracles-Sandon. In Fig. 14 Perseus is represented at an altar performing a ceremony of the ritual of Apollo, whose image is raised on a lofty column. Opposite Perseus is the City goddess, extending both hands towards the image of the god. The subject is perhaps the initial stage of a sacrifice to the god in presence of the Tarsian people (indicated by two

men behind the altar, and the goddess of the city). The ox
which is to be sacrificed waits placidly beside the altar; it
was a good omen that the victim should show no reluctance
and offer no resistance.

The quaint device of Perseus and the fisherman (Fig. 16)
is perhaps a representation of some unrecorded Tarsian
legend about the hero; but probably it indicates only that
fisheries were an important source of revenue at Tarsus, just
as a merchant-vessel is represented on the coins of a city
that possessed a harbour and sea-borne trade. The fisher-

FIG. 18.—Coin of Tarsus Metropolis., First, Greatest, Loveliest, struck
    under Gordian III., 238-242 A.D. Mithras with raised dagger about to
    slay a bull.

man is associated with Perseus on the coins, because that
hero was brought up by a fisherman, and the Tarsian presents his fish to the Divine personage who is most favourable to his craft.

A variation of this type, struck about A.D. 230, shows the
fisherman and Perseus in reversed position; and Perseus
holds up on his left hand the archaic image of Apollo with
his two dogs (or wolves). An inscription adds Apollo's title
Patrôos. The epithet Patrôos, god of our fathers and our

fatherland, was peculiarly appropriate to the old Ionian Apollo, and was frequently given to Apollo by the Greeks. The other epithet Boêthos, the Helper, taken in conjunction with this, proves that special sanctity and veneration belonged to Apollo in Tarsus, as the god of the city, its founder and its ever present aid.[22a]

How far Persian influence exercised any permanent effect on Tarsus, it is impossible to say; but it has left few traces that we can discern. The numerous coins struck by Persian satraps during the fourth century show little distinctively Persian character: but they certainly show that the Asiatic spirit grew more powerful in Tarsus under their rule, and the Hellenic tone grew weaker. As was shown in § VII., they were Oriental with a touch of Persian (some few cases of Greek types being due to exceptional circumstances).

One type, however, is thoroughly Persian. The Persian deity Ahura-mazda (or Ormuzd) appears on Tarsian coins struck under the satrap Tiribazus about 386-380 B.C. (Fig. 17). He has the body of a man terminating below in the broad winged solar disk; he carries a wreath in the right hand, and a flower in the left. The type on the obverse of this coin is the ordinary representation of the Lord of Tarsus with his title in Aramaic letters. We cannot doubt that the intention is to express the equivalence of the two Divine forms: he who to the Tarsians is Baal is to the Persian Ahura-mazda, a very characteristic pagan view.

Mithras appears in the third century after Christ on a coin of Gordian III.; but, though of Persian origin, this deity cannot be regarded as introduced by the Persians. He appears in Tarsus under Roman official influence, as the god of the army and of the anti-Christian Empire (Fig. 18).

§ X. THE REVIVAL OF GREEK INFLUENCE.

In a sense this revival begins with the entrance of Alexander the Great into Tarsus in 334 B.C.   We cannot doubt that this event strengthened the influence and numbers of the Greek element, which under the Persian rule was apparently in process of being slowly eradicated.   Yet the revival of the Greek Tarsus was very slow.   It is not even certain, though it is probable, that coins with the types of Alexander the Great were struck at Tarsus.   At any rate no coins seem to have been struck by Tarsus as a city during the later fourth or the third century.   Freedom and autonomy did not fall at that time to the lot of Tarsus.   It was evidently regarded by the Greek kings as an Oriental town, unfitted for the autonomy that belonged to a Greek *polis*.

Cilicia was subject throughout the fourth century to the Greek kings of Syria of the Seleucid dynasty; and those kings were much influenced in their policy by Oriental fashions. They administered the outlying provinces through officers who bore the Persian title of Satrap ; and they were not disposed to encourage generally within their Empire the development of Greek autonomy with the accompanying freedom of spirit and conduct.   Wherever the growth of an autonomous city in the Seleucid Empire can be traced, its origin is found to lie in the needs of the central government, requiring a strong garrison city in a district which was threatened.   In such cities the Seleucid kings planted new colonies of strangers and foreigners.   The interests of these strangers lay in maintaining the Seleucid power, to which they owed their privileges and their favoured position in their new country.

It is unnecessary here to describe the way in which those
Seleucid garrison cities were organised : that has been done
sufficiently in the *Letters to the Seven Churches*, chapter xi.
A right understanding of their character is essential to a
correct appreciation of the society in the Eastern Provinces
during the Roman period—the society in which the Christian churches of Asia Minor took their origin.   Without a
thorough study of those Hellenistic cities, the student of
early Christian history of Asia Minor has his view inevitably
distorted to a serious degree by preconceptions and prejudices, derived from the classical Greek period and other
causes.   Almost every city that plays an important part in
the early Christian history was founded, or at least refounded
and increased in population, by a Seleucid or other monarch
from one or another of the various dynasties that ruled over
parts of Asia Minor.

The cities are easily recognised as a rule by their names,
which were almost always derived from some member of the
royal family : Antiocheia, Seleuceia, Apameia, Laodiceia,
appear with extraordinary frequency all over the Seleucid
Empire.   In some cases the new dynastic name soon fell
into disuse, and the old native name revived, showing that
certain cities which had a great early history, clung to their
identity with real Greek municipal pride.   Tarsus was one
of this class.   Coins prove that for a time it bore the name
of Antioch-on-the-Cydnus.   But the pride of birth and past
history among the Tarsians maintained the individuality
and continuity of the city ; the new citizens, filled with a
sense of its dignity and honour, soon made themselves a
real part of the ancient city ; and the new name was quickly
disused.

§ XI. Tarsus as the Greek Colony Antiocheia.

During the third century Cilicia lay near the centre of the Seleucid Empire, which extended far beyond it westwards to include Lycaonia, Phrygia and parts of Lydia (during part of the century down even to the Aegean coasts). In this period Cilicia was the helpless slave of the dynasty; no danger was to be apprehended from it; and there was no reason to make any of its towns into garrison cities. Accordingly, none of the Cilician cities struck autonomous coins during the third century : the imperial Seleucid money was the only coinage.

The peace of 189 B.C. inaugurated new conditions in Asia Minor. Lydia, Phrygia and Lycaonia were taken from the Seleucid king Antiochus the Great; the Taurus was now made the limit of his Empire ; and Cilicia became a frontier country. It was not long till these new conditions began to produce their inevitable effect. The Cilician cities, especially those of the western half of the country, could not but feel conscious of their growing influence. They saw that across the frontier on the north-west there was a much freer country, subject only to the mild Pergamenian rule, and barely to that, for Lycaonia was so distant from Pergamum that the kings could not exercise real authority over it. The very sight and neighbourhood of freedom in others produces an ennobling effect ; and we cannot doubt that some of the Tarsians after their long hopeless slavery began now to remember that their city had once been great, energetic and free.

These changed conditions resulted at last in the reorganisation of Tarsus as an autonomous state striking its own coinage. This is a decisive event for the whole future

history of the city.   The evidence, therefore, must be carefully scrutinised.   Fortunately, a brief reference in 2 Maccabees iv. 30 f., 36, when taken in connection with the rest
of the evidence bearing on this subject, enables us to restore
with practical certainty the date and circumstances in which
the change was brought about.

In the first place we notice that the new name, under
which Tarsus began its autonomous career, was Antiocheia-

Fɪɢ. 19.—Coin of Antiocheia-on-the-Cydnus with the head of the City goddess
wearing turreted crown.   Reverse : Hellenic Zeus sitting ; city name.

on-the-Cydnus.   It was, therefore, refounded by a king
named Antiochus.   The coins were struck under Antiochus IV. Epiphanes,[23] and, therefore, the name must have
been given either in his reign, 175-164 B.C., or in that of
his father, Antiochus III. the Great, between the peace of
189 and his death in 187.   It is quite improbable that
the effect of the changed conditions would be realised in
Cilicia and at the court of Antiochus within so short a
time as two years, 189-187 : moreover, if the refoundation
of Tarsus as Antiocheia took place during those two years,
it might reasonably be expected that coins struck under

the founder or his son Seleucus IV., 187-175, would be known.[24]

The fair and reasonable conclusion is that the refoundation took place under Antiochus IV. Epiphanes, 175-164 B.C., and that it was followed at once, and as it were ratified, by the issue of coins, which demonstrated to all the world the existence of this new city. It required about fifteen or twenty years till the effect of the changed relations between Cilicia and the Seleucid Empire caused by the peace of 189 became obvious and demanded a change in the dynastic policy. The coins are quite Hellenic in character. The autonomy of the city is symbolised by the City goddess. The Greek Zeus takes the place of the Oriental Baal on the reverse, and carries none of the Oriental symbols, which appear on the coins of the Persian time.

All this is so natural, and follows so plainly from the facts and coins, that it might have been stated in a sentence as self-evident, were it not for the rigid and almost hostile scrutiny to which everything is subjected that bears, however remotely, on the books of the New Testament and on St. Paul.

In the second place we turn to 2 Maccabees iv. 30 f., 36. About 171 B.C., "they of Tarsus and Mallos made insurrection, because they were given to the king's concubine, called Antiochis.[25] Then came the king in all haste to appease matters." . . . "And when the king was come again from the places about Cilicia," etc.

It was quite a regular practice under the Persian kings (and doubtless long before the Persian Empire began) for the monarch to give to his favourites the lordship and taxes of some town or towns in his dominions. This Oriental way was followed by Antiochus IV. in regard to Tarsus and

Mallos: we have already pointed out that various other Oriental customs persisted under the Seleucid kings. It is clear that those two cities were not autonomous, otherwise Antiochus could not have bestowed them on Antiochis. It is equally clear from the resistance which was offered, that the cities were no longer mere unresisting, slavish Oriental towns, resigned to live under the heel and the all-powerful will of a despot. In the third century, so far as we can judge, the word of the king had been the law in Cilicia, and the Cilician towns would necessarily have accepted their fate, which after all was not likely to be worse under Antiochis than under Antiochus: there is no appearance that cities given in this fashion by a king were worse off than their neighbours. But now, in 171 B.C., the Greek spirit of freedom was reviving. Those two cities were precisely the two old Greek settlements in Cilicia, according to the view already stated ; and that view makes the action which now followed seem quite natural.[26] The Greek spirit revolted against the indignity of being handed over at the caprice of a despot to be the private property of a woman. Mutiny broke out, and became so dangerous that the king had to intervene in person.

Another remarkable feature about this incident is, that there was no thought in the king's mind—on this point the very clear statement is conclusive—of military force or compulsion to be exercised against the two cities. The king saw at once that it was a case for arrangement and diplomacy. He went "in all haste to appease matters". Arguing from the facts stated above, we must infer that the new conditions in Cilicia had already attracted his attention ; and he had recognised that he had gone too far, and that he must strengthen the feeling of friendliness in Cilicia to himself and his dynasty by conceding something to the claims of the cities: we must also infer that he saw at once what form his action must take, and that he proceeded to get the consent of, and arrange terms with, the two cities.

Following the account which has been stated above as to the methods of Seleucid policy, we can therefore say with confidence that a compromise was arrived at. Tarsus was recognised as a self-governing city, but a body of new citizens, who owed their privileges to the king and were likely to be loyal to him, was added to the population. Tarsus now obtained the right to strike coins, the symbol of municipal independence and proof of autonomy; and it received the new name Antiocheia-on-the-Cydnus, in recognition of its loyalty. This name, however, lasted only a few years, till the death of Antiochus.

It has a distinct bearing on this subject that Antiochus made sweeping reforms and changes in other Cilician towns. Alexandria-near-Issus begun at this time to strike autonomous coins; and Adana, Aegeae, Hieropolis-on-the-Pyramus and Mopsouestia all were permitted to strike coins with the effigy of Antiochus IV. on the obverse, but with their own types and names on the reverse—a privilege beyond what they had before possessed, though much less honourable than the purely autonomous coinage which was permitted at Tarsus and Alexandria-near-Issus. Adana was honoured with the name Antiocheia-on-the-Sarus, but this more purely Oriental city did not receive such a degree of freedom and self-governent as Tarsus.

Mopsouestia, at the crossing of the Pyramus, on the one great road leading from east to west across Cilicia, occupied a peculiarly important position, yet one in which it could never become a great city. It was not strong defensively,

and yet it must inevitably be defended and attacked in
every war that occurred for the mastery of Cilicia. It barred
the road; but it was too weak in situation to bar it effectively.
When, after 189 B.C., the kings began to recognise that they
must study and prepare to defend Cilicia more carefully
than in the previous century, this guardian city of the road
had been the first to attract attention. Seleucus IV.,
187-175, perceived its importance, and called it Seleuceia-
on-the-Pyramus. The bestowal of this name implies a
certain honour and privilege, which we cannot specify. It
did not apparently carry the right of autonomous coinage, but
beyond all question it was accompanied by a strengthening
of the fortifications and improvement of the roads beside the
bridge and the city. Under Antiochus IV. Epiphanes,
175-164, this new city struck legal coins on the same footing as Adana, Aegeae, and Hieropolis; the coins at first
bore the name of Seleuceia-on-the-Pyramus, but quickly
the old name reappeared, and even before Antiochus died the
coins began to resume the name of Mopsus.

It would illuminate this subject further, if the action of
Antiochus at Mallos could be certainly determined. A city
named Antiocheia was founded at Magarsus or at Mallos,
but the exact situation of this new city, and the relation of
Mallos to Magarsus, are uncertain ; probably Magarsus was
simply the port-town of Mallos, and the relation between
the two was as intimate and to us as obscure as that between Notion and Colophon or between Athens and Piraeus.
It is certain that Mallos was treated far less generously
than Tarsus. Mallos was more remote from the frontier,
and less important, than Tarsus; perhaps also the Greek
element, always prone to discontent and mutiny, was too
strong there[27]; and Mallos sank into insignificance during

this period, reviving again to a small degree in numismatic history about 146 B.C. It seems highly probable that Antioch on the Pyramus, like those on the Cydnus and the Sarus, was founded by Antiochus Epiphanes at this time as part of his scheme for pacifying and reorganising Cilicia. It is possible that this new city was founded at Magarsus with the intention of depreciating and ruining Mallos.

This long survey of the facts has been necessary in order to prove conclusively the importance of the epoch of re-organisation about 175-170. Cilicia was then recast, and its cities were reinvigorated. New life was breathed into a country which for centuries had been plunged in Oriental-ism and ruled by despotism. But, of all the cities, Tarsus was treated most honourably (setting aside Alexandria as unimportant). It now stands forth as the principal city of the whole country, with the fullest rights of self-govern-ment and coinage permitted to any town in the Seleucid Empire. The Tarsus of St. Paul dates in a very real sense from the refoundation by Antiochus Epiphanes.

Now at last Tarsus had the status of an autonomous city, choosing its own magistrates and making its own laws, though doubtless subject in all foreign relations to the king. For its future history much depended on the new citizens and the terms of the new constitution; and we must ask what evidence there is as to them.

§ XII. THE GREEKS IN TARSUS—ANTIOCHEIA.

The events in Cilicia in 171 B.C., described in the previous section of this study, introduced a new period in the history of Tarsus. It was henceforth a Greek City-State, govern-ing itself in all internal matters through its own elective magistrates, and exercising certain sovereign rights such as the striking of its own autonomous coins. In various respects, and especially in all relations to foreign states, Tarsus undoubtedly must have been subject to the Seleucid kings: that was a necessity of the Empire. The relation of a free city such as Tarsus now was, to the central government of the Seleucid Empire is, however, quite obscure; and until some of the cities of this class are excavated and the whole subject carefully studied, it is impossible to speak about details.

For our present purposes it is extremely important to determine what was the character of the constituent population of the free city of Tarsus. It would consist of the former population together with a certain body of new citizens, introduced in the manner and for the purpose already described. All that can be learned or conjectured about the older population has been already stated in the preceding sections. It now remains to ask what evidence can be found as to the citizens introduced in 171-170 B.C.

It has been shown[28] that in their colonial foundations the Seleucid kings were obliged to trust mainly to two peoples, the Greeks and the Jews, "to manage, to lead, to train the rude Oriental peasantry in the arts on which city-life must rest, to organise and utilise their labour and create a commercial system". This class of colonists was even more necessary than soldiers in those colonies.

The Greeks in those Hellenic foundations of Asia Minor were drawn from very diverse sources. The coins, which are our chief authority, mention Achaeans at Eumeneia, Dorians and Ionians at Synnada, Macedonians frequently. We know that Pisidian Antioch was colonised by settlers from Magnesia, and many other examples might be quoted. How and in what circumstances it was that the settlers were selected in each case, no record exists. We can only conjecture in what manner the superabundant population of Greece, finding their own narrow, barren country unfit to offer a career for their energies, poured forth now at one outlet, now at another, as the opportunity was offered in the new foundations established by the Greek kings in western Asia. Such had been the history of Greece in earlier centuries, when Greek cities founded their own colonies. Such is now the case in modern times, when new Greek cities on the Mediterranean coasts can no longer be founded, and still Greek emigrants go forth in numbers to push their fortunes as the trade of the neighbouring countries open up.

The Greek settlers in Tarsus and in Cilicia generally at this period seem to have been Argives. Dion Chrysostom addresses the Tarsians as "colonists of the Argives". Strabo, who had visited the city, and Stephanus give the same account. The chief magistrates in Tarsus and in several other Cilician cities bore the Dorian title Demiourgos, which may be taken as a definite proof that the Greek element in the population was mainly Dorian. It is therefore certain that the Tarsians prided themselves on being Dorians of Argos, and that their municipal institutions had something of a Dorian character. It seems also not impossible that some Doric tinge may have marked the Greek that they spoke; and, though the few late inscriptions show no trace of this, such evidence could hardly be expected. The Koine, the common Hellenistic dialect, would naturally establish itself quickly in a city like Tarsus; and only a few traces of the Doric dialect may perhaps have lingered. Elsewhere I have used this Doric character in Tarsus as foundation for a suggestion that the origin of the Western

text of Acts should perhaps be sought there: [29] the word
ναοκόρος used for νεωκόρος in Acts xix. 35 in the Bezan
Greek is just such a trace as might have survived in Tarsus.

An Argive connection dating only from 171 B.C. did not
satisfy the Tarsian pride of antiquity. The Hellenistic
cities of that time loved to invent an origin for themselves
in remote Greek mythology. The Tarsians claimed to be
descended from the Argives who had gone forth along with
Triptolemus in search of the lost Io, the beloved of the god,
transformed into a cow by the anger of Hera. It belonged
to the ancient Greek mind to seek a mythological proto-
type and Divine guarantee for historical facts; the first
Tarsian Greeks from the Argive land readily believed that
they were doing what their ancestors in the heroic age had
done ; and this mythological fable soon established itself
as the faith of the city. But the same people, who spoke
of themselves as descendants of those ancient Argive
wanderers, felt no inconsistency in declaring that Tarsus
was the foundation of Sardanapalos and an old Oriental
city. Both Strabo and Stephanus of Byzantium repeat these
diverse legends, as if they were quite harmonious; and,
when the Assyrian foundation is understood in the sense
described in § VIII., there is no contradiction between a
Greek and an Assyrian foundation.

Modern writers about Tarsus have usually interpreted
the mythological tale as furnishing evidence that Tarsus
was really colonised from Argos in the remote beginnings
of Greek settlement on the Cilician coast. This is a false
view of the nature of Greek myth, and inconsistent with
known facts (§ VI.). The primitive Greek settlers on this
coast were " Sons of the Ionian," and came to Cilicia under
the direction of the Clarian Apollo, a god of the Ionian

coast. They had necessarily and inevitably melted into the Cilician ground-stock, and Tarsus had long become an almost purely Oriental town, in which there is no reason to think that Demiourgoi or any other Greek magistrates were elected. When the new Hellenic city of Tarsus was founded in 171 B.C., the titles and character of the magistrates were determined by the facts of the situation and the origin of the only Greek population in the city, *viz.*, the newly enrolled Greek citizens—not by mythological inventions, which grew more slowly and took their tone from the established institutions of the city.

The use of the term Demiourgos in other cities of Cilicia suggests that Antiochus established some connection about this time with the land of Argos, and settled bodies of Argives in other Cilician cities whose constitution he remodelled, though in smaller numbers than at Tarsus.[30] Only in Tarsus were the numbers and influence of the Greeks sufficient to constitute at this time a really sovereign Greek City-State, so far as imperial control permitted sovereignty in such a city. The inscriptions of Soloi-Pompeiopolis, near Tarsus, contain considerable traces of Doric dialect.

§ XIII. THE JEWS IN TARSUS.

This section is the most important and fundamental, so far as St. Paul is concerned, in the study of Tarsian history. On the results of this section must depend all our ideas as to the position which the Apostle's family occupied in Tarsus, as to his own origin and birthright, and as to many allied questions.

It is clearly the presumption in the book of Acts that there was a considerable body of Jews in Tarsus. Paul was at home there among friends of his own race. That this is true to fact hardly any one is likely to dispute; and it may seem not worth while to prove it by formal evidence. Yet so jealous and sometimes so arbitrary is the fashion in which the book of Acts is usually treated by scholars that a passage of Epiphanius may be quoted about the Jews of Tarsus. In the first book of this treatise against Heresies, No. xxx. (Migne, vol. 41, Epiphanius, i., pp. 411-427), he gives an extremely interesting account of a Jew named Joseph, born at Tiberias about A.D. 286,[31] whom Epiphanius had himself known, and from whose lips he had heard the whole story of his life. Joseph, who belonged to a family of high standing and influence in Tiberias, became interested in the Christian teaching, but his thoughts were for a long time carefully hidden from his co-religionists; he was entrusted with the honourable dignity and duties of an Apostle among them, and finally despatched on a mission with letters to the Jews of Cilicia. He collected from every city of Cilicia the tithes and the first-fruits paid by the Jews in that Province. In a certain city he chanced to be lodged in a house beside the church, and he thus became acquainted and even intimate with the bishop. From the bishop he borrowed a copy of the Gospels, and read the book.

Now Joseph had exercised the powers of the Apostolate with such strictness that he became extremely unpopular with many of the Jews, who began to scrutinise his conduct carefully in the hope of finding some charge to bring against him. Seeking their opportunity, they rushed suddenly into his abode, and caught him in the act of reading the Gospels. They snatched the book out of his hands, seized him and dragged him with blows and curses and other ill-treatment to the synagogue, and there flogged him. The bishop, hearing of this, hurried to the scene and rescued him from the hands of the Jews.

On another occasion the Jews caught Joseph while travelling, and threw him into the Cydnus. He was carried away by the current, and they thought with delight that he was drowned; but he escaped. Shortly afterwards he joined the Christians, was baptized, and afterwards promoted to the dignity of a count (*comes*) and member of the Privy Council (*amicus*) of the Emperor Constantine.

In this account Tarsus is not named, but it is mentioned that there were Jews in every city of Cilicia. It is clearly implied, too, that the Cilician Jews were numerous and powerful, otherwise they could not under Christian rule have ventured on such vigorous action against one who was suspected of a leaning towards Christianity. The story plainly shows that no punishment or prosecution took place on account of their assault, though its illegal character is evident (even allowing that considerable freedom was permitted by law to Jews in dealing with a Jew). The fact that the bishop was able to rescue Joseph as soon as he heard of the first assault proves that even in flogging a presumed Christian convert, the Jews were overstepping the authority of the synagogue: while the second and murderous assault was in any circumstances and with any provocation a serious breach of Imperial law. These facts are inexplicable, unless the Cilician Jews had been a powerful body.

Tarsus would certainly be their chief seat in the Province, because it was the centre of trade and finance, and offered the best opportunities for money-making. It would also, naturally, be the place where Joseph took up his abode,

when he went to Cilicia on public duty, for it was the one
city from which all the rest could be best affected and
where there was most frequent opportunity of coming into
contact with the whole of the Cilician Jews. Finally, the
Jews of the town where he lived threw him into the Cydnus,
therefore they were the Tarsian Jews. They watched their
opportunity when Joseph started on a journey towards
Mallos or some place on that side, and threw him into the
river.[32] He must have been travelling in that direction,
because the river is not deep enough to carry away a man
in its current, except in the lower part of its course, and
Joseph would not have touched the lower course of the
river, unless he had been going towards Mallos. Why
Epiphanius avoids mentioning the name of Tarsus, and
merely speaks of "a certain city," I cannot explain. Perhaps he wished to avoid bringing such a charge against the
city by name. Perhaps it is due simply to his idea of
what was good literary style: so Basil of Seleuceia in his
history of St. Thekla mentions Tarsus in circumlocutory
fashion as the city of Damalis and Sandes.[32a]

In passing we observe several interesting points in the
story as told by Epiphanius. In the first place the feeling
was very bitter between Jews and Christians, but it was
almost as strong between Jews and pagans or Samaritans.
The Jews would not permit any Greek (*i.e.*, pagan), or
Samaritan, or Christian to live in the district of Galilee
where they were strongest; it had been impossible to build
a church in any of the towns or villages there, and especially
in Tiberias, Sepphoris, Nazareth, and Capernaum. Such a
fact is not favourable to the existence of an unbroken
Christian tradition in those towns.

On the other hand there was some intercourse privately

between individual Jews and Christians. Joseph was on friendly terms with the bishop of Tarsus, while he was still a Jewish Apostle. Hillel, the Patriarch of Tiberias, when near death, summoned the bishop who was nearest that city to visit him.[33] The pretext was that the bishop's services as a physician were required; but every Jew in Tiberias must soon have been aware that a Christian bishop was attending their Patriarch, even though they did not know that he was secretly administering the sacrament. In later times such a visit could hardly have occurred. We observe, also, that it is assumed by all that the bishop was qualified to act as a physician. The importance of the medical profession in the Lycaonian and Cappadocian Church during the fourth century has been described elsewhere.[34] It would almost appear that the bishop was expected to possess some medical skill, which should be at the service of his congregation and of strangers.

There is, accordingly, no doubt that a strong body of Jews inhabited Tarsus. The only question is as to their status in the city: were they merely resident strangers, or had they the full rights of citizens, *i.e.*, of burgesses? The difference in a Hellenic city was profound. There were in the chief commercial cities of the Mediterranean coasts large bodies of such resident strangers. Many of these became permanent inhabitants of the city, and their families lived there generation after generation. But the descendants of such persons did not become citizens merely by right of their old hereditary connection: they all remained outside of the city (in the Hellenic sense). They had no share in its patriotism and its religion. They could freely retain and practise their own religious rites, however alien these were to the religion of the city where they lived. It was usual for a group of such resident strangers to form themselves into a religious association for the proper celebration of their own ritual.   Thus they carried their own religion with them into the heart of Greece, and were protected by Greek law in the performance of ritual which was forbidden to true citizens—though that prohibition was rarely enforced and practically almost inoperative.   It was in this way that foreign and Oriental religions spread in the Greek cities, though nominally forbidden on pain of death and stigmatised as unworthy, superstitious and un-Hellenic by the more educated among the Hellenes.

Jews especially dwelt in considerable bodies in various Hellenic cities, where they did not possess any rights 'as burgess-citizens, but formed a simple association with synagogue or place of prayer by the seashore or on the bank of a stream (as at Philippi), which aroused attention and attracted proselytes, though it repelled and was hated by the majority of the pagan populace.

The question arises whether the Jews at Tarsus were mere resident strangers of this kind.   This seems disproved by all that can be gathered about that city.

The view which we take is that the Jews of Tarsus were, as a body, citizens with full burgess rights.   That does not, of course, exclude the possibility that there were some or even many resident stranger Jews in the city.   The right of citizenship could only be got by inheritance from a citizen father, apart from exceptional cases in which it was bestowed by a formal law on an individual as a reward for services rendered to the city; but such cases were comparatively few in any one city, for the right was jealously guarded.   There was no desire to increase the number of citizens, but rather the general wish was to keep the number small: philosophers and social theorists taught that the ideal of a city could be attained only in a comparatively limited size, while the ordinary selfish individual thought that the advantages of citizenship would be diminished if they were shared with new citizens.

There were occasional crises in the history of a Greek City-State, when the number of citizens was enlarged by the incorporation of considerable groups of new members. Such crises were, naturally, exceptional and rare: they occurred from various causes—sometimes on account of a great disaster, which had seriously weakened the State and diminished the body of citizens to a dangerous extent, sometimes through external causes and the interference of a power outside the State. In such cases the body of new citizens was not, as a rule, incorporated in any of the older Tribes of the city, but in a new Tribe or Tribes instituted for the purpose.[35]

Now there is no evidence, and no probability, that the body of the citizens of Tarsus was ever enlarged in this way, after it had been founded as a Greek City-State by Antiochus Epiphanes in 171. While we are only imperfectly acquainted with the history of Tarsus, there is no sign that any such crisis ever occurred. The reasonable probability is that the foundation of 171 was permanent, and determined the constitution of the city until the time of Augustus, when there was an oligarchic and timocratic movement, limiting the number of burgesses instead of increasing them, and introducing a money qualification.

The reasons for the view that there was a body of Jewish citizens in Tarsus are as follows.

In the first place, Paul was a citizen, as he himself asserted most emphatically in very dramatic circumstances at Jeru-

salem (Acts xxi. 39). This implies that he was a member
of one of the Tribes into which those Hellenic Colonies
were always divided. Now the members of a Tribe were
closely bound to one another by common religious rites,
which were performed at every meeting of the Tribe. In
every Hellenic city the common religion of the Tribe was
an extremely important element in the life and the thought
and the patriotism of all citizens. No man could be a
citizen except as a member of a Tribe; and the tribal
bond was intimate and sacred. Now no Jew could possibly
become a member of an ordinary Tribe in a Greek city,
because he would have been obliged to participate frequently
in a pagan ritual, which even the most degraded of Jews
would hardly have faced. There was no possible way by
which Jews who retained any religious or patriotic feeling
or national pride—and what Jew does not?—could become
citizens of a Greek city, except by having a Tribe set apart
for them, in which they could control the religious rites and
identify them with the service of the synagogue. This
method was adopted in Alexandria, where the Jews were all
enrolled in the Tribe called "the Macedonians"; and there
can be no doubt that the same method was followed in all
the Seleucid foundations, where a Jewish body of colonists
was settled. (See p. 257 f.)

Accordingly, inasmuch as Paul was a Tarsian citizen
and his father before him was a citizen, there must have
been a body of Jewish citizens constituting the Tribe in
which they were enrolled. There can never have been a
single and solitary Jewish citizen of a Greek city: if there
was one Jewish citizen, there must have been a group of Jews
forming a Tribe, holding together in virtue of their common
Jewish religion; and it may be regarded as practically

certain that the synagogue was their Tribal centre, where
they met not only for religious purposes, but also for judging
all cases affecting their tribal union and rights. In this way
Joseph of Tiberias was dragged to the synagogue and there
flogged, as has just been described.

This train of reasoning seems indisputable; and it has
been fully accepted by Professor E. Schürer.[36] Yet such
indirect arguments, however unanswerable they be, never
can carry the same complete conviction to the reader as a
definite and direct proof that there was in Tarsus a body of
Jewish citizens; and our next argument is that such a proof
is furnished by Romans xvi. 7-21, where six persons are
called "kinsmen" by St. Paul. The word can hardly mean
here kinsmen by right of birth and blood in the ordinary
sense ("kinsmen according to the flesh" in Romans ix.
3); for there is reason to think that the family to which
the Apostle belonged had not come over to the Christian
Church in such numbers, but rather had condemned his
action and rejected him.[37] Nor can it here mean simply
members of the Jewish nation, for many of the others who
are mentioned in this passage without this epithet were undoubtedly Jews. The careful distinction between the various
epithets in the passage is very instructive. The writer was
deeply moved, and his tenderest feelings were roused, when
he was writing the words, and each epithet is full of emotion,
a piece of his heart and his life, as it were. There is in this
term "kinsmen" an instance of the same strong deep feeling
for his native city which is found in Acts xxi. 39 (see § III.).
The word "kinsman" here means fellow-citizen and fellow-
tribesman, for all the six were doubtless Jews and therefore
members of the same Tribe in Tarsus. This use of the word
"kinsmen" was idiomatically Greek, and seems to have

12

risen in other cases to the mouth of the Greek when his feelings of patriotism were moved.[38]   Thus, for example, when the Greeks of Ephesus came to Agrippa to ask him to eject their Jewish fellow-citizens from participation in the rights of citizenship,[39] they declared that "if the Jews are kinsmen (*i.e.* fellow-citizens) to us, they ought to worship our gods," *i.e.* to practise the religion of the city, participation in which was the natural and (to the Greek mind) necessary expression of patriotism and kinship.   This kindred and common citizenship was based on religion.   It was in the same sense that Paul calls those six men his "kinsmen" in Romans xvi. 7, 11, 21.

In the third place, a proof of the existence of a body of Jewish citizens in Tarsus can be drawn from a passage in Philostratus's biography of Apollonius of Tyana, vi. 34. Not long after the end of the Jewish insurrection and the capture of Jerusalem, Titus, as co-Emperor with his father, chanced to be offering public sacrifice on behalf of the State (probably in Rome), when delegates representing the city of Tarsus approached him with a petition about some important interests of their city.   These ambassadors must have been, it is needless to say, citizens of Tarsus.   Titus answered that he would himself act as their ambassador to his father Vespasian, and lay their case before him.   Hereupon Apollonius, who was present in the train of his friend Titus, intervened and said to him, "If I prove to you that some of these delegates are enemies of your father and yourself, and went as envoys to Jerusalem to promote an insurrection, making themselves secret allies of your most openly declared enemies, what treatment shall they receive of you?" "What," said Titus, "but death?"   "Is it not then disgraceful," replied Apollonius, "to take vengeance on the spot, but to postpone kindnesses to a later time, to inflict death on your own responsibility, but to reserve favours until you consult another about them ? "

This dilemma which Apollonius put to Titus depended for its effect on the fact (which must have been well known) that many Jews were citizens of Tarsus. Apollonius was on bad terms with that city, as Philostratus mentions. Apollonius on his visit to Tarsus had sternly rebuked the Tarsians for their luxury and wealth, and became extremely unpopular in the city. Titus was therefore quite prepared to hear him denounce the Tarsians. Further, as there were many Jewish citizens in Tarsus, he was quite ready to believe that some of the envoys were Jews, and that the suggestion that they had been plotting treason in Jerusalem was seriously intended. No person would have suggested, or believed, that Greeks could have gone on an embassy to Jerusalem to plot treason with Jews : the race hatred was notoriously too strong and bitter.

The seeming accusation which Apollonius made with such ready wit must have been a plausible and probable one in itself, otherwise Titus would not have been taken in by it. Its plausibility arose from the Jewish citizenship in Tarsus, and the known fact that many wealthy and prominent Tarsians were Jews. When Apollonius retorted with his sharp-pointed dilemma, Titus was charmed. Though he had been caught in the act of threatening death as the punishment for a superstitious and pretended crime, he extricated himself from the unpleasant situation with the genial humour characteristic of both his father and himself, granting the Tarsians' petition, and saying that his father would pardon him for yielding to truth and to Apollonius. After this incident, Tarsian feeling towards Apol-

lonius changed, and he was reverenced as a benefactor and
" founder " of the city.   (On this use of the term " founder,"
see p. 132.)

All these three arguments unite in this, that each shows us
a situation and words which are full of meaning and point,
if there were Jewish citizens in Tarsus, but pointless and
insipid if there were not.   Considering how scanty is the
information that has come down to us about the constitution of Tarsus and the other Hellenic cities of Asia Minor,
it is fortunate that on this important matter so much
evidence has been preserved, proving that a body of Jewish
citizens formed an important element in the Tarsian City-
State.

§ XIV.   The Jews Settled in Tarsus in 171 b.c.

The next question is when this body of Jewish citizens
was settled in Tarsus.   We have seen that they must have
been settled there as a body, and not from time to time as
individuals ; that the settlement must have formed part
of a general reconstruction of the city ; that there was such
a reconstruction of Tarsus in 171 b.c. ; and that there is no
sign or evidence of any later reconstruction having occurred.
The natural inference is that a body of Jews was settled in
Tarsus by Antiochus Epiphanes, as part of the free self-
governing city which he founded in that year.   I see no way
in which this inference can be evaded.

Such a settlement was in accordance with the regular
Seleucid practice.   Similar settlements of Jews had been
made in many other cases by the predecessors of Antiochus,
and on an especially large scale by his father in the cities
of Lydia and Phrygia not long before.   Even if there were
no record of Jewish citizens in Tarsus, it would be safe to

speak of the probability that he followed the established Seleucid principle, and settled Jews as citizens there.

Professor E. Schürer, however, though he cannot suggest any way of evading this inference, argues that it "appears very improbable in view of the hostility of Antiochus to the Jews". Antiochus, it is true, became the enemy of the rebel Jews in Palestine; but that was at a later time. In 171 he considered himself as the best friend of the Jewish race, and was so considered by many of the most influential Jews in Jerusalem. He regarded Jerusalem with special interest, and as a token of his favour bestowed on it his own name. To the Jewish reactionary party, who raised the successful revolt, it seemed an outrage to rename Jerusalem "Antiocheia"; but Antiochus was innocent of any intention to insult the Jews. The truth was that the king merely carried into effect a great scheme of national education in Palestine, the best that the philosophers of the time could conceive; and that the scheme was highly popular with the aristocracy, but hated by the common people of the country. This scheme of national education was not even originated by Antiochus. It had been the settled policy of the Seleucid kings since they became the lords of Palestine. Antiochus Epiphanes merely walked in the beaten path, the ultimate aim of which was to educate Palestine and all the rest of the Seleucid dominions in Greek civilisation, language and manners. Those who still regard the study of Greek as so valuable that it should be enforced in every school in our remote age and land, ought not to accuse Antiochus of outrage and hostility because he wished to teach Greek in Jerusalem and to bring the Jews up to the level of what he and others believed to be the highest civilisation of the time.

This way of describing the situation in Palestine before the Maccabaean rising is no frivolous trifling with a serious subject. It is the literal truth, and it is also the spiritual truth. The Seleucid policy, which Antiochus Epiphanes continued, was a noble and generous one, and produced excellent results in Western Asia generally. It attempted, wisely, deliberately, and with full consciousness, to produce a conciliation and amalgamation of Oriental ideas and Western education; and in many ways it still offers a model of the best method of essaying this most important problem in social development. But the same policy which is wise and beneficial in one country may be unwise and hurtful in another. It is quite true, as Antiochus and his predecessors saw, that the Jews had much to learn from the Greeks; but they had more to lose than to gain by being Hellenised, if Hellenisation meant the abandoning of all that was distinctive in Judaism. The Maccabaean rising was guilty of many faults and was far from being an unmixed good to the world; but it preserved the Jewish race from being merged in Hellenism and kept it free for its great destiny.

The unification of the Empire was the aim of Antiochus, as it had been of his predecessors, and as it was afterwards in the Roman Empire. The aim was a worthy and a noble one. As it is stated in 1 Maccabees i. 41 f., about 167 B.C. "King Antiochus wrote to his whole kingdom, that all should be one people, and every one should leave his laws," *i.e.*, that national differences and customs should be done away with and a uniform Hellenistic system of civilisation and education should be established.

So successful had the Seleucid policy already been that the "advanced" party among the Jews urged Antiochus

to take more decided steps.   He acted in concert with the
Hellenising Jews, who claimed to be the most enlightened
and certainly were the wealthy and the powerful part of
the community.

The passage in 1 Maccabees proceeds, " So all the heathen
agreed according to the commandment of the king.   Yea,
many also of the Israelites consented to his religion, and
sacrificed unto idols, and profaned the sabbath."   The
penalty for resistance to the policy which Antiochus now
resolved to enforce was death.   But he had been encouraged
and prompted to this enforcement of the Hellenising policy
by some of the Jews themselves.   About 175 Jason, eager to
be appointed high priest, offered large sums of money to the
king (who was in sore need of money for his wars), " if he
might have license to set him up a place for exercise
(Gymnasium) . . . and to write them of Jerusalem by the
name of Antiochians " (2 Macc. iv. 9).   When the king
granted permission, Jason " forthwith brought his own nation
to the Greekish fashion. . . . For he built gladly a place
of exercise under the tower itself, and brought the chief
young men under his subjection, and made them wear a
hat."   This process of voluntary Hellenisation is described
as proceeding to great lengths for several years in Jerusalem
even among the priests.

The building of a Grecian gymnasium, the introduction
of the fashion of young men wearing hats and in general
making themselves as Hellenised as possible—such were
the outrages of which Antiochus had been guilty when the
rebellion first began.   These cannot be condemned by us
as grave offences in themselves; but they were an attempt
to force Hellenic customs on the Jews.   The gymnasium
implied the Greek fashion of practising athletics naked;

and this fashion was the cause of real evils in Greece. The hat has always been and still is an abomination to the true Asiatic; it is still the mark of a European in Mohammedan lands; the uneducated Turks call a European a Shapkali, "one with a hat". For Jews to wear the hat was to denationalise themselves.

Antiochus, therefore, even after 171, was in no true sense an enemy of the Jews. He was only an enemy of what appeared to him to be a violent and reactionary party among the Jews; and repression began about 170 with Oriental severity. That party became dominant in Palestine, and hence arose war with Palestine. But none of this had taken place in 171; and the same policy which made the king eager to Hellenise Palestine made him introduce Jewish colonists into Tarsus and doubtless into other Cilician towns. It is, indeed, highly probable that there were already Jews in Cilicia, and that Antiochus both bestowed the rights of citizenship in the remodelled cities on the old resident Jews, and increased their numbers by bringing into the country more families of Jews. Even after the Maccabaean war began, it is not probable that Antiochus ceased to trust or favour the Jews in the northern part of his realm. He would do so only if they joined or sympathised with the rebellion; and at first they were not likely to do so, for the extra-Palestinian Jews were rather on the Hellenising side. They could not live in a Hellenic city without learning that many Hellenic customs, hated by the zealots, were harmless and even good. They did not regard games and athletics with such horror as the zealots did. St. Paul draws his metaphors and similes so freely from such Greek customs that it is impossible to think even he, strict Pharisee as he claimed to be, felt any detestation of Greek games and Greek ideas : had he been the narrow Jew that many scholars fancy him to have been, he must have regarded all those Greek things as an abomination.

The conclusion is that Dorian Greeks from Argos and Jews formed the main body of the new colonists settled there by Antiochus Epiphanes. From 171 onwards there was in Tarsus a body of citizens of Jewish blood. They were a privileged class in many ways. Josephus points out emphatically that the Seleucid kings showed great favour to all the Jewish colonists, conceded many things which Jewish scruples required, set them free from all obligation to do anything contrary to their religion and their law. We must therefore regard St. Paul as sprung from one of the families which got the Tarsian citizenship in 171 B.C., and reject the story (in itself an impossible one) recorded by St. Jerome, that he or his parents had emigrated from Gischala in Palestine, when it was captured by the Romans.

If the Jewish colonists had been settled so long in Tarsus, and if they were so favourable to a Seleucid king in the beginning, how could they be a strongly Hebraistic and national body, some or many of them strict Pharisees, nearly two centuries later ? That is only part of the Jewish miracle over the whole world. It was strange that they should have survived and revived in Tarsus ; but it is equally strange that they have maintained their national feeling elsewhere for so many centuries. In Tarsus we observe that they were within easy reach of Jerusalem. The restoration of Hebrew nationalism by the Maccabaean revolt must have exercised a powerful influence on them. The family gathering of the Passover, the household instruction about it origin, and similar influences, kept alive their national feeling, and made them revisit as often as possible the national centre at the ceremony in the month Nisan. Contact with a free Hebrew nation in a Hebrew capital city strengthened their national pride, and fanned it into a flame.

§ XV. Tarsus the Hellenistic City.

In the two centuries which followed the foundation of the new Hellenised Tarsus the surroundings and environment amid which St. Paul was educated were in process of development. But this period of Tarsian history is, if possible, more obscure than the earlier period. It was the fortunate coincidence of literary and numismatic evidence that illuminated the foundation of Antiocheia-on-the-Cydnus. Hardly a ray of light illuminates any point in the following period, until we come down to the time of the Emperor Augustus and the great Tarsian philosopher and statesman Athenodorus. A very brief section will suffice for the end of the Greek period.

The oblivion into which the Greek name Antioch quickly fell, and the speedy restoration of the native Anatolian name Tarsus, may be taken as indicating that the Greek element had not attained a marked predominance in the newly founded city. The continuity of Tarsian history was not interrupted seriously : the city felt itself to be the ancient Tarsus, and not the new Antioch. Tarsus could never be a thoroughly Hellenised city: Antioch-on-the-Cydnus might have been so.

Upon the coins we read the same tale. The few coins struck by Antioch-on-the-Cydnus are thoroughly Hellenic in character: the head of the City (idealised as a Divine figure wearing a crown of walls and turrets) and the sitting figure of Zeus have on the surface nothing Oriental about them. The sitting Zeus had long been a Tarsian type; but formerly, even when no Aramaic letters gave him the Oriental name of Baal, there were usually symbols or adjuncts unsuited to the Greek Zeus, which gave an Eastern and non-Hellenic character to the representation.[40] In the period 171-164 the Tarsian Zeus appears almost purely Greek. The symbols of Anatolian character, corn, grapes, and censer, have disappeared. He is Zeus, and not the Baal of Tarsus. There are no Aramaic letters; but the Greek inscription giving the name of a self-governing people, " the Antiochians beside the Cydnus". (See Fig. 19, § XI.)

Even the coins of the following period, on which the old name Tarsus reappeared, were distinctly more Hellenic than those of the older time. On some coins the Antiochian types remained, when the name of Antioch disappeared. Another common type showed the Good Fortune of Tarsus seated on a chair, with the river-god Cydnus at her feet: it was imitated from a famous statue by the Greek artist Eutychides, representing the Good Fortune of Antioch, the Syrian capital. But the Tarsian figure has something about it which stamps it as the Oriental imitation of Greek work. The Greek sculptor had showed the Fortune of Antioch seated on the rocks, at whose feet was the river Orontes: the Tarsian imitator placed his goddess on a chair, with which the Cydnus is out of keeping. The harmony of a Greek ideal is wanting here, but the aim is to show a city seated on the plain. The reverse shows the Hellenic Zeus, not the Anatolian god. It is the coin of a Hellenic city, and the name of a magistrate is inscribed on it (Figs. 20, 23).

Another type, which now appears for the first time on Tarsian coins, and which henceforward became very common,

is strikingly Oriental and Anatolian.   This is a young male
god, who stands on a winged and horned lion, wearing a tiara
and holding in his hands sometimes bow-case and sword,
sometimes flower and double-edged battleaxe as described
above in § IX., and shown in Figs. 11 and 13.   Such an
utterly un-Hellenic figure as this god stands in marked contrast with the Greek head of the City goddess, which appears on the other side of the same coins.   It is as if the
double character and mixed population of the city, Greek and
Oriental, appropriated each one side of the coins.

Fig. 20.—The Good Fortune of Tarsus; River-god Cydnus at her feet.   She
   holds ears of corn, wears veil and crown of towers.   Magistrate's
   name, "of Arsaces".   Reverse: Zeus sitting.

In Fig. 21 an example of this class of coins is shown,
belonging to the period following 164 B.C., but probably
later than the one shown in Fig. 11.   The obverse shows
the head of the City goddess, the Good Fortune of Tarsus,
whose full-length figure appears in Fig. 20.   The reverse
shows the god of Tarsus, within a pyramidal structure (described in § IX.).   But the inscriptions that accompany this
thoroughly Anatolian type are purely Greek, the name of
the people and the monogram of a magistrate.

Tarsus, with the rest of Cilicia, long remained a part of the decaying Seleucid Empire. The dynasty grew weaker; disorder and civil war tormented the State; but the arrogant ambition of princes, who could hardly maintain their position at their capital on the Orontes, still prompted them to seek to enlarge their empire by adding foreign lands to their inheritance, as, for example, when the Egyptian throne was vacant in 123 B.C. The Hellenic grasp on Asia was relaxing. There was little enough of Hellenism at a court like

Fig. 21.—Obverse: head of the City goddess. Reverse: the Tarsian god standing on horned lion between two small altars within a pyramidal structure, on which perches an eagle. Name of the city and monogram of a magistrate's name.

that of the last Seleucid kings; yet it was all that remained of the Greek sovereignty in the East.

During this period we hear practically nothing about Tarsus; but it continued to coin its own money as a free city. Between 150 and 100 B.C. silver coins of the Seleucid kings bearing Tarsian types, but not the name of Tarsus, were sometimes struck. In the growing weakness of the sovereignty this can hardly imply that the Seleucid kings were tightening their grasp upon Tarsus: more probably the choice of Tarsian types was meant by way of compliment to the city as a main support of the dying Seleucid State.

About 104 B.C. the Roman influence, which had been gradually increasing in Asia Minor, laid its grasp definitely on Cilicia, and made part of it a Province. But the history of this Province was for a time complicated by a new factor, the revival of the Oriental spirit under the leadership of Mithridates, king of Pontus. As the Greek element in Asia grew weaker, the Asiatic spirit revived and attempted to throw off the bonds that European domination had placed upon it. About 83 this Asiatic reaction overwhelmed Tarsus. No authority records whether the city was affected internally by the revival; but it seems natural and probable that at least the original native element would be stirred to sympathy with the Mithridatic movement. The Jews, however, were not likely to be deceived by the specious appearance of Orientalism, which this purely barbarous and destructive invasion wore. All is, however, mere conjecture, except the fact that during the following years the armies of Tigranes, king of Armenia, swept over Cilicia and Northern Syria. Tarsus, though not named in the brief record, must have fallen under his power, as did Soloi which lay farther away to the west.

Nothing could have happened which was more calculated to strengthen the Western spirit in Tarsus than the conquest by a barbarian like Tigranes. There was inevitably a revulsion in the city towards Hellenism. Now Roman policy always was directed to encourage and strengthen the hold of Hellenism on the Eastern Provinces. The trained and practical instinct of the Empire did not seek to destroy Greek civilisation in Asia in order to put Roman civilisation in its place, but treated the two as allied and united in the task of training the Oriental. Hence the reaction from the barbarism of Armenian rule was in favour of Rome as well as of Hellenism. When the European hold on Cilicia was renewed by the issue of the Mithridatic wars, and the East was reorganised in the Roman interest by Pompey the Great in 65-4 B.C., the restoration of the Province was probably welcomed in Tarsus. The Province of Cilicia now became much larger and distinctly more important than before.[41]

§ XVI. Tarsus as Capital of the Roman Province Cilicia.

When the Roman province of Cilicia was first instituted about 104 B.C., neither Tarsus nor the Cilician plain was made part of Roman territory. They continued, apparently, to belong to the Seleucid kingdom, though the hold of the effete monarchy on this now outlying part of its shrunken territories can have been only nominal. This situation of affairs tended to strengthen the municipal government in Tarsus, which would probably deal directly with the overshadowing power of Rome.

The Province was instituted chiefly in order to control the pirates of Cilicia Tracheia (the mountainous region west of the level Cilician plain), and to maintain peace on the coasts and the waters of the Levant. Harbours and stations on the land of Tracheia were necessary for this purpose, but the plain and the cities of Cilicia proper were not occupied.[42] The Cilician Province was not as yet a strictly territorial district: the term was used rather in the older sense of "a sphere of duty". The Roman governor of Cilicia was charged with the care of Roman interests generally in the south and east of Asia Minor and on the Levant coasts and

waters.   He went wherever the pressing needs of the occasion called him.   He seems, when it was necessary, to have
been in the habit of marching through lands which were not
as yet in any real sense Roman ; and this implies that some
vague right to free movement across those regions had been
conceded to, or assumed by, the Romans.   The two Provinces of Asia and Cilicia divided between them the execution of Roman policy in Asia Minor ; and apparently the
only principle of division was that what did not clearly
belong to the Province of Asia fell within the Cilician sphere
of duty.

The limits of the Cilician Province under the Republican
administration were vague and undefined : they varied widely
at different times.   The governor of Cilicia was sometimes
active on the Pamphylian and Lycian coast and in Lycaonia.
At one time even great part of Phrygia was detached from
Asia and placed in the Cilician Province : such was the
case, for example, when Cicero governed Cilicia in 51 B.C.
This extension, evidently, originated during the time when
the pirates constituted a danger so great that Roman ships
were afraid to sail along the Levant coasts.   The governor of Cilicia was then obliged to land at Ephesus and go by
road into Cilicia.   As he passed across Phrygia it was convenient for him to hold the assizes in the great cities.   After
Pompey put down the pirates in 67 and opened the sea
once more, the connection of Phrygia with Cilicia was maintained for a considerable time, and Cilicia was then the
most important of the Eastern Provinces in a political view
as well as the largest, for its governor directed the whole
foreign policy of Rome on the north-east frontier.

The varying character of the Province Cilicia reflected the
confused condition of Roman politics and government.   Be-

tween 104 and 49 B.C., Roman policy was uncertain in its
aims and generally ineffective; when the Civil War began
in 49, there was no policy at all, until the issue of the struggle
was determined.

In the decay of all the Greek dynasties, which marked the
later second century and the earlier half of the first century,
there was in Asia Minor no possible rule except either
Roman or Asiatic; and, not unnaturally, the Roman government shrank from the gigantic task of administering the
affairs of the East, while it was also reluctant to withdraw
its hand and power from the country altogether. The uncertainty of Roman aims weakened its power; and the
necessary result of the slackening of its grasp was that the
Asiatic princes, like Mithridates of Pontus and Tigranes of
Armenia, seized the opportunity to assert their freedom
against Roman dictation and to enlarge their kingdoms by
western conquest. At first they even found allies among
the Hellenic states and cities. Dread and dislike of Rome
united Hellene and Asiatic. Mithridates not merely overran the whole of the Province of Asia, but even sent his
armies into Greece and was welcomed for a moment as a
deliverer by cities like Athens. He had, however, mis-
calculated his power, and he only succeeded by over-ambi-
tion in compelling the Romans to exert their strength and
in making it clear that no compromise, no partition of Asia
Minor between Rome and the Asiatic princes, nothing but
war to the knife, ending in either the subjection of Asia to
Europe or the ejection of all Europeans from Asia, was
possible at that time.

The task imposed on the Roman government, however,
was too great. It could conquer, but it could not administer.
Its general, Pompey, destroyed Mithridates and Tigranes,

13

and regulated after a fashion the East. He set up kings and dethroned kings, founded cities, gave constitutions and laws; but his work was ineffective when the central government was paralysed. Some fixed purpose and definite policy was needed, but the Roman Senatorial government had no clear ideas in Eastern policy, and was powerless to maintain order.

To establish a permanent peace, it was necessary to conciliate in a single State the warring elements, Oriental and Western. These elements cannot be adjusted and conciliated by any government acting from above and from outside ; but they will work out their own balance and equipoise, if a strong hand simply enforces order—a truth which modern European governments in Asia and Egypt are slow to learn, but which the Seleucid kings from 300 B.C. onwards had roughly understood.

Augustus at last, with his clear practical sense, seems to have divined the nature of the situation. Like the Senate, he shrank from undertaking the task of administering the East. He did not at first greatly enlarge the Roman territory. He continued the traditional Roman policy of entrusting frontier lands to dependent kings. But he insisted that these kings must maintain order and peace, and that they must administer their charge to Roman satisfaction. He regarded them as agents, entrusted with the duty of civilising and training their subjects up to the level of orderliness suitable for incorporation in the Roman Empire as Provinces.

So he allowed a large kingdom in central Asia Minor to remain under charge of Amyntas, king of Galatia, until 25 B.C. Then, on the sudden and unexpected death of Amyntas in battle, he took the inheritance of this kingdom, and formed it into the province Galatia, while the private property of the king, including the vast estates of the god round Pisidian Antioch, were added to his own private fortune. With the formation of this new Province of Galatia the importance of the older Province Cilicia disappeared. For about a century Galatia included the charge of Roman interests and policy in central and eastern Asia Minor, while Cilicia was now made by Augustus a mere adjunct to the great Province of Syria.

In the Cilician Province, Tarsus necessarily played its part as the capital; but its name is rarely mentioned in the Republican time. It exercised little influence on a policy which was frankly Roman and almost regardless of the rights or interests of the subject people. Tarsus is practically unknown to us during the republican period, except as a point on Cicero's journeys through his Province, and a place where he occasionally resided.[43]

In strong contrast to the policy of the Republican government, the Imperial policy was from the beginning keenly alive to the duty that Rome owed to the subject races. These non-Roman races were to be treated fairly, governed honestly and for their own benefit, educated up to the level of Roman citizenship, and gradually admitted to the citizenship year by year, now one person, now another, as each individual earned in one way or other this honour and privilege. Such was the ideal which the Empire set before itself, and which the great Emperors, like Trajan, tried to realise. In the Imperial period, accordingly, there was far greater opportunity than before for the prosperity and development in its own line of a provincial city. Both the individual subjects and the cities of the Provinces had a career opened to them in aiding the well-being of the whole

Empire. A provincial city henceforth could have a history of action, and not merely a history of suffering.

It would be too little to say that there was general contentment with the new order. The older Provinces in general, and Tarsus in particular, were filled with enthusiastic loyalty to the Empire, which had brought with it peace, order, justice, fair collection of a not too burdensome taxation, and good government generally, in spite of isolated exceptions and failures.

It accords with the new spirit of government that with the Empire Tarsus emerges once more into the light of history. We hear of it frequently from the moment that Julius Cæsar, the true founder of the Empire, entered its gate for a brief visit in 47 B.C., during his march from Egypt northwards against the Pontic king. Then the feelings and desires of the Tarsians began to appear, and we find that they were frankly and enthusiastically for the Empire and against the Senate. They were so devoted to Julius Cæsar, that they called their city Juliopolis, and afterwards they were well disposed to his nephew, the future Emperor Augustus, on his uncle's account. Cassius, acting on behalf of the Senatorial party, compelled the Tarsians and Tarkondimotos, the client-king of the eastern parts of Cilicia, to come over to his side in 43 B.C., when he was preparing for the campaign which ended in the battle of Philippi during the following year. But when Cassius marched on into Syria, and Dolabella approached Cilicia in the interests of the Cæsarian party, Tarsus gladly joined him and took an active part in the war against Cassius and against the neighbouring city of Adana, which they considered to be favourable to Cassius. On the approach of troops sent by Cassius, however, Tarsus yielded without fighting. The

Tarsians could make war on a rival town, but they dared not resist the Roman soldiers.

Municipal jealousies and the old rivalry between Tarsus and Adana (§ III.) were thus mixed with the wider politics of the time, and were with many people more powerful, because nearer at hand, than the larger interests of the great world-struggle. Dion Chrysostom, a century and a half later, speaks of the old feud between Tarsus and Adana.

Cassius soon afterwards entered Tarsus, and requisitioned all the money he could from the State and from private individuals, but did not make any massacre.

When Antonius came to the East in 42 B.C. to represent the power of the victorious Triumvirs, in accordance with the arrangement which assigned to him the command of the Eastern Provinces, and to Augustus the command of Italy and the West, Tarsus reaped some reward of its sufferings. It was complimented for its loyalty; it was granted the status of a " free city," *libera civitas*—which implied that while continuing to be part of the Empire, *i.e.* of the Province, it was governed according to its own laws and not by Roman law—along with the right to duty-free export and import trade. Antony resided for some time at Tarsus, and here occurred his famous meeting with Cleopatra, when the Egyptian queen sailed in her splendid galley up the river Cydnus and entered Tarsus in all the pomp of Oriental luxury.

The privileges which Antony had bestowed on Tarsus were renewed or confirmed by Augustus, when he became master of the whole Roman world after the battle of Actium in 31 B.C. Hence it was open to Dion Chrysostom, who naturally ignored Antony and took account only of the recognised line of transmission of the Imperial authority, to speak to the Tarsians about Augustus as the author of all their privileges. Augustus recognised the importance of Tarsus and treated it with great favour.

It is clear from the preceding account that Pompey, Julius Cæsar, Antony, and Augustus are all likely to have given the Roman citizenship to a certain number of important Tarsians. Those who received this honour from Antony would doubtless have to pay for it. Any Roman Tarsian born about the time of Christ would probably have as his Roman names either Gnaeus Pompeius, or Gaius Julius,[44] or Marcus Antonius, for he would bear the praenomen and nomen of the official to whom he owed the citizenship (see § XVIII.).

§ XVII. The Oriental Spirit in Tarsus.

It has been pointed out that the balance in the constitution of Tarsus depended on the presence of both Greeks and Jews in the State. The older native element (into which the original Ionian Greek stock had melted and been lost) was doubtless the larger numerically, but was probably more inert and passive, not guiding but following. The control and guidance lay in the hands of the two enterprising and vigorous races. This view implies that the Greeks and the Jews tended to opposite sides in municipal politics. In the Seleucid time it may be regarded as practically certain that the Greeks insisted on autonomy and laid more stress on the liberty and right of self-government in the city, while the Jews clung to and championed the Seleucid connection. The Greeks always and everywhere in the world tended to exaggerate the rights of the individual. The Jews were more likely to remember that they

had been placed in the city by the kings, and depended
on the kings for protection against Greek dislike and
enmity. The sense of common interest made the Jews
trusted and trustworthy colonists in the Seleucid foundations.

Now comes the question that is of the most vital importance for Tarsian municipal history. What form did
this balance and opposition between Greek and Jew take in
the Roman Tarsus? As always, the Greeks must have
insisted on the rights of the individual, and on the freedom
of the citizen from external control; wherever the Greek
element is strong the law is weak, and the government is
guided rather by caprice than by principles. That has been
the fact throughout all history; the Greeks are more prosperous under almost any other government than they are
under their own.

This Greek spirit was diametrically opposed to the Roman
law-making and law-abiding spirit. We should expect to
find that the Roman administration in Tarsus trusted most
to the Jewish element as more conservative and more
serious, more consistent and less capricious, than the Greek.
As regards the Republican period there is no evidence. In
the beginning of the Imperial time the city as a whole was
agreed in support of Julius Cæsar, and afterwards of the
Triumvirs, against the Senate. Partly the rivalry with
Adana, still more the hatred against the tyranny of the
Senatorial government, made the general body of the citizens unite. The Jews throughout the Roman world seem
to have been enthusiastic supporters of Julius Cæsar; Suetonius [45] mentions that in Rome the Jews mourned vehemently throughout successive nights at his tomb; and
naturally they took an active part in the popular move-

ment on his side. Naturally, also, the Jews of Palestine remembered that Pompey had profaned the Holy of Holies, and that Julius Cæsar had avenged them of their enemy. There is no reason to think that the Tarsian Jews differed from the rest of their race.

The later history of Tarsus, however, as will be recounted in a following section, shows the Greek element about the time of Christ in strong opposition to the policy of Augustus; and a suppression of popular liberty was carried through by Athenodorus, the friend of Augustus, armed with authority from the Emperor himself. The change in the constitution was emphatically anti-Hellenic in character, and could not but strengthen the Oriental element in the city.

That brings up another question: what was the attitude of the large native population, the old Tarsian 'stock, in the Roman time? We may take Athenodorus as a specimen. He was born in a country village near Tarsus, from which he took his surname Kananites. He was trained in the Greek philosophy, but his school was the Stoic, which had a marked Oriental complexion and numbered among its leaders many men of Oriental birth. He was in strenuous opposition to the democratic principles of the Greeks, who, from eagerness to secure the freedom of the individual, were too apt to sacrifice order, law, and the true liberty of the community as a whole. In his struggle against the violence of faction, and his final suppression of popular licence and liberty, he would probably and naturally carry with him the native population, which was strongly Oriental in character, and therefore had little eagerness for that freedom of the individual, which was so dear to the Greeks. The opposition which, during the second century B.C., naturally existed between the old native population and the new colonists, both Hebrews and Greeks, must have gradually disappeared as the generations passed; and new grouping of the Tarsian parties came into being to suit new conditions. The Oriental element, including both Jews and the old Cilician people, stood over against the Greek element. The latter was distinctly weaker, and the Oriental character in Tarsus must therefore have been strongly accentuated.

That this was so is proved by the evidence of Dion Chrysostom in the two orations which he delivered to the Tarsians about A.D. 110. He had come with the approval of the Emperor Trajan on an informal mission to several of the great cities of the East; thus his position was not unlike that of Athenodorus in the time of Augustus. Neither held any regular office or was armed with formal authority, but both carried with them the immense informal influence that the personal friendship and support of the Emperor conferred in the eyes alike of Roman officials and of the provincial population. Dion Chrysostom was a Greek of Bithynia, Greek not by race, but by temperament, by education, and by a really deep and genuine admiration for the ancient Hellenic literature and achievements in all departments of life. His evidence about Tarsus, therefore, is peculiarly valuable.[46]

Dion was struck with the non-Hellenic character of Tarsus and of Cilicia in general. He acknowledges that Tarsus was a colony of the Argives; but its spirit was not Greek; one asked, as one surveyed the Tarsian populace, whether these people were Greeks or the worst of the Phoenicians. In speaking to the Rhodians Dion praised their Hellenism; even a barbarian who visited Rhodes would be impressed by the old Hellenic spirit, and would recognise at once that he had entered no Syrian or Cilician city, but one that was truly Greek. In speaking to the Tarsians, on the contrary, he recognised nothing that was Hellenic among them, and little that was good in their manners. Only one Tarsian characteristic does he praise unreservedly, and that he praises, though it was, as he says, utterly different from the Hellenic custom. He was much pleased with the extremely modest dress of the Tarsian women, who were always deeply veiled when they went abroad. As Tarsian ladies walked in the street, you could not see any part either of their face or of their whole person, nor could they themselves see anything out of their path. They were separate from the public world, while they walked in it.

Now the difference of spirit between one race and another is nowhere else so strongly marked as in their treatment of women and their customs regarding the conduct and dress of women. The complete veiling of women in the Oriental style was practised in Tarsus; and thus even this Græco-Roman city was marked as an Oriental, not a Greek town. The Greek was swallowed up in the Oriental. That seems to be a law of nature : wherever the two elements meet in Asia, either they must hold apart or the Greek is gradually merged in the Oriental.

We may notice in passing how strong an effect was produced on the mind of St. Paul by his Tarsian experience in this respect. It is, as a rule, the impressions of childhood that rule one's prejudices in regard to the conduct of women; and the Apostle prescribes to the Corinthians a very strict rule about the veiling of women (1 Cor. xi. 3-16). Whereas men are to have their heads uncovered in Church, it is disgraceful for women to be unveiled there. Now it would be quite possible that a Greek or a Roman should reach this opinion about women's dress and conduct in church. So far as this command goes, it was quite in accordance with the ideas of the most orderly and thoughtful among those peoples and quite in keeping with the customs of good society. But there is one little touch in St. Paul's sermon about women that reveals the man brought up amid Oriental custom. He says that " the woman ought to have authority ($\dot{\epsilon}\xi ov\sigma \acute{\iota}a$) upon her head ". This seems so strange to the Western mind that the words have been generally reckoned among the most obscure in the whole of the Pauline writings. A vast amount has been written by commentators about them, almost entirely erroneous and misleading, and sometimes false to Greek language and its possibilities. Most of the ancient and modern commentators say that the "authority" which the woman wears on her head is the authority to which she is subject—a preposterous idea which a Greek scholar would laugh at anywhere except in the New Testament, where (as they seem to think) Greek words may mean anything that commentators choose. Authority or power that belongs to the wearer, such power as the magistrate possesses in virtue of his office, was meant by the Greek word $\dot{\epsilon}\xi ov\sigma \acute{\iota}a$. So Diodorus, i. 47, describes the statue of the mother of the Egyptian king Osymandyas, wearing three royalties upon her head, *i.e.* she possessed the royal dignity in three different ways, as daughter, wife and mother of a king.[47] The woman who has a veil on her head wears authority on her head : that is what the Greek text says. To the European the words are unintelligible ; but that is because he is a European. He must cease for a moment to be a European and pass into the realm of life and thought in which the words apply. Then he will understand them.

To the Oriental the words are simple and clear: they describe the ordinary fact of life. Their meaning has been well described by Rev. W. M. Thomson, in his work *The Land and the Book*, p. 31, in which he has set down the ripe knowledge acquired during thirty years' residence in Syria and Palestine. It was my good fortune not to read this book until I had been visiting Turkey for many years and had learned enough to appreciate the intimate knowledge which guides the thought and expression of the author. The book seems now to be little read; but scholars would find it far more instructive and educative than many of the more learned and more ignorant works produced by Palestinian tourist savants, who see only the surface of the land and people among whom they make hasty excursions, and then judge about custom and character. I have no prejudice (as many young travellers have) against the tourist who dwells in the tents of Cook. On the tour he learns much, if he has been previously studying the subject; his ideas gain precision and vividness during a few weeks or months of travelling. But sometimes, conscious how much he has learned in the line of his competence and how much more real the history of Palestine has become to him, he fails to appreciate the limits imposed by the circumstances of his tour. Mr. Thomson puts in his book the intimate knowledge about details that he had gathered in half a lifetime.

In Oriental lands the veil is the power and the honour and dignity of the woman. With the veil on her head, she can go anywhere in security and profound respect. She is not seen; it is the mark of thoroughly bad manners to observe a veiled woman in the street. She is alone. The rest of the people around are non-existent to her, as she is

to them.   She is supreme in the crowd.   She passes at her
own free choice, and a space must be left for her.   The
man who did anything to annoy or molest her would have
a bad time in an Oriental town, and might easily lose his
life.   A man's house is his castle, in so far as a lady is
understood to be there; without her it is free to any stranger
to enter as guest and temporary lord.

But without the veil the woman is a thing of nought,
whom any one may insult.   The true Oriental, if uneducated in Western ways, seems to be inclined naturally to
treat with rudeness, to push and ill-treat, a European lady
in the street.   A woman's authority and dignity vanish along
with the all-covering veil that she discards.   That is the
Oriental view, which Paul learned in Tarsus.

§ XVIII.   ROMANS OTHERWISE TARSIANS.

With Pompey's settlement of the East in 64 B.C. began
probably the long series of Tarsian-Roman citizens, one of
whom is known to us as "Saul otherwise called Paul".
In the Republican time Roman citizenship was not so frequently given as in the Imperial time; but it is natural
and probable that Pompey, when he conquered the Cilician
plain in 66, may have found some of the leading Tarsians
useful to him in regulating the country for the new system,
and rewarded them with the Roman citizenship.   It was a
matter of pride and also of real advantage in various ways
for a Roman noble to have clients and connections in the
great provincial cities; he aided them and acted for them
in Rome, while they added to his dignity as a Roman and
furthered his interests in their respective countries.

Such new citizens would naturally take his name, Gnaeus
Pompeius, retaining generally as a cognomen or third name

their original Hellenic designation. The Roman name Gnaeus Pompeius would thereafter persist in succeeding generations as a family name, and all male descendants of the family would bear it, being distinguished from one another by their various cognomina or additional names. If we had any lists of Tarsian citizens during the first two centuries of the Empire, we should probably find in them more than one family bearing the name Pompeius.

Hence arises a difference between Roman names in strict usage and these Roman names in the Provinces. In proper Roman usage Gnaeus was the name of the individual, Cornelius or Pompeius or so forth was the name of the *gens* of which he was a member, and the cognomen was often the name of his family (*e.g.*, Scipio), though sometimes a personal epithet given to himself, as Magnus was to Pompey. But when a large number of families took such names universally as Gnaeus Pompeius, Gaius Julius, Tiberius Claudius, Marcus Antonius, these wholly ceased to be distinctive, and the third name or cognomen alone was individual and distinguishing. Hence the third name was in this latter usage far the most important. A person was generally designated by his cognomen (which in a Hellenic city was usually a Greek name), whereas if he were mentioned by the more dignified appellation of Gnaeus Pompeius, this would leave his personality uncertain, for other members of a good many families were so designated. In some inscriptions it may be noticed that the more familiar part of the name, the cognomen (or even in some cases a fourth name, given as a still more familiar and distinguishing name), is engraved at the top in a line by itself in larger letters, while the full name is stated in letters of ordinary size in the body of the inscription. This, it may be observed, is one out of many ancient usages, in which large letters were employed to mark superior importance or direct the reader's attention to the words so emphasised (compare Gal. vi. 11).[48]

The result was that in the Greek-speaking Provinces the triple name was used only in more formal and compliment- ary designation, and especially was required as a legal designation ; but, in the ordinary life of Hellenistic cities like Tarsus, the full name sank almost out of use and out of notice. Hence no full Roman names occur in the New Testament, although it stands (according to our view) in such close and intimate, though often hidden, relation with the Roman life and policy in the Provinces ; because the New Testament moves on the plane of everyday life, and is ex- pressed in the common speech, sometimes in quite colloquial style. This is most noticeable in the personal names. In many cases the familiar abbreviated or diminutive form of a name was used in place of the full and correct form, as in Apollos, Silas, Loukas, Epaphras, Priscilla : in some of these the correct form of the word never occurs in the New Testament, in others we find both, as in Epaphras and Epaphroditus, Apollos and Apollonius, Priscilla and Prisca.[49] Where both are attested, it will be observed that either the natural tendency to more formal and elaborate politeness made some speakers use the formal correct name, whereas other speakers tended to use the more colloquial and familiar name, or the occasion sometimes demanded more formality from a speaker who at other times employed the familiar name. Thus, for example, Paul uses the formal names Silvanus and Prisca, but Luke always speaks of Silas and Priscilla : Paul uses the name Epaphras in writing to the Colossians and to Philemon, for they were familiar with the personality of their fellow-townsman, but to the Philippians, who were strangers, he speaks of Epaphroditus. In these examples, which might be multiplied, we see the variations characteristic of ordinary social usage ; some people tend to use diminutives more freely than others, and the same person will designate another according to the occasion, now more formally, now by the diminutive.

But the formal Roman triple name was simply not em-ployed at all in the ordinary social usage of Hellenic cities. The Greeks never understood the Roman system of names, and when they tried to write the full triple Roman designa-tion of one of their own fellow-citizens, who had attained to the coveted honour of Roman citizenship, they frequently made errors (as is shown in many inscriptions). So at the present day foreigners frequently misuse English titles, and speak of Sir Peel or Lord Gladstone. The reason why the Greeks failed to understand the Roman system of names was because they never followed the Roman fashion except under compulsion. Greek custom gave one name to a man, and knew nothing of a family name, still less of the Roman gentile name (such as Pompeius); and so all Greeks spoke of their fellow-townsmen who had become Romans by their Greek names, as if they were still mere Hellenes and men of one name.

Thus it comes about that, although Paul and Silas and Theophilus,[50] and probably various others mentioned in the New Testament, were Romans, the full Roman name of none of them is mentioned. This silence about the full legal name is no proof of ignorance or inaccuracy : it is just one of the many little details which show how close and intimate is the relation between the New Testament and the actual facts of life. But just as certain is it that Paul had two Roman names, praenomen and nomen, as it is that he was a Roman citizen. No one could be a Roman citizen without having a Roman name; and, though he might never bear it in ordinary Hellenic society, yet as soon as he came in contact with the law and wished to claim his legal rights he must assume his proper and full Roman designation. The peculiar character of the double system and civilisation, Greek and Roman at once, comes into play. In Greek surroundings the Tarsian Roman remains a Greek in designation; but in Roman relations his Roman name would necessarily be employed.

If Luke had completed his story and written the narrative of St. Paul's trial in Rome, we may feel confident of two things, first he would probably have mentioned the Roman name at the opening of the trial; and, secondly, he might perhaps have made an error in setting down the name in Greek. The strict legal designation required the father's name and the Tribe to be stated, and these had a fixed order: the Greeks constantly make some error or other in regard to order, when they try to express in Greek the Roman full designation.

Not merely had Paul a Roman praenomen and nomen, but he was also enrolled in one of the Roman Tribes. This was a necessary part of the citizenship, just as enrolment in one of the city Tribes was a necessary part of the citizenship of a Greek city. Now it may seem inconsistent that, after we have in a previous section proved so carefully that it is for religious and patriotic reasons inconceivable that a Jew should ever become a member of an ordinary Greek city Tribe, we should now lay it down as an assured and certain fact that Paul was an enrolled member of an ordinary Roman Tribe. There is, however, no inconsistency. No Jew could become a member of a Hellenic city Tribe, be-

14

cause every such Tribe was a local body, meeting at regular intervals and bound together by common religious rites, in which every member must participate. But the Roman Tribes, though originally similar in character to the Greek Tribes, had long ceased to be anything more than political and legal fictions: they were mere names, from which all reality had long passed away; their members were scattered all over the Roman world ; they never met, and therefore had no religious bond of union. It is indeed the case that, so long as the Roman people continued to vote, those members of the Tribes who wished to vote and lived near enough to Rome must meet to exercise the vote, and some religious formality must have been practised at this meeting. But few of the widely scattered citizens could meet and vote. The Roman citizenship had other value than mere exercise of a vote, and citizens who lived in the Provinces could never make any use of the vote. Moreover, after Tiberius became Emperor in 14 A.D., the Roman people ceased to meet in *comitia*, and the popular vote had no longer any existence. In Tribes like these there was nothing to forbid a Jew from having himself enrolled; and all Jews who became Roman citizens were *ipso facto* made members of a Tribe, but membership was a mere matter of name and law, free from religious duties.

Inasmuch as the Tarsian Jews were citizens of a Hellenic city, their language was necessarily Greek, and all who were citizens bore Greek names (or at least names which were outwardly Greek). In some cases they may have taken names which were Grecized forms of Hebrew words; but no certain example of this is known to me, though some may be suspected.[51] Some Jews in Hellenic cities certainly bore names which were equivalent in meaning to

Hebrew names, as Stephanus to Atara, Gelasius to Isaac, Theophilus to Eldad or Jedidiah, among women Eirene to Salome: in such cases probably the Hebrew name was used in Jewish circles and the Greek translation in Hellenic society. But the great majority took ordinary Greek names, and hence arises the difficulty of tracing the history of the many thousands of Jewish families who settled in Lydia, Phrygia, and Cilicia. Only in a few cases can we trace a Jewish family through some accident betraying its nationality; for example the curious name Tyrronius, found at Iconium, Sebaste and Akmonia (in all of which Jews were numerous), is proved to be Jewish, and at Akmonia the wealthy pair, Julia Severa and Servenius Capito, who are so often mentioned on coins, were almost certainly Jews.[52] But, as a whole, the large Jewish population of those regions disappears from the view of history owing to their disuse of Hebrew names, at least in public.

In Roman Imperial times, when the Jews were protected and powerful, there was in some degree a revival of purely Jewish names. The name Moses is perhaps found at Termessos in a remarkable inscription of the third century: "I Aurelius Mo[s]es, son of Karpus, having been everywhere often and having often investigated the world, now lie in death no longer knowing anything; but this only (I say) 'be of good courage, no man is immortal'."[53] Another case is Reuben in a long Eumenian epitaph, also of the third century.[54]

Even in Greek times, however, it is probable that most of the Jews of Anatolia had a Hebrew name, which they used in their private life at home and in the circle of the synagogue. The Hebrew name was an alternative name, not an additional or second name. The bearer was called by one or by the other, according to the occasion, but not by both: to use one of the few certain examples, the Jew was "Paul otherwise Saul," "Paul *alias* Saul". In Greek surroundings he bore the one name, in Hebrew surroundings the other.

Whether there was any principle guiding the selection of the two names is uncertain. Sometimes (see above, p. 211) the Greek translated the Hebrew. The topic is part of a wider question, the evidence on which has never been collected and estimated. In the Greek cities and colonies in alien lands, Thrace, Russia, the Crimea, and Asia generally, numerous examples occur of the alternative name. In many cases these belong evidently to the two languages of a bilingual city, one is Greek, one of the native tongue; but that is not a universal rule; there are plenty of cases, especially of a later time, in which both are Greek. The fact seems to be that, as time passed and one language established itself as predominant in the city, the alternative names still persisted in popular custom, but were no longer taken from two different languages. The original rule, however, is the important one for our purpose: *viz.*, that in a bilingual society the two names belong to the two languages.

It was natural that the Jews should often take the names of those kings who had favoured them so much and opened to them the citizenship of many great cities. Alexander was certainly a common name among them, and perhaps also Seleucus, for both Alexander and Seleucus favoured and protected the Jews; [55] but we can well imagine that, after the restoration of Jewish power by the Maccabees, the name of Antiochus may have become unpopular among the Jews (though it does not seem to have been entirely avoided). But, allowing that Alexander and Seleucus were popular names among them, it would be absurd to conjecture that every Alexander in Central Anatolia was a Jew. Even negative inferences are impossible. There is no reason to think that the Jews objected to names connected with idolatry, such as Apollonius, Artemas (or Artemidorus), Asklepiades, etc. Examples can be quoted of Jews bearing names of that kind, such as Apollonius or Apollos.[56]

Epigraphy, generally speaking, was public, not private; and in a Hellenic city public matters were expressed in Greek. Hence, as it is almost solely the public epigraphic memorials that have been preserved, we rarely know more than the Greek names of the Anatolian Jews, only occasionally the alternative name is stated. In the later Roman period, when a purely Jewish name was sometimes used in a public memorial, this may imply either that the alternative Greek (or Roman) name was disused by the individual, or that he had throughout life borne the Jewish name alone without a Greek name. The examples of Moses and Reuben have been quoted above.

When a Jew who was citizen of a Hellenic city was honoured with the Roman citizenship, the matter of nomenclature was complicated by the Roman triple name. As a Greek and as a Jew, such a citizen had a single name in each case; as a Roman he had three names; but the third of these names was, as a rule, identical with the Greek name. Thus we find a Jewish Christian at Hierapolis named " M. Aurelius Diodorus Koriaskos,[57] otherwise called Asbolos ". We may conjecture that Asbolos was the Christian baptismal name, "he whose sins had been black like soot ". Diodorus was the Greek name, M. Aurelius Diodorus the Roman, and the second cognomen is of uncertain character, perhaps a familiar name in private life.

The Jews who became Roman citizens might naturally

be expected to have Greek names as their *cognomina* in ordinary familiar use; and especially the earliest of them must assuredly have had such Greek names. Latin cognomina, however, came into use occasionally; and are more likely to have been employed in families where the Roman citizenship had been an inheritance for some generations. The one early instance which is known with certainty is Paul, whose Roman first and second names are unknown; his cognomen was Latin, not Greek; and he had an alternative Hebrew name Saul. Yet he was a citizen of a Hellenic city, and therefore legally a Hellene (except in so far as Hellenic citizenship gave way to Roman citizenship), but in Greek society he passed under his Latin cognomen. As his father, and possibly also his grandfather, had possessed the Roman citizenship, the use of Latin speech and names was an inheritance in the family.

§ XIX. The Tarsian Democracy.

The importance attached to Tarsian citizenship and expressed in the hasty words of St. Paul, Acts xxi. 39, quoted in § V., was greatly increased by the changes introduced during the reign of Augustus into the constitution of Tarsus. The changes were introduced through the instrumentality of Athenodorus, the only Tarsian besides Paul himself who stands out before us as a real person; and an account of them will make the municipality of Tarsus more intelligible, and will at the same time illustrate to the reader the personality of a noteworthy Tarsian and the surroundings amid which Paul was born and brought up.

Under the careless and corrupt rule of Antony in the East, Tarsus was exposed to suffer from the caprices and

the favourites of an idle despot.   A certain Boethos, "bad
poet and bad citizen," as Strabo calls him, a native of Tarsus,
was patronised by Antony, whose favour he had gained by
a poem celebrating the battle of Philippi.   The vice of
Greek democratic government was the careless readiness
to embark in any new scheme that caught the popular taste
and to employ any leader who suggested himself as likely
to further the enterprise of the moment.[58]   Boethos knew
well how to make use of the Tarsian democracy for his own
benefit, and he allied himself with a gang of corrupt associ-
ates to plunder the municipality.   After the fall of Antony
in the end of 31 B.C., the personal influence of Boethos in
Tarsus was weakened; but the gang evidently had got
possession of the machinery of government, and there was
no great improvement in the administration.   Then Athenodorus came back to Tarsus, invested with the influence
that belonged to a personal friend of the Emperor Augustus,
and apparently holding also in reserve a commission from
the supreme ruler empowering him to reform the constitution of Tarsus as he might find expedient.   The way in
which Athenodorus had risen to this high position in the
Imperial administration is interesting in itself, and gives
a remarkable view of the character of that period and of
the importance which then belonged to education.   (See
§ XX.)

   As to Boethos, nothing is known except what we can
gather from the brief account in Strabo.   He stands before
us a type of the worst product of Greek democracy, the
skilful manipulator of popular government for the benefit
of a clique of corrupt and unscrupulous partisans.   It is
true that we know about him only from a friend and admirer
of his opponent, Athenodorus; but the facts stand out so

natural and so life-like in Strabo's pages that they are convincing. Tarsus fell under the control of a ring similar to that Tammany ring which long controlled New York in our own time; and the situation was the same in both cities. The influence of the more educated body of the citizens was weakened, in the one case through the disorders of the Civil War, followed by the capricious and corrupt rule of Antony, in the other case by the absorption of the educated citizens in other pursuits and their withdrawal from the work of municipal government.

The name Boethos might suggest the suspicion that he was a Jew. It is known to have been borne by Jews, and it was undoubtedly favoured by them as a Greek translation of the Hebrew name Ozer or Ezra.[59] But there is no reason to think that the name was confined to Jews ; and the skill which Boethos showed in manipulating the machinery of municipal administration, though characteristic of the worst class of Jews, was not, and never has been, confined to that race. This bad poet is perhaps more likely to have been a Greek. It was at any rate through clever handling of the most worthless elements of Greek city life that he obtained his position in history.

§ XX. ATHENODORUS OF TARSUS.

Athenodorus was a citizen of Tarsus born not in the city itself, but in "a certain village" of its territory, as Strabo says. The village origin and the name of his father, Sandon —a thoroughly Cilician name—mark Athenodorus as belonging to the native element in the Tarsian state (see § XVIII.). The name of the village must have been Kanana ; and therefrom was formed the epithet Kananites, by which this Athenodorus was distinguished from another Tarsian philosopher, of slightly earlier date, who bore the same name. Both lived long in Rome; each was the confidential friend of a noble Roman, one of Cato, the other of Augustus; both were Stoics: and confusion between them was easy.[60]

The life of Athenodorus extended from about 74 B.C. to 7 A.D. He died in his eighty-second year,[61] and he was the teacher of the youthful Augustus at Apollonia in Epirus. Now the residence of Augustus at Apollonia ended in the spring of 44 B.C., and it is hardly possible that Athenodorus was less than thirty years of age at that time. Eusebius, in his chronicle, says that he was famous in 7 A.D.; this statement must be understood of the culmination of his career in Tarsus (to which he returned in old age), and his death may be placed in the same or an immediately following year, 7-9 A.D. He was born, therefore, between 74 and 72 B.C.; and the earlier dates 74 B.C. and 7 A.D. are probably preferable for the limits of his life (as will appear in the sequel), and as such will be here adopted.

Athenodorus is mentioned in such close relation with Posidonius,[62] the leader of the Stoic school of philosophy at Rhodes, that he may be confidently called his pupil. He studied, therefore, at Rhodes under that teacher before A.D. 51, when Posidonius migrated, near the end of his long life of eighty-four years, to Rome. After concluding his studies Athenodorus may be presumed, according to the usual custom, to have travelled, completing his education by acquiring experience of the world and life. His writings (as we shall see) prove that his travels extended beyond the Greek world into the Eastern desert.

We may also confidently assume that he must have given lectures in some of the great cities of the Mediterranean lands. It was in this way that young aspirants to philosophic distinction made themselves known in educated circles, and in time found a home and a career in some part of the Greek world; and it was as one of those travelling philosophers that Paul afterwards found a hearing in those Greek cities. After some years spent in this kind of probation as a lecturer, Athenodorus settled at Apollonia on the coast of Epirus. During his *Wanderjahre* he acquired so high and widespread a reputation that Cicero, writing from Asia Minor in February, B.C. 50, to Appius Claudius, then censor in Rome, advised him to direct his attention to what Athenodorus, son of Sandon, says about nobility.[63] As it seems highly improbable that Athenodorus had come to Rome before 51 B.C. (when Cicero went away to the East), it is evident that the latter must have learned about his opinions from his writings, and advised Claudius to study some treatise by him on moral philosophy. We can hardly suppose that this great reputation had been acquired before he was twenty-three ; and therefore 74 must be assumed as the year of his birth. An earlier date is impossible, for he was living as late as A.D. 7.

Athenodorus was lecturing at Apollonia when the youthful Augustus came there to finish his education in the autumn of 45 B.C. In the six months which Augustus spent there the Tarsian philosopher acquired a life-long influence over his mind. It can have been no ordinary man who so deeply impressed a subtle and self-reliant character like Augustus. When the latter returned to Rome to take up the inheritance of his uncle Julius Cæsar in March, 44 B.C., Athenodorus followed him. In November of that year he was consulted by Cicero, and prepared for his use in his treatise *De Officiis* an abstract of Posidonius's opinions on duty: it is clear from Cicero's words[64] that Athenodorus was then in Rome.

He remained many years in Rome, enjoying a position of trust and influence with Augustus. The relations between them were creditable to both. Augustus is said to have been guided by the wise advice of the philosopher; and Athenodorus never abused the influence that he enjoyed. A story which is related by Dion Cassius, and more fully by Zonaras,[65] shows that he had the courage to run serious risk in his determination to rebuke and curb the faults of his Imperial friend. He chanced one day to enter the house of a noble Roman friend, and found the family in affliction. An order had come from Augustus that the wife of this noble must go instantly to meet Augustus in the palace, and a closely covered litter was waiting to convey her. It was not doubtful that the purpose was a dishonourable one; but no one in this Roman high-born family dared to think of disobeying the autocrat. It was the village-born philosopher who was bold enough to do so.

Athenodorus immediately offered his services. He took his place in the litter, with a drawn sword in his hand. When he had been carried thus into Augustus's chamber and the litter was set down, he leaped out suddenly, sword in hand, exclaiming, "Are you not afraid lest some one may enter like this and assassinate you?" Augustus was convinced, and Athenodorus's influence was increased by the emperor's gratitude.

In this incident we recognize a man who possessed a clear insight into character, quick wit, decision and courage. He knew both what he ought to blame, and how the blame should be conveyed so as to impress the cautious and subtle mind of Augustus.

In his old age Athenodorus obtained permission to retire to his native city, and, as he was taking leave and embracing his old pupil, he imparted his last piece of advice, "When you are angry, Cæsar, say nothing and do nothing until you have repeated to yourself the letters of the alphabet". Here again we observe the watchful affection which noted and tried to guard against the faults of his friend. Augustus, taking his hand and saying, "I have still need of you," detained him a year longer, quoting the Greek poet's word, "Silence, too," *i.e.* the silence of trusty companionship, quite as much as military service, "brings a reward, gained not through the dangers of war, but in the life of peace". This was a principle of Augustus's policy, expressed by Horace in the second Ode of the third book (one of a group of six thoroughly political poems), *est et fideli tuta silentio merces :* [66] the emperor recognised and rewarded two careers of duty, one in war, one in the civil service.

As Athenodorus seems to have spent his life near Augustus from 45 B.C. until he retired to Tarsus about 15 B.C., it must have been during those early years which (as we saw) he probably spent in travel, that he visited Petra, in the desert east of the Dead Sea. He related with admiration that, whereas the many strangers whom he saw there, Romans and others, were frequently engaged in lawsuits against one another or against the natives, none of the natives ever were involved in any dispute with each other, but all lived in perfect mutual harmony. Clement of Alexandria quotes from him a statement that Sesostris the Egyptian king, after conquering many peoples among the Greeks, brought back artists with him to Egypt, and thus explained the origin of a statue of Sarapis. He may, therefore, have visited Egypt as well as Petra, and thence derived illustrations for his philosophical writings and lectures.[67]

Athenodorus is called a philosopher of nature (φυσικός) by Eusebius, and with his master Posidonius, he is twice quoted by Strabo for his opinions on the ocean and tides.[68] Whether he or the other Athenodorus of Tarsus was the author of a work on his fatherland, quoted by Stephanus Byzantinus, is uncertain; but as the work gives a different account of the origin of Tarsus from that which is stated by Strabo, the friend of our Athenodorus, Muller infers, with much probability, that the author was a different Athenodorus.

The work by which he impressed the world was in the department of moral philosophy; and in his treatises he embodied a noble and dignified view of human life and duty. On that account he was commended by Cicero and quoted by Seneca, from whom is derived the little that we know of his teaching.

Seneca, when he mentions that in society some reckon to our account the social attentions which we pay them as if they were putting us in their debt by admitting us to the privilege of their acquaintance, quotes the saying of Athenodorus that he would not even go to dine with a person who would not think the guest was conferring an obligation by resorting to his house (*de Tranquill. Animae,* 7). In another place Seneca quotes at considerable length his opinion that, in a better state of society, it would be the best way of life to exercise and strengthen one's character by engaging in public life; but, as society is at present constituted, since ambition and calumny are rampant, and the simple, candid person is constantly exposed to misrepresentation, a noble nature is bound to abstain from public life: yet even in private life a great mind can find free scope, and be useful to private friends and to the whole body of the people by wise speech and good counsel (*de Tranquill.*

Animae, 3).   This passage, with its lofty view of life, bears a distinct resemblance to that conception of life as a warfare against evil, which Seneca and Paul express in remarkably similar terms.[69]

Again, in his *Moral Epistles*, i. 10, 5, Seneca quotes from him the striking sentiment, "Know that you are free from all passions only when you have reached the point that you ask God for nothing except what you can ask openly," and he goes on to say, in the spirit if not in the words of Athenodorus, "So live with men, as if God saw you; so speak with God, as if men were listening".

He wrote a treatise addressed to Octavia, the sister of Augustus, of which nothing is known, but which may, perhaps, have been a consolation on the death of her son, Marcellus—a kind of work which was reckoned specially appropriate for philosophers in Roman society, and of which Seneca's Consolation to his own mother Helvia may be taken as a specimen.

In this summary of the few known events of his life Athenodorus stands before us as a personage of real distinction and lofty character, no mere empty lecturer and man of words, but a man of judgment, good sense, courage and self-respect, who stooped to no base subservience to a despot, but rebuked his faults sharply, when the greatest in Rome were cowering in abject submission before him, a man of affairs who knew what were his limits and did not overstep them, and a writer, every one of whose few preserved sayings is noble and generous.   The opinion has been stated in *St. Paul the Traveller*, p. 354, and is still maintained by the writer, that the remarkable resemblance, both verbal and in spirit, which has often been observed between the sentiments expressed by Seneca and the words of St. Paul [70]

is due at least in part to the influence exercised on both
by Athenodorus ; and if this be true, every one must admit
that no writer of antiquity, so far as we know, better deserved, both by his life and by his sentiments, to exercise
such an influence on two of the greatest figures in the history
of the first century after Christ.   Paul can hardly have been
more than an infant when the greatest of pagan Tarsians
died.   But the influence of Athenodorus did not die with
him.   He was long worshipped as a hero by his country,[71]
and his teaching was doubtless influential in the University
of Tarsus after his death.

This account has been strictly confined to the exact facts
that are recorded.   It would be possible from the analogy
of other cities and from the general circumstances of contemporary history to restore something like a picture of
Athenodorus in his Tarsian activity—for his retirement from
the work of a teacher in Rome was merely the beginning of
a new period of practical work.   But that imaginative way
of picturing what is likely to have occurred belongs to the
province of historical romance rather than of history.

Athenodorus was succeeded in his commanding position
in the Tarsian state by Nestor, another Tarsian philosopher
(of the Academic, not the Stoic, school), who had risen at
Rome to influence and trust in the Imperial family and had
been tutor to Augustus's nephew and intended successor
Marcellus about 26-23 B.C.   Nestor lived to the age of
ninety-two and was still living when Strabo wrote about
A.D. 19.   He had doubtless been recommended by Athenodorus to Augustus.   Thus Tarsus was swayed in a critical
period of its history by a succession of philosophers, who combined the learning of the schools with that practical sense
which alone could have won the confidence of Augustus.

§ XXI.　The Reform of the Tarsian Constitution by Athenodorus.

It is not possible to fix the time when Athenodorus returned to Tarsus; but, as he was an old man (so both Plutarch and Strabo say), it can hardly have been earlier than 15 B.C., when he was in his sixtieth year; and it is not likely to have been much later, as he found Boethos still influential in the city and busied with his gang in harrying the State. The terms in which Strabo describes the situation when Athenodorus returned, suggest that the interval since the fall of Antony had not been very long. In Tarsus it was a case of democracy run to seed, emancipated from the limits of order and even of decency, contemptuous of obedience or principle : such was always the result of Greek institutions when divorced from a general sentiment of patriotism and religion (the two were almost the same in the Hellenic thought), which might enforce a certain standard of public action and morality.

Greek democratic government demanded a high level of education and thought among the population, and quickly resulted in anarchy when this condition was not supplied. The demand for education was strong in the democratically governed cities and the care taken to provide it was the best feature of their administration; but the amalgamation of democratic government and the capricious autocracy of Antony had been fatal.

Athenodorus tried, first of all, the method of constitutional agitation for reform, attempting by reason and argument to restrain Boethos and his gang, and to reintroduce a higher standard of municipal morality. After a time, finding that such means were unavailing, and that his appeals were only met with the grossest insult, he made use of the supreme powers [72] with which he had been armed by Augustus and which, at first, he had apparently kept private. He condemned the whole gang to exile and ejected them from Tarsus, and revolutionised the constitution of the city. [73] This event may, perhaps, be dated about 10 B.C., allowing a space of five years (which is probably the extremest possible limit to the patience of the philosopher).

Strabo does not state the character of the new system which Athenodorus introduced, but merely describes the intense love for education which characterised the Tarsians in his time—he was writing about A.D. 19—and evidently regards the reforms of Athenodorus, who was his personal friend, as having been extremely successful.

The general character of the new constitution which was introduced into Tarsus can be determined from the tone of the Imperial policy throughout the Empire and from the slight references made incidentally in the two speeches which Dion Chrysostom addressed to the Tarsians about A.D. 112. Although the Roman Imperial system was established through the victory of the democracy, it was a democracy led by a dictator; and Augustus recognised from a very early stage in his career that he must found his autocracy on oligarchy, not on democracy. His aim was to substitute for the old oligarchy of Roman nobles, who had formerly opposed him and could not be trusted to support his rule, a new oligarchy of official service and merit. [74] He did not try to force his policy on too rapidly, and he was ready and eager to admit into the new oligarchy all members of the old oligarchy, who could be induced to accommodate themselves to it; but he and the rest of the early Emperors were fully aware that their greatest danger lay in possible

15

rivals among the old nobility, and they encouraged and developed the rise of an official class, whose career should lie within the limits of the Imperial system, and who should be servants, not rivals, of the reigning Emperor.

A bureaucratic oligarchy is the necessary accompaniment of an autocracy, which cannot maintain itself alone without some body of devoted agents and servants to rest upon; but an educated people is its enemy.[74a] Thus when the popular party under the leadership of a dictator had triumphed, the power of the people ended; and a narrow oligarchy aided the Imperial despot to rule over and for a people among whom education gradually died out. The saving grace of the Empire was the memory of its origin and the compelling force of that memory. Centuries elapsed before the Emperors were able quite to forget that they had been placed in power as the champions of the people, and that the theoretical expression of their authority was the Tribunician power by which the years of their reign were reckoned. In numerous edicts the Emperors expressed their conception of their prime duty, to be ever on the outlook for opportunities to benefit their people, to think for them, and to direct them for their own good; but it was no part of the Imperial duty to educate the people up to the level of thinking for themselves and governing themselves.

In the cities of the Empire the same process was encouraged: the power of the people was curtailed, and an oligarchical regime was gradually introduced. Tarsus was one of the first examples of the new system, and Athenodorus was the instrument through whom the Emperor acted. A certain property qualification was required for citizenship. Those who had less than the requisite fortune were degraded from the roll of citizens. In the time of Dion Chrysostom these unclassed people of Tarsus were called "Linen-workers," probably a cant name which had gradually established itself in common use. They were the plebeians of Tarsus, in a sense citizens, because they were inhabitants of the city, but yet (as Dion says) not citizens, because they had not the civic rights.

The citizens or burgesses of Tarsus, therefore, were a timocratic aristocracy, whose status rested on a property qualification, and who exercised the power of government and held the right of election and voting generally. Within this oligarchic body, again, there was an inner aristocracy consisting of the Roman citizens, *viz.*, the families which had raised themselves so conspicuously in the city by wealth or by high office or, as was usually the case, by both, as to be admitted into the governing class of the Empire. In estimating the position of the young Paul, as he grew up in Tarsus, this privileged and aristocratic position which he inherited must be taken into account.

As a general rule it was from the local aristocracy that the leading figures in Anatolian history during the Roman period sprang. The lower classes were cut off by a chasm difficult to cross from the opportunity of gaining the education that was indispensable to advancement. For example, the aristocratic tone of Basil and his brother Gregory, during the fourth century, makes itself clearly felt in their writings. They belonged to the class of landed proprietors whose fortune opened to them the path of education. The scorn of Gregory for the low birth and poverty of the heretic Eunomius is quite as conspicuous as his hatred for the heterodoxy of his opponent's religious views.[75] Education was indispensable to advancement and influence under the Empire; even a soldier could rarely rise without education; a civilian practically never. The vice of the Imperial system was that the distinction of educated and uneducated became a matter of birth and caste, and that the lines of class distinction grew harder and deeper until they became impassable barriers. The able freedmen were only partially an exception ; they could make money, and a career was open to their sons ; but their opportunities were in considerable degree due to the aristocratic families of which they were dependents.

§ XXII. THE UNIVERSITY OF TARSUS.

No evidence about the relation of the Tarsian city government to the higher education of the inhabitants has been preserved. From the analogy of other Greek and Græco-Asiatic cities we may infer with confidence that the State exercised some authority over education, and that systematic arrangements were made to ensure that a proper supply of teachers and lecturers was ready to meet the requirements of the people : the intention was to provide public instruction by qualified lecturers in all the branches of science and literature [76] recognised at the time. This involved financial responsibilities to meet expense incurred by the State, officials of various kinds, in short a certain organisation ; but of the details of this organisation in Tarsus we are entirely ignorant. There are some isolated facts mentioned in inscriptions regarding other cities, but this is not the place to attempt to collect them and to use them in illustration of the facts recorded in literature, especially in the biographies of the Greek philosophers. In general terms it may be stated that in accordance with the Greek ideal of city life, the sole ultimate authority over the University lay in the hands of the people. All teaching in the city was for the benefit

of the people, and the popular assembly alone had the right
to dictate the manner and the terms according to which it
should be given. This authority was similar to that which
Parliament exercises in the last resort in our country, but
more direct and practically effective; and the State was then
much less willing to permit a University corporation to
regulate its own affairs in ordinary course. Such regulation
as did then exist was to a much greater degree exercised by
the municipal authority than is now the case. Edinburgh
University, in its close subordination to the Town Council—
as was the rule until about the middle of the nineteenth
century—showed more resemblance than any other of our
Universities to the old Greek system.

How the authority was exercised in Tarsus we have no
means of determining. The story of Athenodorus (see § XX.),
who was undoubtedly authoritative in the University and in
the city alike, shows that there was a real connection between
them; but it was only under exceptional conditions that
a man who ranked primarily as the leading man in the
University could exercise such influence in the city. When
he returned to settle in Tarsus he tried the experiment of
relying on the natural influence which a man of his standing and experience enjoyed in a free community; and this
experiment was a failure. He then had recourse to the exceptional and unconstitutional powers which the Emperor
had entrusted to him.

In the Greek cities generally, to a much greater extent
than with us, the lecturers in the University looked directly
to the city authority, so far as they looked to any controlling
power. To a much greater extent than with us they attained
their position by a sort of natural selection and survival of
the fittest. A lecturer was permitted to enter any city as a

wandering scholar, and might begin publicly to dispute and to lecture (as Paul did in Athens and in Ephesus and elsewhere), if he could attract an audience. The city could, if it thought fit, interfere to take cognisance of his lecturing, and either stop him, if it seemed advisable, or give him formal permission to continue. Apparently there was no definite or uniform rule in the matter, but each individual case was determined on its own merits. Any person was free to call attention in the public interest to a new lecturer; that was a practically universal rule in ancient cities: the State depended on individuals to invoke its intervention. When thus called upon, the State authority decided whether there was any need to take cognisance of the matter: the decision would depend partly on the information laid before it and on the weight which the informer carried, partly on the appearance made by the newcomer when he was examined. All that is a universal and necessary feature of Greek city government; and it implies that there was some public board or council or individual magistrate before whom information could be laid. In Athens it seems certain that the court of Areopagus was the authoritative body. In Ephesus it may possibly have been a court of Asiarchs, Acts xix. 31, men of the highest standing, though not officials of the city. As to Tarsus we have no information.

If the new lecturer, when attention was called to him, was found suitable and approved, this must have given him a regular and legal standing. If disapproval were expressed, he would probably find that it was advisable to try his fortune in another city. Paul apparently did so even when his case was adjourned for further consideration; and possibly in such cases that verdict may have been understood as one of mild disapproval. In cases where grave disapproval was felt the city had always the right to expel any person whose presence was for its disadvantage ; though, under Roman rule, such right of expulsion was certainly liable to revision at the hands of the Imperial officials, if the expelled person was sufficiently influential to be able to appeal to a high Roman officer.

As to the position of a lecturer who had been approved, we have very little information ; and practice doubtless varied in different cities. In some cases he enjoyed a salary from the State. How far he was allowed to charge fees is uncertain ; probably there was no uniform rule ; Paul charged no fees, and his practice was probably not unique, but he certainly makes rather a merit of the fact that neither individuals nor communities were put to expense by him, and he distinctly states it as a general rule, that the labourer was worthy of his hire and that payment for instruction was deserved. It would however be in accordance with the spirit of ancient life that the lecturers depended for their livelihood more on special gifts from grateful individuals than on fees charged universally for the privilege of listening.

To speak about the University of Tarsus is to a certain degree a misnomer, applying a modern name to an ancient institution. But there are really quite as great differences in character among the various modern Universities as there are between a typical modern and a typical Greek University. The essential facts of University life, freedom for the teacher to give instruction, freedom for the disciple to listen, to study and to learn, were Hellenic ; and the restriction of that freedom in various ways in many modern Universities might with greater justice be deemed a good reason for refusing the title to them, than the looseness of organisation in an ancient Hellenic University for denying it the same title.

Strabo, who is practically our sole authority, gives a very

sympathetic and favourable picture of the University of
Tarsus.   He was perhaps biassed to some extent by his
friendship for Athenodorus; but he was an eye-witness and
an authority of the first value.   He praises highly the
zeal for philosophy and the whole range of education which
characterised the people of Tarsus in his time.   In this
respect they surpassed Athens and Alexandreia and every
other seat of learning, for they not merely formed the entire
audience in their own University (to which no students ever
came from outside), but also sought to complete their education by resorting to foreign Universities; and those who
educated themselves in that way were glad to remain abroad
and few of them returned home.   On the contrary, other
educational centres attracted many eager students from outside, who remained there gladly; whereas few of the population in those centres sought education either abroad or at
home.   Only Alexandreia both attracted many foreign
students and sent forth a large number of her own young
citizens to study abroad.

This account is far from suggesting that the Tarsian University was one of the great Universities of the Hellenic
world.   On the contrary, Strabo evidently regarded it as a
young seat of learning, rather provincial and obscure, situated
in a great commercial centre, where there was an eager
desire for knowledge, and where people had the travelling
instinct strongly developed, so that they filled their own
University and after gaining from it all that it could give
went forth in large numbers to study in the more famous
Universities and often to settle there permanently.   Yet it
is sometimes stated by modern writers that the Tarsian
school of philosophy at the beginning of our era surpassed
those of Athens and Alexandreia;[77] it surpassed them only

in respect of the eagerness of its students and in filling its class-room with its own people, but it did not surpass them in equipment or in standing and fame as a seat of learning. Nor is it even correct to say that Tarsus was one of the three great University cities of the Mediterranean world.[78] It may perhaps be inferred from Strabo's words that Athens and Alexandreia were the two outstanding Universities of the Hellenic world; but it is clear also that various other Universities were known to him, which drew foreign students to study in their halls.

While Strabo shows clearly that Tarsus was not one of the great Universities in general estimation, he shows also that it was rich in what constitutes the true excellence and strength of a University, intense enthusiasm and desire for knowledge among the students and great ability and experience among some at least of the teachers. The collision between Athenodorus and the gang of Boethos (as already described) may be taken to some extent as a struggle for mastery between the University and the uneducated rabble, which had attained power partly through exceptional circumstances and partly through the deep-seated faults of the Greek democratic system. The coarseness and vulgarity of the latter ought not to be quoted (as they have been quoted by Dean Farrar) as an example of University conduct and life in Tarsus.

Strabo's account of the Tarsian enthusiasm for Hellenic education is very different from the picture given by Dion Chrysostom, who describes Tarsus about a century later as essentially a non-Hellenic and Oriental town, devoid of all the true qualities of Hellenism, and possessing only one excellence, *viz.*, that it enforced the strictest and closest veiling of women when they walked in the streets. Strabo suggests in his rather highly coloured picture that the Tarsians crowded their own and foreign Universities. Rome itself " was full of Tarsians," some of whom exercised a real power in Roman history through their personal influence with the Imperial family, and with other Romans of high rank. Besides Athenodorus and Nestor, already mentioned, the older Athenodorus, surnamed Kordylion, was the friend of the younger Cato, and died in his house. Strabo names many other Tarsians who had been distinguished in literature and philosophy, Antipater, head of the Stoic School in Athens and the chief opponent of Carneades, Ploutiades and Diogenes, both much-travelled philosophers, the latter also a poet, Artemidorus and Diodorus, and also a tragic poet Dionysides, one of the seven writers called " the Pleiad". Later, Plutarch mentions Diodorus as having visited Britain and Egypt and the Erythraean Sea and the land of the Troglodytes, led by his scientific curiosity.

Philostratus, however, writing at the beginning of the third century, gives a very unfavourable picture of the University of Tarsus in the reign of Tiberius (about the year that Strabo was writing), and mentions that Apollonius of Tyana, when he went to study there, was so offended with the manners of the citizens, their love of pleasure, their insolence, and their fondness for fine clothing, that he left the University and went to continue his studies at Aegae, on the Cilician coast farther to the east. But the work of Philostratus is unhistorical; in some degree he may be expressing the opinion entertained about the wealthy Tarsus in his own country and time, but to a large extent he was guided, I think, by the criticisms which Dion Chrysostom freely uttered in his two Orations to the Tarsians; and cannot be seriously weighed against Strabo's authority.

Tarsus in the reign of Augustus is the one example known in history of a State ruled by a University acting through its successive principals. For that reason alone, as a unique experiment in government, it has a permanent interest for modern scholars. Unfortunately, it is not easy to determine whether the experiment worked well. According to Strabo, a singularly good witness, it succeeded. The facts of history show that the city was extraordinarily prosperous for centuries afterwards. The faults which Dion describes in it are those that accompany overflowing prosperity; and the lack of the Hellenic spirit, which he blames, was really a proof that Hellenism had met and accommodated itself to Orientalism. It is characteristic of the general tendency of University life in a prosperous and peaceful Empire, that the rule of the Tarsian University was marked by a strong reaction towards oligarchy and a curtailment of the democracy: that also belongs to the Oriental spirit, which was so strong in the city. But the crowning glory of Tarsus, the reason for its undying interest to the whole world, is that it produced the Apostle Paul; that it was the one city which was suited by its equipoise between the Asiatic and the Western spirit to mould the character of the great Hellenist Jew; and that it nourished in him a strong sense of loyalty and patriotism as the " citizen of no mean city ".

§ XXIII. TARSUS UNDER THE EMPIRE.

For several centuries after the time of Augustus Tarsian history is a monotonous record of even, uneventful prosperity and peace. The faults which Dion Chrysostom blames in his two Tarsian orations are those which are fostered by too great prosperity, *viz.*, haughtiness, unwillingness to obey the government, and disposition to quarrel with rival cities: the last

fault was common to most of the great Græco-Roman cities
of the East. There was little real and healthy competition
between Tarsus and the cities which it regarded as rivals,
Mallos and Adana in the first century, Anazarbus at a later
time. Municipal quarrels were chiefly empty rivalry about
titles and dignity and precedence, and were calculated rather
to make the cities a subject of contemptuous ridicule in the
estimation of the Romans than to stimulate them to surpass
their rivals in real magnificence and great public works.
Yet even under these foolish quarrels there lay a basis of
reality, as Anazarbus represents a new growth in the upper
Cilician plain, Mallos at least a historical memory.

In truth Tarsus during the first century was the one great
city of Cilicia. The others were quite secondary. The
coinage of Tarsus far surpasses in mass that of all the other
cities of the Cilician plain combined. Strabo mentions that
it ranked as metropolis (of Cilicia); and it continued to be so
throughout the Imperial time. During the greater part of
the first century Cilicia was not a separate Province, but an
adjunct to Syria. Syrian troops were employed there in case
of need, and the supreme authority rested with the Imperial
Legate of Syria. The Province contained three parts, united
in loyal service to the Emperors and in the ritual of the
established Imperial religion as "the Commune of Syria-
Phœnice-Cilicia". In the time of Vespasian, probably, this
union was dissolved: in 74 A.D. the dependent kingdom of
Tracheia Cilicia was taken into the Empire as a Province
conjoined with the Cilician Plain, and Tarsus was metropolis
of the Province.

The organisation and the civilisation of the Roman Empire
laid a strong and compelling hand upon the country, and
produced remarkable results in the way of a balance and equi-

librium between the opposing forces of East and West, which were thus united in a mighty harmony. The two forces, the Oriential spirit and the Western, continued each in full strength, after the East had revived and begun to influence the Empire anew in many ways, by peaceful interpenetration, in art and in religion. The first attempt of the earlier Empire to impose European character on the land and its Provinces was abandoned definitely by Hadrian. It was in all probability under his rule, about 130-35, that the south-

Fig. 22.—The Two Temples at Tarsus "Common to Cilicia" with a garland above them ; both are hexastyle. Coin struck under the Emperor Commodus. The city bears the names of Hadrian and Commodus.

eastern region of Asia Minor was reorganised as the Triple Province Cilicia-Isauria-Lycaonia. Tarsus was the metropolis and president of the " Three Eparchiæ ".[79]

This title appears for the first time on its coins under Septimius Severus, 195-211 A.D.; but there is no reason to infer that the title was then first instituted ; on the contrary, there is every probability that Tarsus was metropolis of the Triple Province from the beginning. It was only in the third century that the habit of inscribing long boastful titles on the coins of the city was carried to such an extreme. The

Three Eparchiæ were never united in a single nation politically or a single Commune in the Imperial religion. The Koinon (Commune) of Lycaonia was distinct from the Koinon of Cilicia, and the latter probably included all parts of Cilicia. Temples of the Cilician Commune were erected at Tarsus,[80] which in the time of Commodus places on its coins the type of two temples "Common to Cilicia"; these temples evidently were dedicated to Hadrian and to Commodus, and they carried with them the title Neokoros, and Twice Neokoros (Fig. 22).

Fig. 23.—The Three Eparchiæ, Cilicia, Lycaonia, Isauria, crowning the Goddess of Tarsus. Coin struck under the Emperor Gordian, 235-238 A.D. Tarsus bears the names of Hadrian and Severus.

On the coin shown in Fig. 23 the three Eparchies, Cilicia, Isauria, Lycaonia, approach the enthroned genius of Tarsus to do homage. The city is represented seated on the rocks, not on a chair, as in the older coins (Fig. 20 and p. 187). There can be no doubt that a statue of the City goddess adorned some public place in Tarsus.

The nature of the Commune as the organised provincial cult of the Emperors, so to say the "State Church" of the Province, was shown on the golden crown which the provincial high priest wore. It was adorned with busts of the Emperors, which stood up from the golden circlet round the head of the wearer. On some coins of Tarsus, one of which is given in Fig. 24, this crown is shown. The artist was unable to represent properly the form of the crown, or the position of the busts above the circlet : one must understand that the Imperial heads rose straight from the circlet and fitted close round the high priest's head. There were certainly more Imperial heads than six on the crown. The deified Emperors

Fig. 24.—The Crown of the Chief Priest of Cilicia in the Imperial Religion ; a circlet of gold surmounted by busts of the Emperors. Coin struck under the Emperor Gordian, 235-238 A.D.

of the past, and the reigning Emperor or Emperors, should all have a place ; but on coins exactness in such details is not to be expected.[81] The figure of Victory holding a garland, also, is an addition made by the coin engraver, and does not belong to the real crown.

Such was the crown worn by the high priest and high priestess of every Province throughout the Empire. Such was the crown worn by the Galatarch, the high priest of Galatia, when he met St. Thekla in the street of Pisidian Antioch and rudely accosted her.[82] Here on a coin of Tarsus it denotes the office of Kilikarch or high priest of Cilicia, and the word Eparchikôn, in the genitive, within the crown, is to be construed with the word Kilikarchia, which is implied by the crown.   It means that in compliment to Tarsus the office had been held by Governors of the Province.   The same compliment is mentioned in the inscription quoted in note 79, where it is recorded that Tarsus alone of all the cities of the Province had been honoured by having Governors filling the offices of Demiourgos and Kilikarch.   It must be understood that the various cities had in succession to supply a person or a married pair to fill the Kilikarchate ; besides being a great honour, this was a great expense to the holder, and few could afford to take the office.   More than once, when Tarsus had to supply a Kilikarch, provincial Governors had paid the city the compliment of accepting the nomination.

The rivalry between Anazarbus and Tarsus belongs to the third century.   It had its origin in the growing divergence of character and interests between the Western sea plain with its three great cities and rivers and the upper or eastern plain on the Pyramus : the divergence grew more marked until at last it compelled Imperial recognition, and brought about the division of Cilicia Prima with its capital Tarsus from Cilicia Secunda with its capital Anazarbus about 395-9 A.D.[83] Anazarbus on its coins arrogated many titles, which Tarsus also used, *e.g.*, " Metropolis of the Nation," *i.e.*, the Province Cilicia, where the word Nation is the translation of the Latin Provincia : [84] it called itself " First, Loveliest, Greatest ": it claimed to be a meeting-place of the " Free Council of the Commune of the Province".   But it never claimed to be " Metropolis of the Three Eparchiæ " ; that title was reserved for Tarsus alone ; and this abstinence must be regarded as a proof that to Anazarbus had been formally granted the title of " Metropolis of the Province Cilicia," with the right to be a meeting-place of the Provincial Commune, but not the higher title, which was reserved for Tarsus. It was a great occasion for Anazarbus when Elagabalus honoured it by accepting the office of Demiourgos, as the chief magistrate was called. It boasted of this unique title about 218-220; and Tarsus could record no similar honour on its coins for some years, until Alexander Severus accepted the magistracy of the city.[85]

The loyalty of Tarsus to the Emperors was obtruded on

Fig. 25.—Athena and Nemesis surrounding the Fortune of Tarsus, " First, Loveliest, Greatest ". Coin struck under the Emperor Gordian III.

the notice of the world by the titles which it assumed with the permission of the Imperial government. It was Hadriane under Hadrian, Kommodiane under Commodus, Severiane under Severus, Antoniniane under Caracalla,[86] Makriniane under Macrinus, Alexandriane under Severus Alexander. Some of these titles were long retained, especially Hadriane ; but most of them were dropped at the accession of a new Emperor.

Fig. 25 is an example of the quaint groups of allegorical figures which were fashionable in later art. The Good

16

Fortune of Tarsus stands between Athena and Nemesis.
Nemesis has a cubit-rule in one hand, and plucks at the
shoulder of her tunic with the fingers of the other. At her
feet a griffin places his right fore-foot on a wheel at the feet
of Fortune, who carries the horn of plenty and the rudder,
the symbols which are appropriated to her in numismatic art.
Athena wears her usual crested Corinthian helmet, and is
armed with spear and shield. The purport of the associated
three figures is evident.

The picture of a ship under full sail, which appears on

FIG. 26.—Ship carrying from Egypt the "Corn of Tarsus". Coin struck
under the Emperor Caracalla, 211-217 A.D.

some coins of Tarsus, "Antoninian Severian Hadrianian," in
the time of Caracalla, might be interpreted as alluding to its
possession of a harbour (for that is the usual meaning of
this type on coins of a city, *e.g.*, at Ephesus in the coin
pictured on p. 229 of the *Letters to the Seven Churches*). But
at Tarsus it is only by inadvertence or from want of space
that the legend "Corn of Tarsus" is omitted in some coins,
though it occurs on most of them (Fig. 26). The legend
"Corn of Tarsus" with the type of a ship implies that the
corn which is meant was borne across the sea. One of

the interesting economic facts in the administration of the world-wide Empire was that scarcity in one Province was compensated by bringing into it the harvest of another Province. Egypt had been in Hellenistic times the granary of the Eastern Mediterranean; but under the Empire this source was closed to the Provinces, because the Egyptian harvest was reserved for the capital, and Egypt was under the absolute personal control of the Emperors. In some rare cases, however, the Emperors as a special favour gave a supply of corn from Egypt to some city—probably on occasion of a bad harvest. This favour was granted twice at least to Tarsus, once under Caracalla and once under Alexander Severus. The situation is clearly explained by comparison of two other coins. One bears the same type of the ship under sail; but the legend is "The Gift of Alexander to Ta(rsus) Me(tropolis)," and the Emperor represented is Alexander Severus. The other is a coin of Caracalla with the reverse type of Triptolemus in his car drawn by winged dragons, carrying over the world the knowledge of husbandry, and the legend "Corn from Egy(pt) for Tarsus".

In coins the small space available for lettering could contain only one statement; and on each of these coins one fact of a complex situation was singled out for commemoration. By combination of the various legends the whole situation is comprehended. The corn was a gift by the reigning Emperor, who was the lord of Egypt as his private property. He gave one or more shiploads to relieve the need of his dutiful city of Tarsus. The ships were the large transport vessels, which ordinarily conveyed the corn from Alexandria to Puteoli. In ordinary years the rich land of Cilicia doubtless produced sufficient corn for its inhabitants; but an occasional failure of the harvest had to be met by importing corn from abroad. In Egypt itself there sometimes occurred a famine, when the Nile failed; and the remote Pisidian town of Pogla, far from the sea, boasts in an inscription of having on one occasion sent corn to Alexandria.[87]   Even when the harvest was short in Egypt, the corn for the city of Rome must be provided, and Alexandria had to import from a different Province.   Pogla was an Imperial estate at that time, and the Emperor relieved the scarcity of the Egyptian city by sending corn from his Pisidian property, but did not interrupt the regular Roman transport service.

The Tarsian artists were not attentive to detail in representing ships.   In many cases they picture the ship with the large sail swelling out towards the stern; but in this case, Fig. 26, the artist represents the sail rightly impelled by the wind towards the prow.   He always represents the ship as moving under the force of sails and oars combined; but the large corn transports were certainly moved by sails alone, oars would be of no use in ships of that size.

PART III.

ANTIOCH.

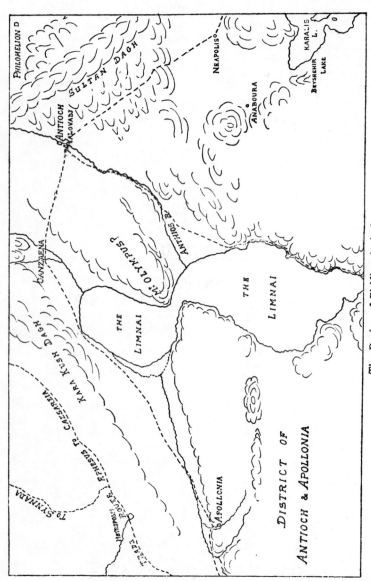

The Region of Pisidian Antioch.

ANTIOCH.

THE history of Pisidian Antioch falls into three periods: first, the early Hellenistic city from 300 to 25 B.C.; secondly, the Roman Colonia Caesareia Antiocheia during the first three centuries after the Province Galatia and the Colonia were instituted; thirdly, the re-Hellenised metropolis Antioch, after Roman language and custom died out and the Oriental spirit (but Orientalism modified by long contact with Hellenic and Roman customs) revived, probably somewhere about or soon after A.D. 212. Some would add an earlier period and the history of a pre-Hellenic and Phrygian town; but this depends on a doubtful interpretation of Strabo's description of Antioch, which we cannot accept. There was a Phrygian population around, and an important hieron of the Phrygian religion in the neighbourhood; but there is no reason to think that a city existed on the site before the Seleucid foundation about 300-280 B.C.

In Antioch we shall find elements of population similar to those which we have been observing in Tarsus, chiefly Anatolian, Greek and Jewish; but, owing to the difference in the proportion of the elements and in the general circumstances, there is a marked difference in the character and spirit of the two cities.

§ I. THE CITY AND ITS FOUNDATION.

The situation of Antioch is very fine, but the locality is now deserted, forlorn and devoid of ruins that possess any interest or beauty. The city occupied a low oblong plateau, varying from 50 to 200 feet above the plain that lies in front. It is lowest on the west side, where it faces the plain, and highest on the east, where it rises very sharp and steep from the bank of the river Anthios. The surface of the plateau has been so much transformed by the needs and works of life in a great city, the cutting down of hills, the doing away with slopes that were too steep, the filling up of hollows, the scarping of the outer edge to strengthen the defences—which always take place on a site long inhabited by a civilised and ingenious population, partly from plans of city improvement, partly from the action of nature—that in wandering over the site of Antioch in 1905 the writer was unable to form any conception of its original form before the transforming hand of man was applied to it. It lies about 3,500 to 3,800 feet above the sea level.

In shape the plateau of the city approximates to a rect-angle. On the east (one of the long sides) it is bounded by the deep, narrow, slightly curving glen of the river Anthios, which has chosen to cut its way from N.N.E. to S.S.W. between this outlying plateau and the higher hills that rise sharp from its opposite bank. The long glen of the Anthios is very picturesque, and in time of flood must present an impressive spectacle, when the waters rise high and fill the bottom of the narrow glen, far down below the edge of the plateau. The plateau must be nearly two miles in cir-cumference, and as it presents a fairly steep outer face, even where it is lowest, it must have been an imposing fortress when high strong walls crowned the outer face on all sides.

Coins of Antioch give a picture of the river-god ANTHIOS (p. 316) in the form consecrated by Greek art to the repre-sentation of the god of a river. He reclines resting his left

PLATE VI.

The desolate site of Pisidian Antioch.

See p. 249.

To face p. 248.

arm on an urn turned sideways, out of which water pours.
Behind him grows a reed.   On this coin, and on many
others, the river-god's body is more erect than in statues of
the same type; and this change sacrifices in some degree
the gentle slope of the figure from the raised head downwards to the feet, an artistic expression of the gentle down-
ward flow of the stream.   But the change accommodates
itself better to the shape of the coin: a figure which is too
much elongated does not fill the field of a coin so well as
one that is more bent.

The strength of the fortress was needed to withstand
attack from the Pisidian mountaineers, an unruly and
dangerous race.   Antioch was calculated to present an
almost impregnable front to such raids and sudden attacks
as enemies of that type were likely to make.   The ordinary
water supply was by an aqueduct which conducts the water
from a distance of several miles away in the Sultan-Dagh,
partly by an underground conduit, but for the last mile
borne on arches above ground.[1]   It would, of course, be easy
in case of war for besiegers to cut the aqueduct, and divert
the flow; but this would not cause more than great incon-
venience to the besieged city.   The river Anthios flows for
a long distance close under the city wall, and it would hardly
be possible for besiegers to prevent the garrison from ob-
taining water out of the river in sufficient quantity for the
necessities of life.

The photographs reproduced on Plates VI.-X. give some
idea how desolate the site of Antioch now is.   Plate X.,
taken from the north, shows the entrance to the gorge of the
Anthios, looking over the fertile and level ground towards
the northern edge of the city-plateau (which rises towards the
river), the cleft through which the Anthios finds its way, and

the higher hills on its left bank.   In Plate VI. the featureless
character of the site is painfully evident.   Plate VIII. shows
the scanty remains of the only Hellenic building of any consequence that we saw on the plateau.   It is on the western
side of the site, towards the north end ; and the view, which
is taken looking to the south-east, shows how high the plateau
rises on the eastern side towards the river.   Plate VIII.
reproduces a photograph of the best preserved part of the
aqueduct, a work of the best period.

In Plate IX. is shown the unsightly ruin, which Hamilton [2] thought might be the principal temple of Antioch, the
shrine of the God Men.   Near the highest part of the city,
which is on the north-east part of the plateau, a semicircular
hollow has been cut in the rocky side of the hill in such a
way that the rock walls of the semicircle rise quite perpendi-
cularly at the back, to the height of nearly 30 feet in parts,
while the front is open, except that a large mass of rock 20
feet square, with a square chamber cut in it, has been left in
the centre.   There is a row of holes, rather more than a foot
square, cut all round the rock walls, and it seems evident that
these holes were intended to receive beams.   These beams
reaching inwards towards the central square must have formed
a level platform.   It appeared to me in 1905 that some sort
of an Odeon or small Theatre must have been constructed in
this hollow, though I could not understand why a floor standing nearly 8 feet clear of the ground was wanted.   Hamilton
saw also the remains of a portico in front, "with broken
columns, cornices and other fragments," and regards the
whole place as "the adytum of a temple".   But a portico
would have been needed in front of a Theatre or Odeon.
Most of these remains have since Hamilton's time been carried
away for building purposes; and the same fate has happened

PLATE VII.

Remains of a Hellenistic building at Antioch.

To face p. 250.

to the remains which he saw in the hollow, "masses of highly finished marble cornices, with several broken fluted columns, 2 feet 8 inches in diameter".

The town has been much enlarged during the last few years, and a good waggon-road has been built to connect it with the Anatolian Railway at Ak-Sheher (Philomelion), while the road to the Ottoman Railway terminus at Dineir (Apameia) was also much improved. These useful works were executed, not by the government, but in great part by the railway companies, competing for the trade of the district.

The modern town of Yalowatch is also situated on the Anthios, a little lower down and on both sides of the stream. It is a widely scattered town, divided into twelve separate quarters (called *Mahale* in Turkish). Professor Sterrett suggests very ingeniously [3] that these correspond to twelve divisions or vici in the Roman city; and this may be regarded as highly probable in view of the permanence of ancient religious facts, for the political division in ancient times had always a religious foundation. This modern town extends nearly up to the edge of the ancient site, but from the middle of the modern town to the centre of the ancient site the distance must be quite a mile and a half.

Beyond doubt the ancient population of Antioch lived a good deal in the open country. The land is pleasant, part of it is rich and fertile, part contains high-lying pastures, and the territory stretches from the lofty range of Sultan-Dagh on the north-east away down in the direction of the great double lake called Limnai, about fifteen miles or more to the south-west. It is, however, doubtful whether Antiochian territory reached so far as the Limnai. The lake shore seems to have been occupied with villages, scattered over the great Imperial estates which will be described in a later section.   Those estates had originally been the property of the god, and Antiochian territory had been part of the estates, until the first Seleucid king gave part of the god's land to the garrison city which he founded on this magnificent site.   It is, however, possible that the city territory touched the Limnai at some point; but this depends on the interpretation of an uncertain symbol on a coin (Fig. 38), described in § IX.

Nothing is recorded about the date and circumstances of the foundation; but there can be little doubt that the city owed its origin to the first of the Seleucid kings, Seleucus Nikator, who named it after his father Antiochus, the deified head of the royal family.

An inscription[4] shows that the worship of Seleucus Nikator was established in the valley of Apollonia (which opens to the west from the Limnai); and, as this cult lasted into the Roman period, it must have been founded on a considerable scale with an insured revenue.   This establishment proves that Seleucus took an active interest in the important route which runs from Apameia through the valley of Apollonia by Antioch to Syria.   On this road the critical point is Antioch, where the path turns round the Limnai, and a sovereign who was strengthening his hold on the road could not miss this point, unless he chose some other place in the neighbourhood.   The water supply determined the exact site chosen; other defensive points could easily be found, but they were all disqualified by their weakness in respect of water during a siege.

The foundations made by the first Seleucus were intended to be a means of establishing and glorifying the whole family and not merely his single self.   They were certainly

PLATE VIII.

The Aqueduct of Pisidian Antioch.

See p. 249.

To face p. 252.

laid out on a comprehensive plan to bind together the whole Empire, and they were to be dynastic, not personal monuments. Hence the later Seleucid rule, that the city bore the name of the king who founded it[5] or of his royal consort, does not apply to the cities of Seleucus Nikator. Some he called after himself, but the most important bore the name of his father Antiochus as the head and guardian genius of the family; one at least on this same road took its title from Apollo[6] as the patron god of the dynasty (the successive kings being considered as manifestations of Apollo in human form on the earth), others of his mother Laodice and his wife Apama. The inclusion of the latter was significant, for it was she, an Asiatic, who conveyed the right of succession in Asia to her husband.[7]

Antioch was thus surrounded by a sea of purely Phrygian population and custom. The situation was, of course, similar in all Seleucid garrison cities : they were founded to be strongholds of the royal power, of a more Greek type, though far from purely Greek, amid Asiatic peoples. But it remained characteristic of the Pisidian Antioch that it continued to be the one centre of the Seleucid form of civilisation for a very large territory, as well as a bulwark against the whole strength of the Pisidian mountain tribes, while the land around continued to be mainly Anatolian and Phrygian in manners and religion, hardly affected even in the most superficial way by Hellenic influence (p. 294 ff.). This situation, by isolating the Seleucid colonists in Antioch so thoroughly, must have made them even more vividly conscious than the colonists in many Seleucid garrison-cities were of their dependence on the support of the kings and of the Seleucid capital Antioch in Syria, more opposed to their ever-present enemy the Phrygian and Pisidian

barbarian, and more devoted supporters of the Græco-
Asiatic type of civilisation which they represented. The
evidence, scanty as it is, points in this direction.

We have spoken of Pisidian Antioch as surrounded by
Phrygians and bordering on the Pisidian land. Such are
the topographical facts, and such are the accounts given by
the ancients, Strabo, Ptolemy, etc. In an inscription of
the city it is called "Mygdonian," from the old Phrygian
chief or king Mygdon.

Thee, Dionysios, here (in marble), the city Mygdonian Antioch has
[adorned with] the garland symbolic of justice and peace.[8]

The ornament of a garland, symbolical of the peace which
Dionysios, a soldier acting as chief of police for the Region
round Antioch, had produced by his good service, was placed
on the basis which supported the statue of Aurelius Dionysios, Regionary Centurion. The text belongs to the third
century, and is in Greek, though dedicated to an officer of
the Roman service. By that time Roman Antioch had
reverted to the former condition of a Hellenic city, and
even the official documents had come to be expressed in
Greek, whereas during the first and second centuries Latin
was (as we shall see below) the language not only of official
documents but also to a large extent of private inscriptions.

In another inscription the city is said to be in Phrygia.
Not until the Province Pisidia was formed about A.D. 295
was Pisidian Antioch in any strict sense a city of Pisidia.
Under the Romans it was geographically a city of Phrygia,
politically a city of the Province Galatia.

It is our first task to determine to what race belonged
these Seleucid colonists of Antioch. It was they who determined the character of the city.

PLATE IX.

Rock-cutting, generally supposed to be the Sanctuary of the God of Pisidian Antioch, perhaps only the site of an Odeon.

See p. 250.

To face p. 254.

§ II. THE JEWS IN PISIDIAN ANTIOCH.

In the other Pauline cities the presence of Jewish inhabitants is either proved by the authority of the Acts alone (as at Derbe and Lystra), or confirmed by clear evidence from other sources, but their status and rights in the city are either unknown or demonstrated only by indirect arguments. Even at Tarsus, where the evidence is most complete, the proof that there was a body of Jews, possessing the full rights of citizens and burgesses, results from a series of concurrent arguments, all pointing towards the same conclusion; but no record of any family of Jewish citizens remains except the family of Paul himself. The deficiency in this last respect may seem serious only to those who are on the outlook for opportunity to throw discredit on the trustworthiness of Acts; but, as a matter of fact, epigraphy rarely records such matters, and moreover hardly any Tarsian inscriptions have been preserved. In Iconium, Lystra and Derbe it remains uncertain whether the Jewish population had the status of resident aliens or of citizens; the former being more probable in Lystra, the latter in Iconium, while Derbe is wrapped in complete obscurity through absolute lack of evidence.

In the case of Antioch alone complete evidence has survived, and that in a curiously accidental way. The fact of citizenship is not often formally recorded in the epitaphs of any city, and, when it is recorded, there is usually some special reason; moreover Jews can rarely be traced in the epigraphy of such cities, because the men usually adopted Greek or Roman names, and thus have become undistinguishable. The inscriptions of Antioch are wholly taken up with matters of other kinds, and in none of them can any Jew be identified with certainty; but an epitaph of Apollonia reveals a Jewess of Antioch by her name Debbora. It belongs to the late second or the third century after Christ.

An Antiochian [by race], sprung from ancestors who held many offices of state in the fatherland, by name Debbôra, given in marriage to a famous man Pamphylus, [I am buried here,] receiving this monument as a return of gratitude from him for my virgin marriage.[9]

The evidence given in this brief inscription is singularly complete. Debbora was an Antiochian citizen by race, but was married to Pamphylus of Apollonia.

That Debbora was a Jewess seemed placed beyond reach of doubt by her name. The spelling is that of the Septuagint, whereas the spelling Deborah in the English Version is taken from the Hebrew text.

Debbora, an Antiochian citizen by descent, did not reside in Antioch, and the formula is therefore used which indicates the real citizenship of a person who resided in an alien city.[10] In her case the situation may possibly have been complicated by an additional fact; Pamphylus, her husband, may have been a citizen of Apollonia; and if that were so, the question of the right of intermarriage between citizens of the two cities would come up. This is a most difficult subject, and information fails us. If there were such right of intermarriage, Debbora would take the citizenship of her husband, and cease to be an Antiochian. But it is quite uncertain whether Pamphylus (whom we may suppose to have been a Jew,[11] probably) was a citizen of Apollonia: he may have been only a resident alien. It is also uncertain how far Roman custom or law interfered to permit intermarriage between citizens of different Eastern provincial cities; but after 212 A.D., when all citizens of provincial cities became Roman citizens, intermarriage certainly must have been legal. The epitaph of Debbora, however, to judge from the form of the letters, cannot be later than 212.

From whatever cause it resulted, the fact seems clear that Debbora did not become a citizen of Apollonia, but remained a resident alien, "Antiochian by race".[12]

The most significant words in the epitaph are the two which describe Debbora's ancestors as "having held many honours of the fatherland" (πολυτείμους πάτρης). The term "honours" (τιμαί *honores*) was regularly applied to the higher magistracies in self-governing cities. The word which we have rendered "ancestors" (γονεῖς) is used ordinarily in prose epitaphs in the sense of "parents"; but here in the language of verse it designates the male ancestors, who entered on the career of office (*cursus honorum*), and it looks back on a line of such ancestors for generations. The epitaph of Debbora may belong to the first or second century after Christ, more probably the first.

The inscription just mentioned is the only certain indication of a Jewish colony in Antioch; and it is fortunate that its evidence is so complete and far-reaching. It shows that for generations Jews of one family had been citizens of Antioch and had attained high offices. Elsewhere the proof had been pointed out that the existence of one single and solitary Jewish citizen in a Greek city was impossible[13]: there must be a separate class or "Tribe" of Jewish citizens in order to make it possible for any Jew to be a citizen. Such a "Tribe," bearing some Greek title, formed the means through which Jews could be members of this Hellenic city (for the early Antioch was Hellenic, a centre of Hellenism as adapted by Seleucid policy to Oriental conditions); it was by making the Jewish religion into the religious bond of their

17

own "Tribe" that the Jews could enter Greek city life and
hold offices of State. (See p. 176.)

The Jew who was a magistrate in any Greek city must
have been willing to shut his eyes to a good deal, tacitly to
acquiesce in a great deal of idolatrous ritual which was performed at every meeting for political or social purposes
under his presumed patronage. He must also have been
ready and successful in the conduct of public affairs and in
the art of wooing a constituency. In no other way was it
possible to win votes and gain an election. When Paul
visited Antioch, the original Jewish Colony had been for
three centuries and a half exposed to the influence which
such practices exert on the character of men, and a profound
effect must have been produced on a race naturally receptive
and progressive. It was inevitable that the Jews of Antioch
should become very different in character from the narrow
class of Palestinian Jews; they were Hellenised, Greek-
speaking, able to move freely and win success in the free
competition of a Hellenic self-governing city. Yet that
standing miracle always remains: they were still Jews in
feeling and religion, citizens of the Hellenic city of Pisidian
Antioch, yet men of Judaea, as the centuries passed. The
religious teaching of the home and the synagogue held them
firmly in the national character.

It may seem strange that no memorial of the Jews at Antioch should have been found among the considerable number
of Antiochian inscriptions, and that the accident of a Jewish
woman residing at Apollonia should furnish the only proof
that Jews were citizens at Antioch. But the same dearth
of information exists about the Jewish colonies in Phrygia
and Lydia: only the rarest and scantiest references exist in
epigraphy to those large and important bodies of people,

Elsewhere it has been suggested [14] that a certain P. Anicius Maximus, commander of the army in Egypt under Claudius, to whom in his native city of Antioch an inscription of honour was raised by the citizens of Alexandria, may have been a Jew; and that the influence of the large body of Jewish citizens in Alexandria may have been the originating cause of this action in the remote Phrygian city. Anicius Maximus served as an officer of the Second Legion Augusta in Britain, A.D. 44, and was decorated for his conduct there. He then was promoted to the command in Egypt; and it was perhaps about A.D. 50 or soon after that the dedication in his honour was ordered by the great city of Alexandria. The inscription was engraved on a basis, which may have supported a statue. But without further evidence this suggestion must remain a mere empty hypothesis.

§ III. THE GREEK COLONISTS IN EARLY ANTIOCH.

It has been shown [15] that Jews and Greeks were the two educated races, to whom especially the Seleucid kings trusted as colonists and makers of a higher civilisation in the Anatolian garrison cities. Strabo mentions that Antioch was a colony from Magnesia on the Maeander, but gives no information as to the manner or date of the foundation. We must understand that in some circumstances otherwise unknown, Seleucus Nikator brought a body of Magnesians to people his new city. Strabo says nothing about any other class of inhabitants; and this would suggest that the Magnesians formed the bulk of the population, and that the city was really a new foundation, not a mere transformation of a previously existing city. Both these inferences are in agreement with all the rest of our vague and scanty information. Strabo would not be likely to have

any information about a Jewish element in the city; for, as
we have seen, that element was concealed under Greek
forms and names, and the Greeks were never ready to acknowledge that Jews had any part in founding a Hellenic
city.   Only when complaining to some over-lord against
their Jewish fellow-citizens as not taking fair part in the
life of the city,[16] do they seem ever to have admitted that
Jews formed an element in a Hellenic city.

Strabo's evidence is entirely confirmed by the epitaph
found in Rome of an Antiochian who had travelled to the
great city of the Empire, and probably settled there :—

A Magnesian of Phrygia (am I); and Appe, devoted as a virgin to the
Scythian goddess (Artemis Tauropolos), nursed me in the olive-clad Anthian
plain.[17]

That "Magnesian of Phrygia" should be a poetic equiva-
lent of "Antiochian" is in exact agreement with Strabo.
In both authorities all thought of a native Phrygian or a
Jewish element in the population of the city is lost.

§ IV. The Phrygians of Antioch.

That in the Seleucid garrison cities generally there was
a native element in the population may be taken as practically certain.   A city peopled purely by foreigners might
have been efficient as a military stronghold, but could never
have been serviceable in the other purpose for which those
colonies were intended, *viz.*, in acting as a civilising centre
from which the type of manners and education favoured by
the Seleucid policy might spread over the surrounding land
and people.   The native element in the cities acted as an intermediary between the foreign colonists and the surrounding natives; the Phrygian citizens shared in the rights and
in the education of the colonists, while blood and feeling and

language united them at first with the surrounding population, until the Hellenised civilisation proved too strong, and
they began to feel themselves real Hellenes.   At Antioch,
whether it be that the proportion of colonists to natives was
unusually large, or that the early date of foundation and
other causes had resulted in thorough Hellenisation of the
native element in the city by the colonists, or that certain
influences had kept the surrounding population from being
affected by the Græco-Asiatic education of the city, there
seems to have been a very distinct separation and contrast
between the urban and the rustic people.   Probably all three
reasons contributed to produce this result.   Here we have
not the usual state of relations which elsewhere existed
between country and Seleucid city; there is not such a
simple uniform progress as is usual in Seleucid States, where
the rustics were uneducated and ignorant persons, who by
degrees acquired an interest and share in the civilisation
of the city as education gradually spread from the centre of
population.   There is apparent, especially on the north-
west and west of Antioch, a totally different kind of custom
and society, non-Hellenic in character (p. 293 f.); and there
was a broad and growing gap between the Hellenic city
Antioch and the population of the country district around.

The evidence, then, scanty as it is, points to the conclusion that the Hellenistic Antioch was rather a Greek
colony than a Phrygian city Hellenised.   The Greek colonists predominated; and, although a Phrygian element in the
city must be supposed, yet either it was not so numerous as
to affect the character of the city, or it was so thoroughly
Hellenised as to acquiesce in the Hellenic spirit.

Now we observe that Apollonia, the neighbouring city,
which we take to be a companion foundation made by

Seleucus Nikator, retained something of the same character
throughout the Roman period. It was never Romanised by
Italian colonists, as Antioch was; and hence its inscriptions
of the Roman time show us the character of the Hellenistic
Apollonia, whereas the inscriptions of Antioch in the Roman
time show a Romanised and Latin Antioch. Apollonia
regularly styled itself a " colonial " city, as no other Seleucid
foundation does. Its inhabitants boasted on coins and inscriptions that they were entirely strangers and colonists:
" the Apolloniatai (who are) Lycian and Thracian colonists ".[18]
We are warranted in assuming, on the authority of Strabo,
that the people of Hellenistic Antioch had a similar feeling.

§ V.   Antioch a City of Galatia.

That Pisidian Antioch was a part of the Roman Province
Galatia in the first century needs now no proof, since Professor E. Schürer, the warmest and most distinguished
opponent of this view, has withdrawn his opposition. The
only doubt that remained was as to the date when this
connection ceased. A large part of south-western Galatia
was taken from it and incorporated in the new Province of
Lycia-Pamphylia in A.D. 74. Another large slice of south-
eastern Galatia, including the cities of Derbe and Isaura,
was transferred to the new Province called the Three
Eparchies (Cilicia-Lycaonia-Isauria) somewhere about 138
A.D. After deducting these parts from the southern half
of the large first-century Province, there remained a narrow
strip of territory running along the west and north and east
coasts of the Limnai, and the north and east and south
coasts of lake Karalis (Bey-Sheher-Giol), with regard to
which evidence was defective. On the one hand this territory was almost completely separated from the main part

of Galatia by a great wedge of the Province Asia which intervened. Especially the extreme western part of the territory, including Antioch and Apollonia, a long and narrow strip of land, almost entirely surrounded by the two Provinces Asia and Pamphylia, seemed singularly unsuited to be a part of the Province Galatia. Moreover Ptolemy mentions Antioch as a city of the district Pisidia in the Province Pamphylia.

On the other hand, Ptolemy mentions both Apollonia and Pisidian Antioch as cities of the Province Galatia, and this fuller statement outweighs his other mention of Antioch in Pamphylia, suggesting that the latter is erroneous. Moreover, these cities must either have been left to Galatia or transferred to Pamphylia or to Asia : now they were not assigned to Pamphylia, for epigraphic proof is abundant at Antioch that the city belonged to Galatia long after the enlargement and reorganisation of Pamphylia in A.D. 74; and there is not the slightest reason to think that Antioch could ever have been given to Asia. Finally, the lost Acta of the martyrs Alphius and others seem to have showed that Antioch was still part of Galatia in the time of Diocletian (*Acta Sanctorum*, 28 Sept., p. 563), and the brief quotation from the Acta in the Menologium Sirletianum, to the effect that Antioch was part of Phrygia Galatica, seems trustworthy.[19]

As we shall see in Part IV., § IV., the Roman colonies Iconium and Lystra were retained in the Province Galatia in order to effect a continuity between the two far-distant parts of the Province, which without Iconium would have consisted of two territories wholly disjoined from one another.

On these grounds I ranked Antioch as a Galatian city (and with it Apollonia, which must be classed with it) throughout the second and third centuries, in *Historical Commentary on Galatians*, pp. 177 f., 209 f., though quite acknowledging that a certain doubt might still be felt. All doubt, however, was removed by the discovery in 1905 of a group of milestones eight miles west of Apollonia on the great road, Antioch-Apollonia-Apameia, described above ; one of them, dated A.D. 198, contains the name of the provincial Governor, Atticius Strabo, who is known to have governed Galatia in that year and to have renovated the roads of that Province.   It is therefore certain that the whole Region of Antioch belonged to Galatia throughout the first and second centuries, and there seems no possibility that any change in organisation of the Province can have occurred between 198 and 295.   About the latter year Diocletian broke up the Province Galatia ; he took South Galatia, including Iconium, enlarged it by adding parts of Asia and Pamphylia, and constituted it as the Province Pisidia.

Along with Antioch the whole of the large Imperial estates adjoining the Limnai and Lake Karalis must be reckoned to Galatia, so far as such estates belonged to any Province. They doubtless formed part of the *Regio* of Antioch already alluded to ; and the soldiers stationed at the Colonia were charged with the maintenance of order in the estates, if called upon by the Imperial representatives who managed those vast properties.

§ VI. CHARACTER OF THE ORIGINAL HELLENIC CITY.

Apart from the few facts mentioned in the preceding sections, the history of the Hellenistic city Antioch is extremely obscure.   Strabo mentions that in 189 B.C., when the Seleucid power over Asia Minor was destroyed, Antioch was made a free city by the Romans.   For 150 years it

seems to have remained in this condition, a self-governing sovereign state, maintaining the Hellenic system of autonomy and education in the borderland between the
servile country of Phrygia and the free but barbarous
Pisidian mountain-tribes. We can only vaguely infer what
was the spirit of the city in this period, for not a single
memorial is preserved above ground, though doubtless
excavation would disclose in a deeper stratum monuments
which belong to that earlier time.

The facts from which we have to judge are the following.
In the first place, it continued to feel itself a Hellenic city.
It did not sink back to the level of a mere Oriental and
Phrygian town. Centuries later we find that its people
spoke of themselves as Magnesians residing in Phrygia:[20]
the Magnesian origin of the Greek colony was still living in
their minds. The same thought was fresh in the memory of
the surrounding population, when Strabo travelled across
Asia Minor and passed through Philomelion, the city on
the other side of the lofty ridge of Sultan-Dagh.

The geographer did not visit Antioch or see it with his
own eyes: he only heard about it as situated on the opposite side of the mountains from Philomelion. His description of the two cities and of the intervening mountain-ridge
shows clearly that he knew only the Philomelian side, and
assimilated in imagination the Antiochian side, which he
had not seen, to the side which he knew. On the latter
side the landscape is a deep-lying, perfectly level valley
from which rises sharp and steep the great ridge of Sultan-
Dagh. On the Antiochian side there is neither a level
valley nor a well-defined mountain ridge: it is only in the
more distant view from the west that the continuity and
grandeur of Sultan-Dagh is realised: the country near the

mountains is very rough and undulating, with ridges of hills considerable in size, which reach back to merge themselves gradually in the superior mass of Sultan-Dagh.

Strabo's description, therefore, is founded, not on what the Antiochians thought of themselves, but on what other people beyond the mountains thought of them. He describes Antioch as a free Hellenic city, and this means a great deal; it implies free institutions, elective form of self-government, popular assemblies, and above all a certain well-established system of education for the young, which was continued throughout their later life by their experience as citizens and voters, producing in them a general knowledge of and interest in political facts and in questions of domestic and foreign policy, on which they had often to vote in the Assembly or Ekklesia—and producing in them also a pride of birth as Magnesians, a pride of education as Hellenes, and a contempt for the slavish Oriental Phrygians or the barbarous Pisidians. All this has to be inferred, but can be inferred with perfect confidence. Excavations to prove the facts by the discovery of written documents of the period are much to be desired.

The only epigraphic evidence which bears on the history of the first Antioch is an imperfect inscription found at Magnesia on the Meander, the parent-city of Antioch: this document is one of a long series of decrees passed by many Hellenic cities in recognition of the privileges of the Magnesian goddess Artemis. In one of the decrees, where the name of Antioch occurs without any distinguishing epithet, Kern (who has published the whole series) understands that the document emanated from Pisidian Antioch; and there can be no question that he has good reason for doing so.[21] These decrees were made during the last years of the third century before Christ in response to courteous messages conveyed by Magnesian ambassadors to the leading Hellenic cities of Asia and of Greece, and among others to Pisidian Antioch.

This decree in honour of the Magnesian Artemis entirely confirms the account which we have given, of Antioch, proving that it was recognised as a Hellenic city by its neighbours, that it remembered its relation to its parent-city and acknowledged its obligations to Hellenism generally.

This event belongs to the third century before Christ; but there is no reason to think that the Hellenic spirit died out in the following century. Antioch lay on a great commercial highway. It was in easy and constant communication with many other Hellenic cities, accessible readily to ambassadors from them (such as had brought the request from Magnesia regarding the worship of Artemis), and this intercourse exercised a strong influence in maintaining the spirit of Hellenism. The whole course of contemporary history shows that Hellenism was an undiminished power at that time in Western Asia. The whole burden of proof would lie with one who asserted that Hellenism died out in Antioch during the last two centuries before Christ, for the assertion is contrary to all the probabilities of the case and the analogy of other west-Asian centres of Hellenism.

In 39 B.C. Antioch with Apollonia and the whole of Pisidia and Pisidian-Phrygia, was given by Antony to Amyntas the last king of Galatia; and thus this large district became part of the Galatian realm. While Antioch now ceased to be a free city, it is not probable that any serious change was made in its internal affairs. It was no longer a sovereign state; it ceased to have a foreign policy; it was controlled by the king, and probably paid tribute to him. But all analogy points to the opinion that it continued to administer its own internal affairs by its own elected magistrates. In any case the kingly period was too short to affect seriously the spirit of the city, for Amyntas was soon killed in battle against the Pisidian mountaineers; and he bequeathed his whole property and realm to the Roman Empire.

§ VII. The Roman Colony of Pisidian Antioch.

A new period in the history of Antioch began in 25 B.C., when the country passed into the possession of Rome at the death of Amyntas. The city was then made a Roman Colony. The exact date of the foundation is not recorded, and absolute certainty cannot be attained; but there can be little doubt that the statement which is usually made by the numismatists is correct, and that the establishment of the Colony took place as soon as the Roman dominion over the kingdom of Amyntas, which now became the Province Galatia, was organised. The name Caesareia Antiocheia, by which the city was henceforth designated, marks it as separate from the other Pisidian Colonies, which were all called Julia, most of them Julia Augusta [22]; and if its foundation belonged to a different time, it must have been earlier and not later than them. Now the other Pisidian Colonies were founded about 7-6 B.C., and probably are connected with the government of Quirinius (Cyrenius), who commanded the armies of the Province Syria in the war against the Pisidian mountaineers at that time.[23] Antioch, being older, may therefore safely be connected with the first organisation of the new Province.

It was a real elevation in rank and dignity that was conferred on the Hellenic city Antioch, when it was constituted and refounded as a Roman Colony. It was thus placed in the highest class of provincial cities: it was made, so to say, a piece of the Imperial city, a detached fragment of Rome itself, separated from Rome in space, but peopled by Romans, *i.e. coloni*, who were of equal standing and privileges in the eye of the law with the citizens of Rome—*cives optimo iure*, according to the technical formula.

The *coloni*, or citizens of the *Colonia*, new inhabitants introduced from the West, for the most part veteran soldiers of the legion Alauda,[24] must be clearly and broadly distinguished from the older Hellenic population, who now ranked only as dwellers, *incolae*, in their own city, and who did not possess the same rank and rights as the *coloni*. The Antiochian Hellenes did not forthwith become Roman citizens and *coloni*; the latter were Roman citizens in their own right before they became *coloni*. But still even the old Hellenic citizens had some share from the first in the increased dignity of the city. They were certainly on a more favoured and honoured footing than the citizens of ordinary Hellenic cities. They were, probably, freed from direct taxation and enjoyed some other privileges; but no evidence remains on the spot, and it is not possible to do more than speak in general terms from the analogy of the *incolae* in other Roman *coloniae*. Their most important privilege, however, lay in the future: they had a more favourable opportunity than the citizens in ordinary Hellenic cities of attaining the coveted honour of the Roman citizenship. The success of the Roman government in permanently conciliating the loyalty of the provincial population [25] was founded on the settled principle of Imperial administration, according to which the peoples were regarded as being all in a process of education and training to fit them for the honourable estate of full Roman citizenship. The ultimate destiny of the Empire was that all freemen should attain this honourable position; and that destiny was achieved, perhaps rather prematurely, by Caracalla about A.D. 212; but, whether or not he hurried on the final stage too rapidly, this was the goal to which the Imperial policy had been tending from the beginning. As a first stage nations on the outer fringe of the Empire were commonly placed under the rule of client kings, whose duty it was not merely to preserve order, but to instil a habit and spirit of orderliness into their subjects and to naturalise among them the first principles of Roman systematic method in government. After a certain time of such training the people was reckoned worthy of being formed into a Roman Province.[26] Such was the history of Palestine under Herod, of Pontus under Polemon, of Galatia under Amyntas, of Cilicia Tracheia under Antiochus IV., and of many other countries.

When a new Province like Galatia was organised, its different parts and cities were variously treated according to their fitness for the duties of loyal service to the Empire. The most backward parts were left in the old tribal condition, as was, for example, the case with the Homonades, who had killed Amyntas and were at a later time subdued by Quirinius: at a much later time such tribes generally received the city organisation. The city was the proper unit in Roman administration; and wherever there existed a Hellenic city in the new Province, it was made a city in the Roman system and a unit in the Province. In such a city the most influential, wealthy and energetic citizens were gradually elevated to the Roman citizenship; and these

formed a city aristocracy, whose weight and authority in the
city rested on wealth, privilege, energy and ability. The
highest and most honoured class among the Provincial cities
consisted of the *Coloniae*. These contained a considerable
body of Roman citizens, and their whole tone and spirit
was thereby affected and Romanised. The amusements,
the public exhibitions, the education, were more Roman in
the *Coloniae* than in the surrounding Hellenic cities: so
also were the magistrates, the public language, the law and
the institutions generally. In this Roman atmosphere the
rest of the population, the *incolae*, lived and moved; they
caught the Roman tone, adopted Roman manners, learned
the Latin tongue, and were promoted to the Roman citizenship more freely and quickly than were the people of
Hellenic cities. In most cases, probably in almost every
case, Roman citizenship was made universal among the free
population (including the original inhabitants of the city) at
an early date.[27] That seems to have been the case at Antioch. The inscriptions, Greek and Latin alike, show no
trace of Hellenes, but only of Romans. Every free inhabi-
tant of the city, of whom epigraphic record survives, bears
the full Roman name, which marks him as a Roman citizen.[28]
This seems to constitute a complete proof that the entire city
became Roman at a comparatively early date, though later
than the Pauline period.

Wherever and whenever the number of Roman citizens
became large, their position as a local aristocracy necessarily
suffered. It was no longer possible to maintain that standard
of wealth on which the influence of an aristocracy must be
supported. Under the early Empire, when there were in
an Eastern city only a few Roman citizens, some of Italian
origin, others from the leading families of the old Hellenic

city, these formed a true aristocracy in the city. But when all freemen became Roman citizens in A.D. 212, there was no longer any distinction; there were no people to whom the Roman citizens could be superior except the slaves. The lines of class distinction in the third and later centuries were drawn anew. It was no longer an honour to bear the three names of a Roman, for all had an equal right to the three names; and the old system of Roman personal names gradually ceased to be attended to or maintained in the Eastern Provinces. A new period and new fashions had begun.

To a certain extent a similar change took place in Pisidian Antioch, when the whole free population of the city attained the honour of Roman citizenship; and this honour necessarily ceased to be an object for the older population to aim at. But the lustre of Roman citizenship did not disappear, for though all free Antiochians were now Romans, yet the surrounding world of Phrygia and Pisidia still remained outside the pale of Roman citizenship, and thus all the Antiochian Romans could feel their superiority to the mass of the Provincials; they were proud that Antioch was a Roman town, a part of the great governing Imperial city.

When did this change take place? When were all the old population of Antioch raised to the rank of Romans? It is not possible to specify the date; but one cannot suppose it was much, if at all, earlier than the second century. The cities of Spain were honoured by Vespasian with mere Latin rank, a step on the way to Roman rank, in A.D. 74. The full Roman honour was accorded to Antioch probably later, and not earlier. Hence we must conclude that in the time of St. Paul's visits to Antioch, the mass of his hearers were still not Roman citizens, but they all looked forward to that rank as a possible honour to be attained in the future.

PLATE X.

The Plateau of Pisidian Antioch, and the Glen of the River Anthios, looking from the north-east.

See p. 249.

PLATE XI.

Looking across Konia to the Twin Peaks of St. Philip and St. Thekla.

To face p 272. *See pp.* 318, 376, 380, 389.

The mere presence in their city of a considerable Italian population gave them higher privileges, and was a distinction to all the inhabitants of every class. Even those who were not Romans were on the way to become Romans in course of time, as a reward of merit and loyalty.

Not merely gratitude for the past and hope for the future made the Antiochian population strongly philo-Roman, but also the keen sense of daily advantages produced the same result. As chief city of the southern half of the Province Galatia, Antioch was the governing centre of a large country; it was frequently visited by the Roman governors of the Province [29] with their large train of attendants (which would cause considerable influx of money into the city and thus tend to enrich the merchants and shopkeepers); great public exhibitions of games and wild beasts and gladiators were held there, which would attract large numbers of visitors and sightseers, all spending their money; the courts of justice held by the governors in the city likewise brought to the city many litigants and enriched the population. The description given by Dion Chrysostom in his oration delivered at Apameia-Celaenae of the crowds and the wealth which were brought to that city owing to its position as a leading Roman centre of administration, may be applied to Antioch in a higher degree. The dignity and the wealth of almost every person in Antioch depended mainly on its rank as a Roman city in the Province Galatia; and its Provincial standing was the most important factor in its history during the first century. Hence "the Province," *i.e.* Rome as it appeared in the land,[30] must have bulked largely in the minds of the Antiochian populace; and, if the Church of Antioch claimed to represent its city,[31] it felt itself to be a Church of Galatia.

18

The tale of St. Thekla, when read in the light of Dion Chrysostom's oration, gives a pretty picture of the assemblage which gathered in Antioch at a great festival of the Imperial religion, presided over by a high priest of the Emperor (*Church in the Roman Empire*, p. 396).

The pride of Antioch in its colonial and Roman character inspires many of the representations on its coin. Most of the types usual and characteristic in Roman Coloniae occur, *e.g.*, the founder ploughing the furrow that marked its limits when it was founded (a specimen of which at Lystra is

FIG. 28.—The Roman Standards at Antioch.

shown in Fig. 53); the she-wolf with the twins (as at the Colony Iconium, Fig. 45). The military character of Antioch is blazoned as Roman, not Greek, in the standards, which are a common type, especially on the late coins of Antioch. They are not to be interpreted as the standards of troops stationed at Antioch; they are simply reproductions of the typical Roman flags seen especially on Imperial coins; the coinage of the Colonia was modelled on that of Rome itself. The most frequent group of standards is the widespread one of a *vexillum* (the flag of a detachment of troops serving apart from the main body) between two *signa* (flags of single companies or maniples of a legion). Sometimes, as in Fig. 28, eagles perch over all the three flags: these are to be understood in a general sense as symbols of Roman war and victory, not as imitated from the standard appropriate to any particular unit in the Roman army. There is no system to be observed in the variations of the standards on coins of Coloniae like Antioch: they seem purely capricious, and only imply that the artists were not skilled in these military details and did not aim at accuracy and truth. It

Fig. 29.—The Emperor Gordian offering Sacrifice beside the Standards.

is doubtful whether in Fig. 28 the coin artist intended mere round bosses, or medallions with heads of Emperors (as the draftsman has taken them); the former is more probable and would be truer to Roman facts.

In Fig. 29 the Emperor Gordian III. stands beside the standards, pouring a libation on a burning altar (whose two handles characterise it as portable). Two of the standards are surmounted by upright crowns, the third by a Victory carrying a crown in her hands: the details of these standards are very uncertain, owing to the poor preservation and the

original rudeness of the coin. The Emperor has one end
of the toga like a veil over his head in the archaic fashion
of priestly service : he is to be understood as performing the
religious ceremonial of the army at the holy place in the
camp where the standards were stored together. On his
dress compare Fig. 53.

In accordance with the purpose for which the Colonia had
been founded, its coins frequently bear the type of Victory
in many varieties. Sometimes the goddess advances, bearing

Fig. 30.—Two Victories fixing a shield on a palm tree : at its foot two
captives (coin of the Emperor Gordian III.).

in her hands a wreath and a palm branch. Sometimes she
stands, carrying a trophy: or the patron god of the city,
Men, raises this figure of Victory on his hand (Fig. 33).
Sometimes (as in Fig. 30) two Victories place a shield on a
palm tree, at the foot of which two captives are seated.
Sometimes the goddess sits on a cuirass, and writes on a
shield, which she holds on her knees: this type may be
compared and contrasted with the coin of Derbe (Fig. 52),
where the goddess stands and writes on a shield.

The outward appearance of the city was made as Roman

as possible. Instead of the old classification into Tribes, the population and the town were divided into *Vici :* the names of six of these are known, and they are purely and obtrusively Roman, *Patricius, Aedilicius, Tuscus, Velabrus, Cermalus, Salutaris*—among them several of the most famous street-names of Rome; and it is a plausible conjecture of Professor Sterrett that there were twelve *vici*, as there are twelve quarters (*mahale*) in the modern town. The magistrates were those usual in Roman Coloniae, Duoviri Iure Dicundo and Quinquennales, Aediles, Quaestors and Curators. There was a priesthood of Jupiter Optimus Maximus; also one or more flamens. The senators were called Decuriones, the senate was an Ordo.

The tale of St. Thekla affords the proof that exhibitions, euphemistically called *venationes*, in which criminals were exposed to wild beasts, were usual; such exhibitions were never as popular in Greek as in Roman cities. The Ordo and the Populus concurred in paying honours to distinguished citizens or strangers, instead of the Boule and Demos of a Greek city. The Populus seems to have expressed its will more by acclamation in the theatre than by formal voting in public meetings.

It is in agreement with the strong Roman feeling and custom which characterised Antioch in the first century of our era that the population are not called by Luke Hellenes or Greeks, but only the Plebs or the Gentiles. The latter is a wider term, which included at once Greeks and Romans and Phrygians and other native races.

§ VIII. HELLENISM IN PISIDIAN ANTIOCH.

While the spirit and tone of Roman loyalty was thus dominant in Pisidian Antioch during the first century, there is no reason to think that Hellenic civilisation and manners were entirely displaced by Roman. It is much to be desired that excavation should be made on the site, in order to give some clear objective evidence on this point; but analogy and general considerations tend to show that Greek ways and Greek education must have maintained themselves in the city, even while the Roman spirit was most thoroughly dominant. Rome was never hostile to Greek custom and Greek law in the East: it recognised that in Asia Greek civilisation was an ally, not an enemy, nor even a competitor. The civilisation which Rome sought to spread over western Asia was bilingual. Accordingly, all probability points to the opinion that Greek was the familiar language spoken at Antioch in the home life, except among the Italian immigrant or colonist families, and, even among these, the knowledge of Greek gradually spread in course of time. Thus it came about that as the Roman vigour died and the Oriental spirit revived during the third century, Greek seems to have become the practically universal language of the Antiochian population, though some few inscriptions recording government documents were written in Latin as late as the fourth century. Hence also it is quite in accordance with the circumstances, that Greek was the language used in the synagogue.

To trace the disuse of Latin and the recurrence to Greek as the public and formal language of the *Colonia* would be a useful task, but as yet this cannot be essayed. Though the inscriptions are numerous, no regular system of dating them was ever employed in Antioch and no era seems ever to have been used there. The want of any chronological system here shows by contrast how useful even a bad system of dating by some local era was in many cities of

Asia Minor; still more, how important a step was made
when a uniform era of the Province came into general use
throughout a whole region, as, for example, in the cities of
Asian Phrygia, or when the Seleucid era, reckoning from
312 B.C., was brought into widespread employment in the
Seleucid Empire and lasted in some parts of Syria for many
centuries. This invention of a useful general system of
chronology was one of those apparently small things which
lie in reality at the basis of the social fabric and help to
form the foundations on which educated society rests. It
was in the Græco-Asiatic cities that this important advance
in the methodical organisation of society was made. It
was among them that common employment of a uniform
era for a large country was first carried into practical effect. The cities of Greece thought it a point of honour to
employ a purely municipal system of dating by the name of
the annual magistrates of the city where the document was
executed. This Greek method, which naturally was unintelligible beyond the limits of the single city, was imitated
in Rome; and owing to the wide Imperial sway of Rome,
the dates by consuls became generally intelligible over the
Empire, though such a complicated system formed a serious
bar to practical usefulness, as it gave no indication of the
interval that lay between any two dates.

Neither Latin nor Greek inscriptions in Antioch were
dated by any system or in any way. A number of the
Latin documents, however, can be assigned to a narrow
period or a definite reign by internal evidence and the
mention of some known person, but the Greek inscriptions
are almost all quite vague, and internal evidence is rarely
of any use for dating them. The lettering furnishes little
evidence under the middle and later Empire, for forms were

at that period employed capriciously and without any uniformity or principle of development. It is possible to argue in some cases from the forms of letters that an inscription, or a group of inscriptions, is late and belongs to the third or fourth century, or that it is early and belongs to the first century ; but it is unsafe to go beyond such vague inferences. Above all, it is utterly impossible at this period to arrange a series of inscriptions in chronological sequence on grounds of lettering alone. We can however state confidently that the Antiochian Greek inscriptions of the Roman time belong in general to a later period than the Latin ; so that Greek must have strengthened its footing in the Colonia as time passed. By an indirect argument, also, it can be shown that the use of Greek in the public documents of the Colonia can hardly have occurred earlier than the third century after Christ.

The Colonia Lystra dedicated a statue of Concord to its sister Colonia Antiocheia,[32] thus claiming to stand in the same category with the great Roman capital of Southern Galatia. The inscription on the basis of this statue was in Greek. The date is uncertain. The excellent shape and clear cutting of the letters favour a fairly early time ; but the public nature of the monument would demand very careful engraving at whatever period it was made. Still one may confidently rank it, so far as extant remains go, among the earliest in the series of Greek inscriptions of Roman Antioch, and certainly the earliest public Greek inscription of the Colonia. It may be regarded as certain that Lystra would have been very chary of using Greek in addressing her sister Colonia and claiming kinship with the Roman metropolis of the Province ; and we must infer that, when this inscription was composed, Lystra had entirely lost the ability to write Latin and engrave a document in that language.   Now, Latin was employed in Lystra for inscriptions at least as late as the reign of Trajan, A.D. 98-117.[33] The dedication of the statue of Concord, therefore, could not be dated much earlier than about 150 A.D.   Further, the colonial coinage of Lystra was still maintained under Faustina the younger and Marcus Aurelius, 161-75 A.D.   Those coins were struck in Latin; and that language, therefore, was still not forgotten entirely in Lystra.   Accordingly, the Antiochian dedication is not likely to be much earlier than

FIG. 31.—Peace (or Concord ?) hurrying to Antioch carrying olive branch and sceptre (coin of the Emperor Decius, about 250 A.D.).

about 200 A.D.; and, inasmuch as none of the other Greek inscriptions of colonial times in Antioch seem to be earlier than this, they may all be assigned with considerable confidence to the third and fourth centuries after Christ.

If the figure of Concord were represented on Antiochian coins, one might infer that the statue dedicated by Lystra had suggested the coin-type, and thus get some evidence as to date : but Concord has not yet been recognised on any of the coins.   It cannot be assumed that Lystra would follow the ordinary Roman representation of Concord, as a standing figure very similiar in attitude to Fig. 32, but carrying the horn of plenty over her left arm, and holding a flat cup (patera) in her outstretched right hand. It is possible that the running figure carrying an olive branch, and a sceptre (Fig. 31), who appears on coins about 248 A.D. and later, may symbolise the one Colonia hastening to greet the other. Although the olive branch was, strictly speaking, appropriated rather to Peace than to Concord, yet the two ideas are closely akin, and Lystra might readily use the one for the

FIG. 32.—Allegorical Figure (the Genius of the City as Concord? or as Good Fortune, or as Plenty?) holding caduceus and cornucopia (coin of the Emperor Decius).

other.   Also, the standing goddess of Fig. 32, with cornucopia and caduceus, who is by some interpreted as Peace, by others as Good Fortune,[34] but who does not agree with the regular type of either goddess, may have been the Lystran conception of Concord.   This figure also belongs to the middle of the third century.   Such suggestions, however, are mere vague possibilities ; but they do not tend to discredit the conclusion to which we have come.   See also § IX.

Those public documents of Antioch expressed in the Greek language are usually of the class intended to be read by the people, as, *e.g.*, the dedication of a public weighing-machine in the Forum, which one could hardly date later than the third century. On the other hand inscriptions of a more purely governmental character were in Latin even during the fourth century.[34a] The distinction shows that the use of Latin was retained for formal purposes, after it had ceased to be understood by the mass of the population.

The disuse of Latin was coincident with the revival of the Oriental spirit in the East; and to a certain extent Antioch must have been affected by this revival. But throughout central Asia Minor the new Orientalism was strongly Hellenised; the further west one goes in the country, the stronger is the Hellenisation, and in Pisidian Antioch of the fourth century we find a Hellenic, not an Oriental civilisation: the city was Pisidian only in name, and the name meant only that it was the capital of the Imperial Province Pisidia, but it was still the centre of Hellenism in a wide district. But in its Hellenism there was mingled a certain Anatolian element with the Greek tone, due to a recoil from the more purely European tone of Rome, which had not assimilated, but only dominated the East. Domination of one by the other is a fragile basis on which to arrange a State mixed of East and West. Greek civilisation, on the contrary, had amalgamated with the Eastern races and coalesced with Orientalism in a mixed Græco-Asiatic system of law and custom.[34b] The new Orientalism was however far from being unaffected by the lesson of Roman organisation. It had caught up ideas and elements from the Roman systems, and applied them in its own way to its own purposes.

In this way the later Roman Antioch gradually ceased to be a Roman city, and took on the character of a Græco-Asiatic

city. It no longer styled itself a Colonia but used the Greek
term Metropolis. Its magistrates gradually disused the Latin
title duumvir and took the Greek title strategos. It is an
interesting parallel that when the Greek Luke describes the
action in the Roman Colonia Philippi, he calls the duumvirs
strategoi. The senate no longer called itself an Ordo, but
a Boule. These changes are not merely a matter of name;
they are the outward indication of a deep-lying and complete
change of spirit. The Roman spirit was dying out, and the
Provinces were establishing their supremacy in the administration of the whole Imperial body.

These facts, though belonging to a later time, indicate the
permanent vitality of the Greek civilisation in Antioch,
underlying the Roman character which was so triumphant
in appearance during the first century. A right instinct led
Paul to appeal in Greek to the Greek side of Antiochian
feeling; but the facts of the city at the moment guide the
historian and prevent him from using the term Hellenes
about the auditors to whom Paul appealed. The municipal
government of Antioch in St. Paul's time was Roman in its
feeling; the governing classes were proud of their Roman
character. But the Romanisation was only superficial. The
Italian colonists gradually melted into the mass of the population, which was Hellenised Oriental, but the Roman character though only superficial lasted long, as appears from
a fact observable in the coinage. The letters S. R., which
occur regularly on coins of Antioch from about 200 A.D.
onwards, indicate the Senatus Romanus, and this interpretation, which cannot be doubted, points to some closer
relation to Rome and the Senate. The same letters occur
on coins of Iconium: see Part IV., p. 366, where their meaning is discussed.

The truth is that the Romans of Antioch were the upper
and governing class, a local aristocracy; and their character
must be distinguished from that of the non-Roman population, the Hellenised Anatolians, both Magnesians and
native Phrygians, who amalgamated more readily. The
distinction between the governing aristocracy and the mass
of the population appears clearly in the narrative of Acts
(see § X).

§ IX. THE RELIGION OF ANTIOCH.

The chief god of Antioch was Men, as Strabo mentions,
and his authority is confirmed by the coins and by the inscriptions of the city. One of the commonest types on the
very numerous and varied coins of the Colonia shows the god
(named on many *Mensis* in the Latin translation), a standing,
fully draped figure wearing the Phrygian high-pointed cap on
his head, with the horns of the crescent moon appearing
above and behind his shoulders: he rests his left arm on a
column to bear the weight of a Victory which stands on his
hand, and raises the left knee to plant the foot on a bull's
head lying on the ground: in his right hand he holds a long
sceptre: beside his right foot a cock stands on the ground
(Fig. 33). The complicated symbolism is difficult to interpret;
but certainly it shows the effort of Hellenic anthropomorphic
art to indicate a complex Divine idea, remote from any
strictly Greek conception. The bull's head often appears on
tombstones in Asia Minor, and was certainly widely employed
as a symbol that was efficacious to avert evil. The cock also
occurs alone as the type on the reverse of some small Antiochian coins: in such cases it is doubtless to be understood
as a part standing for the whole of the Divine image, when
the representation had to be simplified and abbreviated on a

small coin. The meaning of the symbol is obscure. The Victory bearing a trophy which the god bears on his hand marks him as the supreme deity and victorious power.

The resemblance of the name Men to the Greek word Men (month) led to much confusion and even error which was made already by the Greeks, and has been commonly followed by modern scholars, regarding the correspondence between Anatolian and Greek religious ideas. It was falsely supposed that the Anatolian deity Men was simply the Moon-god. Hence also his name was mistranslated in

Fig. 33.—The God of Antioch, Men, holding Victory on his right hand.

Latin as *Mensis* on coins and *Luna* in an inscription,[34c] and the objects above his shoulders were misunderstood as the horns of the crescent moon, whereas originally they were probably only wings as represented in archaic art. The symbolism shows that the Men of Antioch was not the mere embodiment of a single object like the moon, but an envisagement of the general Divine idea, supreme and many-sided. He was simply the great god ; and his name Men was probably a shortened form of the longer Manes, which also occurs widely as the name of an Anatolian deity.

The variety of Greek names that were applied to Men at Antioch (as seen in the inscriptions) also indicate that his nature was very complex, so that he could be plausibly identified with widely diverse Greek gods. He is called Dionysos, Apollo and Asklepios; and he must therefore have been the giver of wine, the god of prophecy (or the sun-god), and the great physician. In short, he is the Anatolian supreme god, the impersonation of their entire conception of the Divine nature and power.

In the religion that was characteristic of Central Anatolia generally and of Phrygia especially, the principal deity was not male but female. The Great Mother was to the Phrygian peoples the true and supreme embodiment of the Divine nature. The god was secondary and subordinate, though always a necessary element in her life, inasmuch as the Divine life was the model and prototpye of human life and human society. In various districts of the country we find that the god stands forth most prominently in the exoteric form of the religion; but even there, if we can penetrate beneath the surface, we find that in the esoteric ritual of the Mysteries the goddess was the prominent personality, and the god was only secondary. The exoteric form of the religion was largely determined by historic conditions and especially by mixture of races. New peoples, among whom the female sex occupied a less honoured and influential position than it did in the primitive Anatolian society, came to be widely dominant in Central Anatolia. These new peoples must, of course, acknowledge the old religion of the country; and generally they recognised it as their supreme religion; but the new social conditions demanded new religious forms to correspond to them, and the god was publicly more acknowledged and regarded than the goddess.

It might, therefore, be plausibly conjectured that in the more secret ritual of the Antiochian god, the Great Goddess would assume prominence. We are, however, not reduced to conjecture ; clear evidence exists that such was the case.

On a coin about 238 A.D. the well-known image of Cybele appears, seated on her throne, holding the small drum (tympanon) which was needed in the ritual of her worship, and with her favourite animals on each side of her chair, the lions. This is the Phrygian goddess in the form that is commonest over the Græco-Anatolian lands (Fig. 34).

FIG. 34.—Cybele seated with her Lions at her feet; she wears a crown of towers and holds in her hands a tympanum (coin of the Emperor Gordian III.).

It is not possible in Antioch, as it was in Tarsus, to trace the successive settlers in the city by their various patron deities and guardian heroes. The population of Antioch was far simpler in its composition than that of Tarsus. The colonists of the Hellenistic city did not succeed in Antioch to an ancient inheritance of fame and achievement, as they did in Tarsus. They made a city amidst a multitude of villages, each featureless, all having one common character, all the servants of the central hieron, knowing nothing of self-government and individuality, content to have their life ordered for them by hieratic authority. The new settlers of the Hellenic city, apart from Jews (whose religion was private and never left any trace on public monuments of that period), were Hellenes of Magnesia, wholly devoted to their own goddess Artemis, who was essentially Anatolian, closely akin to the Ephesian goddess and differentiated from the Phrygian merely by certain local characteristics of no serious importance. The goddess of the new population was practically the same as the goddess who already had her

FIG. 35.—The Genius of Antioch holding cornucopia and olive branch (coin of the Emperor Severus).

home in this region. No other stratum of population has left any recognisable impression on Antioch, except the Roman colonists in 25 B.C.; and they seem to have brought no gods with them except the Majesty of Rome and the Emperors: soldiers of a legion in the Civil War, of various origin, united only by their common loyalty to the Roman State and the gods of the legion, they seem to have accepted readily the existing religion of Antioch.

The city then was devoted, not merely to Men, but also to a goddess of the Artemis-Cybele class, sufficiently Hellen-

19

ised in external character to suit a Hellenic people and city. The Genius of the city, who is represented on a very large number of colonial coins, is distinctly different in type from the ideal representation of other Græco-Asiatic cities. She stands, a matronly figure, in a Greek lady's dress—a long-sleeved chiton confined by a girdle, carrying a horn of plenty and a branch, the symbol of purifying power; the kalathos on her head is the symbol of Divine might (Fig. 35). In a rather different and more maiden-like image she stands with long sceptre supporting her raised left hand, while with

Fig. 36.—The Genius of Antioch, holding sceptre, emptying her cornucopia over an altar (coin of the Emperor Verus, A.D. 161-166).

the right she empties her cornucopia over an altar (Fig. 36). In Fig. 37 the Emperor Gordian III. holds the Genius of Fig. 35 on his left hand, while he extends his right hand to clasp the hand of the city. Antioch is here represented by the City Genius of the second type, a young virgin with sceptre in one hand; she has laid aside the horn of plenty in order to be free to extend the right hand to welcome the Emperor. Between them is a small altar. Both figures stand on pedestals: and the first letter of the name is inscribed on that on which Antioch stands. From the pedestals we may infer that the coin type is derived from a pair of statues publicly exhibited in some open place in the city.

These two types of the Genius of Antioch were evidently both familiar in the city, doubtless in sculpture. One approximates more to the type of the virgin Artemis, the other to the type of the matron Demeter, a Hellenised form corresponding to Cybele. The double conception of the goddess is quite in keeping with the ancient Divine ideal: the Divine nature is at once youthful and mature, " maiden and

FIG. 37.—The Emperor Gordian III. in A.D. 235 holding the Genius of the city in his right hand and greeting the Goddess of the city (marked A[ntioch]). The latter holds a sceptre. Between them is an altar.

mother and queen "; the mother is the same person as the daughter.

The two ideal figures described near the end of § VIII. approximate to one or other of these two types; but neither is marked on the coins by name, as Genius of the Colonia; and both probably are to be understood as embodiments of aspects of the city's nature and purpose. The city's duty was to preserve peace in the country, and cherish concord among the Roman towns; and it is possible that those two figures represent Peace and Concord; but they are also in a sense embodiments of the colony as the guardian of the land and chief of the associated colonies.

One other idealisation of the Colonia still must be mentioned, as it marks the close connection between the Genius of the city and the native goddess (Fig. 38). This is a somewhat complex and enigmatic representation. The goddess sits on a throne, like Cybele in Fig. 34. She carries a palm branch like a Victory; Eros runs towards her knee, as to Aphrodite's; in her left hand she holds a large object,

Fig. 38.—The Goddess of Antioch as the Lady of the Limnai (coin of the Emperor Gordian III.).

which seems to be the stern of a ship. If this interpretation is right, the authority of Antioch must have extended over the Limnai, and probably also the city territory touched the east shore; and the Colonia is represented in the character of the goddess whose home was on the Lakes.

A glance into the history of the Antiochian cult is necessary to show the character of this goddess.

The region of Antioch and the Limnai [35] was the property in primitive times of an ancient hieron and priestly establishment [36] which exercised theocratic authority over a wide district and a large subject population. Strabo says that Antioch was the centre and seat of this priestly establishment; but this is not exactly correct. Antioch was a Greek foundation within the territory of the hieron; and there was in the city a temple of the local religion in an outwardly Hellenised form. The true seat of the old cult was nearer to the north-eastern corner of the great double lake called Limnai; but exact localisation can hardly be made without excavations.

A cave, simply an arched opening in the rock, on the north side of Mount Olympus, where it extends out into the Limnai, was visited by Miss Gertrude Bell in 1907. It is regarded by the Greeks as sacred, and a panegyris is still held by them there every year, to which the Christians gather from a distance, for none live in the immediate neighbourhood. The cave is sacred to the Virgin Mother of God, the Panagia, who has taken the place of the pagan goddess. That this cave was once a sanctuary of the Virgin Artemis of the Limnai may be regarded as certain; similar holy caves of Cybele or of Artemis are well known; but it does not follow that this was her sole or even her principal seat. There was probably also another centre of her worship at some point north-east of the Lakes, from which are derived the numerous inscriptions described below. The relation between those two centres was similar to that between the great temple of Artemis at Ephesus and her old holy place in the mountains to the south.[36a]

In the island near the cave Miss Bell also saw an inscription on a block of marble covered by the water of the lake. This ought to be extracted and read.

The territory of the deity was probably taken possession of by the Seleucid kings, part being used to found Antioch.

When the Romans destroyed the Seleucid rule over these
parts of Asia Minor in 189 B.C., they set Antioch (and
doubtless also Apollonia) free.   The property of the god,
except the portion assigned to Antioch, was then restored to
the priests ; and the old theocracy lasted until the formation
of the Province Galatia in 25 B.C., when the vast estates of
the god became Imperial property, as Strabo mentions.[37]   In
place of government by the god through his priests (a system
which apparently had not been changed by the kings, who
doubtless made the priests the representatives and agents of
the reigning king), a more Roman method of administration
was inaugurated.   The inscriptions are not sufficient to furnish
conclusive evidence, but they point to the view that the Imperial administration through a Procurator (an Imperial
freedman) and Actor or Actores (Imperial slaves) was veiled
to some degree under old forms, so that the Procurator was
priest of the cultus.   The cultivators of the estates [38] were
subjects directly of the Emperor, and did not form part of the
Provincia.   They were enrolled in a religious association
(*collegium*), worshipping the Emperor and the ancient Phrygian deity.   The supreme deity is frequently mentioned as
Great Artemis.   She was the old Phrygian Mother Goddess,
the unwedded mother, nourisher, teacher and ruler of all her
people ; and the forms of the cult, so far as allusion occurs
to them, are those of the old Phrygian religion, with a body
of subordinate priests or ministers called by the ancient title
Galloi and an Archigallos as their chief.   All these, Galloi and
Archigallos, were under the Procurator's authority as chief
priest.

The Roman administration and the old Phrygian system
on these estates are treated, as far as the evidence per-
mits, in the writer's paper on the Tekmoreian Guest-friends,

Studies in the History of the Eastern Provinces, pp. 305-377, where all the evidence is collected.

It is there shown how the ancient system of life and society, as organised not in the cities but in the villages grouped round the central temple, acquired new strength during the third century, and some of the many causes which combined to produce this change are described. The Provinces were no longer so much under the influence of Rome, nor the East so submissive to the West: the subjects were asserting themselves, not to break up the Imperial unity, but to modify its character. A religious element was combined with the social. The great struggle between Christianity and the Emperors dominated everything in the Roman world: wherever any opposition existed between two parties or groups or interests, either one side became Christian, the other Imperial, or they sank their opposition and united to resist the enemy and defend the Empire. The Imperial policy sought to strengthen itself by alliance with the national cults and the national life in Anatolia; and the Imperial estates were made strongholds of the anti-Christian action, which in the third century took a more energetic form and imitated the rival religion by becoming a propaganda. The Hellenic ideal of city life decayed, as freedom and self-government disappeared from the Hellenic cities; and the spirit of Hellenism could not survive when liberty had left the Roman world. Thus the citizens of Antioch degenerated towards the level of the people on the estates; and some of them abandoned the city and adopted village life. The standard of education rose on the estates and in the villages; and the Greek language was gradually adopted in place of Phrygian or Pisidian. A monotonous level of education, midway between the old Hellenism of the cities and the ignorance of the rustics, was established over the whole region. It is this mixed system, containing elements taken both from Orientalism and from Hellenism, and some even from Roman life, which is presented to us in the later third century and which we have sometimes spoken of as a reviving Orientalism, sometimes as the new Hellenism victorious over the Roman spirit in Antioch. The East absorbed the European, but the new product spoke the language of Europe and was in other ways altered in character.

The religion of Antioch was in origin identical with the Artemis-worship of the native population on the estates; but Hellenic education and custom imparted a certain superficial alteration to the cult without giving any really Greek character to it. The "very manifest god Dionysos," as the deity is styled in one inscription, is not really more Greek in character than Men himself. The citizens were Hellenes in education. They had the tone inevitably nurtured in freemen, who for generations had exercised the sovereign rights of self-government through elective magistrates, and had met for free discussion in public meetings. Thus they were raised intellectually far above the level of the still half-enslaved Phrygian population on the Imperial estates around Antioch, and in such a position the Hellenic pride of birth and intellect must have been fostered and strengthened. But in religion and in racial temperament they were Anatolian (except the colonial Romans, who were still a separate and superior caste in the time of St. Paul).

§ X. First Appearance of Paul and Barnabas in the Antiochian Synagogue.

We turn now to study the visits which Paul paid to Antioch, and to compare the information given in the Acts with the results attained in the preceding sections.

On his first visit in company with Barnabas he crossed the broad and rugged mountain region of Taurus, coming northward from Perga to Antioch probably in the late summer or autumn of the year 46 [39] after Christ. As the narrative of Luke states the circumstances, the two Apostles entered the Synagogue as comparative strangers on the first Sabbath after their arrival, and took their seat. The Rulers of the Synagogue, after the lessons for the day (probably from Deuteronomy i. and Isaiah i.) [40] had been read, sent them an invitation to address the congregation: "Brethren, if ye have any word of exhortation for the people, say on".

It cannot be supposed that the Rulers would have invited any chance stranger to speak in public. We must therefore conclude either that Paul and Barnabas took their seats in some special place, showing thereby that they desired to address the people, or that previously they had made known to these Rulers their character and mission as teachers: perhaps both these preliminaries had been observed. The former alternative is adopted by J. Lightfoot, who supposes that they sat down in the place appropriated to the Rabbis. The example of Jesus in Luke iv. 16 shows that a person who desired to speak in the Synagogue had the opportunity permitted him by Jewish custom, just as is the Quaker custom still; but there was this difference, that among the Jews the Rulers were charged with the superintendence of public worship, the choice of speakers, and general care for the order of the proceedings, whereas among the Quakers any one whom the Spirit prompts is free to rise and speak. It seems therefore probable that the Rulers satisfied themselves previously as to the qualifications of Paul and Barnabas; and this implies either that some private communication had taken place before the public worship began, or that the

Apostles had already been some time in Antioch and acquired a reputation as teachers and preachers.

Formerly I took the latter view,[41] and supposed that the inattention to precise statement of the lapse of time, which characterised Luke in common with most ancient writers, made him here slur over a certain interval during which the Apostles lived and worked in Antioch till they had become noteworthy figures in the city. This supposition would explain how it came that the Rulers on a certain Sabbath invited the Apostles to address the congregation; and it is quite in keeping with Luke's style of narrative that he should hurry over the early days of the residence in Antioch, and concentrate attention on the critical moment. At that time it seemed to me to be impossible and incredible that already, on the second Sabbath of their residence (xiii. 44), Paul and Barnabas should have succeeded in catching the ear of "almost the whole city" and in alienating the Jews. But further study has gradually brought me to a different view. That which once seemed impossible and incredible must be accepted as the fact. A similar change of opinion has come about in regard to many things during the last years of the nineteenth and the first years of the twentieth century: hundreds of assertions which would formerly have been pronounced incredible and impossible are now accepted as obvious statements of fact. The word "impossible" should rarely be used in criticism, or only in a different way from that in which it was formerly employed: it is a dangerous and question-begging term.

In this case Luke is quietly explaining and emphasising that instantaneous and marvellous effect on the Galatians, which so deeply impressed Paul himself and which he describes in his letter, "ye received me as an angel of God".

He was welcomed by the native pagan Galatians as one who came bringing the message of God, as one who must be believed and trusted implicitly, as one for whom nothing that they could do was too much, to whom they were ready to give up all that was dearest and to sacrifice their very eyes. Such a reception—that a pagan city should welcome a Jewish stranger as an angel of God—was marvellous, impossible, incredible; but Luke describes how it occurred; and this striking agreement between Acts and the Epistle proves that we must accept to the fullest extreme the strange and at first sight almost incredible account given by Luke. Paul was invited to address the audience in the Synagogue on the first Sabbath after he arrived. Weak and showing traces of an illness which was popularly regarded as a direct infliction of Divine wrath on a guilty and accursed person, he was received by the heathen part of his audience at least, not with contempt or disapproval as outcast and cursed by God, but with enthusiasm as the messenger come from God.[42]

This striking inauguration of the Galatian mission, naturally made a deep impression on Paul's mind, as we see throughout the impassioned outpouring of his feelings in the Galatian letter. While we cannot explain with perfect confidence exactly how it was that the Rulers came to invite these strangers to speak, we must accept the fact that it was so. Just as at Philippi (xvi. 13), so at Pisidian Antioch, the events of the first Sabbath in a new city and a strange land are described with especial interest and minuteness by the historian—a good example of his method in narrative.

§ XI. Paul's First Address to a Galatian Audience.

A speech delivered on an occasion like this must be interesting to the student of history. The question must be asked, whether we have in Acts xiii. 16-41 a report of that speech, or merely an address embodying in Luke's own language his conception of the way in which Paul was in the habit of appealing to a mixed audience such as might gather in a Synagogue of the western Jewish Diaspora. This important question is sometimes put in a misleading fashion, as for example in the long footnote in Meyer-Wendt's *Kommentar*, eighth edition, p. 234, where it is expressed in the form of an alternative; either this address was found by the author of Acts in the written Source on which he was dependent in this part of his work, or it is the author's free invention without any authority. Neither alternative is correct. Both are false. But when the question is so expressed, the unwary reader, like the incautious critic, is readily seduced into the belief that one or other alternative must be right; and, as the style and vocabulary of the Lukan writing have influenced the passage, there is an almost inevitable tendency towards the conclusion that we have in this passage a freely invented oration which the author of ¡Acts considered suitable for the occasion and characteristic of Paul. Luke was not in this part of his work dependent on any written Source, but on information from the actors and eye-witnesses, and on his own personal knowledge.[43] His style has free play, when he is reporting in brief a long speech.

Let us therefore take the address as Luke reports it, and consider its character and its suitability to the audience before whom it is said to have been delivered.

In the first place we observe that it is not addressed to the Jews of the Synagogue alone. From the opening to the close it is addressed to the double audience, the Jews and the God-fearing Gentiles,[44] all pagans by education, but at-

tracted within the circle of Jewish influence in virtue of a
certain natural affinity in them to the lofty morality of the
teaching in the Synagogue.

Nor is the double address expressed in the way of depreciating the second kind of auditors as an inferior class.
There is nothing resembling the tone of the modern Greek
priest in a Greek village of Macedonia, where a small body
of Wallachian settlers, too poor to have a church of
their own, attended the Greek service, and listened to the
address of the priest: "Christian Brethren, and ye Walla-
chians".[45] Paul's opening words are perfectly courteous to
both classes, " Men of Israel and ye that fear God, hearken ".

Incidentally we observe here how inaccurate is the view
taken of this address in the above-quoted footnote of Meyer-
Wendt's *Kommentar:* Dr. Wendt states the opinion that
this address is a free composition by the author of the Acts,
in which he tried to exemplify the way that Paul on his
missionary journey preached the Gospel before the Jews.
The distinguished commentator has failed to observe the
most important fact about this address, the fact which gives
character and effect to it, that from first to last it includes
the Gentiles in its clearly expressed scope. What help for
the understanding of the speech can be expected from a
discussion which leaves out of count the most essential and
remarkable fact in the address?

In the second place, as the orator proceeds and grows
warm in his subject, his address becomes still more complimentary to the God-fearing Gentiles and actually raises
them to the same level with the Jews as " Brethren ". At
first he had distinguished the two classes of auditors, Jews
and God-fearing; but in xiii. 26 he sums them up together
with a loftier courtesy as " Brethren, children of the stock

of Abraham, and those among you that fear God". That Brethren is not confined to the first class, but common to both, is shown by verse 38, by the comparison of the climax from 16, through 26, to 38, and by the terms ἡμῖν and ὑμῖν in 26. The two classes, which were kept separate in the opening words, are now united as parts of the genus "Brethren". Then finally in verse 38 the distinction of two classes in the audience disappears, and all are identified on the higher plane of Christian thought as "Brethren".

Doubtless this was the first occasion on which either in this or in any other Synagogue the Gentiles had been addressed by a Jew as "Brethren". Here we stand on the same level as in the Galatian letter iii. 26-30, "Ye are all sons of God . . . there can be neither Jew nor Greek, there can be neither bond nor free, there can be no male and female: for ye are all one in Christ Jesus".

What a development here appears from the language which Paul had used to Peter in a Gentile city before a Gentile audience only a short time before! "We being Jews by nature and not sinners of the Gentiles." It is, of course, true that the words were uttered dramatically, as Paul was speaking from the point of view of his Jewish antagonists and employing their language. But even with this explanation I feel no longer able to hold the opinion expressed in *St. Paul the Traveller*, p. 138 f., that that scene occurred immediately before the Apostolic Council. After hesitating long I find myself decisively driven over to the view which at first I rejected (but which my friend Mr. F. Warburton Lewis has often urged on me) that the visit of Peter to Antioch (Gal. ii. 11 ff.) preceded the first missionary journey of Paul and Barnabas, and that he was sent from Jerusalem as far as Syrian Antioch to inspect and report on this new extension of the Church, just as he had been sent previously to Samaria along with John on a similar errand.

Accordingly we see that the sermon at Pisidian Antioch was given by Luke in such detail, not merely because it inaugurated an important stage in the development of Paul's sphere of work, *viz.* the beginning of the Galatian Churches, but also because it represented a new step in his thought and method.

§ XII. The Approach to the Gentiles.

But, while the Gentiles are associated on a footing of such perfect equality with the Jews in this address, they are regarded entirely on the side of their approach to the Jewish beliefs, and not the faintest reference is made to their own religious conceptions apart from and previous to Judaism. In that respect this sermon stands in marked contrast to the oration to the Athenians and the brief address to the Lystran mob, in which Christian doctrine is set before the auditors as the development of their own natural conceptions of and aspirations towards the Divine power. Here, on the contrary, the God-fearing Gentiles are addressed as standing on the same plane of thought with the Jews, and the correct text of xiii. 43, followed in the Revised Version,[46] " And as they went out they besought that these words might be spoken to them the next sabbath," shows that the Jews in the Synagogue did not at the moment appreciate (any more than Dr. Wendt appreciates) the importance of the inclusion of the Gentiles by Paul in his address and in his gospel. The topics were so purely Jewish that the appeal to the Gentiles, though clearly marked, was ignored as a mere piece of courtesy or regarded as accidental by the Jews generally. Possibly some of the Jews were offended already by this extreme complaisance to the Gentiles, but they are not alluded to by the historian, who only says that many of the Jews and Gentiles followed the Apostles, when they continued their mission.

But, although the elevation of the Gentiles to the same level with the Jews is so skilfully and delicately introduced in this address, as to have even escaped the notice of so careful a commentator as Dr. Wendt, it is woven in the texture of Paul's words and thought.

It is absurd and unfair to doubt that Luke was fully conscious of this. He places the speech at the beginning of Paul's work among the Gentiles as a typical example of the way in which Judaism and the promises of God were made universal by him.

The Jews as a body did not perceive the deep-lying suggestiveness of Paul's inclusion of the Gentiles; but the Gentiles saw it, and on the next Sabbath almost the whole city flocked to the Synagogue. It was now clearly apparent what interpretation was put on the words of Paul. Even the Gentiles who had not previously been attracted within the circle of the Synagogue came to hear the new message of a widened Judaism. The teaching, which on the first Sabbath had been allowed to pass without open disapproval and had even been welcomed by many of the Jews, was now openly contradicted, when one or both of the Apostles addressed the crowded assembly. The Jews of Antioch were not prepared to admit the Gentiles to an equality with themselves.

No explanation is given in the oration quoted by Luke of the way in which this equality which Paul preached was explained and justified by him. The equalisation is simply assumed and acted upon. " You," throughout the speech, embraces Jews and Gentiles. " We " in xiii. 26 includes all who will. But one cannot suppose that the entire Gospel

was explained in one oration to an audience wholly unprepared for it. The aim of the sermon was to drive home
into the minds of the audience one or two fundamental
principles, and to suggest the universality of the Gospel ; and
the subsequent events showed that this part of the message
was caught with avidity by the hitherto unprivileged Gentiles in the audience. The oration was only the introduction, not the completion, of a course of instruction.

This consideration shows the unreasonableness of Professor McGiffert's criticism of the oration ; [47] he regards it as
composed by Luke, and not as a trustworthy reproduction
of what Paul said. He points out that in xiii. 39, " where
it is said that *every one that believeth is justified from all
things from which ye could not be justified by the law of
Moses*, a conception of justification is expressed, which, if
not distinctly un-Pauline, nevertheless falls far below Paul's
characteristic and controlling idea of justification as the state
of the saved man who is completely reconciled to God and
enjoys peace with Him ". Dr. McGiffert's words are quite
correct, but his inference that Paul could not have made
the statement is incorrect. This statement was a first step
towards making the new idea intelligible to minds wholly
unprepared for understanding the full Pauline conception.
The able modern scholar and writer sees that the statement,
though "not un-Pauline," is incompletely Pauline. But that
is precisely what should be expected in a preparatory an-
nouncement like this. The teaching of freedom, of the
lighter yoke and the easier burden, which as we saw already
(Part I., § IV.) is the most characteristic feature in the letter
to the Galatians, is clearly yet not obtrusively contained
here.

But, when Dr. McGiffert regards " the forgiveness of

sins " (xiii. 38) as sufficiently un-Pauline to excite suspicion, we find no reality in his criticism.   Even if the words were never used by Paul elsewhere, it is mere pedantry to regard the idea as un-Pauline; but they occur (as the learned critic mentions) in Ephesians i. 7 and Colossians i. 14.   They are a simpler and less philosophic expression of a process which Paul dwells on always, but as a rule in a more mystic and more transcendental way—a process which every Christian preacher must in some form or other always dwell on.

The occurrence of such simpler, as one might say pre-Pauline or preparatory-Pauline expressions at the climax of the address, is eminently suitable to the situation, and strongly confirms the character of this oration as a trust-worthy report of the speech actually delivered by the Apostle in the Galatian Synagogue.

It is needless to repeat here the analysis of the topics in this address which are described by Paul in the Epistle as having constituted his teaching to the Galatians.   They are treated in my *Historical Commentary on Galatians*, pp. 399-401, to which I may be permitted to refer.   The common topics there more fully described are :—

(1) The history of the Jewish people becomes intelligible only as leading onward to a higher development : this higher stage came in "the fulness of time" (Gal. iv. 4), and con-stituted the climax of their history, when God fulfilled His promise, and when the Jews by condemning Jesus fulfilled prophecy (Acts xiii. 27, 32 f.).

(2) The promise given originally to the Jews cannot be fulfilled except through Christ.   Such is the burden of the Epistle and of the address.   The Law cannot save: it is incomplete : it cannot justify.   In the address indeed Paul does not actually go further than to say that the Law cannot

justify completely, xiii. 39; but this is already un-Jewish, and suggests much more than it actually says. But through Christ every one that hath faith is justified (Acts xiii. 23, 32 f., 38 f.).

(3) Christ must be hanged on a tree and be accursed (Gal. iii. 13, Acts xiii. 29).

(4) Christ is not dead, though He was slain (xiii. 30, 32 f., 34 f., 37).

This is not a complete outline of Paulinism, but it is a characteristic sketch preparatory to the evangelising of an audience which knew nothing but the Law. It is not what a later writer would compose as a presentation of Paulinism to any audience; but it is the way in which, one cannot deny, Paul might well take the first steps to introduce his gospel to such an audience as this. The idea of liberty, which is so prominent in the Epistle, could not be suggested too explicitly at this stage before a mixed audience. It belongs to the further ministration, which followed xiii. 47.

The Received Text of xiii. 42, which appears in the Authorised Version, " when the Jews were gone out of the Synagogue, the Gentiles besought that these words might be preached to them the next Sabbath," is wholly unjustifiable. In the first place we notice the mistranslation of the first participle (ἐξιόντων), which cannot possibly imply that the Jews " were gone out of the Synagogue," but only that they were in the act of going out or on the point of going out. This stage is antecedent to xiii. 43, when the Synagogue had broken up and the audience had been dismissed. Secondly, this reading misses the delicacy of the situation, exaggerates the share attributed to the Gentiles in the action, and gives a quite irrational picture of the situation. We cannot possibly admit that the Jews could depart first from the

Synagogue and leave the Gentiles alone with Paul in it. Even with a correct translation, " while the Jews were going out of the Synagogue," the situation as described remains almost the same, for the Jews are still represented as beginning to go out and leaving the Gentiles gathered round Paul and Barnabas; and, moreover, this reading anticipates the situation as it developed in the ensuing week, whereas the Jews did not understand its nature until the following Sabbath. Thirdly, the evidence of the manuscripts is overwhelming and indubitable.

It is gathered from xiii. 42 by some commentators that Paul and Barnabas went out beforehand [48] and afterwards the Synagogue was dismissed. But the words "as they were going out," may very well be interpreted as referring to the time occupied in the gradual departure of a large audience. During the breaking up of the audience the hearers in general asked that the address might be repeated, a request with which (as we must understand) the Rulers complied. After the breaking up occurred the scene described in the following verse.

§ XIII. The Door of the Gentiles.

This turning away from the Jews to address the Gentiles directly and alone was a very important step in the development of the Pauline evangelisation. That it was made now for the first time seems certain. It is the method of Luke to emphasise the great stages in the development of the Church; and the attention which he devotes to this address would alone be a sufficient proof that it marked a decisive step in advance. Moreover, on their return to Syrian Antioch, Paul and Barnabas reported about their journey and its results; and the fact on which they laid special stress was that God "had opened a door of faith to the Gentiles" during this journey.

The address in the Synagogue was not the opening of the door: it was only a preliminary that led up to that decisive step. It is only in xiii. 46 that the step is actually described. When Paul took this step, the door was opened for the Gentiles to enter direct into the Church (instead of through the Synagogue).[49] Luke, evidently, understood that it had not been opened in Cyprus, for there Paul and Barnabas spoke only in the Synagogues, Barnabas, not Paul, was the leader, and Paul still appeared in his Hebrew character under the name of Saul. It had not been open in Syrian Antioch, for there also the leader was Barnabas, and Paul appeared only as the Hebrew Saul in a subordinate position; and no reasonable doubt can exist that the Christian teaching in Syrian Antioch reached the Gentiles through the Synagogue and not direct: had the door stood open there already, it would not have been necessary or correct for Paul and Barnabas to report that God had opened a door to the Gentiles on the journey.

Can we gather from the general situation any information to explain how it was that Paul made such a distinct step forward in his outlook and method at this time? It is quite natural that the idea of the gospel of the Gentiles, deep-seated in his mind, should gradually translate itself into action, and grow stronger and more commanding as it becomes more active. That this must have been so lies in the nature of the case; and Luke's narrative marks the gradual development very clearly. It was never part of this author's method formally to state reasons and estimate causes; but he certainly conceived that Paul's missionary aims gradually expanded and developed, and he certainly modelled his

history so as to exhibit the steps by which this development took place : no one has any doubt as to this intention
on the part of the author of *Acts :* the only doubt is as
to his competence and trustworthiness in carrying out his
intention.

What, then, was it that led Paul to take this large and
sudden step onwards in his course at the very beginning of
his Galatian mission ?   The answer to this question must be
to a great extent conjectural and dependent on a more or
less subjective estimate of the preceding conditions.   The
sole authority is Luke ; and we have to try to divine the
purpose in his mind, prompting his choice and his emphasis ;
and this attempt must inevitably be conditioned by personal
judgment about Luke's character as a historian.

In the first place we cannot but notice that this event
comes shortly after the scene in Paphos, where Paul for the
first time became the leader.   At Paphos also he ceases to
be conceived by Luke as a mere Jew among Jews; and
the change in his name marks a change in method and outlook.   The first missionary action which Luke mentions after
this change was the speech in the Antiochian Synagogue, for
the residence in Pamphylia had been rendered abortive by
the illness, which was still affecting him when he spoke in
the Antiochian Synagogue, but which the Galatians over-
looked in their enthusiastic reception.   We must understand
that Luke marks the three steps in the process of opening
of the door as (1) the scene in Paphos, (2) the first Galatian
sermon addressing Greeks and Jews as equal, (3) the turning
away from the Jews to address the Gentiles directly and outside of the Synagogue.

In the second place, Paul was now entering a new country,
where the conditions of life and the relation of Jews to

Gentiles were probably different from those to which he was accustomed. An orator like him must have been sensitive to the new conditions and guided almost unconsciously by them. There was something in the moral atmosphere of the Synagogue at Antioch that led him on to the issue of addressing the Gentiles as "Brethren" equally with the Jews, and exhibiting to them the Gospel ("placarding it before them," as in Gal. iii. 1) as their own. Can we determine what was this electric quality to which Paul was sensitive? Surely, it is to be connected with the friendly relations of Jew and Gentile. We should not expect that in an ordinary Græco-Roman city, almost the whole population would gather to hear a Jew preach to them in the atmosphere of a Synagogue: a certain degree of rhetorical stress and exaggeration may perhaps be felt in the expression; but one cannot doubt that a large and impressive concourse of citizens to the Synagogue took place on the second Sabbath. What was it that made the Antiochians gather in such a vast crowd? That they should do so must be regarded as on a parallel with the general sympathy of spirit that existed between Anatolians and Jews. This sympathy I have elsewhere described.[50] The ancient people of Phrygia was the ground-stock into which both the old conquering tribes of Phryges or Bryges from Europe and the Magnesian colonists of the third century melted and were absorbed: it had marked affinity with the Semitic peoples. In the character of this ground-stock lies the explanation, both why Paul now was drawn on to address them so sympathetically in his first speech, and why later they attempted to reconcile his teaching with a strict and complete obedience to the Jewish Law (an attempt which elicited the Epistle to the Galatians). Only such an affinity could render it possible that almost the whole population crowded to hear the Jewish stranger preach his message to themselves.

A possible objection that may suggest itself on a hasty view may here be alluded to. We have laid much stress on the Hellenised character of Pisidian Antioch, and on its diversity from the purely Anatolian character of the surrounding population; and yet now we are laying stress on the fundamentally Anatolian spirit of the Antiochians. It may be thought that these are inconsistent opinions. There is, however, no real inconsistency between them, and the reader who detects inconsistency fails to conceive rightly the Græco-Oriental character in those Seleucid colonies of Phrygia. In them Hellenic education adapted itself to Oriental peoples, and in doing so was profoundly modified in spirit. Each of those cities was an experiment in the amalgamation of the Oriental and the Western. Therein lies their deep interest. They were attempting to do, and on the whole with remarkable success, what must be achieved on a wider scale at the present day if the peace of the world is to be maintained and progress to be made. The warfare and antagonism between Eastern and European has to be changed for peaceful interpenetration, which will result not in domination of the one over the other, but in harmonious development of a reconciled common civilisation, in which each side contributes what the other lacks (see Part I., § V., and *Letters to the Seven Churches*, Preface).

Accordingly, the mass of the population of Antioch was Hellenic or Hellenised: it was not, however, Greek, but Græco-Oriental. Hellenism is rather an educational than a racial fact. Even the Magnesians who had colonised Antioch were not a Greek people racially; they came from a Hellenised city of Anatolia, in which the mixture of Greek blood can have been only slight. It was precisely in those Græco-Oriental cities that the Jews found themselves most at home. In the strictly Greek cities of European Greece the Jews seem never to have been able to effect such an accommodation with their Greek neighbours.

The appeal which Paul made to the non-Jewish Antiochian Galatians was evidently addressed mainly to the older population, the Hellenized Anatolian, not the Roman, section of the city. Consideration of the circumstances will bring this out clearly.

Not the whole city had come to hear Paul. There was a class that did not come; and it is easy to see what class it was that was not interested. It was the class which included the women of rank to whom the Jews soon after had recourse in order to excite persecution against Paul. That is to say, it was the Roman colonists, the local aristocracy. They were not drawn so much to the Synagogue. An address in Greek would not be so attractive to them, for Greek had not yet become their home language, as it did two centuries later (see § VIII.). They had not the same affinity of spirit with the Semites as the older population had. An aristocracy is, as a rule, not so easily and quickly affected by missionary influence as the humbler classes are. (See also p. 511.)

This class, which did not come to the Synagogue in any great numbers, held the reins of government; it was the privileged burgher class. To it the Jews went for help, moving it through the women who belonged to it.

In conclusion we cannot but observe that the narrative of Acts implies a very marked concord and friendly relation between the Jews and the other two chief sections of the Antiochian people. The mass of the population gathers in

the Synagogue.   The governing *coloni* are easily induced by
the Jews to act against Paul and Barnabas, and it can hardly
be doubted that the charge against the strangers was that
they had disturbed the harmony of the State.   This picture
of the Roman Colonia is very favourable, and is quite in accordance with all that has been gathered from the extra-
Biblical evidence.

PART IV.

ICONIUM.

FIG. 27.—The River-God Anthios on a coin of Antiochia Colonia
(see p. 248 f.).

ICONIUM.

§ I. Natural and National Character.

It would be difficult to find two cities more strikingly
similar in general situation than Iconium and Damascus.
Both lie on the level plateau, high above sea level (Iconium
3,370, Damascus about 2,300 feet). Both are sheltered on
the west by lofty mountains, or, as one might better say, a
mountainous region : Anti-Lebanon in one case, the Phrygo-
Pisidian mountain-land of the Orondeis in the other, each
with peaks of more than 5,000 feet in height, rise from the
level plain three or four miles west of the city. From the
mountains, in each case, flows down a stream right into
the city, making the land around into a great garden, green
with trees, rich in produce; but the water has no outlet
and is soon dissipated in the soil of the level plains which
stretch away to the east of both cities, as far as the eye can
see. Yet the scenery to the east is not monotonous in the
outlook, for mountains rising here and there like islands give
character and variety to the view. (Map, p. 384.)

The mountains on the western side are more varied in
outline at Iconium than they are at Damascus. The flat
table-top of Loras-Dagh (about 6,000 feet) to the west, the
twin cones of St. Philip and St. Thekla (about 5,200 feet)
to the north-west, a larger rounded mountain which rises
over Zizima and Ladik far up to the north, all arrest the eye
and the attention. The Christian form of the local beliefs

(317)

connected with the hills of St. Philip (Takali-Dagh, the Arab Dakalias) and St. Thekla is described in § X.; and the facts there mentioned suggest that all these striking features of the landscape had their religious features. (Pl. XI.)

Iconium and Damascus alike were unsuited for defence, and utterly devoid of military strength, according to ancient methods of warfare. They are cities of peace, centres of commerce and agriculture and wealth, marked out by their natural character for historical and political importance throughout all time. Water is scarce on those arid plateaus, and sites which had an abundant, ever-flowing, natural supply of water, formed centres of human life and history from the beginning of organised society. Their importance, therefore, rested on a sure foundation. No political change could destroy them, though oppressive or inefficient government might temporarily diminish their wealth and prosperity.

Damascus has filled a greater place before the eyes of the world than Iconium; it stands pre-eminent in historical and romantic interest, because it was close to the scene of events and peoples greater in ancient history. In fame it surpasses Iconium as much as its river Abana surpasses in the volume of water that it carries the stream which gives fertility and growth to the gardens of Iconium, and which exhausts itself at the edge of the city. Iconium was at least as important in relation to its neighbouring towns and tribes as Damascus; but Damascus lay nearer the main centres of historic evolution, while we can only dimly conjecture that Asia Minor was more important in the world's history before 1500 B.C. than it has been since, and in that early period Iconium is to us only a legend, hardly even a name.

Only at one period in later history has Iconium rivalled the political importance as a governing city that has several times belonged to Damascus. In the Seljuk period, from the end of the eleventh century to the fourteenth, Iconium or Konia was the capital of the Seljuk empire of Roum. The Sultans of Konia waged war on equal terms with the Emperors of Constantinople : they held great part of Asia Minor, and for a time Nicaea itself was one of their garrison cities, while their armies swept in repeated raids down to the Aegean Sea. The city was then made so splendid with beautiful buildings, palace, mosques and mausolea, that the proverb arose and lasted long among the Turks, "See all the world ; but see Konia".

Both Iconium and Damascus are, therefore, necessarily and inevitably of immemorial antiquity. However far back in history one can penetrate, there one finds standing out clearly in the dimness of primitive history or legend the importance of those two great cities. Damascus has always been famous as the oldest city in the world. But Iconium, though less famous, was as old as Damascus, for both went back to the beginning of history. At Iconium tradition recorded the fame of King Nannakos (or Annakos), who reigned before the Flood, and lived to the age of 300 years. Learning from an oracle that, when he died, all men should perish, he convoked all people to the temple, and "made supplication with tears," and his Phrygian subjects mourned so vehemently that "the weeping in the time of Nannakos" became a proverb even among the Greeks. Herondas of Cos about 270 B.C. makes one of his characters, speaking in the common conversational language of lower middle-class society in a Greek town, quote this proverb.

Soon after "the weeping of Nannakos" came the Flood

in which all men perished. When the earth dried again after the Flood, Jupiter bade Prometheus and Athena make images (*eikones*) of mud, and he caused the winds to breathe on the images, and they became living. Thus Iconium was re-peopled immediately after the Flood, and derived its name from the *eikones*. The last is a Greek addition; in this Phrygian legend, evidently, the city bore the same name before the Flood as after.

Nannakos gave origin to other proverbs. " More ancient than Nannakos," "from Nannakos," "in the time of Nannakos," and similar phrases, were widely used to describe things of great age and survivals of primitive antiquity. The name of the old Phrygian king had passed into the common stock of familiar Greek tradition at some early time in a way unknown to us.

Attempts have been made to show that the story of Nannakos was borrowed from Jewish tradition and record, and was not a native Iconian legend.[1] It is assumed in such attempts that the form Annakos gives the original and correct name, and that it is the Biblical Hanokh, or Enoch; the legend of a flood which destroyed the Phrygian world at the death of Annakos is explained as a version of the tale recorded in Genesis vi.-ix. But this theory cannot be accepted. The correct name is certainly Nannakos, which appears in all authorities except Stephanus (in whose text Annakos is probably a mere error); Nannakos is a name known in Asia Minor, and the cognate names, Nannas, Nannasos, etc., are common in the country round Iconium. The frequent and varied forms of proverb connected with the name furnish strong proof that the legend was one of native origin, and not borrowed from the Bible. The only way in which a Biblical origin could be explained is through

the influence of the Jewish colonists in Lycaonia and Phrygia.
But those Jewish colonies belong to the Seleucid times;
they began under Seleucus Nikator shortly before 281. It
is unlikely that they could ever have acquired such deep-
rooted importance as to influence popular Greek expression
in the degree which those proverbs imply, and certainly they
could not do so before the great foundations made by
Antiochus the Great, about 215-200 B.C.[2] The Jews of
Phrygia were undoubtedly wealthy, influential, and energetic, and they strongly affected the religious ideas of
thoughtful men, as the writer has tried to describe elsewhere[3]; but their influence was not of the kind that was
likely to mould popular language; rather they were disliked
and feared by the vulgar. Moreover, it was in the Roman
more than in the Greek period that they became so influential. Now the proverbial use of the story of Nannakos
was firmly rooted on the west coast of Asia Minor when
Herondas was writing about 270-260 B.C., and it seems
impossible to account for this except through the influence
of an ancient Phrygian tradition familiarly known to the
Greeks from a very early time.

The story of Nannakos, then, although only a fragment
of it has been preserved, belongs to native Iconian tradition,
and furnishes evidence of a primitive Phrygian belief in a
deluge; though it may be freely admitted that the story, as
told by Suidas, has probably been coloured by the Biblical
narrative, which indubitably affected Phrygian legends in
later time.

The precise form of the Iconian legend is irrecoverable,
but it was evidently markedly different from the Biblical
story. The coming of some disaster was predicted to the
people, and their vehement mourning over the impending

catastrophe was the feature that most deeply impressed the Greek mind. Their king, Nannakos, in spite of his tearful supplications, by which evidently he tried to propitiate the god and avert the Deluge, seems to have perished with his people, and the land was repeopled by Divine intervention.

The primitive Phrygian legend can be traced also at Apameia-Celaenae in a non-Biblical form.[4] It was there connected with the remarkable natural phenomena of the locality, the underground waters; and it took the form that Divine intervention saved the city from being entirely engulfed after many had perished. This native legend at Celaenae (of which the details are not preserved) was modified by being blended with the Biblical story, as appears on the coins with the name and type of Noah and the Ark; but there is no reason to think that this occurred until the Roman period; the Noah coins are of the third century after Christ. Here also the Jewish influence was slow and late in affecting popular thought, and the analogy constitutes an additional argument that Nannakos could not be borrowed from Jewish sources. In both cases the earlier allusions reveal a legend unlike the Biblical form, and the Biblical analogies are stronger in the later references.

It seems probable that the Iconian form of the legend was, like the Apamean, adapted to local circumstances. Further exploration is needed to give certainty, but there is every probability that the plain of Iconium was irrigated by water coming from the large lake, Trogitis, about forty-five miles in an air-line to the south-west, separated from Iconium by the high Orondian mountain country. The evidence for this must be stated here.

A scheme has been under consideration recently for bringing the water of this lake to irrigate the plain. In 1882 the writer heard Said Pasha, governor of the Konia Vilayet, speak of the plan and the surveys which he had caused to be made in preparation for it ; and the scheme has been revived in the last few years as a private enterprise to be carried out by a European company.[5] It was stated on good authority to the writer in 1905 that the engineers, who reported on the practicability of the scheme, found that it could be carried out at moderate expenditure, because an ancient cutting which had formerly carried the water through the mountains at the only difficult point, still exists, and can readily be cleared again.[6] That a channel exists by which the water of lake Trogitis can flow into the Konia plain, has long been known to the archæological travellers in Lycaonia ; but, until I was informed by an excellent authority that it was artificial, I had been under the impression that it was purely natural. It discharges into the river Tcharshamba, which flows across the plain of Konia about twenty-four miles south of the city. This river is described by the Arab geographer Ibn Khordadhbeh in the ninth century under the name of Nahr-el-Ahsa, River of Subterranean Waters,[7] and the name seems to prove that the connection with the lake was still open at that time. In more recent time the channel has been allowed to become blocked up, and the connection with the lake has ceased, except when the water of Trogitis (which varies greatly in volume) is very high. Professor Sterrett, in the account of his exploration of this district,[8] reports that the water was flowing from the lake through the channel in 1885, but he unfortunately did not follow its course. In May, 1905, the river was carrying a large body of water into the plain of Konia, but I was assured that no connection with the lake was open, and that the water came entirely from the Isaurian mountains, which drain into this river.

Hearing at Konia, in May, 1905, the report about the ancient cutting, I perceived at once that if such a great engineering work existed, it was likely to have affected Iconian legend; and being hopeful also of finding evidence of the period when it was executed, I went to investigate; but after two days, it became evident that more time than was at my disposal would be necessary, and I had to abandon the quest. But, whether the channel was wholly natural or in part artificial, there is every probability that in ancient times the course of the water was kept clear, and that the plain of Iconium was dependent for its fertility on this water supply. Strabo contrasts the fertility of the Iconian plain with the barrenness of northern and eastern Lycaonia; and the reason for the difference lies in the water supply. The soil of those Lycaonian plains is, as a rule, very fertile, but the productiveness depends on the supply of water by human agency.

The river Tcharshamba sometimes brings down in flood a large body of water from the Isaurian mountains. Moreover, the lake Trogitis varies greatly in level, and sometimes rises so high as to cover a considerable extent of country which in ordinary years is cultivated; and, when this is the case, as has often been stated to me by natives of the district, its waters run into the Tcharshamba Su. The statements must, I think, be accepted, though I cannot vouch for the facts from personal observation. The river, which in most years carries a fair body of water, has no outlet. It pours its water into the plain of Konia, to stagnate and evaporate there. Every spring the river forms extensive inundations in the region on the north-west and north of the Kara-Dagh; and these greatly impede travel in modern times from Konia to Barata in the northern skirts of Kara-Dagh and beyond that to Cybistra and the Cilician Gates, making the most direct road impassable. On exceptional occasions, when the river is very high, the water extends far to the north, and covers even the road from Konia to Kara-Bunar. In June, 1891, when travelling along that road, my wife and I had to make a detour to the north; and even then our horses waded for some miles through deep water, which covered the level plain like an inundation.

Such a state of the country and the waters interrupts communication, blocks roads, and renders a very large tract of flooded land permanently incapable of cultivation, while the rest of the plain (except where the waters flowing from the Orondian mountain region are diffused) suffers from lack of moisture; and is dependent entirely on rainfall to produce light crops. The water is near, but it needs the hand of man to unite it to the dry soil by irrigation.

This was the original and the natural condition of the country; and the improvement of the Iconian plain by conducting the water over it and preventing it from stagnating in marshes was a great work, requiring much skill, knowledge, patience and labour, one of those great engineering achievements on which were built up the prosperity and wealth of the Mediterranean lands: see Part I., § III. Such works were attributed to the god; and from the religious belief originated, as usual, a growth of mythology and popular legend.

We conclude, then, that a religious myth was attached to the irrigation of the Iconian plain. It was through Divine helping power that the water was not a destructive deluge, as it once had been. The gods themselves saved the land and the people whom they had made, moderating an ever-present danger of flood into a beneficent irrigation. We find traces of similar legends wherever in Asia Minor any remarkable water supply exists, as at Apameia-Celaenae or in the valley of Colossae.[9]

The form which the Deluge-story took at Iconium is adapted to bring into strong relief the great antiquity of the city. The Iconians prided themselves on their ancient origin : their city was the first founded after the Flood, and it had been great before the Flood ; the belief that Phrygian was the primitive language of mankind—a belief which was proved to be true by a scientific experiment conducted on the order of the Egyptian king Psammetichus, who found that infants brought up out of hearing of human speech spoke the Phrygian language—was probably shared by them. It was evidently through this pride in their antiquity that some tradition of their Phrygian origin was preserved. Most of those Hellenised cities of Asia Minor claimed to have a Greek origin, and invented legends to connect themselves with Greek history and mythology. In this legend the Iconians claimed to be pre-Greek, the ancient city, the beginning of history.

There was, however, another Iconian legend, which attributed a Greek origin to the city. It is recorded in such confused and self-contradictory fashion by late Byzantine authorities (the Paschal Chronicle, Cedrenus, and Malalas), that one would be tempted to set it aside as mere scholastic trifling, if it were not proved by the Iconian coins to be the accepted legend in the city during the Greek and the Roman period. The Nannakos legend throws no light on, and receives none from, the coinage of the city ; but the tale told so badly in the Paschal Chronicle, Malalas, and Cedrenus, stands in the closest relation to the coins, which form the surest indication of the current views in Iconium.

We shall, for brevity's sake, relate this Greek legend only in the form that best suits the coinage, tacitly omitting all the variations that are mixed up in the three versions. Perseus came to Lycaonia, and vanquished the opposition of the people by the power of the Gorgoneion, which turned his enemies to stone. He then made a village called Amandra into a Greek city, and called it Iconium from the eikon or image of the Gorgon, which he received there before the victory. This seems to point to Divine help granted to him before the battle began. He erected in front of the new city a statue representing himself holding up the Gorgon's head ; and this statue (the authorities say) is standing there to the present day. The coins show us the same statue which these authorities mention, and which was doubtless an ornament of the city ; there can be little doubt that it was a Hellenistic work modelled after the famous statue of Perseus by the great Attic sculptor of the fifth century B.C., Myron.

The representation on the coin is shown enlarged in Fig. 39. This representation must have been imitated from a statue (which doubtless stood in some public place at Iconium) ; this seems proved by the square basis which can be clearly seen under the feet. That coin-types of Phrygian cities were sometimes imitated from works of art in the porticos or other public places is an established fact ; so, for example, reasons have been stated for thinking that several picturesque types on coins of Apameia (including the famous type showing Noah and the Ark) were taken from paintings in a public building of that city : see the *Cities and Bishoprics of Phrygia*, ii., p. 431 f., where other cases of Phrygian coin-types imitated from local statues are mentioned. No sculptural copies of the statue by Myron have

as yet been found; two copies of a head of Perseus are
regarded by Furtwängler, *Masterpieces of Greek Sculpture,*
p. 200, as taken from this statue; but coin-types at Argos,
Iconium and Asine, are regarded by him as imitated from
Myron's work or from copies of it.

The hero stands holding up the head of Medusa to destroy
his enemies, while he himself looks away in order to avoid
suffering from the sight of that head which turned to stone
all who gazed upon it. The Iconian coin makes the hero
hold the Gorgoneion higher in the air than the Argive coins,

Fig. 39.—Perseus destroying the opponents of Hellenism : coin of the
Emperor Hadrian, imitating a statue at Iconium.

and this attitude is certainly truer to the action of the statue.
In Fig. 40 the distinguishing characteristic of this Iconian
type is lost. Perseus holds the Gorgoneion low; and the
energy and spirit of the statue are lost in this milder attitude.
But this attitude accommodates itself better to the shape of
the coin; and hence it is usually adopted by the artists,
as at Tarsus (Fig. 8) and at Argos in the example just
mentioned.

We saw in Part II., § IX., that the Tarsian and East Anatolian Perseus seemed to be a Hellenised form of a native

god conceived as young and active; this Hellenic hero is mythologically represented as the founder of the Hellenic city who conquered the older native population by the help of his patron goddess Athena. Yet at Iconium, as we shall see, Athena was merely a Hellenisation of the ancient Phrygian local goddess. The transformation of the religious ideas accompanies the transformation of the Anatolian town into a Hellenic city. The old deities remain, and yet are modified to a certain degree, less in real character than in outward show and name. The deep-lying nature of the

FIG. 40.—Perseus in the commoner type (see Fig. 8): coin of the Emperor Gallienus.

religion was not permanently changed; and the older Phrygian character recurred, as the Oriental and national spirit was re-invigorated in the early centuries after Christ.

Now it must be asked how there could be two legends in the city about its origin, a Phrygian and a Greek. What is the relation between the two? The analogy of many other cases leaves practically no doubt that the two legends belong to different sections of the population; one belongs to the Hellenised and educated section, partly Greek immigrants but chiefly Grecised natives, and the other to the humbler, uneducated native Phrygian population. This becomes clear also if we glance at the religion of Iconium.

§ II. THE RELIGION OF ICONIUM.

The religion of an ancient city was the most complete expression of its spirit and ideals and aspirations, and a full knowledge of its religion would be an epitome of the evolution of its social organisation. About the religion of Iconium little information has been preserved. To judge from the evidence of inscriptions, the deity whose worship was most deeply rooted in the popular mind was a form of the Phrygian Mother-Goddess, Cybele. She was known as the Zizimmene Mother in all this region from Iconium northwards to a distance of thirty miles or more. The name is derived from her chosen home at Zizima among the mountains, about five hours north of Iconium, where she had revealed her presence by the underground wealth which she taught men how to recover. The copper and the quicksilver mines beside the village (which still bears the old name under the form Sizma) have been worked from a remote period, as is proved by the extensive old shafts; and the latter are still productive.

The underworld, with its abundant wealth, as seen in mines, and its marvellous powers seen in the hot springs and medicinal waters and cool refreshing fountains which it tenders for the use of man, was the abode of the Divine nature, and the ultimate home from which man comes and to which he returns in death. This thought was strong in the Phrygian mind, and the serpent which lives in the earth was regarded with awe as the intermediary between the Divine power and mankind, and as the bearer of the healing and kindly influence of the Divine nature. Wherever signs

PLATE XII.

The Sacred Village and Mountain of the Zizimmene Mother of Iconium.

To face p. 330.   See pp. 330, 336, 378.

of the wealth and power under the earth were most clearly manifested, there the Goddess Mother had her seat; and she assumed a certain local character according to the nature of the place and the people, though the same fundamental Divine conception underlay each of these local forms. Thus Zizima was marked out as the home of the great deity of south-eastern Phrygia. In Iconium she was styled also the Mother Boethene and the Mother of the Gods: Boethene is apparently some old Anatolian epithet, Grecised in form, so as to suggest the meaning "the Mother who comes to

Fig. 41.—Athena Polias, the Goddess of Iconium: coin of Gallıenus.

help" (as Apollo was the Boethos of the Tarsians, Part II., § IX.); but its real meaning was local, derived from some village, where the goddess had a sanctuary, though it is now impossible to recover the original form. The usual accompaniments of the Phrygian Cybele worship are found at Zizima, reliefs showing the goddess seated between her lions, her priests with an archigallos as their leader, a god named Angdistis, who is an enigmatic figure, sometimes regarded as female, sometimes as male (like the Carian androgynous deity).[9a]

The religion of Zizima has survived in a Christianised form to the present day.

But this native Phrygian conception of the Divine nature has left little mark on the coins of Iconium. Only faint traces of the worship of the Phrygian goddess appear on them. Athena is the important Divine type: she appears in many variations, but the most characteristic represents her standing, holding in her left hand an upright spear, on which she leans and round which twines a serpent. The serpent marks her character as the health-giving deity, and

FIG. 42.—Zeus at Iconium, with sceptre and thunderbolt: coin of the first century B.C.

the Iconian Athena may be regarded as a Hellenised form of the Phrygian goddess, for a Latin inscription is dedicated to Minerva Zizimmene. She was probably styled Polias, the City-Goddess, as an inscription shows. Zeus and Perseus, whom she aided and directed in his travels and his conquest, the other important types are purely Greek.

The bearing of these facts seems clear. Athena with her associated hero Perseus represents the immigrant Greek influence, which became completely dominant in the city, and for a time seemed to have almost expelled the Phrygian religion from the public ceremonial, as Perseus routed and benumbed the natives of the land. But this Hellenic victory was only an outward appearance. The Iconian Athena was a strongly Hellenised form of the Phrygian goddess; the immigrant Greek element made the native goddess their

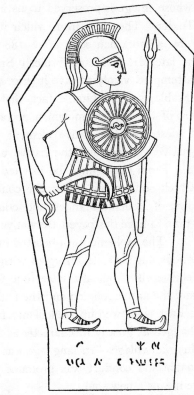

FIG. 43.—Relief at Iconium, now destroyed; after the drawing of Texier.

own and gave her a Greek form; but the common people never lost their hold on their own Mother-Goddess.

This external character as a Greek city belonged to Iconium from the time when its coinage began, probably about 50 B.C. The educated classes and the representative citizens counted themselves as Hellenes, not as Phrygians. The hero of the immigrant Greek civilisation had destroyed the Phrygian character and transformed an Oriental town into a Greek self-governing city. It is highly probable that, just as at Tarsus, so here also Perseus is a Grecised transformation of a native hero, whose image is preserved to us in a drawing published by Texier. The stele from which it was taken was destroyed by a workman soon after 1880, as I was informed by the late Mr. A. Keun, formerly British Consul in Konia, who attempted vainly to save it (Fig. 43).

It is a remarkable, yet indubitable fact, that the patron goddess and hero of the Hellenism which, according to this Iconian legend, destroyed the native element in the city, should be the native goddess and the native hero in their Hellenised form. From this it must be inferred that it was not a body of Greek settlers, but rather the conquering and transforming power of Hellenic manners and education, that seemed for the time to have destroyed the native population by Hellenising it. The Hellenic spirit boasted in the legend that it was victorious, and that the Phrygian village had been made into a Hellenic city; but at a later time the Oriental spirit revived, and the native religion and the native goddess returned. The East swallowed up Hellenism; but the later Iconium was changed as greatly in character as in language from the old Phrygian village. Its language was Greek, and its mode of thought and conduct was profoundly changed. A new language means a new soul.

§ III. THE TERRITORY OF ICONIUM.

In attempting to estimate the character of Iconium and the tone of its population, we cannot follow chronological order so faithfully as in Tarsus and Antioch. The nature of the evidence, which has to be worked out step by step, makes it necessary first to describe the territory and the villages, next to prove that Iconium (which was made a Colonia by Hadrian) was in the Province Galatia throughout the first three centuries, thirdly to describe its constitution as revealed by inscriptions. Thereafter, it will be possible to give a clearer account of the Hellenic city and of the Roman Colonia.

Iconium commanded and formed the centre of a very wide territory. The plain that stretches away to north and east and south was Iconian soil to a great distance from the city. On the south the territory of Iconium bordered on Lystra, among the outer Isaurian hills. The natural features suggest, and Ptolemy is in agreement, that the territory which belonged to Lystra did not extend into the plain (though Lystra was a Lycaonian city).

On the south-east, beyond all doubt, Iconian soil stretched nearly as far as Kara-Dagh, fourteen hours away. On the north-east it reached almost certainly to Boz-Dagh, which divided it from northern Lycaonia, a half-Phrygian, half-Lycaonian district. On the west and north the bounds are not so clearly marked by nature. Iconian territory on that side extended some distance into the mountainous or hilly region which for the most part belonged to the Orondians. Probably the basins of the small streams which flowed into the Iconian plain were included in Iconian territory; and on this principle the limit between Orondian territory and Lycaonia (*i.e.* Iconian) has been marked in the map attached to my article on Lycaonia already quoted.[10] The north-east part of this hilly region, lying between Iconium and Laodiceia the Burnt, seems to have formed part of a great estate belonging to the Roman Emperors.

That estate was originally the property of the Great Goddess, the Zizimmene Mother, or Mother of Gods, already mentioned in § I. As was the case at all the great sanctuaries of Asia Minor, the Mother of Zizima was mistress of the lands around her chosen home; and the people were her servants, the slaves of the sanctuary. During the Roman period the mines and the lands of Zizima became Imperial property, and were managed for the benefit of the Emperor's private purse by his own personal agents, his slaves and his freedmen. The goddess had originally been more closely connected with Iconium, if we may judge from the number of dedications found in that city; but under the Romans the mines were managed from Laodiceia, as is shown by the large proportion of Imperial slaves and freedmen who are mentioned in the inscriptions found there.[11] (See Pl. XII.)

It was usual that the management of such a property should be centred in a city, and not in the rural surroundings amid which it was situated. So, for example, the Phrygian marble quarries (which likewise were Imperial property) were managed, not from the quarries, nor even from the neighbouring city Dokimion, but from the more important city of Synnada, nearly thirty miles to the south. That is proved both by the numerous references to the personal agents of the Emperor in the inscriptions of Synnada, and from the fact that the Phrygian marble was known all over the world as Synnadic, because people heard of it as connected with and managed at Synnada, and orders for it were sent there. Only in the home country was the marble known as Dokimian. The deciding reason for this close relation to Synnada indubitably was that Synnada lay on the road from the quarries to Rome, while Dokimion lay in the opposite direction; and if the marble blocks had been carried first to Dokimion, they would have had to be transported afterwards back past the quarries to Synnada on their way to Rome.

Now, though Iconium was in some respects a greater city than Burnt Laodiceia, and probably more intimately connected with Zizima in primitive times, yet Laodiceia was marked out as the natural seat of management for the Roman estates; it was on the great Trade Route leading to Ephesus and Rome; it was closer to Zizima than Iconium was; and it lay between Zizima and Rome. Had the ore been brought from Zizima to Iconium, it would have had to be carried from Iconium to Laodiceia on its way to Rome. Roman convenience dictated the arrangements in both cases.

This is a typical example of the great principle that Rome was the centre of the world in that period, and that everything was arranged with a view to ease of communication with "the great city, which reigneth over the kings of the earth"—as "she sitteth upon the seven mountains"—her by whom "the merchants of all things that were dainty and sumptuous were made rich" (Rev. xviii. 14), "the great city wherein were made rich all that had their ships in the sea by reason of her costliness," and whose "merchants were the princes of the earth"—the one centre to which flowed all trade and all produce of the earth—over whose destruction "the merchants of the earth were in the end to weep and mourn, for no man buyeth their merchandise any more," to whom resorted all the kings of the earth, and all the wealthy, to enjoy her amusements and be corrupted by her vices (Rev. xvii. 2, xviii. 3). In the list of wares which the merchants carried to the great city (Rev. xviii. 12 f.) we recognise the produce of the mines of Zizima in the "scarlet," for the cinnabar which was exported from the

22

remote village among the mountains was the vermilion pigment widely used in the Roman world. The name " Burnt," by which the city was distinguished from the many other cities called Laodiceia, becomes full of meaning when we remember that this Laodiceia was the managing centre of the mining trade of Zizima, and that the ore was treated by roasting either at the city or in its territory. The furnaces were a sight striking to the ancient mind, and the city became known far and wide as Burnt Laodiceia. This hitherto obscure epithet reveals to us an important fact of ancient Lycaonian society and trade.

The same epithet " Burnt" (Katakekaumene) is applied to a district of Lydia, on account of its scarred and blackened appearance, due to volcanic action proceeding from craters which have become extinct in comparatively recent time; and it is likely to have had a similar origin in the appearance presented by the city or the neighbourhood. The idea that the name was derived from a conflagration which destroyed the city rests on no authority, and is merely a modern inference from the epithet " Burnt". The character imparted to a landscape by numerous large furnaces may be seen (on a much greater scale) in various places at the present day. The ancients were interested in the appearance imparted by fumes and fire; for example, a recipe is given in a Greek Magic papyrus now in the British Museum, "to make brass things appear gold "; [12] the method recommended is obscure, but it involved the use of native sulphur, the fumes of which impart a richer yellow tinge to brass.

The land of Iconium was extremely fertile, and highly cultivated by irrigation. Those Lycaonian plains, in great part composed of rich and stoneless soil, are dependent for high produce on irrigation. The spring rains, which are generally abundant and make even June a very uncertain month in respect of weather, are in most years sufficient for a certain amount of cultivation—much wider than at the present day. But the crops produced by irrigation are more abundant, far more certain as being independent of the varying rainfall, and more extensive. A large body of water is poured into the plain by several streams. It is at present for the most part dissipated or left to stagnate in marshes; but in ancient times the supply was (as we have seen in § I.) much larger, more regular, and properly distributed by irrigation.

Strabo contrasts the barrenness of the Lycaonian plains in general with the productiveness and wealth of the Iconian territory; and the only possible reason for the difference, when the soil is similar, lies in the irrigation, which was wanting in the one case, and applied in the other. An indication of the abundant artificial supply of water in the Iconian plain is seen in the narrative of the German crusade in 1190, led by the famous Emperor Frederick Barbarossa. When he marched from Iconium towards the south, he spent the second night at a village called Forty Fountains. Now there are no natural springs in the Iconian territory. After careful questioning of many informants, I could not learn of the existence of any natural fountain in the plain, except a small one under the western edge of Kara-Dagh. On or near the line of Barbarossa's march there is no spring; but the village to which his second day's march would bring him was not far from the natural course of the stream that flows from Lystra into the Iconian plain. The Forty Fountains must have been artificial, supplied from the Lystra water, which is still used in a similar way, partly for irrigation, partly

to supply the large village of Ali-Bey-Eyuk [13]; and Forty
Fountains must have been at or a little north of that
village. The modern village, which takes its name from
a large tumulus (eyuk), "the mound of Ali-Bey," close
beside it, is indubitably the site of an ancient village.

The population of this widely stretching Iconian land
—at least 200 square miles in extent, probably considerably more—was, of course, not entirely concentrated in
the central town. To the ancients the city was not merely
the circle of the walls, but the entire state of Iconium,
with all its territory and the dwellers on it. We have
just given an example of one village, Forty Fountains.
Another was situated about twelve miles further to the
south-east, some distance beyond the river Tcharshamba,
beside a poor modern khan, halfway between Konia and
Laranda. This village must have been not far from the
extreme southern limit of Iconian soil. Except for the
khan, the place is now entirely deserted.

On the road to the north-east, crossing Boz-Dagh towards
Colonia Archelais (Ak-Serai) and central and northern
Cappadocia, there was a village four hours from Iconium,
out of whose ruins the grand old Turkish khan called
Zazadin (perhaps Zaz-ed-Din) [14] has been built. So many
of the stones from the village church, evidently a large and
fine building, have been built into the khan, that an
architect, if allowed to demolish the khan, could probably
rebuild the church almost complete. The ancient village was
close to the khan; but its remains are now wholly covered
by soil. The site is now absolutely deserted. The entire
series of inscriptions built into the walls of the khan have
been published by Rev. H. S. Cronin (who travelled with
me in 1901) in the *Journal of Hellenic Studies*, 1902, p. 358 ff.

A second village on the same road lay at the edge of the plain, just below the point where it begins to ascend the low pass over Boz-Dagh. This site is described more fully in the following section. It has been entirely deserted in modern times, until a small khan, called Ak-Bash, was built (after 1901, before 1904) to accommodate travellers on the road, which is more traversed since the railway has begun to revive the prosperity of the country. An old khan called Kutu-Delik or Dibi-Delik stands about half a mile west of Ak-Bash. It has been built out of the ruins of a village which stood here (see § IV.).

The villages of the Iconian territory have not been carefully or exhaustively examined ; no part of Asia Minor has been explored with proper minuteness. There would be no difficulty in constructing a fairly accurate map of the territory, showing most of the villages ; but much time would be required, with careful and skilful work. The villages were numerous, but the traces are slight. A few examples only are here given of those whose remains are most familiar.

Out of the many Iconian villages which we have examined all but two have yielded inscriptions. Others I refrain from mentioning, whose traces are plain. These ancient villages do not always coincide with the modern villages. Some are now absolutely uninhabited, while in many modern villages I saw no trace of ancient life except occasional stones, which had probably been carried. The ancient villages lay mostly on the roads. Hence they played a part in the spread of Christianity, as will be shown in another place.

Villages like those of the Iconian territory must be pointedly distinguished from the old class of Anatolian villages. The latter were real centres of population and life, possessing a certain individuality and character which differed utterly from the character of the Hellenic City or self-governing State; such villages were Oriental, and not Hellenic, in character; and the native Anatolian "organisation on the village system" is often mentioned as diametrically opposed to the Hellenic social and political ideals. Those villages of the Anatolian type had certain officials, such as komarchs, brabeutai, etc., varying in different districts: so, for example, the villages on Imperial estates, like Zizima, retained their ancient native character, and were absolutely non-Hellenic in type. But the villages on the soil of a Hellenic City-State were, so to say, outlying parts or detached fragments of the central city. The free inhabitants were not villagers, but citizens of the city, and they shared in the political rights of the State. Such villages had no individual character or organisation; it is their nature to look away from themselves to the city of which they are parts. Each free villager was expected to take his share in the politics and administration of the city.

It is true that some traces of individual and separate character may be found in the Iconian villages. Thus a village headman ($\pi\rho\omega\tau\sigma\kappa\omega\mu\dot{\eta}\tau\eta\varsigma$) is mentioned,[15] but only during the fourth century or later, when the Hellenic City-State had lost almost all its nature and power; while during the Roman time, perhaps, there was in the villages of this class only a "first man of the village" ($\pi\rho\hat{\omega}\tau\sigma\varsigma\ \tau\hat{\eta}\varsigma\ \kappa\dot{\omega}\mu\eta\varsigma$), who possessed a certain influence by rank and seniority without definite official position. The exact status of the Iconian villages is, however, not quite certain. In certain cities of Asia Minor the villages seem to have retained more

of their individuality than in the true Hellenic City-State;
such cities, however, were hardly so strongly or early Hellenised as Iconium seems to have been ; Hierapolis, near
Laodiceia on the Lycus, is an example, and it was apparently
strongly Anatolian in character as late as the time of Augustus.[16] The evidence at Iconium, though too scanty to
permit certainty, favours the view that the villages were of
the Hellenised type, mere outlying parts of the central city :
see the account of the village Salarama in § IV.

§ IV. ICONIUM A CITY OF GALATIA.

That Iconium in the time of St. Paul was a city of the
Province called Galatia, is now admitted by every one, even
by Professor Schürer, the most stubborn opponent of Galatic
provincial unity. The question now is, how long that connection lasted. The view has been stated in my writings
on this subject that Iconium and Lystra were included in
Galatia until the reorganisation of the provinces in the latter
part of the third century. Monsieur Imhoof-Blumer, on the
contrary, in his great work on the coins of Asia Minor, places
Iconium in the Eparchia Lycaonia, which was formed (as
we saw in § II.) about 138 A.D. No one, as a rule, is more
accurate in such matters than the great Swiss numismatist ;
but the evidence is here against him.

That Iconium belonged to the Province Galatia until the
end of the third century can be proved, not indeed with the
conclusive certainty with which the date of the colonial
foundation has been demonstrated in § II., but at least with
an approximation to certainty much closer than is possible
for many universally accepted facts of ancient history. The
best authority for the limits of the Province about the end
of the third century is the very brief *Acta* of St. Eusto-

chios in the time of Maximian. Eustochios was a pagan priest at Vasada, who adopted Christianity after seeing the steadfastness of the martyrs, and came for baptism to Eudoxius, bishop of Antioch. Afterwards, as a Christian presbyter, he went to Lystra, where he had relatives. He was arrested, taken to Ancyra, tried and executed with his relatives and children. It is here clearly shown that Vasada was subject to the bishop of Antioch, and that Lystra was in the Province of Galatia, of which Ancyra was the capital.[17] Had Lystra been reckoned as a city of Lycaonia, a prisoner arrested there would have been taken for trial to the metropolis of the Province, whether this was some Lycaonian city, or (as is more probable) Tarsus in Cilicia.[18] Now, if Vasada and Lystra were in Galatia, much more must Iconium, which lay directly on the way from both cities to Ancyra, have been in Galatia. On this saint see also p. 378.

Some writers may refuse to be convinced by this evidence, as the tale of St. Eustochios is not preserved in an independent form, but is merely related in Greek Menaea under 23 June, and the Menaea are confessedly not an authority of high character. But, although the form in which the tale has been preserved is quite late, it must rest on some good and early authority. Somewhere about the end of the third century Lystra ceased to be under Ancyra; and after that time such a tale could not have been invented.

Moreover, other authorities confirm the *Acta* of Eustochios. Ptolemy indeed is confused and self-contradictory: he says quite rightly that Vasada and Lystra were in the Province of Galatia, but he assigns the district Lycaonia to the Province of Cappadocia, and gives in it seven cities, one being Iconium. This absurd and utterly unhistorical classification is due to his mixing up authorities of different periods. His

Galatian list is good ; and, though not a complete enumeration, is correct so far as it goes, whereas the Cappadocian
list is full of inaccuracies and blunders, to explain which so
as to gain any knowledge from the list involves elaborate
argument and a good deal of hypothesis. We therefore
leave Ptolemy aside for the moment.

All doubt, however, is set at rest by a milestone, found
at Salarama close under the south slope of the Boz-Dagh
in Iconian territory (§ III.). It was erected at the order of
the governor of the Province Galatia, C. Atticius Strabo, in
198 A.D.

It is unquestionable that this milestone originally stood on
Galatian territory ; and we may confidently say also that
it stood from the beginning close to its present position in
the plain below the Iconian end of the pass. There was
here a village or settlement under Iconian jurisdiction, and
the ruinous old Turkish khan,[19] in which the milestone is
built, has been constructed out of the stones of this village,
in the same way as Zazadin Khan (see § III.) was built.
The name of the village was (as will be shown below) probably Salarama.

It is true, indeed, that stones are often carried from a considerable distance to be used in modern buildings ; but the
stones which are thus brought are chosen because their shape
and size make them suitable for the purpose ; and moreover
transport is now more necessary because the supply close at
hand has been exhausted. But any observant traveller—few
archæological travellers, however, are observant in such
matters—can in almost every case determine whether the
stones in a large building, situated in a now lonely and
isolated situation like this khan, have been transported from
a distance or found on the spot. Such evidence should

always be noticed and recorded ; but how rarely is it that any explorer condescends to observe details of this kind. Yet out of such details history is built.

A milestone, obviously, is the kind of stone which no one would carry far, especially over a mountainous pass, to build a wall : an irregular column, very rough in surface, thicker at one end, large and weighty, it is as unsuitable for building purposes as any stone can well be. Not far from it is a large flat slab, on which once stood the altar or table in the village church : it shows the four square holes at the four corners and a larger central hole, circular, surrounding an inner smaller square hole, in which the five supports of the sacred Trapeza were fitted, with a dedicatory inscription on the front edge, "the vow of Cyriacus". Had this stone been transported from a distance it would have been broken, either for convenience of transport, or from accident by the way. If it were broken into small fragments, too, it would be far more useful for building; but, as it stands, it is nearly as unsuitable as the milestone. The mere weight of these stones is prohibitive. They were put into the walls, in spite of their inconvenient shape, because they happened to be lying near at hand, and it entailed less trouble to utilise them as they were than to break and trim them, or to transport other more suitable stones from elsewhere.

Still more important and conclusive evidence is got from another huge block, in the wall of the khan, which must weigh many tons and could not be carried far by Turkish builders. It bears the Greek epitaph of C. Aponius Firmus, who had served as a cavalry soldier in the Roman army and attained the rank of a petty officer. Aponius belonged to a family which lived in this village of Iconian territory, and he was buried in the family burying-place here. It was a family of some wealth and importance, as can be gathered from the facts: this huge block of fine limestone must have belonged to a large mausoleum, and the inscription extended over two blocks at least, and is engraved in large finely-cut letters of the second or third century. Considerable expense was required in constructing such a tomb, as the limestone must have been carried a good many miles: such transport was commonly practised in Roman times, though Turkish engineering was rarely capable of it. Moreover the "large letters" of the inscription[20] imply some pretension and a desire for conspicuousness. Another fine limestone block (not so big or weighty as this) from the same village cemetery, perhaps part of the same mausoleum, certainly from the grave of a member of the same family, has been carried seven or eight miles south across the plain to another old Turkish Khan, called Sindjerli. It was the gravestone of C. Aponius Crispus, who had been duumvir (*i.e.* supreme magistrate) of the colonia Iconium somewhere about 155-170 A.D. It also is written in Greek.[21]

The family of Aponius was therefore possessed of, and resident ordinarily on, a property in this northern part of the Iconian territory. Members of the family entered the Imperial service, and held office in their own city; but their burial place was at their country residence, about twenty-five miles north-east from Iconium. The relation of the villages in the Iconian territory to the central city has been treated in § III., and this Aponian family furnishes an excellent example. It received the Roman citizenship, and took the name of a Roman family, well known in the first and second centuries,[22] some member of which had been in relations with the first member of the Iconian family that attained the citizenship. The name and the rights were transmitted to

his descendants in the usual way. This family has nothing
cf the village character about it : it was evidently Iconian in
one generation after another, using the Greek language, and
following the usual course of municipal office, like other
members of distinguished Iconian families.

Another inscription in Sindjerli Khan, a dedication to
Zeus Salarameus, shows the local name. This Zeus, according to a common custom, derived his name from the locality,
and as both inscriptions are likely to have been brought
from one place,[23] there is every probability that the village
at the foot of the pass was Salarama.

Thus our argument has afforded a decisive proof that the
village at the south end of the pass formed part of the
Iconian City-State, and that the whole State, like this
part, was still included in the Province Galatia as late as
A.D. 198 ; and this practically means that the connection
between Iconium and the Province Galatia lasted unbroken
from the institution of the Province in 25 B.C. until about
the end of the third century after Christ.

Incidentally, this result gives a pleasant confirmation of
the trustworthiness of the *Acta* of Eustochios ; and it is to
be hoped that some fuller record of the martyrdom may
hereafter be discovered ; in all probability the *Acta* would
throw some welcome light on the condition of Vasada and
Lystra about A.D. 270-300.

It may appear immaterial as regards the Pauline period,
whether Iconium was Galatian in the second and third
centuries after Christ; but such a way of looking at the
case is essentially superficial. Though the point does not
directly concern the interpretation of Acts, it has indirectly
an important bearing on it. You cannot get a proper
conception of the character of a Hellenic city by looking at

it in one period alone: you must regard it as a living
organism, you must understand the history and law of its
growth, and to do so you must " look before and after " the
period that immediately concerns you.

In regard to Iconium the critical question in recent discussion undoubtedly has been whether its incorporation in
the Province Galatia was merely nominal and external, or
was a real and vital fact of Roman organisation which
would affect the character of the city, *i.e.*, of the Iconian
people. In thinking of a Hellenic city one must always
keep clearly in mind the principle of city life as stated by
Thucydides : a city is constituted not by walls and buildings
but by men. The Hellenic city was an association of free
citizens, taking action voluntarily for the common good by
choosing individuals out of their number to whom they
should entrust for a limited time certain powers to be exercised for the benefit of the whole city, leaving the individual citizen free and uncontrolled except in so far as all
by common consent curtailed their own rights in order to
make the city safer and stronger.

The question as to the Galatian character of Iconium,
then, really amounts to this—was the Roman provincial
organisation in the first century a mere fetter on the free
Hellenising development which had begun in the city at
least two centuries earlier, an institution too alien in character to touch the heart and spirit and life of the citizens ?
or was it a real influence affecting their thoughts and life and
conduct ?

The answer to that question is of prime consequence both
for the historian and for the student of the New Testament.
The character and the measure of Roman influence on
Western Asia is involved in it: the meaning of the terms

"Galatia" and "Galatians," with all the numerous consequences for the life, chronology, sphere of influence and
direction of missionary effort of St. Paul, turns upon it.

In the first place we observe that, if the influence of the
Roman organisation on Iconium and the rest of the group
of the Pauline cities of South Galatia had been so essentially weak as writers like Prof. E. Schürer and Professor
Zöckler represent it to have been, it must have been
evanescent and could not have lasted. As we have seen,
Hadrian modified the organisation of south-eastern Asia
Minor, to give freer play and stronger effect to the racial
and national spirit. There was then a favourable opportunity to separate Iconium from the Province Galatia, if
the connection had previously been only external and
fettering. But, inasmuch as the connection of Iconium
with the Province Galatia persisted through the reorganisation, the probability that the connection was strong and
real is much increased. The Romans had hitherto always
thought and spoken of Iconium as situated in the half-
barbarian, half-Romanised Lycaonia, one of the component
parts of their Province Galatia. But about 130-138 A.D.
they separated it from Lycaonia, and left it in the Province
Galatia, at the time when they were forming a Commune of
the Lycaonians in a new Province to attach them more
closely to Rome. The Iconians themselves had all along
distinguished themselves from Lycaonia as being citizens of
a Phrygian Hellenic city; and now the Romans recognised
Iconium as a Roman colony, with the highest class of Roman
rights permissible for a city of the East, in their old Province
of Galatia.

Secondly, Iconium had been attached to the Galatian
State before the Roman Province of Galatia was constituted.

Amyntas, king of Galatia, ruled over it; and the view has been maintained elsewhere that Iconium was taken by the Gauls about 165-160 B.C.[24] Now, it is true that very few references to the Galatian connection have been found in Iconium: but extremely few inscriptions of Iconium are known earlier than the colonial foundation, and the only document which bears on the provincial connection mentions the Galatic Province. In considering·whether the people of a city in the Galatic Province would accept for themselves the address "Galatians," we may appeal to the analogy of another city of the same region. Take the case of Apollonia in Pisidian Phrygia, far further distant from northern Galatia than Iconium was, handed over by the Romans to Amyntas, the last Galatian king: the Galatian connection must inevitably have been far weaker there than in Iconium. Yet at Apollonia in A.D. 222 a citizen spoke of his city, in an inscription that has fortunately been preserved, as his "fatherland of the Galatians,"[25] and mentioned his son's career of honourable municipal office among the noble Trokmians. It is not necessary to remind the reader that the "fatherland," to the Greek mind, was one's own city, and not a country or a region. Moreover, in a monument exposed to public view in Apollonia it was impossible to speak of any place except Apollonia as "fatherland".

Apollonia, therefore, geographically a Phrygian city, by education a Hellenic city, was politically so thoroughly a Galatian city in the third century, that an ordinary citizen could speak of its people in this simple and direct way as Galatians; to hold a magistracy in Apollonia was "to be glorified among the Trokmoi".

In this last phrase the name of one of the three Galatian tribes is used as a mere poetic variation of "Galatai"; a second term was needed both to avoid the repetition of Galatai in two successive lines and for metrical reasons.[26] Now, if in Apollonia people could speak in this tone and spirit, there cannot exist a doubt in the mind of any one who is guided by evidence and not by antecedent prejudice, that in the southern cities of the Province generally the Romanising spirit was strong enough to affect thought and expression, and to make the address "Galatai" acceptable to an audience gathered out of several Galatian cities.

It may be objected that the actual examples which can be quoted are rare, one in Iconium, and one in Apollonia ; but this is a valueless argument. These are the only cases which exist, there are no other cases to quote on the other side, and these are of the kind where one is practically as good a proof as a score, for one shows what was the familiar public custom.

Thus from these details, recovered one by one through many years of travel and study—during which the isolated facts, insignificant and almost worthless in themselves, have acquired meaning and value through juxtaposition with one another—there is gradually built up a unified conception of Iconium as a city of Hellenised character, situated in the extremest corner of the Phrygian land (where the Phrygians had encroached on what was in a geographical view really part of the great Lycaonian plain),[27] but so strongly penetrated with Roman feeling and loyalty that it was honoured with the Imperial name about A.D. 41, and finally raised to the dignity of a Roman Colony about A.D. 135. It always held aloof from its Lycaonian neighbours and fellow-provincials, and clung to its first Roman connection with the Province Galatia for more than three hundred years, for Galatia was much more thoroughly Romanised than the

"Three Eparchies". Its coins show that in the first and second centuries it boasted especially of its semi-Greek origin from the Greek hero Perseus conquering the native population. Later a more distinctively Phrygian origin seems to have been claimed in popular legend. But through all times and authorities the mixed character of the city is apparent.

§ V. THE CONSTITUTION OF THE HELLENIC CITY ICONIUM.

The number of Tribes in Iconium is shown by the strange expression employed in an inscription, "the four *stemmata* of the Colony"[28]; these *stemmata* must be interpreted as the four garlands of honour placed upon the monument by the four Tribes into which the Colony was divided, and the number apparently corresponded to the four elements out of which the population was composed. Unfortunately the names of only three of the Tribes are known, and some of them only in later forms of Imperial character.

One was the Tribe of Athena Polias. Now a dedication to Minerva Zizimmene has been found at Iconium,[29] which proves that, as has been already stated in § I., the Athena or Minerva of Iconium was merely a Hellenised form of the Phrygian Mother-Goddess; and therefore there can be little doubt that the Phrygian part of the population was enrolled in the Tribe of Athena. This would be in point of numbers a very large tribe.

Another Tribe bore the name Hadriana Herculana, and a third was styled Augusta. It is impossible to say what racial elements were incorporated in these Tribes, but perhaps the Roman citizens were placed in the Augustan Tribe. There are analogies that favour this supposition. The Roman citizens, however, could not have been suffici-

23

ently numerous under Augustus to constitute even a small Tribe, and other racial elements may have been incorporated in subdivisions of the Tribe.

This Augustan Tribe was doubtless an older institution renamed in honour of Augustus. It may have contained also some new population introduced when Iconium became a Hellenised self-governing city. Iconium was in the territory granted to the Pergamenian king Eumenes by the Romans in 189 B.C.; and it was the invariable custom of those Greek or semi-Greek kings to maintain their power

Fig. 44.—Heracles at the Colony Iconium: coin struck under the Emperor Gallienus.

by establishing Hellenised cities, with an accession of population devoted to the founders' interests, as centres of Hellenism.[30] It is, however, practically certain that Lycaonia, though given to Eumenes, was too remote to be firmly held by him or his successors; and thus Iconium was likely to acquire that self-centred and individualised character, differentiating it from other foundations of the Pergamenian time, which is apparent in the scanty records of its constitution and history.[31]

The Tribe Hadriana Herculana was evidently an old

Tribe, united in the worship of Hercules, which received an additional title in honour of Hadrian.   On coins of Iconium Hercules appears in a purely Greek form, as the hero with the club and lion's skin (Fig. 44).   But in those regions the Hercules who was actually worshipped was an Oriental deity who gave a new name, Heracleia, to the Cappadocian town Cybistra, and was similar in character to the Cilician Sandon.   No evidence justifies even a conjecture as to the character of this Tribe.

The name of the fourth Tribe is unknown ; but when we take into consideration the long Galatian connection, beginning probably about 160 B.C., and remember that a monastery "of the Galatians" existed at Iconium,[32] the probability is evident that a Galatian element was introduced into Iconium, and this element naturally must have been formed into a distinct Tribe, whether that of Hercules, or some other.

The ancient Phrygian origin and the new Hellenism of Iconium stand out clearly in the foundation legends. But those legends are not to be misinterpreted as giving any trustworthy information about the primitive history of Iconium.   They show what was popularly thought about Iconian history at the time when they were current in the city and in that part of the Iconian population among which they circulated.   The Hellenes talked of their origin from the conquest by Perseus, the hero who represented the immigrant population : the Phrygians prided themselves on their antiquity and doubtless on their autochthonous origin. This latter detail is not mentioned in the brief record ; but it cannot be doubted that in ancient times a people who believed they were settled under the rule of kings before the Flood, also believed that they were sprung from the earth.

The legend of Perseus was firmly rooted in the Iconian belief before 50 B.C., for it affected the earliest coin-types (which belong to that time).

About the time of Christ Iconium was a Hellenic city, proud at once of its ancient pre-Greek origin at the very beginning of history, and of its transformed and thoroughly Hellenic character. Its free, self-governing constitution is marked by the magistrate's name, which appears on some of its early coins, Menedemos son of Timotheos. The spirit here is Greek. Whereas the Phrygian was quite Oriental in character, a slave of government, submitting to the rule of a king or of the god through his priest, the Greek was a free citizen, master of his own life, joining by vote and lively interest in the administration of his own city, his fatherland.

How and when the transformation of Iconium from an Oriental town to a Hellenic self-governing city was actually accomplished in history is unknown. That Greeks must have gradually settled as residents in the town from the time of Alexander the Great onwards may be assumed as certain. That process was going on all round the Eastern Mediterranean lands, and Alexander's victory made Asia Minor easily accessible. But this alone does not account for the transition in government that came about.

It may be regarded as improbable that the Seleucid kings made any formal refoundation at Iconium, such as they made at Laodiceia, twenty-seven miles to the north. Lycaonia was not a frontier land, where it was important to attach the people by favour and gratitude to the sovereign (see Part II., § XI.). Before 189 B.C., a large tract of country reaching far to the west of Lycaonia belonged to the Seleucid Empire. In that year Lycaonia was taken away from the Seleucid sovereign along with all the other districts beyond Taurus. Whether the Pergamenian kings made any formal refoundation of Iconium is uncertain : no evidence remains of such action, and some evidence would have been likely to survive.[33]

It seems probable that Iconium, situated so far from the seat of government and containing a considerable Hellenic population, partly Greek by origin, partly Hellenised Anatolian, wrought out for itself a constitution and widened the citizenship. The Pergamenian kings, whose authority over that distant region was only nominal, would readily acquiesce in the change. This change was the triumph of the Hellenic system over the native Phrygian system, shadowed forth in the legend as the victory of Perseus. The peculiar form of this legend in Iconium seems to require a supposition of this kind. In Tarsus, where Perseus represents a body of colonists introduced all at one moment into a mixed State, the legend has a different form. Iconium attracted settlers gradually.

The best parallel to the Iconian legend is found at the ancient Celaenae, where at an early time without any formal colony Greek population and manners gradually established themselves, and the transformation of the Phrygian town into the Hellenic city was shadowed forth in early legend as the victory of the Greek Apollo over the Phrygian Marsyas. This legend was far older than the refoundation of Celaenae as the Seleucid city Apameia (*Cities and Bishoprics of Phrygia*, ii., p. 414).

The want of any coins of the second century B.C. might be used as an argument against the theory that the Hellenisation of Iconium occurred so early as that period ; but the weakness and uncertain status of the slowly growing Iconian

constitution render the argument weak.   Moreover, northern
Lycaonia with Iconium seems to have fallen under Galatian
rule about 164 B.C., and to have been named "the Acquired
Land " (προσειλημμένη)[34] ; and it is probable that Iconium
was part of a Galatian Tetrarchy, and therefore incapable
of striking its own coins.   It is, however, quite possible that
a certain degree of home rule should prevail in the city under
the loose tribal Galatian system, without the higher sovereign
rights.

The Hellenisation of Iconium is, as we have seen, clearly
marked in its earliest coins.   Zeus and Dionysos are the
principal types, two Hellenised expressions of the principal
native deity.   Perseus holding the Gorgoneion or the Gorgoneion alone are the reverse types.   The names and letters
on the coins are Greek, like the subjects, showing that the
victory of Hellenism in the city was complete.   The presence of a magistrate's name in some cases (as above mentioned) proves the existence of a constitutional form of city
government.

The period to which these coins belong is probably about
the middle of the first century B.C. or slightly later.   Iconium,
with at least central and southern Lycaonia, had been taken
over by Rome and incorporated in the enlarged Province
Cilicia (perhaps by Pompey in 65-4 B.C., perhaps even earlier).
The relaxing of Roman authority during the Civil Wars
after 49 B.C. may have encouraged Iconium to assume the
sovereign right of coinage.   In 40 B.C., when Roman power
was reviving under the tyranny of the Triumvirs, Antony (to
whose share the East was assigned) gave Iconium and a
large kingdom comprising part or the whole of southern
Lycaonia and Tracheia Cilicia to Polemon.   This sovereign
seems to have proved incapable of ruling his large realm,

which was to a great extent peopled by unruly Isaurian
tribes of mountaineers; and in 37 he was transferred to
Pontus. The more able and warlike Amyntas of Galatia
was entrusted with the government of Lycaonia and Pisidia,
while Tracheia Cicilia went to swell the vast kingdom which
Antony presented to Cleopatra.

The robber Antipater, an acquaintance of Cicero's, had
made himself master of Derbe and Laranda; but these were
soon conquered by Amyntas, armed with Roman authority
and Galatian troops. In 25 B.C., however, Amyntas was
killed in battle; and his whole kingdom, including North
Galatia, Lycaonia, and Pisidia, was formed into the Roman
Province Galatia. The right of coinage was confirmed to
Iconium by Augustus; and the coins just mentioned might
be assigned to this period, were it not for the magistrate's
name. The cities of Galatia seem not to have been permitted to put the names of their magistrates on their coins,
a right which was enjoyed by all the cities of the Province
Asia.[34]

Iconium was now a Græco-Roman city; and Rome in
accordance with its usual policy made no attempt to introduce the Latin language and custom, but accepted the
Hellenism of the Græco-Asiatic cities as a friendly power.
It is therefore one of the many slight and almost accidental
examples of accuracy in details, which abound in the book
of the Acts, that Luke gives the name Hellenes to the population of Iconium, alone among the Galatian cities. In Lystra
and Antioch the people are called "the multitude," ὄχλοι
and ὄχλος. This term, used as the Greek translation of the
Latin *plebs*,[35] was suitable for the people of Roman Colonies.
If the modern German scholars had been right in making
Iconium a Claudian colony, the term Hellenes used in Acts

xiv. would be unsuitable. Luke rightly uses the same term about the people of Thessalonica, Corinth and Ephesus.

That a body of Jewish settlers existed at Iconium is certain ; but whether these Jews were citizens or merely resident strangers is as yet unknown. If they were citizens, they could hold the right only as a distinct Tribe or as a special and exclusive division of a Tribe.[34] Evidence is still very defective ; but any day may reveal a decisive document. The names of the three Tribes just enumerated, and the fact that the Tribes had each a *prostates* as its official head, were revealed by inscriptions discovered in 1905 and still unpublished. Previously the constitution of Iconium was wholly unknown.

§ VII. ICONIUM AS A ROMAN CITY.

The Emperor Claudius paid a good deal of attention to the organisation of Lycaonia (see Part V., p. 387). It is a sign and a result of this attention that he gave three Lycaonian cities the right to add his name to their own. Thus we have Claudio-Derbe, Claudiconium, and Claudio-Laodiceia. This of course does not imply that those cities become Roman *coloniae*, for those names are Greek and unknown in Latin usage. It might seem hardly necessary to guard against such a mistake, yet a number of highly distinguished German scholars have made the error ; and it seems hardly possible to eradicate it. It is stated in the fundamental German text-books, which are in every one's hands, that Claudius refounded Iconium as Colonia Claudia Iconium ; and this groundless and false statement is repeated by one writer after another, Marquardt, Pauly-Wissowa's Encyclopaedia, Zahn, and most of the recent commentators on the Acts and the Epistle to the Galatians : the older

commentators are free from it ; the blunder is one of the
triumphs of recent scholarship ; but Professor Knowling
carefully disclaims it, and the leading numismatic authorities
are free from it. The title Claudia Iconium is a fiction of
Marquardt's, adopted on his authority by his followers ; [36]
the title never occurs in that form.

The constitution of Klaudeikonion continued to be that of
a Greek city; and the powers of the State were exercised
by the Demos, the Greek assembly of all citizens. Had
the city been a Roman Colony, the public authority would
have been exercised by the Colonia, *i.e.*, the body of Coloni
in assembly.[37] The language of public documents continued
to be Greek. If the city had been a Roman colony, Latin
would have been used on coins and in inscriptions erected
by the State. It is true that a Roman Procurator who
held office under Claudius and Nero was publicly honoured
by the Demos as " Founder," [38] and this has been quoted
as a proof that he had founded the Colony ; but the title
" Founder " was given very widely, and in honorary inscriptions means little more than " benefactor " (Part II., p. 132).
Moreover, a mere Procurator would not have founded a
Colonia. That honour would have been reserved for an
officer of higher rank.

While it is wrong to infer from the titles Claud-Iconium,
Claudio-Derbe, that those cities were Roman Coloniae, yet
the assumption of such a title implies a great deal of Roman
feeling and an enthusiastically demonstrative loyalty in the
population. To understand how significant such titles are,
a modern example is helpful. Let us imagine Queen Vic-
toria bestowing on the Irish capital the title Victorian Dublin,
or the Irish people accepting such a title. If such giving
or accepting had been possible, how utterly different would

Anglo-Irish history have been during the nineteenth century. Under the Roman Empire such things were possible; and the necessary inference from this must not be ignored.

§ VIII. The Roman Colony of Iconium.

The Greek city Klaudeikonion retained its character and status until the time of Hadrian, 117-138 A.D. Most of the Iconian coins struck in his reign are of the Greek city; but some few are of the Roman Colonia. It is therefore clear that at some time in the later part of his reign Iconium was elevated to the rank of a Colonia, the highest dignity which could be conferred on a provincial city. It then began to use officially the Latin language on coins and in public inscriptions. It disused the honorary title derived from Claudius, and recurred to the simple ancient name; and its full style was *Colonia Aelia Hadriana Augusta Iconiensium* (or *Iconensium*).

The time when Iconium became a Roman Colonia is demonstrated conclusively by an inscription found in 1905, which records the career and public services of the first supreme magistrate of the Colonia (*duumviro primo Coloniæ*).[40] His name was M. Ulpius Pomponius Superstes, and he was son of M. Ulpius Valens. The names are sufficient proof of the date. Evidently the father Valens received the Roman citizenship under Trajan, 98-117 A.D., and took his Roman name, M. Ulpius, from the Emperor. It must therefore have been some time after A.D. 130 before the son of M. Ulpius Valens could be of legal age to be appointed duumvir of a Roman colony. The son M. Ulpius Pomponius, as a leading Roman of Iconium, was appointed one of the two chief magistrates in the year that the Colonia was founded, 130-138 A.D.

The course of events which led up to the foundation of the Colonia was probably as follows : Hadrian, during his second eastern journey, A.D. 130, formed the plan of re-organising south-eastern Asia Minor. He saw that the older principle of provincial division, on which Asia and Galatia especially had been formed—disregarding national divisions, in one case breaking up one nation among two provinces, in another uniting many nations in one province, with the apparent intention of trampling on national patriotism as non-Roman, and substituting the Roman unity, Asia or Galatia Provincia, for the national unity—he saw that this principle had failed, and that national feelings were gradually reviving. He was not prepared to reorganise the whole eastern world ; but he made some changes of the provincial arrangements in the direction of paying more respect to national distinctions and feelings. About the last year of his reign he instituted the new Province of the Three Eparchiae, Cilicia-Isauria-Lycaonia. As the name and organisation show, these Eparchies were to be really three Provinces conjoined under a single head, each retaining its individuality and national character. Thus there was a separate Koinon or provincial Council of the Lycaonians, and no common Council of the three Eparchies.

Iconium was not included in this new Triple Province. For the sake of convenience it had to be left in the Province Galatia ; which, without that city, would have consisted of two separate parts, far distant from one another, Pisidia and North Galatia. But, as a compliment to Iconium, it was made a Colonia, and thus received the highest privileges and rank permitted to a provincial city.

No Italian population seems to have been introduced into Iconium by Hadrian. His foundation of the Colony was

purely a compliment and an honour, which undoubtedly conferred on the citizens some advantages and improved rights.
This kind of merely complimentary Colonia had been unknown in Republican and early Imperial times, when
Coloniae had a Roman purpose and were formed by a body
of Roman *coloni*.[41]   Hadrian made Iconium a Colonia by a
species of legal fiction.

As might be expected from its former loyalty to Rome,
the city had such a lively sense of the honour conferred on
it by Hadrian, that the municipal government tried to act
as if the city were genuinely Roman.   They abandoned the
use of Greek and employed only Latin in official documents,
coins and inscriptions (and doubtless also in documents
written on more perishable materials, like paper, though
these have all perished, and positive certainty is therefore
not attainable).   This remarkable fact shows how real the
distinction was between a Greek and a Roman city, and
how much, as regards the pride of Iconium and patriotism
and sense of dignity, was involved in the question whether
it was a Greek city or a Roman Colonia in the time of St.
Paul.   The account which is given of Iconium in my *Church
in the Roman Empire*[42] and in *St. Paul the Traveller* would
be fundamentally inaccurate if it had been a colony founded
by Claudius.

The people, of course, could not change their language
so easily as the municipality could.   They continued to
speak Greek and to write in Greek.   The epitaphs, with
the rarest exceptions, are Greek after 138 A.D., as they were
before.   In this respect Iconium offers a strong contrast
to Pisidian Antioch (where the epitaphs were for the most
part Latin throughout the first two centuries of the Empire),
and even to Lystra, where Latin epitaphs are quite as

numerous as Greek, the Greek epitaphs being later and the Latin older.

The Roman city or Colonia Iconiensis formed a new ideal for itself. The statue of Marsyas, the emblem and pledge of Roman rights and liberty, was erected in the Iconian forum, and represented as a type on its coins. The other usual Colonial types, the she-wolf with the twins and the founder of the Colony guiding the plough, blazoned the Roman character of Colonia Iconiensis. The type of the

Fig. 45.—The Roman Wolf at the Colony Iconium : coin struck under the Emperor Gallienus.

she-wolf was imitated from the famous Roman statue by many, perhaps by all Roman colonies, and a copy of the statue was probably placed in the forum of Iconium. The last type represents the ceremony of founding the Colony. After the auspices had been taken, the high official who was charged with the duty marked out the limits of the new city and the line of the foss by ploughing a furrow. Every detail of the solemn religious act had to be performed with the due ritual. The plough was drawn by a yoke of bull and cow, both white : the cow was on the left, the bull on the right. The

officer wore the toga girt in the ancient fashion called after
the old Latin town of Gabii, and a fold of it was passed
over his head like a veil; Fig. 53 shows the same type at
Lystra, and it occurs also on coins of Colonia Antiochia.

The name of the Roman Senate (S. R.), which is inscribed
on Iconian coins of the third century, recalls the Roman
connection. The same initials are placed on the coins of
Antioch in that century. Mallos places on its coins after
it became a Colonia either the full legend SACRA SINA-
TUS, misspelt and ungrammatical, or the letters S. C., "by
decree of the Senate". These facts point to some new
arrangement whereby the Roman Senate was granted some
rights in connection with the coinage of these eastern
Coloniae in the third century, showing how real their relation to Rome was throughout the Imperial time. It was
a point of honour in those Coloniae to claim recognition of
their character as no ordinary provincial cities, but outlying
parts of Rome itself.

Yet the Greek character was not expelled, and could not
be expelled, for Iconium had been too strongly affected by
Greek education and feeling; it was still a Greek-speaking
city (except perhaps among the humbler classes, where
the Phrygian language may have still lingered), and so
far as it contained works of art, they were Greek works.
The later coins reflect this side of the city's life, when they
occasionally employ Perseus as a type, or show us the three
Graces (probably taken from a group of statuary in one
of the public places or halls). Athena, too, was the chief
Divine type, and not any Roman god. The Emperors were
the sufficient envisagement of Roman divinity.

But the native Phrygian character found no admission
on the coins, in spite of its growing strength among the

people. It remained always inarticulate, strongest among the uneducated, living in the popular heart. We can only dimly trace it on the lips of the people, as when the Iconian Hierax, a slave in Rome condemned as a Christian in 163 A.D., informed the Prefect who was trying the case that he had come from Iconium of Phrygia; or when Bishop Firmilian mentions that the Council of 232 A.D. was held at Iconium in Phrygia (doubtless repeating the description which he heard in the city, when he attended the Council).

FIG. 46.—The Good Fortune of the Colony Iconium: coin struck under the Emperor Gordian III.

Yet the national character was not eradicated. Hellenism was here only a superficial stratum. The deep-lying character gradually re-emerged. The revival of the national Anatolian character after the first century of our era is a general and striking feature in Asia Minor. The Hellenistic character grows weaker and the Oriental stronger; or perhaps it would be more correct to say that a new and mixed type was developed, in which Oriental, Greek and Roman characteristics were all blended.

The name of the city reflects its character. It never abandoned its ancient name: it held too firmly to its glory

as the oldest of cities to give up the name that marked its
origin. Similarly in Lydia the ancient capital Sardis never
abandoned its name and its Lydian primeval fame; but
Philadelphia, á Grecised refoundation of an old Lydian
town, changed its name to Neocaesareia (though this did
not last long), and Hiera Kome permanently assumed the
name Hiero-Caesareia. Sardis indeed added an epithet
to mark its Roman character and its favour with the
Emperor Tiberius, and styled itself "Caesarian Sardis";
and for the same reason Iconium styled itself "Claudian

Fig. 47.—The Good Fortune of the Colony Iconium: coin struck under the
Emperor Gordian III.

Iconium". In both cases the epithet lasted for a time,
and gradually passed out of use. But such epithets
indicate the tenacious clinging to the character of the
Greek constitutional state: Sardis or Iconium was still a
Greek city qualified by a Roman honorary appellation, a
Greek constitution modified by Roman admixture.

While the Phrygian religion never appears in the coinage,
it affects the ideal representation of the city. The Good
Fortune of Iconium appears always as a matronly figure
seated on a throne, after the fashion of Cybele (Figs. 46,

47); she wears the Kalathos on her head and the full dress of a Greek lady; supported in one arm is the cornucopia, while her other hand holds the rudder; under her chair is the wheel. These are the usual attributes of Good Fortune; but the ordinary Roman type shows the goddess standing. The Iconians preferred the seated figure, under the influence partly of Cybele representations, partly of the established Hellenistic figure of the Good Fortune of the city. The standard of this last type was the statue of Syrian Antioch, seated on the rocks with the river Orontes issuing from

FIG. 48.—The Empress Poppaea as the Goddess of Iconium, A.D. 60-62.

beneath her feet. From Antioch this type spread through Tarsus to Lystra and to Barata in Lycaonia, and was more faithfully imitated in those Lycaonian cities than in the Cilician metropolis (p. 187).

It was certainly the influence of the widespread Antiochian type that made the Iconian artist sometimes add the river-god at the feet of the city goddess: this adjunct is doubly unsuitable at Iconium, for not merely is the river out of harmony with the chair (as at Tarsus, p. 187), but also there is no river at the city. Several small streams flow out of the western mountains, but even the nearest and largest is exhausted for irrigation purposes before reaching the walls. The Tcharshamba Su, which is far distant on the extreme limits of the city territory, is the only Iconian river of any consequence.

Accordingly the Good Fortune of Iconium is a sort of compromise between the Roman type and the Hellenistic. This Iconian type shows that the portrait of Poppaea on coins struck under Nero (Fig. 48) represents the Empress under the form of the city goddess, holding the sceptre in the right hand, and flowers, perhaps poppies, in the left : compare the Antiochian goddess, Figs. 34, 38.

§ IX. St. Paul at Iconium.

The account of Paul's work at Iconium is couched in very general terms—a period of successful work, followed by a riot and expulsion from the city. But even in this vague outline it is clear that the circumstances were markedly different from what happened at Antioch. The Apostles resided a considerable time at Iconium ; the stress laid on this point implies that they stayed there longer than at any other place on this journey. Future history shows that Iconium was one of the most influential seats of the new religion in Asia Minor. Through inscriptions we can trace the ways by which a uniform type of religious custom was diffused over a very large region of central and southern Anatolia, and Iconium was indubitably the centre from which it spread.[43] May we suppose that the long residence in Iconium was more permanently effective than the sudden rapid impression produced in Antioch ? Or shall we prefer to think that the importance of Iconium as a centre from which Christianity spread was due to the ease of communication between it and the country round ? Perhaps both causes had some share in the result; but personally I feel inclined to lay some stress on the first.

It must also be observed that there was no ruling oligarchy in Iconium, like the Roman colonists in Antioch. Iconium was a Hellenic city, where the power lay in the hands of the whole body of citizens. In Antioch Paul's Jewish enemies accomplished their object by appealing privately to the oligarchy through the ladies of high rank who were within the influence of the Synagogue. In Iconium they gained the same end by gradually working on the feelings of the masses. "The Jews that disbelieved stirred up the souls of the Gentiles and made them evil affected." This was a slow process, and during it Paul "tarried there a long time, speaking boldly". Gradually "the population of the city was divided and part held with the Jews and part with the Apostles". There can be little doubt that the uneducated mob was the part that held with the Jews; that is shown both by the example of Lystra and by the issue in Iconium.

One must observe the art with which the method of narration brings out the slow gradual growth of the disaffection: the Jews begin it, thereafter occurs a long period of work, and then at last a popular riot breaks out. The Bezan editor misunderstood the method of the narrative; and, through the comments which he adds to the text, describes two riots in Iconium: one was stirred up by the Jews when they began to excite the minds of the mob: soon this was pacified, for "the Lord quickly gave peace": thereafter followed the period of successful work, and then the great second riot which expelled the Apostles.

In Pisidian Antioch the expulsion was produced by magisterial action; in Iconium it was brought about by mob

violence, for it may be assumed that the attempt at stoning
the Apostles came from the lower classes under Jewish in-
stigation.   One sees how well the difference corresponds to
the contrasted characters of the two cities, one governed
by a Roman aristocracy, the other by a Hellenic body of
citizens.

Taking into account the character of ancient life and city
government, we have material in the narrative of Luke to
form some picture of the expulsion of the Apostles from
Iconium.

In judging about such a situation as this, one must bear
in mind the great difference between ancient and modern
facts.   The magistrates of an ancient city were the bearers
of sovereign power.   During their term of office they exercised the authority which belonged to an independent, self-
ruling, supreme people, and which that people had entrusted
to them by free election.   In particular, large and undefined powers of acting to preserve order rested in their
hands.   The safety of the people was the supreme law.   If
the magistrates considered that the presence of any stranger
was a cause of disturbance, they were empowered in the
interest of public order and safety to eject the stranger by
summary process, without formal trial ; public opinion entirely justified this kind of action, and even regarded it as
a proof of good spirit in the magistrates.   Roughly speaking,
the magisterial power, being sovereign, was such that all
action not expressly forbidden to them was permitted,
always supposing on their part the good intention to maintain order and authority and peace.   In modern times, on
the contrary, all action not expressly permitted to magistrates is forbidden to them, for their power is not sovereign.
In thus expelling obnoxious individuals the ancient magis-

trates were quite justified in summarily inflicting personal chastisement. Much depended on the character and standing of the persons expelled ; the humbler they were in station, the more likely was it that expulsion would be accompanied by blows and even regular flogging.

Thus, on one side, the power of the ancient city-magistrates was immensely wider than that of modern magistrates. On another side, it was more restricted. Their action had merely temporary effect: it was not a lasting condemnation of persons or of teaching. It was also narrow in its sphere : it applied only to one town, and carried no force beyond.

Further, this expulsion, being merely ordered by the magistrates in virtue of their power to do what they considered needful to preserve order in the city under their charge, carried with it no permanent disqualification from returning to Iconium. It did not always imply that the persons expelled had done anything wrong ; but their presence in the city had been productive of discord, and the quickest and easiest way of quieting the discord was to remove the cause outside of the city territory. The disorder in Iconium had arisen because of the coming of these strangers : if the strangers were expelled, the disorder would cease. Such was the easy way of administration, which sought peace, not justice. It would depend on the personal feelings of the magistrates whether or not the expulsion was accompanied by personal chastisement.

Such an expulsion was simply an order to move on ; though it was likely to be repeated if Paul and Barnabas returned to Iconium while the matter was still fresh in the magistrates' memory. But, after a reasonable interval, and especially after a new year had begun and new officers had come into power, the Apostles were not likely to be interfered with, except on a fresh occasion if other disturbances began and fresh complaints were made against them.

Accordingly, considering the excellent opening offered in Iconium and Antioch, one would not be surprised that the immediately following journey was regarded by Paul not so much in the light of a new enterprise, but rather as a useful way of spending the interval that must elapse before he could return to Iconium.

§ X. THE CHRISTIAN CULTS OF ICONIUM.

Iconium, with its neighbourhood, is the one place in Asia Minor where the pre-Turkish ecclesiastical system remains in force to the present day with little change. The Christian population has remained in continuous possession of its own shrines, free to practise its own religious ceremonial with little restriction. In the Seljuk realm there was no tendency to oppress or ill-treat the Christian population, on which the industry and trade of the Mohammedan state largely depended. A Greek built the most beautiful college (Medresse) in Sivas, a leading city of the Seljuk Empire, and his name Kaloyan (*i.e.* Kalo-Yanni or Joannes) is inscribed upon it. The Christian heretics, who abounded in Phrygia and Lycaonia, preferred the mild Seljuk rule to the persecuting bigotry of the Orthodox Emperors. Hence the ritual of Iconium was not actively interfered with by the Moslems, while Konia lay too far apart from the Christian world to have its old customs modified by change of religious feeling or by the growth of new needs. In such a city as Smyrna, the existing facts of religion cannot safely be taken as evidence of the Byzantine system; for there foreign influence and close relation with other Greek ecclesiastical centres have caused a certain amount of change (it cannot well be called development) in the local church arrangements. In Konia, on the contrary, we can confidently regard the present facts as preserving the Byzantine ecclesiastical ritual. Hence a sketch, even imperfect, of the chief Greek ceremonial at Konia presents some interest as a record of historical survival.

There are four popular festivals (*panegyris*) among the Orthodox of Konia.

1. St. Chariton has a monastery, now uninhabited, except at the time of the festival on 28th September. The buildings, however, are kept in repair by a custodian (who is not a monk, but a layman). They are situated in a narrow rocky glen, which extends up from the plain of Konia into the mountains, about five miles north-west of the city, and close under the hill of St. Philip (Takali Dagh). This glen is parallel to the one in which is situated the large village of Sille, inhabited by many Christians and a smaller number of Mohammedans; but the glen of Sille is nearly a mile further north. The monastery of St. Chariton, situated under a perpendicular precipice on the north side of the glen, is regarded as holy even by the Moslems; a small mosque stands in the centre of it; and the Tchelebi-Effendi, the chief of the Mevlevi Order of Dervishes, makes a donation of olive oil every year. The legend explaining the origin of the Turkish veneration is mentioned in *Pauline and Other Studies*, p. 188; but according to the best form of the legend it was the son of a former Tchelebi Effendi, or of the founder of the Order, Djelaled-Din himself, who fell over the precipice and was caught in his fall by the saint and so preserved. (See Plate XIII.)

St. Chariton was a real personage, but the biographical details which are preserved about him (*Acta Sanctorum*,

28th September, p. 575) are wholly legendary. The only facts that can be trusted are that he was born at Iconium and that he founded a famous monastery near Jerusalem. His date is stated under Aurelian (about 272 A.D.) by most authorities, which is impossible, under Julian (363-5 A.D.) by one, which may be correct.

Besides the Turkish mosque there are in the monastery shrines of the Virgin, of St. Saba, and of St. Amphilochius. The last was much venerated in Iconium also (see below). St. Saba also was a founder of monasteries in Palestine; and therefore he was suitably associated with St. Chariton in this monastery.

2. St. Philip has given his name to the nearer of the twin peaks, which tower above Iconium about six or seven miles to the north-west. In the photograph, Plate XI., their height is dwarfed, because the view is taken too close to the city. From a distance of ten or twenty miles, St. Philip seems to stand over Konia like a guardian. The broad and lofty summit of Loras Dagh alone is in some respects an even more striking feature of the scenery; but about the religious ideas which were doubtless connected with it I have learned nothing.

The hill of St. Philip had, beyond all question, religious meaning and awe for the Iconians of pre-Christian times; but about this nothing is known. The great Byzantine fortress, which crowns the mountain, has obliterated all signs of pagan work. The Turkish name, Takali Dagh, is evidently identical with Dakalias, as the Arabs of the ninth century called a great fortress near Iconium.[44] In July, 1907, I heard from one informant that the name Gevele is also applied to Takali; but had not the opportunity of verifying this report. Gevele is the modern form of the ancient name Kabala or Kaballa.[45]

The *panegyris* at the hill of St. Philip is in my notes dated 24th November; but this must be due to a slip on the part either of my informant (who made several other small inaccuracies, which he afterwards corrected) or of myself. The day of St. Philip the Apostle is 14th November in the Eastern Church, 1st May in the Western.

That St. Philip of Iconium was the Apostle, not the Deacon (whose festival was on 6th June), seems certain. It is possible that tradition told of the journey of St. Philip to Hierapolis and to Ephesus by way of Iconium; and there is in fact a probability that a missionary would prefer the land route to the sea way, and the longer road through the Christian cities to the short "Syrian Route" from the Cilician Gates by Savatra. Why St. Philip should be preferred to St. Paul as the guardian of Iconium is a matter of local superstition, which is always capricious and irrational. Possibly Loras Dagh, which overhangs St. Paul's road for many miles, was connected with the great Apostle of Iconium. So far as I could learn, no other cult of St. Philip exists near Konia except on the mountain, where he is certainly the successor and heir of a pagan deity.

3. St. Eustathius has a small church on the western outskirts of Konia: it is of late mediæval or early modern time and possesses little architectural interest, except that it is restored or rebuilt from an older church. How the worship of St. Eustathius was become connected with Iconium, it is impossible to tell. According to the legendary biography, which is quite untrustworthy, Eustathius was the Christian name given at baptism to an official at Rome under Trajan. He was converted through the appearance of Christ to him when he was hunting; and his wife and two sons followed his example. In order to avoid partici-

pation in the celebration of Trajan's Persian victories, he
fled by ship to Egypt with his family. He was expelled
from the ship, and came to a place named Badyssus, where
he lived fifteen years, when he was brought to Rome and
roasted with his wife and sons in a brazen bull, like that of
Phalaris (*Acta Sanctorum*, 20th September, p. 123).

This Iconian cult is an enigma; the celebration of the
festival on 20th September distinguishes it from the worship of St. Eustochius of Lystra and Vasada on 23rd June
(p. 344); yet the Bollandists have remarked on the possibility of confusion between the two names; but I found
out nothing further regarding it. It is noteworthy that the
name Badyssos is distinctly Anatolian in type.

4. St. George of the Car, Araba-Yorgi, is a local form of
St. George of Cappadocia, the patron Saint of England.
The reason of his association with the waggon at Iconium
I cannot explain from Christian causes. Saints on horse-
back are common; but a saint on a car is unknown to me.
This St. George on the Car is a remarkable, and so far as
my knowledge goes, unique figure. He is apparently a
revival of the Sun-God, Helios, who was worshipped on
mountain-tops, and who generally takes in Greece the
Christianised form of St. Elias, the saint usually worshipped
on the summit of hills. Helios was the god on the car;
the usual representation of him shows him in a four-horse
chariot. On the mountain five hours north of Iconium St.
George takes the place which in Greece was given to St.
Elias.

The festival of Araba-Yorgi on 23rd April is celebrated
on a mountain above Ladik. I have not visited the spot,
but it seems to be not far from Sizma, and the cult may be
regarded as the Christianised form of the religion of the

Zizimene Mother. On this mountain at sunrise milk and
water flow in a dry place: such is the story told me by a
Greek who had not himself been present at the annual
miracle. The legends of St. George may be found in the
Acta Sanctorum, 23rd April, p. 123 ff. (See Plate XII.)

The Christian festival takes place at sunrise on 23rd April,
when a new year and a new summer are beginning. That milk
should, on this occasion, flow in a dry place is a familiar phenomenon in pagan religion, an illustration of the bounty and
power of the god. Usener has collected examples of this
religious belief (as Professor Strzygowski reminds me) in an
article on "Milk and Honey," printed in the *Rheinisches
Museum*, 1902, p. 177 ff. In the panegyris on the mountain
north of Iconium (if my informant is correct), water takes the
place of honey; but in a land where water is so precious, and
where artificial irrigation is absolutely necessary for agriculture, a bountiful flow of water was as valuable and divine a
gift as nectar or honey. In fact there is a great ancient dam
for storing water, a work of wonderful size, in the plain on
the north side of the mountain, some hours east of Laodiceia.
Usener has given many examples of the effect which this
old pagan belief exercised on Christian ritual, where it even
affected in some cases the Eucharist, so that bread and wine
with milk and honey were given to the communicants.

Besides these four popular festivals (all doubtless Christianised forms of older pagan feasts), there are many churches
and holy places which are indubitably survivals of Byzantine
cults.

Amphilochius was made Archbishop of Iconium, when it
was raised from the position of second city of the Province
Pisidia to be metropolis of the new Province Lycaonia,
about 371 A.D. He retained a high place in the veneration

of the Iconian populace, probably not so much on account of his literary eminence and personal character, as because of his opposition to the Arians and support of Basil. The firm hold which the struggle against the Arians had on the popular mind is shown by the inscriptions on a Cappadocian rock-church, specimens of which are published in the *Supplementary Papers* of the Society for the Promotion of Hellenic Studies, i., p. 22. These rock-churches are certainly much later than the time of Basil and Amphilochius; yet they apostrophise the Arian Emperor Valens as if he were still living. Besides the shrine in the monastery of St. Chariton, St. Amphilochius has a church on the acropolis of Iconium, which is architecturally the oldest and the most interesting in the city (Plate XIV.). The quaint legend connected with the transformation of the church into its present form is told in *Pauline and Other Studies*, p. 170 f.

Thekla was the earliest Iconian saint. Her name is a common personal name in Lycaonian inscriptions of the fourth and fifth centuries, and has been given to one of the twin peaks near Konia, which rises behind the village of Sille. At the southern edge of the ravine in which the village stands, also, there is a ridge of rocks in which the place is pointed out where Thekla was received into the sheltering bosom of the mountain. On the opposite side of the ravine is a rocky hillock that bears the name of the Syrian Saint Marina. The worship of Thekla has its origin not in the historical personage, but in the desire of the Anatolian people for a female impersonation of the Divine power.[46] The same feeling leads to the worship of St. Marina, and above all to that of the Virgin Mother of God, the Panagia, who has a church in Sille, besides her shrine in the monastery of St. Chariton. She had also a church at

PLATE XIV.

The Church of St. Amphilochius at Iconium.
To face p. 380.

Konia on the way out to St. Eustathius ; but it fell into ruin, and has disappeared. Plate XI. shows the twin peaks of St. Philip and St. Thekla rising behind Konia (p. 272).

There is, moreover, a cult of St. George of old standing at Konia, and a church of the Holy Transfiguration on the acropolis. The great mosque of Ala-ed-din on the acropolis is also said to be a renovated church of St. Sophia; but this seems a little doubtful.

A garden called Aimanas, on the south side of Iconium, perhaps retains the name of Ai (Hagios) Mannes, a martyr mentioned in an inscription on a column in the Mosque of Ala-ed-din.

At Sille there is a church of the Archangel Michael, the construction of which is attributed by tradition to Constantine and Helena. But Michael, the commander of the heavenly hosts and protector of the Christians, was more probably introduced into the worship of Iconium in the time of the Arab wars, when the populace turned to St. Michael the Stratelates as their saviour during the terrible raids made every year by the Moslems. There are also churches or holy places of the Prophet Elias, of Ayios Panteleêmon and of St. George, and a place called Ayanni (St. John) close to St. Marina.

These remains of Iconian ecclesiasticism take us back, not to early Christianity, but to the Byzantine time, the fifth century or later. There is not a trace of anything that can be called early; even the hills of St. Thekla and St. Philip are probably connected rather with Byzantine superstition and the rehabilitation of paganism in Christian form than with the real historical personages whose name they bear. The one fact that remains in the local legend of St. Thekla is that she was received into the rock ; an evident piece of old pagan belief. The Panagia cult was doubtless later than the Council of Ephesus, 431 A.D.; and that of St. Amphilochius is evidently later than his death, about 400 A.D., perhaps a good deal later.

Considering the character of the Mevlevi Dervish establishment, which is in many respects non-Mohammedan, and has (as we saw) a connection with the monastery of St. Chariton, it is probable that their sacred centre with its splendid pile of buildings (shown in Plate XIII.) has taken the place of a Christian foundation. The holy colour of the Mevlevi is not the Moslem green, but the Christian blue. They do not regard themselves as debarred from drinking the juice of the grape, but openly and publicly offer and drink wine.

It is disappointing that in a place where the Christian power was continuous and the tradition unbroken from the earliest time, there should be such an utter want of early memory. The fact forms one more proof to confirm the general opinion that the Byzantine period was divided by an untraversable gulf from the true old Christian tradition, or rather that the old tradition was overlaid with a vast stratum of paganising superstition of a local Anatolian character, which had never been eradicated from the minds of the uneducated native population. The Orthodox church lost its hold on education. The unchanging East remained : all else had proved evanescent and transitory.

PART V.

DERBE.

The Country of Iconium, Derbe and Lystra.

DERBE.

THE determination of the exact site of Derbe was for a long time a most serious want in the geography of the New Testament. In a general way the situation was practically certain, and the credit for first pointing it out belongs to my friend Professor Sterrett, now of Cornell University, who has done so much to pave the way towards a right knowledge of the topography of this whole country. The territory of all these Lycaonian cities was extensive, and must have been dotted over with villages, which stood in the same relation to the city as we have described above in the case of Iconium.[1] The territory of Derbe was on the extreme south-eastern edge of the Lycaonian plain. It was bounded on the west by the Isaurian hilly country, and on the south by the Taurus mountains. Perhaps it included a considerable tract of the mountain land; but so far as we saw the nearest mountains in ascending one of the front hills of a spur of Taurus, they are singularly rough, rocky, and valueless—in contrast with many parts of Taurus and other mountain regions of Asia Minor, where the glens are often productive and valuable. Further back among the mountains, when the broad, lofty plateau of Taurus is reached, these uplands are probably much more valuable; but there we come to another land, and pass beyond the limits of Derbe, which was essentially a city of the Lycaonian plain (as Strabo describes it), and not of the Taurus mountain-region. The

(385)   25

site of the city must lie either in the plain or on one of the front peaks of Taurus commanding the plain.

On the east the land of Derbe was bound by the two Lycaonian cities of Laranda (which now bears the name of the Seljuk prince Karaman, and continues to be, as it was under the Romans, the principal city of the whole region) and Ilistra (which still retains its ancient name). On the west, as Strabo says, Derbe bordered on the Isaurian country; on the north-west it touched the territory of Iconium, and on the north-east that of Barata, the city of the Black Mountain (the volcanic mass of Kara-Dagh, which rises like an island in the Lycaonian plain). The exact limits towards Iconium are unknown. Towards Barata we followed the boundary stones for a considerable distance. This line of demarcation is unique in my experience, so far as its extent is concerned: even single boundary stones are comparatively rare, and are mostly of Roman time, but here we have a line extending for several miles with no break worthy of notice. It consists of a long series of stones at intervals of about 150 feet.[2] Most of the stones are from one to two feet high, some are flat, a few are not visible, being presumably covered by the soil and sparse scrub of the plain.[3] On the stoneless, dry, dead level soil of the plain, the line of the boundary stones is quite conspicuous; and even where they now barely protrude above the soil, examination by the aid of the spade would probably prove that they have been carried to the spot and placed there by the hand of man.

A few stones belonging to a similar series of termini were discovered in 1901 in Pisidia. The material is harder in them, and they retain the original Latin numbers, showing that they were placed in the Roman time. They probably marked the boundary between the Colonia Parlais and the

Antiochian estates, which passed from the god to the kings and from them into the possession of Augustus and his successors.[4]

The Lycaonian line of stones marks the limit between Derbe and Barata, and was probably placed in the period when Derbe was a frontier city of the Roman Empire, either under Augustus soon after 25 B.C., or under Claudius soon after 41 B.C. (assuming that the bounds were settled at the beginning of one or other of the two periods); and the latter is more probable, as Claudius directed special attention to this district and granted both to Iconium and to Derbe the honourable title of "Claudian". The line would have been the boundary of Roman territory from 25 B.C. to 74 A.D., if the Kara-Dagh was included in the part of Lycaonia which was granted to King Archelaus from 25 B.C. to 17 A.D., and to King Antiochus, 41-74 A.D. But while this assignment is quite probable, it is very far from certain; and in the map attached to a detailed topographical study of Lycaonia[5] I indicated the doubt by making the boundary pass through the city of Barata and along the crest. The title may have perhaps been bestowed when the demarcation of Roman territory (with Imperial properties involved) as well as of the two cities was made. (See p. 360.)

The boundary line crosses the Bagdad railway between the stations of Arik-Euren and Mandasun. Only a few stones can be seen west of the railway; but on the eastern side they stretch for several miles straight to a black volcanic cone called Davdha-Dagh, which protrudes from the plain south of Kara-Dagh. We did not follow them the whole way, as no mark of any kind could be seen on any of the first seventy; and the material is so poor and liable to disintegration that marks could not be expected to last long.

Mr. Mackensen, the Director of Construction of the Bagdad
Railway, first mentioned to me the existence of this line of
stones, for which he desired an explanation; and he made
one of his engineers mark them on a survey plan of the
railway from Konia onwards, which he kindly gave me.
But even without the plan, no traveller who crossed the
boundary could have failed to observe the long straight line
of stones. The fact that it remained unobserved until Mr.
Mackensen noticed the stones and wished to understand
their purpose, was because none of the principal lines of road
crosses or goes near the line, and therefore no traveller came
within sight of them. This is not the only case in which the
railway, by diverging from the commonly used lines of road,
has brought interesting memorials of ancient life within the
range of knowledge. Any one who now travels by the
Bagdad Railway, must be struck with this boundary line, if
he watches the country, instead of devoting his attention to
a guide-book or a novel.

The thin low scrub which covers the plain is characteristic
of Lycaonia generally. Looking from a little distance, one
might imagine that the ground was thinly covered with grass;
but there is in reality hardly anywhere a blade of grass on
the plain, but only low-growing plants of several kinds,
mostly sweet-smelling, the commonest of which is like thyme.
But, wherever there is a slight depression in the level of the
plain with signs of underground moisture near the surface,
grass grows more or less luxuriantly. Sheep and goats find
good food in these shrubs; and the plain is still traversed by
immense flocks of these animals, as Strabo describes it,
when it gave pasture to the great herds owned by Amyntas,
the last king of Galatia. We must understand that the flocks
passed, with the rest of his inheritance, to Augustus and the

PLATE XV.

See p. 389.

Hadji Baba, the Pilgrim Father, the Mountain Guardian of Derbe.

To face p. 388.

succeeding Roman Emperors and formed part of their vast properties in Asia Minor.

The most striking natural feature of the land of Derbe is the lofty conical peak, 8,000 feet or more in height and snow-clad until after the end of June, which overhangs it on the south. This beautiful mountain is conspicuous in the view from Iconium and most parts of Lycaonia, until one crosses Boz-Dagh and gets into northern Lycaonia; and, if one goes far enough north, it again rises into view above the bare, bald ridge of Boz-Dagh. It is called Hadji-Baba, "Pilgrim Father," a name in which the imagination of some of the modern Greeks in Lycaonia finds a reminiscence of the travels of St. Paul; nor can any one regard as impossible the theory that the Turkish name is a translation of a Pauline name attached to the mountain in the Christian time. We remember that the conical peak, about 5,300 feet high, which is the most striking natural feature beside Iconium, bears among the Greeks of Konia the name of St. Philip, and that this name must be regarded as a relic of Byzantine nomenclature,[6] and may fairly be treated as evidence that Iconian tradition made Philip travel from Palestine to Hierapolis and Ephesus by land and not by sea. We remember also that Ephesus stretched from the hill of St. John to the hill of St. Paul. We remember again the probable reminiscence of the journey of St. Paul across Pisidia contained in the modern name Bavlo. In fact, it needs no proof, since many examples are known, that there was a tendency in Anatolia during the Christian period to regard certain prominent peaks as endowed with something of the nature and personality of the Apostles, over whose travels they had stood as silent witnesses. Doubtless the sacred character thus attributed to these peaks had belonged to them long before the Christian period, and the Apostle in each case merely took the place of an older deity to whom the peak had previously been consecrated : so, for example, the hill of St. John at Ephesus had belonged to the Goddess of Ephesus, the hill of St. Paul to Hermes. We are in presence of the same phenomenon which constantly attracts

FIG. 49.—Paul the Martyr of Derbe.

our attention in Asia Minor, *viz.*, the continuity of religious belief and the permanent attachment of religious awe to special localities, to hills, to hot springs, to great fountains, and to other places of various kinds, where the Divine power was most clearly manifested to men.[7]   (See Plate XV.)

In the territory of Derbe remains of city life are chiefly collected along the southern border of the plain, and the site of the actual town must be looked for in this part. They begin on the east at Bossala Khan, under the shadow of the "Pilgrim Father," an early Turkish building with some wretched huts around it, and extend at intervals for about seven miles west, to a mound called Gudelisin. Losta, a village about two miles west of Bossala, contains a great many relics of the late Roman and early Byzantine time ; and several rising grounds between Bossala and Gudelisin are crowned with groups of scattered blocks of cut stone, sometimes covered with Greek inscriptions. The most interesting of these groups is on a sloping ridge, gently rising from the plain about a mile and a half west of Losta. Here there must have stood a church of very large size, and probably other buildings of early Byzantine time. The hillock may be regarded as the site of an ecclesiastical foundation, whose character is to be gathered from the following inscription :—

Nounnos	Νοῦννος
and Vale-	καὶ Οὐαλέ-
rius decor-	ριος ἐκόσ-
ated Pau-	μησαν Παῦ-´
lus the Mar-	λον τὸν Μάρ-
tyr	τυραν
in remembrance	M.X.

The term "decorated" was used commonly in Lycaonia during the third and fourth centuries (perhaps even during a longer period) in the sense of "made the tomb of". This interesting monument, therefore, marks the grave of a Christian martyr, whose body was piously honoured by two of his fellow-Christians, perhaps his pupils. The explanation given

by the Greeks of the district [8]—that the monument com-
memorates the Apostle Paul, and is a proof that he passed
this way and was remembered here—cannot be accepted.
We have here the inscription on a real grave, not on a
cenotaph. Moreover, the monument belongs to so late a
period that it cannot be connected with the Apostle. The
lettering is of the third century, rather than of the first.[9]

This monument evidently belongs to the pre-Constantinian
age, while Christianity was still proscribed. We should
hardly be justified in dating it so late as the time of Diocletian about 300 A.D., for persecution was then so systematic and energetic that the corpse of a martyr could not
have been taken and buried in the ordinary fashion, with a
tombstone of the usual type, and an epitaph openly com-
memorating the facts and names. The incident belongs
either to one of the minor persecutions of the third century
or to the severe but short persecution by the Emperor
Decius, 250 A.D. Several other monuments found in Phrygia
have been interpreted with more or less certainty as placed
over the graves of martyrs of this period; but in none of
them are the facts stated so plainly and simply as on this
Lycaonian gravestone.

The memory of Paul the Martyr of Derbe had not
perished when Christianity became legalised and supreme
in the country; and this incidentally confirms our dating in
the third century, for martyrs of the first or second century
seem rarely to have been remembered in later times as
real personalities at the place of their burial. The hill
became the seat of an ecclesiastical foundation, including a
church of large size, and the pious perhaps chose a burial
place near the martyr, according to a general Christian
custom.

The tombstone of Paul the Martyr has also an interest of another kind. It is ornamented with a pattern of the regular Isaurian type, described by Miss Ramsay in *Studies in the History of the Eastern Provinces*, p. 23 ff : a central pointed pediment flanked by two round pediments, all supported on four columns.[10] Nounnos and Valerius purchased the tombstone ready made, and had the inscription engraved between the central columns. As the letters required more room than the space afforded, the engraver chiselled away part of the column on the right of the central space, and some of the letters extend into the space under the right hand pediment.

The date which has just been assigned to this monument confirms in a most satisfactory way the principle of dating which was stated in Miss Ramsay's article. The origin of the Isaurian scheme of decoration was there assigned to the middle of the third century. As the tombstone of Paul is, plainly and indubitably, an example of an already current and conventional type, we should, on the principle there stated, be bound to infer that it belongs to a date rather later than 250, and that Paul perished in a minor persecution of the period, perhaps under Valerian. Such seems the most probable opinion on a review of all the facts.

The wide extent of the ancient remains that still lie in or close to their original position increases the difficulty of fixing the precise site of Derbe; and the only view that explains the facts seems to be that there were more sites than one. Either Derbe changed its place (as Ephesus was moved more than once [11]), or there were two towns in the locality, with sepulchral monuments lining the way between them. The latter opinion is confirmed by various facts, and the name of a second town can be determined. This was Possala or Passola,[12] which is mentioned as a bishopric in some documents of the fourth century, and later; and the name has remained to the present day in Bossala Khan. It is not necessary to suppose that the Khan stands exactly on the site of the old town. The Khan is on the direct road from Iconium to Pyrgos (Cassaba) and Laranda, and the town stood a little way west from the road at Losta, which is plainly an ancient site; but doubtless buildings and graves extended along the whole way from Losta to the Khan and the great road, so that Losta and Bossala together represent one ancient town. Why the Khan should preserve the old name and the village should lose it, we cannot tell with certainty: it is one of those freaks of nomenclature which are common. The centre of population may have changed its name when its people and its religion changed, while the old name clung to the now separate Khan on the road, along which trade passed, and where Christians were more active and old memories were stronger.

In Losta an old Turkish *Tekke*, a round edifice of religious nature, superior in architectural character and in sanctity to a mere village mosque, indicates the continuity of religion between the ancient Possala and the modern Losta. We notice all over the country that (as a rule) no religious fact was lost in the transition from Christianity to Mohammedanism in Asia Minor. I have seen many cases in which the only evidence of life and human nature still persisting on an otherwise utterly dead and deserted ancient site is the religious awe attaching to some ruinous old Turkish sacred building; the name of some Mohammedan hero or saint is remembered, who lies buried there, for in Anatolian religion there seems always to have been a grave at the central point of the divinely chosen locality; and the inquir-

PLATE XVI.

See p. 395.

The Site of Derbe.

To face p. 394.

ing traveller can detect some signs of a belief in the healing
Divine power that resides at the sacred spot. At such places
the Byzantine Christians used to worship by the grave of a
saint, and the Turks now show the grave of one of their
"Dedes". The outward appearance and the sacred name
change; the essential religious fact persists. Every ancient
city had its religious unity centred at some definite locality,
and this lives on in the minds of men, and the sick and
ailing remember it in their trouble, while the strong and
healthy pass by without a sign of recognition.

Fully five miles west of Losta was the greatest centre of
ancient life in this neighbourhood. Here at and around a
very large mound, called Gudelisin, and chiefly on the low
ground west of the mound, there are plain traces of an
ancient city of moderate extent. Most of the Byzantine or
early Turkish buildings which were seen on the mound by
Professor Sterrett in 1885, and by us in 1890, and which are
dimly visible in the photograph taken then by my travelling
companion, Mr. Hogarth (published as Plate XVI.), were destroyed to build two refugees' villages, one on the south-east
edge of the mound, and the other at a distance of two miles
to the south-east, soon after 1890. Even the larger ancient
cut stones have mostly been carried away. Few sites in the
country are more utterly destroyed; but the surface is
covered with fragments of pottery of all periods from pre-
Hellenic time onwards. In 1901 my wife and I searched
carefully for any scrap of cut stone that might be attributed
to the Greek or the early Roman period, and found only two,
one a small piece of an Ionic volute in marble, the other a
tiny fragment of an inscription with two or three letters in a
good and early style of Cambridge. In 1901 Mr. Cronin
and Mr. Wathen made some excavation in the mound with

eight workmen employed for a day; but they were not fortunate in finding any positive result, and no negative inference follows from investigation on so small a scale.   I believe that here was situated the Derbe where Antipater entertained Cicero, and where St. Paul found refuge and friends, and that much might be learned by excavation even on a moderate scale. The stones and inscriptions from this site, which have been carried westwards to Elmasun three miles away, are Byzantine and late Roman; and the Greek and early Roman work, still more the pre-Greek remains, may yet be found by excavation on and near the mound.

It may be regarded as certain that Derbe was the important centre of population in the Roman period, while Possala was originally a mere village of the territory of Derbe.   A Roman road led from Laranda by Derbe and Lystra to Pisidian Antioch.   A Roman milestone on this road was found by us in 1890 at a bridge over Tcharshamba River, about fifteen miles north-west from Derbe and twenty or twenty-five south of Lystra.   Others have been found close to Lystra, and at intervals on the way to Antiocheia. Only the interval of about twenty-five miles north-west of Lystra still remains unexamined and unknown: [13] the discovery of a milestone in this section would be a welcome completion to our knowledge.   Iconium lay off the line of this road, which was built by Augustus and bore the name Via Sebaste, "Imperial Road," as several of the original milestones show; this term was translated into Greek as βασιλικὴ ὁδός, and in this form survives in the legend of Paul and Thekla.[14]   The original purpose of the road was to connect the two Roman Coloniae, Antiocheia and Lystra, and thus to strengthen the defence of the Province Galatia against the Isaurian and Pisidian mountaineers, especially the Homonades. The road was built in 6 B.C., about the time when Quirinius, Legate of Syria, was engaged in subduing that people.

The "Imperial Road" served only a temporary purpose, and was not in accordance with the natural conditions. Iconium is marked out by nature as the chief centre of life and trade for Lycaonia, and a road which left Iconium to one side could not serve the needs of communication. Thus the direct road from Laranda to Iconium was necessarily more important commercially than the "Imperial Road"; and, as military needs became unimportant after the Isaurian lands were pacified and formed into a Roman Province in 74 A.D., the situation of the village Possala near the principal road gave it growing importance. But Possala and Derbe were always recognised as parts of one state, never as separate cities. The same bishop administered both places, and in the earlier records he is styled Bishop of Derbe, in the later of Possala. The change marks the growth of the latter town and the gradual decay of Derbe. That Possala was the later representative of the decayed Derbe is recorded in a gloss attached to the name of Derbe in a list of bishoprics published by the late Professor Gelzer ; and some list or other record may yet be found in which the full title is given : "Bishop of Derbe and Possala" (ὁ Δέρβης καὶ Ποσάλων).[15]

Professor Sterrett's view approximated to that which has just been stated, and he has the merit of being the first to detect that this locality was the land of Derbe. In his *Wolfe Expedition to Asia Minor*, p. 22, he says: " I consider that the ruins of Bosola and Zosta,[16] being so near together, represent one and the same ancient city. This city I should

like to call Derbe.   Stephanus Byzantinus says Derbe was
a fortress of Isauria, a designation which would suit this site
well enough.   Of course, little can be argued from St. Paul's
itinerary as to the site of Derbe, but in reading the account,
one is impressed with the idea that Derbe cannot be far from
Lystra, and Lystra has been found to be at Khatyn Serai."
The objections to his view are conclusive.   Not merely does
it leave out of consideration the important site of Gudelisin ;
it also ignores the companion town of Possala.   Now, if
Losta and Bossala represent one and the same ancient city,
as my friend and I are agreed in thinking, it cannot be
doubted that Possala was the city in question.   As to Gudelisin, he merely says : " Here a large mound, in every way
similar to the Assyrian Tels, shows many traces of an ancient
village or town.   Most of the remains must be referred to
Christian influence." [17]   The last remark is true of the buildings which he saw on his visit, but not of those below ground
or of the pottery on the surface.

Another village of the territory of Derbe attained some
importance.   It stood about four miles north from Derbe on
the straight road to Iconium ; and the modern name Utch.
Kilisse, " Three Churches," together with the ruins of some
large buildings, prove that it possessed considerable importance in the Byzantine time.   The place is now an uninhabited
mass of ruins, all of a late period, so far as they are visible
above ground : one of the buildings was a church.   Professor
Sterrett, who discovered these remains, appreciates their
character rightly (*Wolfe Exped.*, p. 29).[18]

The description of the roads given above illustrates well
the narrative of St. Paul's journeys.   On his second journey
he came from Syrian Antioch (doubtless through the Cilician
Gates) to Derbe, next to Lystra, and thence to Iconium,

which was about eighteen miles north-north-east of Lystra
and a little way off the " Imperial Road " to Pisidian Antioch.
But, on the first journey, he fled from Pisidian Antioch along
the " Imperial Road ". According to the legend of Paul and
Thekla (as interpreted in the *Church in the Roman Empire*),
when he reached the point where a branch road diverged to
Iconium, a few miles distant, he found Onesiphorus waiting
for him. Onesiphorus, who had been warned in a dream of
his coming, recognised him from the description given of his
personal appearance, and invited him to his own house,
which was next door to that of Thekla's parents. From
Iconium, Paul fled naturally first to Lystra and thence to
the more distant Derbe (Acts xiv. 6).

Little is said about Derbe in the Book of Acts, and little
is recorded of it in other ancient documents. It was one of the
rudest of the Pauline cities, education had made no great
progress in it, and therefore it was not fitted to produce a
strong impression on the history of the Church or of Asia
Minor. Its inscriptions are late in date, and show little trace
of contact with the Roman world. It had, however, a certain
importance about the time of St. Paul as being the frontier
city on a Roman " Imperial Road," and therefore a station
for customs and frontier dues ; [19] and, as it profited so much
by the Imperial system, it had even stronger reasons than
most other Lycaonian towns for strenuous loyalty to the
Empire and for strong Roman feeling. Owing to this
temporary importance it was honoured with the Imperial
title Claudio-Derbe; but it struck no coins until a much
later period.

Although the coins of Derbe are late, they may be quoted
as proofs that Greek art and Greek ways were not alien to
the city. The native Lycaonian inhabitants were educated

in the Greek language, and in all probability regarded themselves as Hellenes in virtue of their education. As a city on one of the great roads, many traders must have passed through it or resided in it, amongst others Jews. There is no trace of any refoundation of the city, at which Jews might have been enrolled in a Tribe as citizens; and we may probably regard the Jews of Derbe as resident aliens. The bestowal or assumption of the title Claudian Derbe does not imply any fundamental change in the constitution, such as took place at Tarsus in B.C. 170 (see Part II., § XI.).

Fig. 50.—The Heracles of Derbe: coin struck under the Emperor Antoninus.

The Heracles of Derbe (Fig. 50) is a Hellenised form of a native god, and proves nothing as to real Hellenisation of the religion. Just as the name Heracleia was applied to Cybistra, not because the Greek god was worshipped there, but because a native god who superficially resembled Heracles was the great god of the region—the peasant-god who is represented on the rock at Ibriz—so Derbe and Iconium and many other Anatolian cities placed Heracles on their coins.

But other types are more indicative of Western feeling.

The Good Fortune of Derbe (Fig. 51) is represented entirely in the Roman style; and the use of such a type is a proof that Roman custom was not unknown in Derbe. The most interesting of the types used at Derbe, however, is thoroughly Hellenistic; a figure of Victory writing on a shield, which she balances on her raised left knee. The attitude and the down-slipping drapery clinging round her middle are strikingly like the Victory of Brescia and the so-called Venus of Melos (the chief ornament of the Greek Galleries in the Louvre), which was certainly adapted from,

FIG. 51.—The Good Fortune of Derbe: coin of the Empress Faustina the Younger.

if it should not actually be restored as, a Victory in this attitude. That wings should be added in the coin is due to the striving for pictorial effect. The figure is a noble and striking one in Lycaonian coinage, and may confidently be regarded as taken from a statue in the city (Fig. 52).

Claudio-Derbe was a city of the Province Galatia till about A.D. 130-135, when it was incorporated in the new triple Province of the "Three Eparchiae," Cilicia-Isauria-Lycaonia. An inscription of the third century at Losta was dedicated to the Emperor Gordian by the three Provinces or Eparchiae.[20]

During this period Iconium and Lystra continued to form part of the Province Galatia. About A.D. 295 the " Three Eparchies" were divided. The southern part of Lycaonia (including Derbe) was now assigned to Isauria, the western and central part (including Iconium) to a new Province Pisidia ; while the northern towns continued attached to the Province Galatia. From an authority of the fourth century Stephanus gathered his description of Derbe as "a fortress of Isauria ". Finally, about 372, Lycaonia was made a Province by itself, and Derbe was included in it.

Fig. 52.—Victory writing on a shield: a statue at Derbe. Coin struck under the Empress Lucilla.

One more point requires notice regarding the site of Derbe. The possibility that the city might have been situated on one of the hills on the southern edge of the plain was alluded to above. We inquired carefully into this, and learned that on one hill only are there any ruins. The second hill west of Hadji-Baba has a huge lump of rock protruding conspicuously out of one side of its summit. This was described to us as covered with walls and houses, built of small stones, with no marble and no inscriptions. The description did not suggest any hope that the Roman

Derbe could have been situated there, but rather that a Byzantine fortress had been built on this lofty point during the troubled times of the Arab raids. In order to leave no doubt however, we ascended the hill. The Kalé, as it is called, is about 1,200 feet above the plain. The ruins cover an oval space of about 150 to 200 yards long by 80 to 100 broad. The walls are not Byzantine work. They are built of small stones, splintered off the native rock, entirely uncut and undressed. The stones are of two sizes. The larger stones were used to form the outer and inner faces of the wall, and rarely, if ever, measure more than a foot in any direction. The smaller stones were mere scraps, piled loosely in to fill up the space between the faces. Not a trace of mortar or any other binding material could be seen in the walls, except that two cisterns for holding rain-water were faced inside with some hard kind of cement. The small size and wretched character of the fortress and the tiny huts of stone inside it were enough to show that this was not Derbe. But the work is early, not late. The impression of date, suggested by the walls, was confirmed by examination of the numerous fragments of pottery scattered over the surface of the ground. Some of these are evidently pre-Hellenic, belonging to a class which is found widely over ancient sites in Asia Minor, ornamented with alternate zones of darker and lighter hue, yellowish or brownish in tint, analogous to some classes of early Grecian pottery which are roughly and not quite accurately described as Mycenæan; others are certainly of Hellenistic time.

One might well imagine that this fortress had been the first stronghold of "the robber Antipater," as Strabo expressively calls him in his brief, incisive way, before he succeeded in making himself master of Derbe, about 60 B.C.

But it is likely to be even earlier in origin, and may have seen the city of Derbe grow and decay again.

In conclusion, it seems right to add that the merit and thoroughness of Professor Sterrett's exploration stand out all the more markedly, when one remembers that two skilful and highly-trained French scholars travelled through the same country about the same time, and placed Lystra at Losta. They argued partly from the name and partly from a short inscription in the village which mentions "Titus and Gaius, brothers, men of Lystra," as the architects of a building. Titus and his brother, however, must have carried their activity and skill from their native Lystra to Possala. Yet the wrong identification might have been accepted on this very specious and tempting argument, had not Sterrett found conclusive proof of the true position of Lystra. (See p. 411.)

Coins of Derbe are extremely rare, and seem to exist only in the cabinets of the Bibliothèque Nationale at Paris.

PART VI.

LYSTRA.

LYSTRA.

§ I. Situation and Character.

THE modern village of Khatyn-Serai, the "Lady's Mansion,"
lies in the acute angle formed by the confluence of two small
streams, which flow down out of the Orondian and the
Isaurian hill-country, one from the north-west, the other from
a little south of west.   They are divided by low hills, which
sink very gently to the meeting of the waters.   The village
lies partly on the point of the hills, partly on their southern
side.   The water-supply, unusually lavish for the Lycaonian
land, keeps the environs green, and makes the trees grow
with a luxuriance known nowhere else in Lycaonia, except
in the gardens of Konia and the mountains of Kara-Dagh.
Khatyn-Serai, therefore, suits the Eastern taste and the
Eastern love of quiet gardens and flowing water better than
any other village of Lycaonia; and doubtless this is the
reason for its name.   Either it was in Seljuk time appropriated to the enjoyment of some great lady (such as the
Sultan's mother for example), or the name has a quite
general sense, "Mansion such as suits a lady".

Two Turkish bridges, mainly built of ancient cut stones,
many of them inscribed, cross the two streams, one on the
road to Iconium and the north, one on the road to the
south-east, and indicate to the explorer, as he approaches
by either of the roads along which travellers come, that an
ancient city lay somewhere close at hand.   The actual site
(407)

lay on the opposite bank of the northern stream, about a mile north-west from Khatyn-Serai, on a small elongated hill in the centre of the valley and in the low ground south and east of the hill.

In such a locality as this a centre of population must always have existed. It is constituted by nature the most charming and productive site in the northern hill-region of Isauria, lying near the open Lycaonian plain, possessing a considerable extent of fertile soil in the valley well watered by the two streams, as well as a large tract of low hilly ground. But the town stands apart from the main róads that traverse the country and are the natural paths of trade. The valley in which it lies is secluded and restricted in development: a great city, known and open to the world, could not grow in so sequestered a spot. The site is marked out by nature for a small rustic town, where the people and the customs would be national not cosmopolitan.

Considering the character of almost all other Pauline cities, the great places of the Eastern world, most of them centres of international intercourse and progress, one must wonder how Lystra came to be one of the list. How did the cosmopolitan Paul drift like a piece of timber borne by the current into this quiet backwater? Beroea is, of all the Pauline cities, the one most closely resembling Lystra in general character, a small rustic town, Macedonian not cosmopolitan. To Beroea Paul retired when obliged to leave Thessalonica; but as we know from himself, he was eager to return at the earliest opportunity, and Beroea was perhaps a place to wait in, rather than an object in itself. Lystra may perhaps have been regarded similarly as a place of refuge for the moment from which it might be possible to return to Iconium (see pp. 372-4). Thus Paul

PLATE XVII.

Khatyn Serai and Lystra and the Bridge on the Southern Road.

See p. 407 1.

To face p. 408.

and Barnabas came to be settled for a time in this small Lycaonian town, which in respect of situation is not unlike Barata (as described in the *Expositor*, Sept.-Oct., 1907).

Hence also it is natural to find that in the narrative of Luke Lystra is the only city in which Paul is brought into immediate contact with the uneducated Anatolian populace, ignorant of Hellenic culture, speaking the Lycaonian tongue, though not wholly ignorant of Greek, for the Apostles appealed to them in that language with some effect, and must therefore have been understood by many of them. But the striking events which occurred at Lystra are associated mainly with the humbler class of the Lycaonian populace; and it is the only city of Asia Minor in which a native language is mentioned. Here, alone, the native Anatolian gods and the native religion are confronted with the new faith. Everywhere else Paul's address was directed to the classes which had shared to some degree in Greek education and were familiar with the Greek tongue.

The adventures of the two Apostles at Lystra have already been described by the present writer in *St. Paul the Traveller and the Roman Citizen* in some detail, and it seems unnecessary to repeat what is said there.

Inasmuch as Iconium ranked itself as a city of Phrygia, Lystra and Derbe stood forth as the two cities of Roman Lycaonia in the time of St. Paul. Besides them there was a large Lycaonian territory which contained no constitutionally organised city, but only villages of the Anatolian type. On the west, in the hill-region of Northern Isauria, there were several places which at a later period ranked as cities and bishoprics, but at that time they either were reckoned to Pisidia or ranked only as villages. On the east Lycaonia contained more than one city; but Laranda, Ilistra and others were not in Roman territory. They were part of the kingdom of Antiochus IV., one of those client-kings who were doing the work of governing outlying regions and preparing the inhabitants to become subjects of the Empire at a later date. Accordingly, when it is said in Acts xiv. 6 that Paul and Barnabas, being expelled from Iconium, "fled to the cities of Lycaonia, Lystra and Derbe, and the region round about," this is exactly equivalent to saying that they took refuge in the Roman part of the country of Lycaonia, in which there were two cities and a region where the Anatolian village-system prevailed: in the technical language of politics and administration the Roman part of Lycaonia was called Galatic Lycaonia, *i.e.*, the part of Lycaonia which was included in the Province Galatia. The use of the term "region" here is similar to that which was described in Part III., when Antioch was called the centre of a "region" (Acts xiii. 49 and inscriptions).

In this territory, Galatic Lycaonia, there were two cities: the term city must here be understood in the strict sense, as a self-governing town with sovereign rights exercised by elected magistrates. How had these two places alone been more or less Hellenised and Romanised, while the rest remained of the ordinary Anatolian type?

As regards Derbe, we have seen in Part V. that the change was due to the Roman Imperial influence, and to the importance of this point on the frontier of Roman territory, which made it a customs-station and a centre of Roman business and official life.

The development of Lystra was due to its being selected as the seat of a Roman Colony, which required the construction of a Roman road to connect it with the other Coloniae and especially with Antioch, the capital of Southern

PLATE XVIII.

Mediæval Bridge on the north side of Khatyn Serai.

See p. 407 f.

Galatia. This road, constructed at first for military reasons, passed near the real trade-centre of Lycaonia, *viz.* Iconium; and thus it became a trade-route as it was continued to Derbe and Laranda, and was thereby connected with Cilicia and Syria. It was, however, never more than a secondary road on the commercial side, and its military importance died out as the mountain tribes were subdued and the country became thoroughly peaceful. In the time of St. Paul, Lystra was still of some consequence from its colonial rank; and we must suppose that both Hellenes and the uneducated Lycaonians of the town were sensible of the dignity and the advantages derived from this rank and from the Roman road (called in inscriptions and in the Acts of Paul and Thekla the "Imperial Road"), which connected it with Antioch on the one side and with Derbe on the other. What has been said above regarding the influence of colonial dignity on the prosperity of Antioch and on the minds of all its inhabitants applies also to the sister Colony of Lystra, though in a much diminished degree. Not merely was Antioch a capital for the southern half of the Province, but also it was an older foundation than Lystra. Now time is needed to plant deeply and strengthen the pride of city-dignity: successive generations have to grow up with this consciousness in their minds; and Lystra, as a Colonia, had only two generations to look back on, while Antioch had three. We must therefore infer that Lystra was a much weaker reflection of Antiochian feeling and municipal pride.

The coins of Lystra are very rare. One was bought on the spot by Professor Sterrett in 1884; and his discovery of an inscription in addition to the coin revealed the hitherto unknown fact that Lystra was a Roman colony, and confirmed the brilliant conjecture of the great geographer Leake that

it was situated at Khatyn-Serai: Leake travelled in 1800,
and did not see this site.   In company with the late Sir
Charles Wilson I visited it in 1882 for one night.   We were
on the outlook for some evidence to test Leake's opinion;
and I inferred from the large proportion of Latin inscriptions
that a Roman Colonia had stood on this site, and that therefore Lystra, which was not a Colonia, could not have been
situated here.[1]   This argument supplies a good example of
the gradual nature of discovery and of the way in which an
inference which at first seems perfectly conclusive and inevitable may be set aside by the irony of fate as knowledge
progresses.   Indirect evidence is always subject to this
chance: it may be set in a quite different light by new
discoveries.   If the colonial coins of Lystra had been discovered a few years earlier, the observation that Khatyn-
Serai was the site of a Colonia would have at once furnished
the needed proof that Lystra was situated here; but the
idea that Lystra could have been a Colonia was so unimagined
and so improbable that, when I communicated Sterrett's
discovery of the first colonial inscription to the greatest
epigraphic and historical scholar in Europe, he at first expressed his disbelief in the trustworthiness of the copy, as
the copyist was then unknown to him; and it was only
when I assured him that the copyist was known to me as
practised and reliable that he began to think of the consequences which must follow from Professor Sterrett's discovery.   At the same time a coin published by the late
M. Waddington and Sterrett's new coin placed the matter
beyond the reach of cavil or hesitation.   A firm footing in
Lycaonian history was now at last reached.   What had been
dark and unintelligible was now brought within the range of
historical study, though still much work and many journeys

were needed before light was thrown on this subject in an even moderate degree; and much still remains to do, before we shall be able to see clearly. Excavation at Lystra is urgently needed in the interests of history and of New Testament study; but the expense would be very considerable, as the accumulation of soil is great and the land is agriculturally valuable. Moreover, permission to excavate can now hardly be gained except through strong Government pressure, and Germany is the only country in Europe

FIG. 53.—The Founder of Colonia Lystra tracing the limits of the new city with plough drawn by a yoke of bull and cow.

which habitually makes the acquisition of knowledge an interest of Government,[2] while public opinion even among scholars in our country is entirely devoid of interest in the life and fortunes of this unimportant Lycaonian town and third-rate Roman Colonia.

The colonial character of Lystra is similar to that of Antioch, only less marked and more evanescent. But, as we saw on p. 280, Lystra presented a statue of Concord to her sister Colony of Antioch, somewhere about the end of the second or the beginning of the third century. A gift like this implies that the smaller and poor colony still retained some pride in her rank and her Roman character; and yet so faded was her memory of her Roman dignity that the inscription was written in Greek, and Latin had evidently ceased to be spoken or known in Lystra. The few coins of Lystra are all colonial. Any little importance which the city possessed arose from its connection with the Roman State and the Roman administration and defence of the Province Galatia. But with its foundation as a Colonia, by Augustus, probably through Cornutus Aquila, governor of

FIG. 54.—The City goddess of Lystra sitting on the rocks, with the crescent on her head and corn-ears in her hand; a river at her feet.

Galatia about B.C. 6, its coinage and its rank as a city of the Roman world began. The coins, so far as yet known, belong to the reigns of Augustus, Titus, Trajan and Marcus Aurelius. Latin and Roman ideas probably ceased about the end of the last-named Emperor's reign (see p. 281).

Yet the only strictly Roman type is the one shown in Fig. 53, the founder ploughing the furrow that marked the limits of the Roman Colonia, as already described (p. 365). The other known types are more or less Hellenic in character, either Hellenised representations of religious ideas, or

imitations of works of Hellenistic art. In Fig. 54 we have
an example of the influence of the famous statue of Syrian
Antioch by the sculptor Eutychides, a type which spread
through Tarsus into Lycaonia and Cappadocia. Fig. 55
shows the same type at Barata; and it occurs also at Tyana.
This diffusion of an artistic type from Tarsus to the north
and north-west recalls and supports the theory advanced
first by the writer in the *Revue des Études Anciennes*, 1901,
p. 358, and quoted in *Studies in the Art and History of the
Eastern Provinces*, p. 60, that a widespread type in the

Fig. 55.—The City goddess of Barata sitting on the rocks with a river at her
feet. She carries the cornucopia, and in her right hand an uncertain object.

earliest Christian art of Lycaonia and Isauria came from
Tarsus along the same path. Professor Strzygowski informs
me that he is disposed to regard Syrian Antioch as the
ultimate source of the type; and the example of Eutychides's statue is quite favourable to his view.

We observed that Tarsus and Iconium, cities of the plain,
modified the Syrian type so far as to make the City goddess
sit on a chair. Barata and Lystra follow the original type
in making her sit on the rocks. Barata was a city of the
mountains, Lystra was a city of the hilly country. The City

goddess of Lystra wears the crescent moon upon her head, and carries corn-ears in her hand : this shows a certain modification of the borrowed type, either to suit the local religious ideas, or possibly (as Mr. G. F. Hill suggests) to identify the City goddess with Isis.

The form of the name Lustra on some, if not all, of the coins and the Latin inscriptions, shows the attempt to Romanise a Lycaonian city. There can be no doubt that the name is Lycaonian, or rather East Anatolian, for Kilistra and Ilistra in Lycaonia, Kybistra and Kizistra in southern Cappadocia, prove that the form is native to this region along the north side of Taurus, and that the nearest approach to a correct rendering in Latin letters would be Listra : doubtless Ilistra is the same word pronounced with a slight vowel sound escaping through the mouth before the L. But the Greeks called it Lystra to suggest a derivation from the Greek verb λύειν, and the Romans named it Lustra to give it an apparent connection with the Latin *Lustrum* : in each case false popular etymology sought to find a fortunate meaning for the name in its own language.[3]

The colonial constitution was doubtless the same as at Antioch (p. 268 ff.) ; but few details are preserved. From fragmentary inscriptions we learn that there were probably duumvirs as the supreme magistrates, and twelve divisions of the burgesses : the name of these divisions is given in a Greek inscription as Tribes (φυλαί), but the name in Latin is not attested.[4]

The evanescence of Roman influence and language and the predominance of Hellenic types in the coinage point to the conclusion that the Roman element in the population of the Colonia was not nearly so strong in Lystra as in Antioch. Lystra was a Lycaonian town with a small admixture of privileged Roman Coloni. Dr. Olmstead of Cornell, who has been making a study of the pottery found on these sites, informs me that only a few fragments of Roman pottery were found on the site : the rest was native, of Hellenistic period or earlier.

The colonial character of Lystra cannot be traced in Acts, as it can be clearly seen at Antioch ; but the comparative weakness of the Roman municipal consciousness, which appears in all the rest of the scanty evidence, fully accounts for this.

Besides the Roman colonists the population of Lystra consisted of the class which was educated in Greek manners and the Greek language, and the uneducated Lycaonian population.

Not a trace of the Roman aristocracy can be detected in the narrative of Acts. They apparently stood completely outside of the influence of Paul and Barnabas, as we saw was the case with the Romans of Antioch, who were appealed to by the Jews as the ruling oligarchy of the Colonia (see pp. 313, 371). In Lystra the Roman burgesses make no appearance in the troubles which led to the expulsion of the Apostles. The riot was engineered through the mob, as at Iconium (Part IV., § VIII.). This confirms the view above stated on other grounds that the Roman element in Lystra was scanty and unimportant.

The Greek-educated inhabitants were called Hellenes⋅ They would naturally be the well-to-do part of the native-born population. There is no trace of any Hellenistic re-foundation in Lystra, and Greeks by race are not likely to have existed there in any numbers. The term Hellenes expresses an educational, not a racial character. These Hellenes would not be fully qualified citizens ; only the

Roman Coloni were burgesses of Lystra at this period (see
p. 271); all the rest of the free inhabitants were mere residents (*incolae*).   But these Hellenes of Lystra may be
assumed to have been the educated class of the city, some
wealthy, others at least belonging to successful commercial
families or to any local native aristocracy which may have
existed in Lycaonia.   Timothy, whose father was a Hellene,
therefore belonged to the well-to-do or the wealthy classes
of the non-Roman population.   Even without this evidence
the fact that the father was accepted as the husband of a
Jewess may be safely assumed to prove that he was a person
of some standing in Lystra.   This is only an example of the
general law that the important leaders in the Church of Asia
Minor belonged to the better class of local families and not
to the humble and uneducated classes: on this see *Pauline
and Other Studies*, p. 375 f.

The uneducated Lycaonian population seems to have
been unusually numerous in this secluded town, and has been
already mentioned.

§II.   CHARACTER OF THE FIVE CITIES.

The history of each of these cities presents a study of
amalgamation, more or less thorough and more or less
successful, between the European and the Asiatic races.
The proportions and the results differ in every case.   There
is an infinite variety in the study of the great Græco-Asiatic
cities, and yet the elements are to a large extent the same.

Tarsus is far the most Oriental.   So it has been throughout history, and so it is still; as you travel over Central and
Eastern Asia Minor far and wide, you are aware of the
Oriental spirit in the population everywhere; but it is only
when you reach Tarsus that you feel at last that you have

entered a really Oriental city. On the other hand, Pisidian Antioch was a Hellenic city, or rather colony; yet even there the Anatolian tone grows stronger and becomes supreme as we come down to the fourth century.

But there is one difficulty in this study which must always be borne in mind by the reader. While directing attention for the moment to the Oriental or the Occidental element in any of the cities, one has to leave the other element too much out of sight; and after a time, when one turns to the other side of the picture, there may appear to be some inconsistency. In one section the city might seem to be described as mainly Anatolian, in another as Hellenic, in another as Semitic, as the evidence bearing on each topic is treated separately. The reader must compensate one section by another.

Moreover, time makes a difference. The Western spirit, active and busy, seems at its first entrance to carry everything before it. The city becomes in outward show entirely Hellenic and Roman during the first century after Christ. But the Oriental nature lies deep and strong under the surface. It revives during the second and third centuries, and becomes predominant in the fourth. The unchanging East swallows up the West, unless the latter is constantly reinforced either by fresh immigration, or by the maintenance of a high education. A true system of education raises both Asiatic and European to a higher level, on which they can mix and meet, each preserving his own individuality, yet respecting and appreciating that of the other; and this is the platform on which Christianity, alone among the religions of the world, claimed in the beginning to move and to work, though too often it has allowed its ideals and its aspirations to sink to a lower level.

PART VII.

ST. PAUL IN THE ROMAN WORLD.

PART III

PREPARING THE BODY OF THE DISCIPLE

ST. PAUL IN THE ROMAN WORLD.

In a subject like this, so wide, so important and so much discussed, it is impossible to avoid an apparently too dog-matic statement of opinions which would not be generally accepted at the present time. The appearance of dogma-tism is due to the desire of brevity: it is easy for the reader to find other views stated by more distinguished scholars. It is not my aim to give a history of opinion, or to balance and weigh the views of the learned. Any small value which this book may have is due to its expressing a judgment formed fresh from the original documents and the actual localities, not from a study of the modern authorities, many of whom I find so antipathetic that they have little for me. Yet many opinions, to which no allusion is here made, have been pondered over long, before they were re-jected. Some I held at one time as a convinced disciple of their leading champions; and I have grown out of them through the force of unconscious life under the impulse of experience, rather than reasoned myself out of them through conscious argument.

But it is the penalty of stating a new view of history that one must inevitably fail to carry conviction at first, however confident one is that the world will one day be convinced. To support a new reading of history, there are needed many subsidiary studies which can be made only by a co-ordinated

(423)

group of scholars, a school of students working in unison, correcting and completing one another, but looking at all the questions of history from the same point of view, and thus building up by organised co-operation a harmonious study. A body of reasoned investigation must form the basis of any new view of history; and that cannot be wrought out by a single person within the limits of human life. The true historian cannot now exist except by founding a school to co-operate with him. One may see, or think one sees; but one cannot by mere brief statement of opinions make others see who have been habituated to a different point of view. The solitary historian at the present day is doomed to failure. Yet I can at least emphasise and reiterate that the history of the Roman Empire has to be re-written from the point of view which I have tried, however inadequately, to set before you in outline in the first part of this work and to exemplify in some individual cases in the following parts.

Before passing from this subject it seems best to give one example, bearing on the conduct and the writings of St. Paul, and showing how easy it is to miss the right point of view in studying the position of the Church in the Empire, and how much the judgment of the most learned historians and the most respected scholars may thus be distorted.

The contrast between the Apocalyptic view and the principles which rule in the letters of Paul is certainly great. Yet sometimes one finds that this contrast is exaggerated in modern opinion and made to appear as if it were a contradiction. I have seen the statement printed by a good scholar that, if Paul had lived to read the Apocalypse it would have broken his heart. Such a statement seems to originate from a one-sided view of the position of the Apostle in the Roman world, and a failure to estimate completely the various forces which were acting on him, and among which he had to steer a steady course.

A study of the situation in its entirety must, I think, lead to the conclusion that Paul would have been in perfect sympathy with the Apocalypse of John, if he had lived to the epoch when it was written, and would even have written his own Apocalypse. Nay, I would even go so far as to maintain that there was an Apocalyptic period in the teaching of Paul, before he had fully understood the position which the Church occupied in the Roman world, and that he has given us an outline of his Apocalypse; but it is so original and so unlike the traditional Jewish Apocalyptic style that its significance is not properly recognised. John was so imbued with the spirit and affected by the form of the earlier Jewish Apocalypses, that very wild theories have been advanced as to the nature of his book ; but John was brought up in Palestine. Paul stood beyond the influence of this class of literature, thanks to his Hellenic education. He shared in the views of John, but he expressed them differently.

The attitude which the first Christians ought to take to the Roman Imperial Government was not one that could be easily determined or clearly defined in a body of rules. The judgment of individuals must have differed considerably : the judgment of the same individual would almost inevitably vary from time to time according to changes in the prevailing tone of administration and alteration in the personal point of view. The attitude of Paul himself altered materially during the period of his life that is best known to us. On the one hand the Imperial system was based on the most glaring and flagrant form of idolatry, the worship of a living man as the incarnate god on earth; it was the direct enemy of Christ: its system was like a parody of the Christian Gospel.   How could Paul do anything but hate it and condemn it?   On the other hand it saved the world from worse evils: every one who lived in those times knew that the Emperor and the Imperial Government alone stood between the civilised world and destruction, and restrained the power of disorder, war and savagery, which had recently nearly overwhelmed society and put an end to civilisation. Something, nay much, was due to the Emperor, and the Lord's command was clear and definite, "Render to Cæsar the things that are Cæsar's".   It was a delicate position for the adviser who had to counsel new converts not very well educated in moral judgment, as to how they ought to regard the Imperial system ; and one can well understand that Paul's earliest words to a young Church should require subsequent interpretation and explanation.

Moreover, Paul at Thessalonica had found the Roman administration the enemy of the Gospel.   He was accused of treason to the Emperor and of setting up a rival Emperor, and was practically condemned in absence by the magistrates. Their action, covered by the name of loyalty to Cæsar, made it impossible for him to return soon to Thessalonica, eager as he was to do so.   This hindrance he speaks of as "Satan" ; and his language approximates to calling the Imperial system by that name (*St. Paul the Traveller*, p. 230 f.).

The treatment which he had experienced in the Roman Coloniae, Philippi, Lystra and Pisidian Antioch, in all of which he suffered severely and was probably beaten with the staves of the lictors who attended on Roman magistrates, was calculated to confirm the unfavourable opinion which at one time he seems to have entertained of the Imperial Government as the enemy of the faith. The Coloniae were outlying parts of Rome, peopled by Romans (for the non-Roman inhabitants were merely residents, not citizens) and governed by Romans; and for years these represented to him the feeling of the Roman State towards the Gospel and its adherents. That he endured violence at Pisidian Antioch as well as at Lystra, and that the vague words of Acts xiii. 50 conceal severe bodily suffering, seems clear from the language of the Apostle himself, 2 Timothy iii. 11: "persecutions, sufferings: what things befell me at Antioch, at Iconium, at Lystra; what persecutions I endured". It was only in Coloniae that he could be beaten with the lictor's staves; and as he had so suffered thrice, and he had been only in three Coloniae, we must infer that his expulsion from Antioch and Lystra had been preceded by chastisement administered by the lictors (which in itself may be assumed as customary when disorderly persons were ejected from a Roman town). Hence, at Philippi, Paul and Silas did not at first claim the rights of Roman citizens. Paul had not as yet begun to feel that Rome and Roman law might be a protection against barbarism and cruelty.

In Corinth we find that Paul's attitude towards the Imperial Government had altered. The decision of Gallio (which owing to the force of precedent in Roman administration was practically a charter of freedom for Christians to preach and teach, valid until reversed by some higher tribunal) had something to do with the change in his attitude towards the Government; but, probably, a more important cause lay in the development and the widening of his own views, as he better understood the problem of the Roman world. He realised that the Empire was for the present the vehicle

destined to carry the Christian Church, and that the Imperial
Government was in a sense necessary to the Church. Further,
he had learned that the Empire was tolerant of the Church;
and there seems to have arisen in his mind the idea that
Christianity might ultimately make itself the religion of the
Empire. But that ultimate aim could not possibly blind
him to the inevitable fact that there must be war against
the great and crowning idolatry of the Imperial cult, which
was the keystone of the Imperial arch, the basis of the
Imperial unity.

Such was the dilemma with which Paul was confronted;
and his letters to the Thessalonians are to me intelligible
only on the view that he was fully conscious of the dilemma.
The Empire was the servant, the bearer, the instrument of
the Church, and yet it was also its irreconcilable and inevitable foe. There could never be permanent peace between
the Church and the Emperor, "who sitteth in the sanctuary
of God, setting himself forth as God". But that war had
not yet actually begun : much had to occur before it should
begin. As yet the Emperor did not stand before them revealed in his real character. He was still the restrainer of a
worse evil, the instrument of God. Ultimately he should be
revealed as he really was, the man of sin, the son of perdition,
the enemy of God ; and then should come the great and final
war. In that future time the Emperor, who now restrains
the forces of disorder and barbarism, shall be disclosed as
himself the great power and leader of barbarism and the
enemy of all that is good. Every enemy of the truth shall
then be allied against the Church, in the great battle which
the seer of the Apocalypse foresaw at Har-Megiddo. But
that is not yet. Such was the way in which the relation between the Empire and the Church developed during the

following centuries, and so Paul foresaw with the eye of a statesman and a prophet.

This is the cryptic message of explanation to the Thessalonians, 2 chap. ii. That message had to be expressed in very cautious and enigmatic language, significant only to the initiated. It was a dangerous truth, which might bring death to the young Church in Thessalonica; the letter might fall into the wrong hands, and such a truth must not be so plainly written that every person could understand it.

Is it too great a stretch of imagination to attribute to Paul such insight into the future course of history, and to recognise in the mystic words of that letter an anticipation of the Apocalypse of John? Surely not. We have seen in p. 73 f. that the Imperial policy as defined by the ablest among the Emperors anticipated the inevitable approach of that conflict with the Church, and recognised the Church while still young and weak as the great enemy of the Imperial system in the future. Paul was much more likely to see the character of the Empire than the Emperors to comprehend the nature of the Church. It is in truth as inconceivable that Paul could be insensible of the nature of the Imperial system, as it is that he could consent to any compromise with the Imperial worship. A purified Empire was the Pauline idea; but a purified Empire meant the elimination of the God-Emperor.

One must therefore guard against the tendency to exaggerate the contrast between the spirit of recognition of and allowance for the Empire, shown in Luke, most of the Pauline letters, and 1 Peter, and the spirit of defiance and detestation that animates the Apocalypse of John. The contrast is a very real one; but it indicates no deep difference of opinion between the various writers. The difference of tone is due to change of circumstances. Paul's hatred of the enthroned lie, the Imperial false god, was as deep and strong as John's; and he knew equally well that in the end the Church must destroy the Imperial tyranny, or be killed by it. But he was content to wait till the future developed. In the meantime the power that maintained peace and order in the world was, in a sense, the friend and protector of the infant Church.

Now as I have begun to speak of the Apocalyptic side of early Christian thought, I should conclude this study by an analysis of a passage in the Apocalypse of John, which rightly understood shows how closely one of his most Hebraic visions approximates to the Pauline point of view, though superficially it seems as far from it as East is from West. In a vision of the Apocalypse (Rev. vi. 2 ff.) John saw Conquest riding forth with War, Ravage or Scarcity (which is its result and not distinguished in Hebrew thought from it), and Massacre in his train. Conquest is imagined after the fashion of the Parthian King, a bowman, mounted on a white horse. The person of the others is not described, but only their work. War is thought of as a combination of discord and slaughter, carrying a great sword and mounted on a red horse. Ravage or Scarcity, the name is indifferent, sits on a black horse and holds a balance. Massacre, whose name is Death, and who is followed by Hades, rides on a pale horse.

The imagery is bold and simple. Conquest rides forth as the great king, clad in glory and holding the might of the bow. But horror and terror attend on the glory of the conquering sovereign : Battle with its bloodshed, Ravage that produces famine, and Massacre go with him. Yet there is a measure to their power. In war there is a stricken field and a fight between combatants. In the most bloody of battles many even of the defeated army escape. The limit here lies in the nature of the case, and there is no need to specify or describe it. Far more terrible are the other two figures; but to them a definite limit is fixed. Massacre has authority over the fourth part of the earth: three-fourths of the conquered country is spared. Ravage carries his own measure with him, for he holds in his hands a balance; and a voice proclaimed, " A measure of wheat at the price of a denarius, and three measures of barley at a denarius; but harm not the wine and the oil ". The crops are to be destroyed to the limit of extreme scarcity, until wheat is sold at seven times and barley at four times the ordinary price; but the vine and the olive trees are to be left uninjured.

In interpreting a series of allegorical figures like this, the general purpose rules the whole. That Conquest brings with it the three companion terrors was the law of life and of war in the Mediterranean world, as it must always be; but a limit to their action existed in every case. The limit set to the Ravaging of the land calls for some explanation.

The Ravaging is confined to the annual crops; but the country is spared the almost irretrievable ruin which would have resulted in the Mediterranean lands from destruction of the vine and the olive. In the northern lands, where fruit-trees are of small account, we do not easily sympathise with or comprehend an image like this. Destruction of the trees means little to us, until we have understood the economy of the Mediterranean world. But there to cut down the olive tree or to burn the vineyards is the last extreme of savagery, which only the rudest and worst of barbarians would perpetrate in the land which they had conquered. The loss of the harvest of wheat and barley means scarcity and high prices ; but a new year brings new crops. The loss of olives and vines means lasting ruin, for new olive trees take about seventeen years to grow, new vines also need a good many years, and in times of uncertainty and danger no one dares to spend labour for a result so remote. In the long series of curses pronounced in Deuteronomy xxviii. against degenerate Israel, the ravaging of the land by savages from the remotest parts of the earth, who shall not leave corn, wine or oil, is described in terrible detail. Only one horror remains to put the climax on the destruction wrought by those ignorant savages, *viz.*, cannibalism, of which a hideous picture is drawn. The noble savages of the Crusading armies, knights and lords and bishops, cut down the olive trees of the Holy Land, and involved it in lasting ruin.

In the picture of the Apocalypse this horror and utter destruction is forbidden : a measure is observed : there is extreme cruelty, much bloodshed, but not the utter savagery of wanton destruction of all property, all means of livelihood, and the entire foundations on which civilised life rests. The bearing of this on the design of the Apocalypse it is not our present purpose to discuss ; surely it is plain. But it falls within the scope of these lectures to indicate the place in history which this idea occupies, and its bearing on the topic of degeneration, which in the present condition of historical investigation is forced on the attention of every student of the Pauline philosophy; for, as we have seen, the very first question which the Pauline student must answer is whether degeneration or progress is the ordinary law of human history. Paul says degeneration is the usual and

normal tendency of man : the sciences of comparative religion, comparative mythology and folklore and anthropology
generally, as they are now conducted, assume at the outset
and throughout that progress is the ordinary and natural
law of human history, and that the phenomena observable in
the world past and present ought to be classified on the
principle that the rude, the barbarous, the ugly and the
brutal is early and primitive.

This part of the vision in the Apocalypse expresses, not
an individual opinion or an isolated phenomenon, but the
conception of the law of war, which lay deep in the nature
of the Mediterranean peoples as far back as we can see.
It is bloody and cruel, it has little care for human life and
it takes no thought for the wounded, but it is not savage,
for it recognises limits and it conserves the permanent prosperity of the land.   It was not a written law, produced by
diplomatists and conventions ; it was the unwritten law of
God, binding men by the sanctions and the terrors of religious awe, stamped deep into the nature of men through
many generations, until it had remade the form of their
minds and become the unconscious law of their action.
Contrast, for example, the conquest of Palestine by Joshua
with that by the chivalry and the religion, an external and
unfelt religion, of Europe in the early Crusades, as regards
the permanent well-being of the country and the world.
The Israelite conquerors, a race partly nomads of the
Arabian desert, partly serfs from Egypt, overran a land
peopled by nations, much more civilised on the whole than
themselves : it was a cruel and bloody conquest, in which
the more civilised inhabitants were slain, or reduced to serf-
dom ; but the land and its powers of production remained
practically uninjured.   The Crusades reduced Palestine

28

almost entirely to the condition of waste land, and so destroyed its recuperative power that it continues to the present day in very large part waste, only a few scattered districts being well cultivated near the few centres of population.

A later period understood the conquest by Joshua differently; the later taste demanded that the purpose and result of the Hebrew conquest should be a universal massacre, and called for the isolation of the people of God in a land where all older population had been destroyed, and it partly explained by the trick of the Gibeonites the obvious fact that the previous population was not annihilated, partly shut its eyes to the actual condition of Palestine, where a considerable remnant of the older races did actually remain.

Here you find, as in every case, that, when you get back to the early stage of Mediterranean history you do not reach a condition of savagery : you get back to a religious law, to a state where order, international ordinances and social organisation were recognised.

This vision is no prophecy for future ages to unfold : it is a declaration of the truth and the law of the world in the emblematic fashion that Oriental thought always loves : it is a statement in the Hebraic style of certain deep-lying principles, which governed the evolution of Mediterranean history. Paul with his Hellenic training would have expressed those principles in more scientific form ; and it is to me unintelligible how so many distinguished scholars in modern times can read his letters and continue to maintain that he was a narrow Jew, ignorant of Hellenic thought and training. But perhaps they read Paul little : one sometimes suspects that they are so busy reading the vast array of modern treatises about him that they have no time to read his own words. The volume of modern comment on Paul is so enormous as almost to bury the original, and we are in danger of neglecting the text while we study the commentary: which is a good reason for bringing this book to an end.

(*Reverse of Fig.* 9, *p.* 140.)
Fig. 9a.—The Emblem of Tarsus: lion killing stag.

NOTES.

ST. PAUL.

[1] E. Curtius, *Gesammelte Abhandlungen*, ii., p. 531 ff.; E. L. Hicks, *Studia Biblica*, iv., p. 1 ff., and *Classical Review*, i., pp. 4 ff., 42 ff.

[2] *Pauline and Other Studies*, p. 72 f.

[3] Since the words were uttered, we have to mourn his too early death.

[4] Fischer, *der Oelbaum, seine geographische Verbreitung, seine wirtschaftliche und kulturhistorische Bedeutung*, Gotha, Perthes, 1904, p. 2. A fuller discussion of the subject is given in *Pauline and Other Studies*, p. 219 ff.

[5] In an account of the Religion of Greece and Asia Minor, in Hastings' *Dictionary of the Bible*, v., pp. 109-56.

[6] The subject of the destruction of agriculture in Asia Minor and its possible restoration was discussed in the *Contemporary Review*, Dec., 1906, pp. 786-800.

[7] I use the term history, not in the narrow sense of history that rests on the written ancient sources, but in the wider sense of all attainable knowledge of the past, whether dependent on literary or on archæological evidence.

[8] The quotation is from the article already mentioned in Hastings' *Dictionary*, v., p. 133.

[9] The subject is discussed more fully in the *Expositor*, Feb., 1900, p. 91 ff.

[10] The thought must have been simmering in the mind of Virgil, but the form was suggested as a reply to a poem of Horace. My own personal view is that the two poems inaugurated the personal relations and intimate friendship of the two poets.

[11] From the translation of Sir Theodore Martin.

[12] The Book of Epodes was not published collectively till 30 B.C.; but it is a well-established fact that important single poems like this were known earlier.

[13] Two others, the Sixth and the Tenth, were also supposed by Schaper to have been composed for the enlarged second edition.

[14] Professor J. B. Mayor collects the resemblances to Isaiah in the *Expositor*, April, 1907, p. 289 ff., and suggests an origin in the Sibylline Books, not in knowledge of Isaiah's writings. I have discussed this in *Expositor*, June, 1907. The present section is based on a paper read to the first international meeting

of the Franco-Scottish Society, 1894, and buried in its Transactions. Monsieur S. Reinach discusses *l'Orphisme dans la IVe Églogue de Virgile* in his *Cultes, Mythes et Religions*, ii., pp. 66-84 ; there is much worth study in his paper, and an element of truth in his view, but it is pushed to extremes and is confined to one side of the case.

TARSUS.

[1] Preface to *The Letters to the Seven Churches*, with chapters xi., xii.

[2] It will be convenient here, once for all, to mention various articles in which the writer has studied Tarsus from other points of view. In an article, " Cilicia, Tarsus, and the great Taurus Pass," *Geographical Journal*, October, 1903, pp. 357-413, there is given a study in considerable detail of the geographical and commercial conditions which helped to determine the history of the three cities of the lower Cilician plain. Two papers in the *Athenæum*, 6th December, 1902, and 1st August, 1903, contain a description of the situation and surroundings of Tarsus, and of the topography of the district. A paper in which the attempt was made to estimate the importance of the relations between sea valley and central plateau, and to classify "the geographical conditions determining history and religion in Asia Minor," *Geographical Journal*, September, 1902, pp. 257-282, bears on the history of Tarsus among other places. The article " Tarsus " in Dr. Hastings' great *Dictionary of the Bible*, gives a summary of the history of Tarsus. I have also written a detailed study of Mallos, the great rival of Tarsus, but refrained from printing it until the opportunity of visiting Mallos may present itself, so that the topographical view expressed in it (which is quite opposed to the opinions, differing from one another, recently advocated by M. Imhoof Blumer and by Messrs. Heberdey and Wilhelm) may be tested by actual experiment ; but in the present study the truth of the view advocated in this unpublished paper must be assumed. We visited Tarsus, my wife and I, in 1902 and in 1891. In August, 1890, also I passed through it, without stopping, when hurrying to catch a steamer at Mersina, the modern port of Tarsus.

[2a] That the bounds about A.D. 200 were at the Cilician Gates, as here stated, and not farther south, seems proved not only by the nature of the case but also by the inscription "Ορoι Κιλίκων engraved on the rocks there. But Strabo (p. 673) says that the boundaries of the Cilicians were only 120 stadia (15 miles) from Tarsus ; and this brings us about the northern edge of the high ground on which stand the late city and the triumphal arch, where we consider that certain Tarsian games were held (see p. 94 f.) : now those games are stated on coins to have been held ἐν Κοδρίγαις ὅροις Κιλίκων, "at the triumphal arch, the boundary of the Cilicians," and this agreement between Strabo and the coins furnishes irresistible evidence for his time. Yet the defensive point for Cilicia was at the Gates ; and in earlier times, as when Alexander the Great invaded the country, the only attempt at guarding the country had its station there.

[3] I take it to be *mansio in monte*, mentioned in the Peutinger Table.

[4] The only alternative to this hypothesis is to alter the text.

[5] The Cydnus rises on the southern face of Taurus: the other two are rivers of the central plateau, which force their way through the Taurus in deep gorges offering wonderfully picturesque scenery, and thus reach the sea.

[6] The Pyramus formerly joined the sea farther to the west, as is described in a subsequent paragraph.

[7] So Dion Chrysostom says, *Or.* 33, p. 13, § 39.

[8] Kara-Tash, Black-Stone, is the name both of the hills and of a village situated on them.

[9] So also Alcmaeon, when struck with madness after he had slain his mother, could find no rest or peace or home, until he went to a place which was neither sea nor land. Such a place he found in the swampy delta of the Achelôos. Bellerophon, afflicted also with madness by the Divine wrath, found his lonely refuge in the marsh land of the lower Sarus. I am indebted to Miss J. E. Harrison, LL.D., for the illustration.

[9a] See Dion, *Or.* 33, § 24; Professor T. Callander on the two Tarsian Orations in the *Journal of Hellenic Studies*, 1904, p. 62.

[10] It is an error of Ritter's to call the harbour town Anchialos. The sole foundation for the great geographer's opinion seems to lie in the derivation ἄγχι ἁλὸς, "near the sea". The references of the ancients show clearly that Anchialos was about twelve miles south-west of Tarsus on the road to Soloi-Pompeiopolis, and a little way inland from Zephyrion, which was situated at Kara-Duwar, on the coast about two miles east from Mersina, the modern harbour which has taken the place of Zephyrion.

[11] I may refer here to the fuller discussion of this scene in my *Pauline and Other Studies*, pp. 59-62.

[12] Another proposed identification of Kittim with the people of Ketis in Cilicia Tracheia keeps the name in the same region. The Hebrew text of Gen. x. 4 has Dodanim, the Septuagint Rodanim: both texts have Rodanim in 1 Chron. i. 7.

[13] The omission of the letter s between vowels is a common phenomenon in Greek: hence Alasia became Ἀλήιον.

[14] No definite proof is known that the Median Empire included Cilicia, but, as it extended to the Halys, it is likely to have embraced Cilicia, though that cannot be assumed as certain, for an extension of Median power across the Eastern Taurus to the Halys without touching Cilicia is quite possible.

[15] The phrase δυναστεύων is used of one Syennesis; and that word was appropriate to priest-kings in western Cilicia.

[16] "Religion of Greece and Asia Minor" in Hastings' *Dictionary of the Bible*, v., p. 128.

[17] We omit entirely some coins of the sixth century, which have been very doubtfully attributed to Tarsus.

[17a] The attribution to Tarsus is proposed by M. Six, and accepted by Mr. V. Head (*Hist. Num.*, p. 612), two of the highest authorities.

[17b] Some scholars, desirous to find some unifying idea in the group of separate types on this coin, understand that the battlemented walls are the fortifications of Tarsus, and that the type of lion and bull, a Tarsian emblem, is placed above to give the name of the fortified city. But two parallel lines of wall seem an unsuitable way of portraying a city. At the "Syrian Gates" there were two parallel lines of wall; other features of the Gates are omitted in this small picture.

[18] See Lehmann-Haupt, *Klio*, 1907, p. 299, n. 5.

[19] As Herodotus and others show, the name Cilicia was formerly applied to a much larger territory, reaching as far north as the Halys and including the two most important cities of southern Cappadocia, Tyana and Mazaka.

[20] Quoted by Eusebius, *Chron.*, i., p. 27 (Ed. Schoene).

[20a] See Plate IV. in *Pauline and other Studies*, and an article on the Peasant-God in the *Contemporary Review*, December, 1906.

[21] *St. Paul the Traveller and the Roman Citizen*, p. 84.

[21a] Disandon in Syncellus, Desanaus in Eusebius. The authorities are fully given in the important articles by K. O. Muller in *Rhein. Museum*, iii., p. 22 ff.; Meyer in *Zft. d. deutschen morgenlaend. Gesellschaft*, 31, p. 736 ff.; Wernicke in Robert, *Aus der Anomia*. That Sandon was Anatolian, not Semitic (against Muller), may be regarded as certain: the name was specially characteristic of Cilicia.

[21b] In *Aus der Anomia*, p. 178 ff.

[22] Fraser, *Adonis Attis Osiris*.

[22b] M. Imhoof Blumer considers that both epithets belonged to Perseus, not to Apollo (*Journal of Hellenic Studies*, 1898, p. 172 ff.). Mr. G. F. Hill sees that Patrôos must belong to Apollo (*Catalogue Brit. Museum*, p. lxxxix.). The fact that where Perseus appears without Apollo no epithets occur, but where the same scenes are represented with Apollo on the hand of Perseus, the epithets are added, suggests that the titles are Apolline. Greek religious ideas point strongly to this connection, and are unfavourable to attributing the epithets to Perseus.

[23] The dates of the coins are, of course, taken from the numismatic authorities, and need no discussion.

[24] The possibility that Antiocheia-on-the-Cydnus was founded under Seleucus IV. and named after his father, may be set aside as too remote: it is an accepted rule that cities which were named after one of the Seleucid kings must be presumed to bear the founder's name. The arguments for this are overwhelming. Clear evidence must be given for any theory of an exception to the rule (p. 253); and in this case the evidence is in favour of the rule, fo several other Cilician cities were refounded and began to strike their own coins under Antiochus IV., as will be shown below.

[25] There is some doubt as to the status of Antiochis. It is possible that she was legally the second wife of the king, and that the disparaging term in 2 Maccabees is due to Jewish hatred of their enemy.

[26] It would have been much harder to understand the facts if such purely Cilician and non-Greek cities as Adana and Anazarba had begun the insurrection.

[27] The rich coinage of Mallos, thoroughly Greek in character during the sixth and early fifth centuries, as M. Imhoof Blumer was the first to recognise it, proves how much more Greek Mallos was than Tarsus. The Greek element in those colonies had to be counterbalanced by a strong Oriental element, before it was sufficiently amenable to Seleucid requirements.

[28] *Letters to the Seven Churches*, p. 130.

[29] *The Church in the Roman Empire*, p. 154.

[30] It is, however, possible that the term demiourgos spread from Tarsus to other Cilician cities, which may have imitated its constitution when they acquired autonomy.

[31] See M. Clermont Ganneau in *Quart. Statement Pal. Expl. Fund*, 1901, p. 382.

[32] The supposition that the Jews of some other city followed Joseph for such a distance as to be able to throw him into the Cydnus is too violent to be accepted.

[32a] Some prefer to interpret this as a designation of Dalisanda in Cilicia Tracheia.

[33] The Latin translation in the Migne edition calls him the bishop of Tiberias; but this is a false rendering of the Greek. No Christians were allowed to live in Tiberias.

[34] *Expositor*, Jan., 1906, p. 42.

[35] On the "Tribes" into which the population of a Hellenic city was divided, see the *Letters to the Seven Churches*, pp. 146-150, or any work on Greek Antiquities.

[36] See his article on the Jews of the Diaspora, in Hastings' *Dictionary of the Bible*, v., p. 105.

[37] *St. Paul the Traveller*, pp. 35 ff., 310-12.

[38] An examination of the meaning and use of συγγενής and συγγένεια in Greek is much needed. The lexicons, even Steph. Thesaurus, rarely give any help in such matters.

[39] See Josephus, *Ant. Jud.*, xii., 3, 2, § 126, and *Letters to the Seven Churches*, p. 152.

[40] Such as grapes and corn-ears, which marked the giver of corn and wine.

[41] The history of the Province Cilicia in this century is treated more fully in *Historical Commentary on the Epistle to the Galatians*, p. 105 ff.

[42] Appian, *Syr.*, 48.

[43] It is only twice named in his writings, *Att.*, v., 20, 3, *Fam.*, ii., 17, 1;

but it is implied as the place where he was residing during certain events; but no light whatsoever is thrown by this Roman governor on the condition of the capital of his Province. He was wholly taken up with Roman matters.

[44] Augustus had the same family names as his uncle the Dictator, who had adopted him. The name Gaius Julius Paulus occurs once, Julia Paula twice, in early Christian inscriptions of Lycaonia.

[45] Suetonius, *Jul.*, 84.

[46] It is collected by my friend and old pupil, Professor T. Callander, in the *Journal of Hellenic Studies*, 1904, p. 58 ff.

[47] ἔχουσαν τρεῖς βασιλείας ἐπὶ τῆς κεφαλῆς. This passage, which is so perfect an example of what Paul did mean, is actually quoted (*e.g.*, in Heinrici-Meyer's *Kommentar*) as a proof that ἐξουσία means the authority to which the woman is subject.

[48] *Historical Commentary on Galatians*, p. 466.

[49] The termination *illa* was often used to form diminutive or pet names. Apollonius occurs in the Bezan text.

[50] On the Roman official, ὁ κράτιστος Θεόφιλος, see *St. Paul the Traveller*, p. 388.

[51] Possibly the strange name Tyrronius may be a Semitic name Grecised, *Cities and Bish. of Phr.*, ii., pp. 639, 647-50.

[52] At Akmonia C. Tyrronius Klados was chief of the synagogue in the second half of the first century, *Cities and Bish. of Phr.*, ii., p. 650: on Julia Severa *ibid*. See note 51.

[53] I propose to restore the text (unintelligible in *Bull. Corresp. Hell.*, 1899, p. 189), Αὐρ. Μω[υσ]ῆς Κάρπου, ὁ πάντη πολλάκις γενόμενος καὶ τὸν κόσμον πολλάκις ἱστορήσας, νῦν δὲ κεῖμαι μηκέτι μηδὲν εἰδὼς · ταῦτα [δ]ὲ [μ]ό[ν]ο[ν] "εὐψύχει, οὐδεὶς ἀθάνατος".

[54] *Cities and Bish. of Phr.*, ii., p. 386.

[55] Seleucus, *Cities and Bish. of Phr.*, ii., p. 545; Alexander, Josephus, *Bell. Jud.*, ii., 18, 7; *Cities and Bish.*, ii., p. 672.

[56] *Cities and Bish.*, ii., p. 672.

[57] ἐπίκλην Ἄσβολος: the reading of the second cognomen Koriaskos or Korêskos is not quite certain, *Cities and Bish.*, i., p. 118, No. 28; ii., p. 545 ff.; Judeich, *Alterthümer von Hierapolis*, p. 142. I still believe against Judeich that the inscription is Christian, and specifically Jewish-Christian.

[58] ἡ εὐχέρεια ἡ ἐπιπολάζουσα παρὰ τοῖς Ταρσεῦσιν ὥστ' ἀπαύστως σχεδιάζειν παρὰ χρῆμα πρὸς τὴν δεδομένην ὑπόθεσιν (Strab., p. 674).

[59] See Herzog in *Philologus*, lvi., p. 45, and Th. Reinach in *Revue des Ét. Juives*, 1893, p. 166 f.

[60] The other Athenodorus was living in extreme old age as late as 47 B.C., and was distinguished by the surname Kordylion. I confused them in *St. Paul the Traveller*, p. 354. Although I have more than once had to write about Athenodorus since then, I did not observe that the error had infected

my own work. The supposition that Athenodorus was of Jewish origin must occur to every one on account of the epithet Kananites (variant in Matt. x. 4, Mark iii. 18, for Κανaναῖos, see Herzog, *Philologus*, lvi., p. 51), but Strabo's statement that the surname was derived ἀπὸ κώμης τινός must be accepted; for Strabo was a personal friend of the philosopher, and therefore his authority, always great, possesses a specially high value in this case. As Athenodorus was a Tarsian citizen, the suggestion which I made in Hastings' *Dictionary of the Bible*, iv., p. 687, that he may have been born in Kanna of Lycaonia and educated in the Tarsian schools, would have to be supplemented by the supposition that the honour of citizenship had been conferred on him by a special decree of the Tarsian people. This great philosopher, favoured of the Emperor, was precisely the sort of person in whose favour such exceptional decrees were made; but although Strabo's account is perhaps not absolutely inconsistent with this, yet it strongly suggests that Athenodorus was born a Tarsian.

[61] See note 71.

[62] Strab., pp. 6 and 55 : in the Epitome Diog. the order of enumeration is Posidonius, Athenodorus, Antipater.

[63] Cicero, *ad Fam.*, iii., 7, 5. He assumes that Appius could find in Rome a copy of Athenodorus's treatise, which in itself implies fame, for books were scarce in that period and hard to procure.

[64] *Ad Att.*, xvi., 11, 4; 14, 4. Cicero asks Atticus, who was in Rome, to urge Athenodorus to hurry.

[65] Dion, lvi., 43; Zonaras, p. 544, B (ed. Dindorf, ii., p. 455).

[66] ἔστι καὶ σιγῆς ἀκίνδυνον γέρας.

[67] Strabo, p. 779 : Clemens Alex., *Protrepticon*, p. 14 (ed. Sylburg).

[68] Eusebius, *Chronica*, A.D. 7. Jerome, in his translation of the Chronicle, modifies the expression and calls him a Stoic philosopher, evidently because he knew from other sources that Athenodorus belonged to that school. Strabo, pp. 6, 55.

[69] See especially Lightfoot's judicious essay " St. Paul and Seneca " in his edition of Philippians (*St. Paul the Trav.*, p. 353 ff.).

[70] *Ibid.*

[71] Lucian, *Macroh.*, 21, δύο καὶ ὀγδοήκοντα ἔτη βιοὺς ἐτελεύτησεν ἐν τῇ πατρίδι, καὶ τιμὰς ὁ Ταρσέων δῆμος αὐτῷ κατ' ἔτος ἕκαστον ἀπονέμει ὡς ἥρωι. Ruhl in *Rhein. Mus.*, 1907, p. 424, throws doubt on the eighty-two years stated by Pseudo-Lucian; but the authority of Strabo and Eusebius proves that the statement is near the truth and is not exaggerated.

[72] ἐξουσία is the word used by Strabo, which illustrates the meaning that necessarily belongs to it in 1 Cor. xi. 6 (discussed above in § xvii.).

[73] κατέλυσε τὴν καθεστῶσαν πολιτείαν.

[74] His principle was expressed in the words quoted from Horace, *Odes*, iii., 2, 25 : see § xx.

[74]a See Part I., § vii.

[75] In the *Pauline and Other Studies*, p. 369 ff., there is an article on Society in the Eastern Roman Provinces during the fourth century in which this is brought out.

[76] ἐγκύκλιος παιδεία, Strabo, p. 673.

[77] Frazer, *Adonis Attis Osiris*, p. 42.

[78] I have been guilty of this error myself in Hastings' *Dictionary of the Bible*, iv., p. 687, following many predecessors therein. I corrected the mistake in the *Expositor*, October, 1906, p. 373.

[79] ἡ πρώτη καὶ μεγίστη καὶ καλλίστη μητρόπολις τῶν γ' ἐπαρχειῶν Κιλικίας Ἰσαυρίας Λυκαονίας προκαθεζομένη, καὶ β' νεωκόρος, καὶ τετειμημένη μόνη δημιουργίαις τε καὶ Κιλικαρχίαις ἐπαρχικῶν ἐλευθέρῳ κοινοβουλίῳ καὶ ἑτέραις πλείσταις καὶ μεγίσταις καὶ ἐξαιρέτοις δωρεαῖς, see Waddington in *B.C.H.*, 1883, p. 281 f.

[80] We should expect that, after Anazarbus became a meeting-place of the Commune, and was able like Tarsus to place on its coins the term Koinoboulion (place of deliberation of the Koinon), it also would have had a temple "Common to Cilicia," and would have been Neokoros; but no coin mentions such a temple, and the title Neokoros, which has been read on one coin, is not accepted with perfect confidence. But probably coins may yet be found which mention both honours.

[81] See Hill in the Austrian *Jahreshefte*, 1899, p. 245 ff., where several illustrations, taken from marbles, show the form of the crown fitting round the heads of high-priests and high-priestesses.

[82] *Church in the Roman Empire before* 170, p. 397.

[83] "Tarsus Cilicia and the great Taurus Pass" in *Geographical Journal*, 1903, p. 357 ff.; above, § v.; on Cilicia Secunda Mommsen in *Sächs. Acad. Abhandl.*, ii., 259.

[84] The same usage occurs often : Asia Provincia, ἡ Ασία τὸ ἔθνος, in Dion Cassius, liv., 30, shows how far the term Nation was from a racial term in this expression; Asia was the most mixed of Provinces (*Stud. Bibl.*, iv. p. 30).

[85] Mr. Hill infers from the shape of the garland worn by Commodus and by Caracalla on some coins of Tarsus, that these Emperors accepted the Demiourgia there; but this seems a narrow basis for such an opinion; had this been so, we should expect that the fact would be mentioned on the coins.

[86] Also Antoneinoupolis and erroneously Antoniane.

[87] Rostowzew in the Austrian *Jahreshefte Arch. Inst.*, 1901, p. 37 ff. (Beiblatt).

ANTIOCH.

[1] It is described with illustrations by G. Weber in *Arch. Jahrb.*, 1904, p. 96 f.

[2] Hamilton, *Researches in Asia Minor*, i., p. 474.

[3] *Epigraphic Journey in Asia Minor*, p. 143.

[4] Sterrett, *Wolfe Expedition*, p. 402; see my *Studies in the History and Art of the Eastern Provinces* (1906), p. 360.

[5] See Part II., § xi.

[6] Apollonia, see *Studies in the History of the Eastern Provinces* (1906), p. 360 (against the opinion of G. Hirschfeld, who regarded this city as a Pergamenian foundation).

[7] *Pauline and Other Studies*, pp. 169, 187.

[8] Sterrett, *Epigr. Journey*, No. 92, where read ρεγεωνάριον and 'Αν[τιόχεια] πό[λις] and [σ]τέμμα (double accusative); see my *Studies in the Art*, etc., p. 278.

[9] M. Chamonard's copy in *Bull. Corr. Hellen.*, 1893, p. 257, is more complete than Professor J. R. S. Sterrett's *Wolfe Expedition*, No. 550. In inscriptions of the Roman time, when divorce was so easy and frequent, it was often added to the epitaph of a married woman that she had only one husband and was *univira*: this is expressed in the last line.

> 'Αντιόχισσα [γένος] πάτρης γονέων πολυτείμων
> οὔνομα Δεββωρά, ἀνδρὶ δοθεῖσα κλύτῳ
> Παμφύλῳ . . . [φι]λοτ[έ]κνω . . . ιητ . . . Εὐμήλ . .
> παρθενικῶν λέκτρων ἀντιλαβοῦσα χάριν.

[10] The opening formula with γένος (a convincing restoration) is discussed in the *Expositor*, 1906, i., p. 506 f.

[11] Marriage between a Jewess and a Hellene was certainly rare, though it sometimes happened, Acts xvi. 1.

[12] The formula denoting the status of an Antiochian who settled in Apollonia and was by a special law in his favour granted citizenship in his new home may be seen in a Eumenian inscription on a grave, where a certain Hermes is styled "Akmonian and Eumenian," *Cities and Bish. of Phr.*, ii., p. 389, *C.I.G.*, 3893.

[13] *Letters to the Seven Churches*, p. 149.

[14] I thought that the suggestion was made in the *Church in the Roman Empire before* A.D. 170; but that is not the case. The inscription is published in *C.I.L.*, iii., 6809, from my copy, and also by Professor Sterrett.

[15] *Letters to the Seven Churches*, p. 130.

[16] *Letters to the Seven Churches*, p. 152.

[17] Kaibel, *Epigr. Graec. Ital.*, etc., No. 933, published this inscription very incorrectly in respect of transcription. Aipe is the name in the copy, for which Kaibel suggests ἀγνή. He misunderstands the phrase, "a Scythian virgin," the meaning of which is given above: on the term "virgin" see *Pauline and Other Studies*, p. 108; *Histor. Comm. on Galatians*, 40, 202 *Church in the Roman Empire before* 170, p. 397 f. Kern understands that Magnesia *Mae.* is meant; but "Phrygia" is against this.

[18] The title 'Απολλωνιατῶν Λυκίων καὶ Θρᾳκῶν Κολώνων is often mistranslated as if three classes of people were meant. The people of Synnada and other cities called themselves "Synnadeis Dorieis," and so on, without adding "Colonists"; this means "The people of Synnada, who are Dorians".

[19] *Histor. Comm. on Galatians*, p. 209 f.

[20] A single example is sufficient proof of the general custom : see § iii.

[21] O. Kern, *Die Inschriften von Magnesia*, No. 80.

[22] They are Coloniae Julia Augusta Olbasena, Julia Augusta Prima Fida Comama, Julia Augusta Felix Cremnensium (or Cremna), Julia Felix Gemina Lustra (the omission of Augusta may perhaps be accidental in our authorities), Julia Augusta Parlais.

[23] See the proof stated in *Christ Born at Bethlehem*, p. 238 ff.

[24] So called from the lark, *alauda*, which was the mark or crest distinguishing it.

[25] The cessation of war and the inauguration of peace at the first established the Empire in the affections of the Provinces (especially of the East); but only good administration could have made this favour permanent.

[26] The essential and fundamental fact in the Roman Province was not the territory, but the people; hence the Greek translation of Provincia was τὸ ἔθνος, the nation; the Latin Provincia Asia is rendered ἡ Ἀσία τὸ ἔθνος by Dion Cassius, LIV. 30. The process is described in *Christ Born at Bethlehem*, p. 120 ff.

[27] One would be disposed to conjecture that Lystra was an exception. Its usefulness as a colonia soon ceased; the Roman blood and tone were weaker there than in Antioch, and perhaps died out naturally during the later second century.

[28] One or two apparent exceptions, such as the magistrate Sekoundos in Sterrett, *Epigr. Journ.*, No. 96, belong to the third century, when Roman names were losing their clear form. Sekoundos was a Roman: Secundus was merely his *cognomen*, but his two first names were omitted in Greek usage, just as St. Paul's two first names are never mentioned.

[29] Probably each of the numerous inscriptions in honour of governors of Galatia marks a visit paid by the official in question to the city.

[30] On the aspect of the "Province" in Asia Minor, see the *Letters to the Seven Churches*, p. 103, about the Province Asia as the Beast that came up from the earth.

[31] Our view is that such was always the claim of the Church: *Letters to the Seven Churches* in many passages.

[32] *The Church in the Roman Empire*, p. 50; Sterrett, *Wolfe Expedition*, No. 352.

[33] See the inscription published by Rev. H. S. Cronin in *Journal of Hellenic Studies* (1904), p. 114.

[34] Hill, *Catalogue Coins, Brit. Mus., Pisidia*, p. cxii.

[34a] Sterrett, *Ep. Journ.*, Nos. 122, 123.

[34b] The mixed Græco-Asiatic law is described in *Historical Commentary on Galatians*, §§ xxxi., xxxiii. ff.

[34c] *C.I.L.*, iii., 6829.

[35] On this subject, compare *Studies in the Art and History of the Eastern*

Provinces (Hodder & Stoughton, 1906), pp. 4 ff., 282, 287, 357 ff.   The centre of gravity of the Roman world was shifting towards the East, and Rome was no longer the real centre.

[35]a χώρα, Acts xiii. 49, Sterrett, *Epigraph. Journey*, No. 92, p. 121 (where ῥεγεωνάριον, i.e. *regionarium*, is the true reading).

[36] The inscriptions afford no evidence of a college of priests ; but the analogy of Pessinus and of the Ormelian *hieron* may be regarded as conclusive.

[36]a *Pauline and Other Studies*, p. 157; *Letters to the Seven Churches*, p. 217.   On caves of Cybele, see Anderson in *Annual Brit. Sch.*, Athens, iv., p. 56 f.

[37] His account is not quite clear, and probably he himself did not exactly comprehend what took place, as he had never visited Antioch.   In all probability the Divine property had been taken by Amyntas, and passed as part of his inheritance to Augustus.

[38] ὄχλος, *plebs collegii*.

[39] *Church in the Roman Empire*, p. 65 f.; *Pauline and Other Studies*, p. 365.

[40] The association between these two passages, which is found in the present table of Jewish lessons, is probably of very early origin.

[41] *St. Paul the Trav.*, p. 99 f.

[42] " That which was a trial to you in my physical frame ye despised not, but received me as an angel of God " (Gal. iv. 14).   The effects of the illness were apparent when Paul came to Galatia, as the quotation clearly shows.   It is quite extraordinary that scholars, in spite of Paul's own words, should maintain that the illness began after he came to Galatia.

[43] See, for example, Harnack's *Lukas der Artzt*, and the review of that work in *Expositor*, December, 1906, February, 1907.

[44] There can be no doubt that this is the meaning of the formula so often employed by Luke.   "Those that feared God" were in a sense pagans still, they had not professedly and overtly abandoned paganism.

[45] I speak of a period fully forty years ago, before racial hatreds became so intense as they are now, when such a mixed audience has become almost an impossibility.   I heard the story twenty-seven years ago from a British subject, speaking Greek with perfect fluency, who had resided for business purposes in Thessaly and southern Macedonia.

[46] The Authorised Version (on which see the end of the section) is due to an ancient alteration in the text intended to bring it into conformity with a mistaken conception of the nature of the situation.   From verse 45 it was concluded that the Jews could not have joined in the invitation to Paul; and "the Gentiles" were introduced as sole givers of the invitation.

[47] See his *History of Chr. in Apost. Age*, p. 186 ff.

[48] So Meyer-Wendt.

[49] The meaning of this step is more fully discussed in *St. Paul the Traveller, passim*.

[50] *Historical Commentary on Galatians*, pp. 194 f., 256, etc.

ICONIUM.

[1] Especially by M. Babelon, *Mélanges Numismatiques*, i., 1892, p. 171.

[2] *Letters to the Seven Churches*, chaps. xi., xii.

[3] *Letters to the Seven Churches*, pp. 145, 149.

[4] This paragraph gives in brief the results of the discussion in *Cities and Bish. of Phrygia*, ii., pp. 415, 432, 671.

[5] The scheme was contemplated by a French company about 1904. It has recently been taken up by the German Railway Company, and the subject is under investigation in 1907.

[6] Other ancient cuttings in a different part of those mountains are described in Professor Sterrett's *Wolfe Expedition to Asia Minor*, pp. 161 and 162.

[7] For this identification of Nahr-el-Ahsa see the writer's "Lycaonia" in the *Jahreshefte des k. k. Oest. Arch. Instituts*, 1904, p. 118 (Beiblatt).

[8] *The Wolfe Expedition to Asia Minor*, pp. 123, 133, 180.

[9] On Colossae and its waters see *The Church in the Roman Empire*, last chapter.

[9a] Angdistis is male on a relief at Sizma, female in an Iconian inscription (*C.I.G.*, 3993). The conjecture Bo[ri]thene, in place of Boêthene (*Histor. Comm. on Galatians*, p. 220), is possible, but not probable. It would imply that here, as beside Thyatira in Lydia, there was a village Boritha or Boreita.

[10] *Oest. Jahreshefte*, 1904 (Beiblatt), p. 67 f.

[11] I have to add that the evidence bearing on the mines is collected in the *Classical Review*, Oct., 1905.

[12] *Greek Papyri of Brit. Mus.*, i., p. 89.

[13] Falsely called Ali-Bey-Keui in modern writers and maps; the error is due to ignorance of Turkish among travellers, who fail to understand the thick and difficult pronunciation of the peasantry. Keui means village.

[14] It is the finest known to me in any part of Asia Minor with the single exception of Sultan Khan (further N.E. on the same road), which is by far the most splendid in Turkey.

[15] Mr. Cronin, *loc. cit.*, inclines to a different interpretation of the term (as I also once did). His chief argument is that no other example occurs in Asia Minor of πρωτοκωμήτης in this sense; but in 1904 I found in this region another example of the term, evidently used in this sense, at Serai-Inn, a village in the territory of Laodiceia.

[16] *Cities and Bish. of Phrygia*, i., p. 97; on the villages of Hierapolis see Anderson in *Journal of Hellenic Studies*, 1897, p. 411 f.

[17] Ptolemy in the middle of the second century likewise places both Vasada and Lystra in the Province Galatia (as Antioch was).

[18] So, for example, Claudius, Asterius, and their companions were arrested at Laranda in Lycaonia in 285 A.D., and carried before the proconsul, who ordinarily resided in Cilicia: they were taken about in his progress through

Cilicia and finally executed at Aigai, many miles east of Tarsus (*Acta Sanctorum*, 23rd Aug., p. 567). The Province of the Three Eparchiai, Cilicia-Lycaonia-Isauria, existed as late as 285.

[19] The name has been almost forgotten. Professor Sterrett in 1884 got it as Dibi-Delik, I in 1904 and 1905 as Kutu-Delik; but Monsieur Cousin in 1898 was told that it was Sindjerli-Khan (as I was by careless informants): there is a village Sindjerli about two hours to the south, and Sindjerli-Khan is near the village.

Since this paragraph was written I copied in Tilki Khan, at the southern end of another pass over Boz-Dagh on the road from Iconium to Psebila, a milestone of the year 199 A.D. It belongs to the same series as the one mentioned in the text, but does not contain the name of the provincial Governor. The omission may perhaps be due to the carelessness of the engraver; but, while this series of milestones shows great ignorance of Latin usage, a more probable reason is that Strabo's term of office expired while the roads were in process of reconstruction, between the time when the milestones at Salarama and Psebila were cut in 198 and the time when the work progressed as far as Tilki-Khan.

[20] See Gal. vi. 11; *Histor. Comm. on Gal.*, p. 464 f.

[21] The name in this case is spelt Apponius.

[22] The best known is Aponius Saturninus, a prominent supporter of Vespasian in the war of A.D. 69, who afterwards was Proconsul of Asia.

[23] Thus, for example, the discovery of Savatra in 1901 resulted from the report that many stones for the Tchelebi Effendi's country house beside Iconium had been brought from a village twelve hours distant.

[24] *Studia Biblica*, iv., p. 51.

[25] See Lebas-Waddington, 1192.

[26] In *Studia Biblica*, iv., p. 52 f., failing to observe the " poetic licence," I inferred that this region of the Galatic Province was incorporated in one of the three Galatian tribes; but that inference seems less probable than the explanation now suggested. I also misinterpreted the date, being afraid, like Waddington, to follow the rule that cities of these regions dated from the organisation of the Province (Asia or Galatia, as the case was); the correct dating does away with one of the witnesses called to prove the scarcity in the days of Claudius, and therefore requires the deletion of three lines also in *St. Paul the Trav.*, p. 49, *Christ Born in Bethlehem*, p. 252; but I am glad that in all three places I spoke of the dating as uncertain, so that the strength of the argument in them is unaffected. I saw this inscription for the first time in 1905, and recognised that it must be placed 150-250 A.D.

[27] So regarded by Strabo, Cicero, Pliny in some passages, and the Romans generally. Pliny's variation is due to his dependence on different authorities.

[28] Τοῖς τέσσαρσιν στέμμασιν τῆ[s] κο[λω]νίας (*C.I.G.*, 3995b, where τῆ[s] οἰκο-[δομ]ίας is restored meaninglessly): the term prostatai, which follows, denotes the heads of Tribes, and proves that the stemmata represent four tribes of the four-headed Colony (*Hist. Comm. Gal.*, p. 219): *stemma* at Antioch, note 8.

[29] It is published in .*C.I.L*, iii., No. 13638.

[31] *Letters to the Seven Churches*, chaps. xi., xii.

[32] *Studia Biblica*, iv., p. 32.

[33] See note 24.

[34] On coins of Parlais, before Augustus made it a Roman colony, the name of Diomedes occurs. This is a case like Iconium, and the coins must be placed similarly, either about 50-40, or with some special privilege contrary to the custom of the Province immediately after 25 B.C.

[35] *Studies in the History of the Eastern Roman Provinces*, Hodder & Stoughton, 1906, p. 308. It is, of course, not meant that ὄχλος is used everywhere in the Acts as translation of *plebs*. It is applied to the mob of purely Greek cities, as at Thessalonica, Beroea and Ephesus. But the fact remains that Hellenes is used at Iconium and not at Antioch and Lystra.

[36] Marquardt, *Roem. Staatsverw.*, i., p. 364 (ed. ii., 1881); Kornemann in Pauly-Wissowa, *Real-Encyclopaedie*, 1900, iv., p. 551; Zahn, *Einleitung in das N.T.*, 1897, § 11, n. 5, and at length with arguments, *Kommentar zum N.T. : Galater*, 1905, p. 13. Numismatists, on the contrary, almost all take the right view, *e.g.*, Head, *Hist. Num.*, p. 593; Hill, *Catalogue Br. Mus. Lycaonia*, p. xxiv.; Macdonald, *Hunterian Collection*, ii., p. 524; Imhoof-Blumer, *Kleinasiatische Muenzen*, ii., p. 418.

[37] See, *e.g.*, Sterrett, *Wolfe Expedition*, No. 352, and *C.I.L.*, iii., 6786, where the Colonia Lystra passes such votes.

[38] See *C.I.G.*, 3991.

[40] The inscription (which I sent to Dr. Wiegand, of the German Institute in Constantinople, through my friend the German Consul in Konia, Dr. Loytved, for publication) contains many points of interest. Two impressions were also sent him, one made by Dr. Loytved, one by myself. To make assurance doubly sure I consulted also my friend Professor O. Hirschfeld, in Berlin, the leading authority on Latin Epigraphy, who considers the meaning of the phrase quoted to be indubitable.

[41] Kornemann in Pauly-Wissowa, *Real-Encyclopaedie*, iv., p. 566.

[42] It is called "a Roman City," p. 45 note; but this phrase means only, as the context shows, a city of the Empire and of the Province Galatia (in contrast to Dr. Farrar's statement that it was excluded from the Province).

[43] In the *Expositor*, Dec., 1905, Jan., Feb., 1906, there is given a first account of the early Christian inscriptions of Lycaonia. We observe also that on coins of the Colonia the spelling is sometimes Iconiesis, instead of Iconiensis. This false spelling is due to the Greek rendering of the Roman adjective: after the Colonia was founded the older Greek ethnic Ἰκονιεύς was liable to be replaced by Ἰκονιήσιος (just as the Philippians are called by Paul Φιλιππήσιοι, the transcription of the Latin Philippenses: *Histor. Comment. on Galatians*, p. 321); and Greek speakers not very well accustomed to Latin made the Latin adjective like the Greek rendering.

⁴⁴ See " Lycaonia " in the Austrian *Jahreshefte* (Beiblatt), 1904, p. 121, where I conjectured that the fortress Dakalias guarded this road, but did not observe the identity with Takali : also *Histor. Geography of Asia Minor*, p. 359.

⁴⁵ See *Lycaonia*, p. 69.

⁴⁶ *Pauline and Other Studies*, pp. 133 f., 158 f.

DERBE.

¹ P. 340 ff.

² I paced a number of the intervals successively, as follows : 130, 137, 140, 67, 68, 140, 66, 134, 69, 67, 73, 60, 65, 68, 62. The five larger measures are where intermediate stones have been destroyed or hidden from view. The intervals, therefore, vary from 60 paces to 73 ; and the stones must have been placed roughly according to eyesight, and not by measurement. I paced the short interval 60 twice, and measured it with the tape-line, 148 feet.

³ Probably most of them might, with care, be traced. The lost stones occur mostly near the point where I began to pace the distances, when I was on the outlook only for taller stones.

⁴ These stones have been described and published by my friend the Rev. H. S. Cronin in the *Journal of Hellenic Studies*, 1902. On the topography, however, it is necessary to consult my paper in the Annual of the British School at Athens, 1902, on " Pisidia and the Lycaonian Frontier," incorporating the results of more recent discoveries.

⁵ See the Austrian *Jahreshefte*, 1904, p. 67 (Beiblatt).

⁶ Konia and the neighbouring village Sille have preserved a continuous Greek population, and continuity in the tradition may therefore be expected, and can almost certainly be traced in the church of St. Amphilochius and the monastery of St. Chariton, etc. See Part IV., § ix.

⁷ See the chapter on " Ephesus " in the *Letters to the Seven Churches ;* the articles on the Ephesian goddess and " The Permanence of Religion, etc.," in *Pauline and Other Studies*, p. 125 ff.

⁸ The few Greeks, who are met with in this neighbourhood, are all strangers engaged in trade. The Christian population of this part of Lycaonia was entirely exterminated or expelled after the Turkish conquest. There is, therefore, no continuity in the local tradition ; and no one among the Greeks knows that Derbe was situated in the neighbourhood.

⁹ There is no absolute impossibility that it might be of the second century ; but, personally, I should not be inclined to date it so early.

¹⁰ The most ornate example of this type was republished in *Pauline and Other Studies*, p. 216. The whole series is published by Miss Ramsay in *Studies in the Art and History of the Eastern Provinces*, p. 22 ff.

¹¹ Compare the chapter on Ephesus in the *Letters to the Seven Churches.*

¹² The chief facts about this name are gathered together in my paper on Lycaonia, in the Austrian *Jahreshefte*, 1904, 73 f.

[13] A general account of it is given in my *Preliminary Report of a Journey in 1905, Studies in the History and Art of the Eastern Provinces*, p. 241 ff.

[14] See the *Church in the Roman Empire*, chap. xvi.

[15] For particulars, and for the spelling of the name, see the Austrian *Jahreshefte*, 1904, 73 f. (Beiblatt).

[16] Professor Sterrett uses here this form of the name; but I heard only Losta, and so also MM. Radet and Ouvré.

[17] *Wolfe Expedition*, p. 29.

[18] He also was, I think, the first traveller that observed the ruins of Gudelisin.

[19] λιμήν was the name for such a station, whether it was a coast-town and harbour, or an inland city like Derbe. Stephanus Byz. is the only authority who has recorded this fact, which he gathered from some lost authority, who described the city as it was between 41 and 74.

[20] Sterrett, *loc. cit.*, p. 23, where the author has not observed that *Provincie* is a plural, and that the names of two of the Eparchiae are lost at the end of the inscription. He mentions that the letters are faint.

LYSTRA.

[1] *Bulletin de Correspondance Hellén.*, vii., p. 318 f.

[2] The new Turkish law regulating antiquarian research and excavation is so strict as to be almost prohibitive without strong Government support.

[3] Lustra occurs in the only two Latin inscriptions which give the name, *C.I.L.*, iii., 6786, 12215. The same form is used in the only legible coins that I have seen; but they are mostly worn and the letters uncertain. M. Babelon prints Lystra in a coin of Augustus (*Coll. Waddington*, No. 4790); but a misprint may be suspected here.

[4] See Cronin in *Journ. Hell. Stud.*, 1904, pp. 113, 115.